Date Due

Springer Series on PSYCHIATRY
Carl Eisdorfer, PhD, MD, Series Editor

Mary Coleman, MD, received her BA from the University of Chicago, an MA from Johns Hopkins University, and an MD from George Washington University.

Affiliated during her career with neurology, pediatrics, and community medicine at Georgetown University School of Medicine, Washington, DC, she is now Professor Emeritus. Dr. Coleman was principal investigator on grants from the National Institute of Mental Health, National Institute of Neurological Diseases and Stroke, and the National Institute of Child Health and Human Development. Her honors have included the Huntington Clinical Foundation Distinguished Lectureship and Theodore D. Tjossem Research Award.

Dr. Coleman has been on the editorial boards of *Biological Psychiatry* and the *Journal of Autism and Developmental Disorders*. She is the author of six previous books, including the first and second editions of *The Biology of the Autistic Syndromes*, coauthored with Christopher Gillberg, MD.

Christopher Gillberg, MD, PhD, received his medical degree from Göteborg University in 1973, after which he specialized in child and adolescent and adult psychiatry. He also trained in psychotherapy for individuals and families. He has been Professor of Handicap Research and Professor of Child and Adolescent Psychiatry, both at Göteborg University. Dr. Gillberg received the Fernström Award, known as the Little Nobel Prize, for his studies in autism. He also received A Fulbright Scholarship for advanced study at New York University. He is currently the Editor-in-Chief of *European Child and Adolescent Psychiatry* and serves as scientific advisor to the Swedish National Board of Health.

The Schizophrenias

A Biological Approach to the Schizophrenia Spectrum Disorders

Mary Coleman

Christopher Gillberg

SPRINGER SERIES ON PSYCHIATRY

Springer Publishing Company, Inc.
536 Broadway
New York, NY 10012-3955

Cover design by Tom Yabut
Production Editor: Pamela Lankas

96 97 98 99 00 / 5 4 3 2 1

Library of Congress Cataloging-in-Publication Data

Coleman, Mary.
    The schizophrenias : approach to the etiology of schizophrenia spectrum disorders / Mary Coleman, Christopher Gillberg.
        p.   cm. — (Springer series on psychiatry)
    Includes bibliographical references and index.
    ISBN 0-8261-9290-4
    1. Schizophrenia—Etiology. 2. Schizophrenia—Diagnosis.
    3. Psychological manifestations of general diseases.
    I. Gillberg, Christopher, 1950–. II. Title. III. Series:
    Springer series on psychiatry (unnumbered)
    [DNLM: 1. Schizophrenia—etiology. WM 203 C692s 1996]
RC514.C582 1996
616.89'82071—dc20
DNLM/DLC
for Library of Congress   95-53058
                                                                CIP

Printed in the United States of America

Illustration on p. xiv by Johnny Johnson, form Elliot S. Gershon and Ronald O. Rieder, "Major disorders of mind and brain," p. 127, copyright © September 1992 by *Scientific America, Inc.* All rights reserved. Reproduced by permission.

To all the young people cut down by mental illness in the flush and promise of youth, relegated to lives of pain, nothingness, or a tragic exit; to all of these afflicted, those to come, and their long-suffering close ones—may this book provide a ray of light, of hope, and of help.

—Blanche Prince, LCSW, BCD

Contents

Foreword

It has been more than 20 years since I first had the opportunity to work with Dr. Mary Coleman. We collected blood from a large number of children with autistic syndromes and analyzed it for antibodies against a variety of infectious agents. Looking back on the research we were doing at that time and comparing it with the present, it seems like at least a century must have passed.

At the time of our first collaborative research in the early 1970s, the biological basis of serious psychiatric illnesses was much less clearly defined. Departments of Psychiatry at most leading medical centers were still dominated by individuals who had been psychoanalytically trained and the emphasis in training programs was on learning how to do proper psychotherapy. Diseases like schizophrenia, bipolar disorder, and autism were taught of course, but no psychiatrist who wanted to be successful would have considered specializing in such disorders because these disorders did not respond to psychotherapy.

By the late 1970s computed tomography (CT) scans began to appear in psychiatric journals and the return of biological psychiatry was underway. It is worth noting that it was a "return," because from the early 1800s until approximately 1920 almost all psychiatry was biological. It was only with the ascendancy of Freudian concepts of early childhood experiences that the biological assumptions of earlier years were laid aside, and they remained there quietly for half a century. The rush from the CT scans of the late 1970s to the introns, G proteins, and limbic interconnections of today has been dizzying. And the blood samples we so laboriously collected 20 years ago can be used now for 100 tests on the same specimen we used then for one test, and each test is 100 times more sensitive.

Two things, however, have not changed much during the two-decade rush to biological psychiatry. First, it is no more clear now than it was then how many schizophrenias there are. It is clear that schizophrenia is not a single disease, just as it is clear that bipolar disorder and autism are not single diseases, but what is the shape of that heterogeneity? Attempts to answer this question using clinical data and symptom subtyping have proved remarkably unproductive, and researchers wait patiently for promised biological markers. Most of us assume that a variety of etiological subtypes will emerge, but always lurking in the corner of our consciousness is the syphilitic spirochete, which, all by itself, can cause a wide variety of clinical pictures.

The other thing that has not changed during the last two decades is the susceptibility of psychiatric researchers to fashions. Although we like to think of ourselves as being beyond the whims of hemlines, tailfins, and hair styles, our research ideas are just as susceptible to the latest showings in New York and London. Genetic theories have evolved from a simple stress- diathesis model to having multiple candidates for gene-of-the-month; neurotransmitter theories have evolved from an all-purpose dopamine theory to knowledge of at least 60 other neurotransmitters, many with several subtypes; the limbic system has evolved from being a relatively simple circuit to including several billion neurons, each connected by dendrites with up to 50,000 other neurons; but always there are fashions. One of the latest fashions is the neurodevelopmental hypothesis that is on display in all the journals. Although it has many attractions, it is in fact more a theory of pathophysiology than a theory of etiology.

The present volume signifies a scholarly and refreshing break with psychiatric fashions, and a return to first principles. What can we learn from studying other diseases regarding changes in the brain that cause symptoms like those seen in schizophrenia? Is an undiagnosed metabolic disease that masquerades as schizophrenia really schizophrenia? After we have identified all the conditions that may mimic schizophrenia, will there be any schizophrenia left? Given the present rate of research progress, it seems likely that we will have answers to many of these questions in the next two decades. Psychiatric research has never been more exciting as we penetrate deeper and deeper into the human brain, the last true frontier on earth.

E. FULLER TORREY, MD
VISITING SCHOLAR
NATIONAL INSTITUTES OF MENTAL HEALTH
BETHESDA, MD

ACKNOWLEDGMENTS

This book was written based on an original concept of Blanche Prince, LCSW, BCD. She has been a constant support during the preparation of this manuscript and has actively contributed to its contents. The authors wish to thank the Harry Stern Family Foundation for their financial assistance toward the writing of this book. We are indebted to the staff of the Crearer Medical Library of the University of Chicago, in particular James Vaughan, for their assistance. The authors wish to thank colleagues who helped in the preparation of the manuscript, especially David S. Rosenblatt, M.D. The staff of Springer Publishing Company, especially Pam Lankas, Louise Farkas, and Bill Tucker, were of great help.

Mary Coleman, MD
Christopher Gillberg, MD

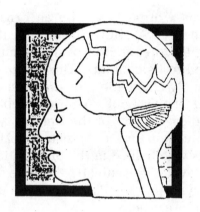

CHAPTER 1

Introduction

Thi is a book about the medical differential diagnosis of
schizophrenia.
There are many studies showing that a significant proportion of patients with schizophrenia and other major psychiatric
disease entities have undiagnosed and unattended medical illness, sometimes illnesses that directly contribute to their psychiatric symptoms (Marshall, 1949; Herridge, 1960; Davies, 1965;
Johnson, 1968; Maquire & Granville-Grossman, 1968; Browning,
Miller, & Tyson, 1974; Hall et al., 1978; Koranyi, 1979; Bernstein &
Andrews, 1981; Maricle, Hoffman, Bloom, Faulkner, & Keepers,
1987; Johnstone, MacMillan, & Crow, 1987; Koran et al., 1989; Sox
et al., 1989; Vieweg et al., 1995; Torrey, 1990). Johnson's study
of 250 consecutive admissions to a psychiatric inpatient service
demonstrated that 12% of the patients had physical disorders
that were productive of their psychiatric symptoms and that
caused their admission. He pointed out that 80% of these illnesses
were initially missed by physicians who examined these patients
as part of their admission to the hospital (Hall & Beresford, 1984).

A medical illnesses may, or may not, be relevant to a particular patient's psychiatric problems. In any given patient, it could
be simple coincidence that the patient has two separate diseases
(a medical disease and schizophrenia) and it is possible that the
medical disease discovered was so stressful to the body that it
precipitated ahead of schedule the schizophrenic breakdown in
someone already predisposed to schizophrenia, their second disease. But it also could be that the underlying medical disease
entity directly contributed to the schizophrenia, a condition *sui
generis* (Slater, Beard, & Glithero, 1963).

In a chapter entitled "One, Two or Many?" Dalen (1972) warned against embracing a multifactorial model that suggests that almost anything may be relevant to the etiology of schizophrenia; to his way of thinking, notions of multicausality or, worse yet, omnicausality are dangerously wrong. Many psychiatrists would agree with Tsuang et al. (1990) who, when they were discussing schizophrenia in families, said that the "evidence for genetic heterogeneity is neither clear-cut or compelling" (page 25). Yet there is ambivalence out there in the field. In the same paper in which Tsuang et al. state that the evidence for genetic heterogeneity is neither clear-cut nor compelling, they also say, perhaps wistfully, "The idea that numerous, perhaps innumerable, factors are relevant to the phenomenon of schizophrenia is congenial to the impression that we have formed in our clinical work with schizophrenia" (pages 24–25). Others also have that impression. Given the diversity of symptoms, the variable course and differential response to treatment, it is not surprising that schizophrenia has been seriously considered by major investigators as a heterogeneous disorder (Himmelhoch, 1978; Bartko, Carpenter, & Strauss, 1981; Helmchen, 1988; Wyatt, Alexander, Egan, & Kirch, 1988).

"One, Two or Many?" is more than an intellectual debate; it has direct consequences. If there are many etiologies to schizophrenia, the physician has a lot to do (full work-ups on patients followed by appropriate treatments when indicated); if there is only one cause, the physician can rely on present therapies until the field develops the ideal drug that hasn't any major side effects and that cures all schizophrenia.

Schizophrenia is one of the most common serious mental illnesses of adult life—the lifetime prevalence rates in the United States have been reported to be 0.7% of the population (World Health Organization, 1973, 1979; Kessler et al., 1994). If this data is correct, this means that for every 1000 adults, 7 are likely to be schizophrenic. It is hard to be sure of the number of people with schizophrenia, however, because despite serious efforts at standardization, there is fluctuation in diagnostic categories. For example, in the United States a major study demonstrated that the proportion of patients diagnosed with schizophrenia fell from the early 1970s to the late 1980s—in six major psychiatric hospitals, the overall proportion of schizophrenic diagnoses among patients discharged from these hospitals fell from a high of 27% in 1976 to 9% in 1989 (Stoll et al., 1993).

Because schizophrenia is so common and is often chronic, the patients who have not become homeless and do receive some care already cost society $33 billion a year in the United States alone (NAMI Advocate, 1994). Dr. William Glazer, a psychiatrist at Harvard Medical School, indicates that "About one-quarter of American hospital beds are for patients with schizophrenia." "About half of those are in the revolving door, with repeated readmissions for relapse" (Goleman, 1994, p. B4). Hospital costs are estimated to exceed $100,000 annually for chronic inpatients and up to $10,000 per relapse (NAMI Advocate, 1994). In fact, schizophrenia's total costs to society are estimated to be six times the costs of myocardial infarction (Andrews et al., 1985) and also exceed the total financial burden of all cancers (National Foundation for Brain Research, 1992) in the U.S. Large costs also burden European societies (Davies & Drummond, 1994).

These cost estimates do not include the individuals with schizophrenia who are homeless; in 1989 a study from the *Journal of the American Medical Association* reported that 42% to 49% of the homeless people on the streets are mentally ill (Lundberg, 1989). In terms of human suffering, there is general agreement that a 30-year-old policy of deinstitionalization has failed, at least in the United States (Goodwin, 1994), leading to the overwhelming suffering of the individuals with schizophrenia and also of the patients' relatives, who love and try to care for them (Winefield & Harvey, 1993). The overrepresentation of persons with schizophrenia in the lower socioeconomic groups also is well known, most likely caused by the downward "drift" phenomenon (Brar, Thorp, Amos, & Nimgaonkar, 1995). This represents an additional uncounted cost as well as misery to the families, particularly the children who have parents with schizophrenia.

Medical therapy for schizophrenia is based on the concept that it is a single disease entity in spite of overwhelming evidence that it is the final common pathway in the brain of a great variety of different illnesses (as will be examined in the rest of this book). For more than a generation now, antipsychotic drugs for this mythical single disease have been the primary treatment (Kane & Marder, 1993). Despite many troubling and disabling side effects (Johnson, 1988), these drugs have often been successful in reducing one part of the symptoms of schizophrenia in suffering patients. Doctors can suppress the hallucinations of many people with schizophrenia, but a number still remain greatly impaired—many remain unable to function independently in normal society. It is a tragic fact of medical history that over the past generation deinstitutionalization of individuals with schizophrenia was begun after these drugs, sometimes only partially effective and often with side effects, became available (Crane, 1973).

It is the goal of this volume to facilitate a program designed to assure that every person diagnosed with schizophrenia has had a full medical evaluation based on the latest information in the field. At an absolute minimum, every person with such a diagnosis should have had the opportunity to be evaluated for the known disease entities that can both present with schizophrenic-like symptoms and have therapies that can reverse such symptoms (see Work-Up of Treatable Diseases in Chapter 16). No longer should any individual diagnosed as schizophrenic who has a treatable disease have the actual disease entity discovered too late for effective treatment or at autopsy.

There are some who admit that schizophrenia may well be more than one illness but will cry "But what is the yield? Is it cost effective to perform a complete medical work-up on every individual with schizophrenia?" This so-called cost-effective argument can then be used to treat each patient as though he or she had only one disease—a mythical disease named schizophrenia—even if the physicians have their doubts.

From the point of view of the patient, the answer regarding cost effectiveness is clear—the expense of the work-up is worth it because the patient wishes any chance possible, no matter how small, for a real reversal of illness rather than to stay ill all of his or her adult life. The patient wants to have a chance for a return to a meaningful and productive life in society.

From the point of view of the community as a whole, the answer also is clear—the lifetime maintenance costs of each patient (short of throwing them into the street and into homelessness) more than justify the cost of a one-time full medical evaluation when the symptoms first present. This is true even if one uses the most conservative figure available—6% of patients with schizophrenia were found to have a medical illness that contributed to their psychiatric symptoms (Johnstone et al., 1987).

Norman Geschwind, a neurologist who made many contributions in the field of biological psychiatry, stated the situation 20 years ago:

> While it has become fashionable to acknowledge the existence of an area of overlap between neurology and psychiatry, this common ground unfortunately bears more resemblance to a no-man's land than to an open border. While neurologists tend to mutter darkly about the failure of psychiatrists to be aware of the brain as an organ of the mind, psychiatrists, perhaps somewhat defensively, have stressed their awareness of the whole man, biologic as well as psychologic. . . . There are some who would like to believe that neurologic causes of psychiatric disorder are rare. Neurologic disorders, however, account for at least 30 percent of all first admissions to mental hospitals. Furthermore, even if neurologic causes of psychiatric disorder were uncommon, this would still not justify their neglect, since some of these conditions are treatable.
>
> (Geschwind, 1975)

Over the last 20 years, there have been changes from that no-man's land into a more open and friendly border. This book aspires to help psychiatrists understand more fully the biological approach to schizophrenia and to aid neurologists in comprehending how very difficult, overwhelming, and sometimes quite murky the diagnostic problems are in so many patients with the devastating disease entity of schizophrenia. We psychiatrists and neurologists urgently need to work together on behalf of these seriously ill people, some of whom are the abandoned homeless of our societies.

REFERENCES

Andrews, G., Hall, W., Goldstein, G., Lapsley, H., Bartels, R., & Silove, D. (1985). The economic costs of schizophrenia. *Archives of General Psychiatry, 42*, 537–543.

Bartko, J. J., Carpenter, W. T., & Strauss, J. S. (1981). Statistical basis for exploring schizophrenia. *American Journal of Psychiatry, 138*, 941–947.

Bernstein, R. A., & Andrews, E. M. (1981). The hospitalized psychiatric patient and the primary care physician. *Psychosomatics, 22*, 959–970.

Brar, J. S., Thorp, G., Amos, K., & Nimgaonkar, V. L. (1995). Further support for the "drift" hypothesis of schizophrenia. *Biological Psychiatry, 37*, 639 (abstract).

Browning, C. H., Miller, S. I., & Tyson, R. L. (1974). The psychiatric emergency: A high risk medical patient. *Comprehensive Psychiatry, 15*, 153–156.

Crane, G. E. (1973). Clinical psychopharmacology in its 20th year. *Science, 181*, 124–128.

Dalen, P. (1972). One, two or many? In A. R. Kaplan (Ed.), *Genetic factors in schizophrenia*. Springfield: Charles C Thomas.

Davies, D. H. (1965). Physical illness in psychiatric outpatients. *British Journal of Psychiatry, 111*, 27–33.

Davies, L. M., & Drummond, M. F. (1994). Economics and schizophrenia: the real cost. *British Journal of Psychiatry, (Suppl.) (25)*, 18–21.

Geschwind, N. (1975). The borderland of neurology and psychiatry: Some common misconceptions. In D. F. Benson & D. Blumer (Eds.), *Psychiatric aspects of neurologic disease*. New York: Grune & Stratton.

Goleman, D. (1994, August 10). Breaking the cycle of schizophrenia. *The New York Times*, p. B6.

Goodwin, F. K. (1994, March 30). The Rip Van Winkle of Psychiatry. *The Wall Street Journal*, p. A19.

Hall, R. W. C., & Beresford, T. P. (1984). Physical illness in psychiatric patients: Areas of inquiry. *Psychiatric medicine* (vol. 2, pp. 401–415). New York: SP Medical & Scientific Books.

Hall, R. C. W., Popkin, M. K., DeVaul, R. A., et al. (1978). Physical illness presenting as psychiatric disease. *Archives of General Psychiatry, 35*, 1315–1320.

Helmchen, H. (1988). Methodological and strategical considerations in schizophrenia research. *Comprehensive Psychiatry, 29*, 337–354.

Herridge, C. F. (1960). Physical disorders in mental illness. *Lancet*, *2*, 949–951.

Himmelhoch, J. M. (1978). What is schizophrenia? In D. Bergsmas & A. Goldstein (Eds.), *Neurochemical and immunologic components in schiozphrenia* (pp. 19–35). New York: A. R. Liss.

Johnson, D. A. W. (1968). The evaluation of routine physical examination in psychiatric cases. *Practitioner*, *200*, 686–691.

Johnson, D. A. W. (1988). Drug treatment of schizophrenia. In P. Bebbington & P. McGuffin (Eds.), *Schizophrenia: The major issues*. London: Heinemann.

Johnstone, E. C., MacMillan, J. F., & Crow, T. J. (1987). The occurrence of organic disease of possible or probable aetiological siognificnce in a population of 268 cases of first episode schizophrenia. *Psychological Medicine*, *17*, 371–379.

Kane, J. M., & Marder, S. (1993). Psychopharmacologic treatment of schizophrenia. *Schizophrenia Bulletin*, *19*(2), 287–302.

Kessler, R. C., McGonagle, K. A., Zhao, S., Nelson, C. B., Hughes, M., Eshleman, S., Wittchen, H-U., & Kendler, K. S. (1994). Lifetime and 12-month prevalence of DSM-III-R psychiatric disorders in the United States. *Archives of General Psychiatry*, *51*, 8–19.

Koran, L. M., Sox, H. C., Marton, K. I., Moltzen, S., Sox, C. H., Kraemer, H. C., Imair, K., Kelsey, T. G., Rose, T. G., Jr., Lewin, L. C., & Chandra, S. (1989). Medical evaluation of psychiatric patients. *Archives of General Psychiatry*, *46*, 733–740.

Koranyi, E. K. (1979). Morbidlity and rate of undiagnosed physical illness in a psychiatric clinic population. *Archives of General Psychiatry*, *36*, 414–419.

Lundberg, G. D. (1989). Fifty hours for the poor. (Editorial.) *Journal of the American Medical Association*, *262*, 3045.

Maguire, C., & Granville-Grossman, K. L. (1968). Physical illness in psychiatric patients. *British Journal of Psychiatry*, *115*, 1365–1369.

Maricle, R. A., Hoffman, W. F., Bloom, J. D., Faulkner, L. R., & Keepers, G. A. (1987). The prevalence and significance of medical illness among chronically mentally ill outpatients. *Community Mental Health Journal*, *23*, 81–90.

Marshall, H. (1949). Incidence of physical disorders among the psychiatric inpatients. *British Medical Journal*, *2*, 468–470.

National Alliance for the Mentally Ill (NAMI) Advocate. (1994, January–February). New schizophrenia drug now available in the U.S. Arlington, VA: NAMI Publishing.

National Foundation for Brain Research (NFBR) (1992). *The care of disorders of the brain*. Washington, DC: Author.

Slater, E., Beard, A. W., & Glithero, E. (1963). The schizophrenia-like psychoses of epilepsy. *British Journal of Psychiatry, 109*, 95–150.

Sox, H. C., Koran, L. M., Sox, C. H., Marton, K. I., Duggar, F., & Smith, T. (1989). A medical algorithm for detecting physical disease in psychiatric patients. *Hospital and Community Psychiatry, 40*, 1270–1276.

Stoll, A. L., Toben, M., & Baldessarini, R., et al. (1993). Shifts in diagnostic frequencies of schizophrenia and major affective disorders in six American psychiatric hospitals, 1972–1988. *American Journal of Psychiatry, 150*, 1668–1673.

Torrey, E. F. (1990). Economic barriers to widespread implementation of model programs for the seriously mentally ill. *Hospital and Community Medicine, 41*, 526–531.

Tsuang, M. T., Lyons, M. J., Faraone, S. V. (1990). Heterogeneity of schizophrenia—Conceptual models and analytic strategies. *British Journal of Psychiatry, 156*, 17–26.

Vieweg, V., Levenson, J., Pandurangi, A., & Silverman, J. (1995). Medical disorders in the schizophrenic patient. *International Journal of Psychiatry in Medicine, 25*, 137–172.

Winefield, H. R., & Harvey, E. J. (1993). Determinants of psychological stress in relatives of people with chronic schizophrenia. *Schizophrenia Bulletin, 19*, 619–625.

World Health Organization. (1973). *Report of the international pilot study of schizophrenia, volume 1*. Geneva: Author.

World Health Organization. (1979). *Schizophrenia. An international follow-up study*. Chichester, UK: Wiley.

Wyatt, R. J., Alexander, R. C., Egan, M. F., & Kirch, D. G. (1988). Schizophrenia, just the facts: What do we know, how well do we know it? *Schizophrenia Research, 1*, 3–18.

CHAPTER 2

Diagnosis and Definitions

In spite of its 85-year history as a diagnostic concept and its even longer presence in the world of clinical realities, schizophrenia is almost as far removed from diagnostic consensus today as it was 50 years ago. The extent of differing opinions pertaining to diagnostic criteria is so diverse that some writers have questioned schizophrenia's existence (Boyle, 1990). Thousands of papers have been published in the field, but very few of these have dealt empirically with the construct of schizophrenia itself.

Since its inception by Eugen Bleuler in 1911, even in times of vociferous diagnostic disagreement, the existence of "schizophrenia" has been taken for granted. The evidence that it exists, at least as a distinct disease, is meager.

It is perhaps significant that Bleuler considered the concept to be without fine distinctions vis à vis other conditions and that he regarded the "schizophrenias" to be an amalgam of psychological disturbances (Bleuler, 1911).

Even though "schizophrenia spectrum disorders" is now, in the mid-1990s, a much-used term, the extent of the literature on schizophrenia "itself" (without the plural) is suggestive of agreement among clinicians and researchers on a core condition that is distinct and may be reliably separated from other severe psychopathological disorders. Nevertheless, the frequent reference to "type I" and "type II" schizophrenias (Crow, 1980), "pseudoneurotic" or "nonregressive" schizophrenia (Nyman, 1975) and the "classic schizophrenias" (hebephrenic/disorganized, paranoid, catatonic schizophrenia, and dementia simplex) is testimony to the generally accepted heterogeneity of the syndrome.

To state it briefly: schizophrenia has been a topic of controversy for many years. Two of the most salient reasons for the debate about schizophrenia are that (1) it has always eluded straightforward definition and (2) its etiology remains obscure. However, research clinicians can assign schizophrenia diagnoses with reasonable reliability and in the individual case, as we shall see, etiology may sometimes be known.

So, what are we to make of these conflicting views? Does schizophrenia exist? Should it be thought of in the plural? Is there a common denominator, psychologically or physiologically? Before we can go on to even start to consider these issues, we need to familiarize ourselves with both the old and current concepts of schizophrenia.

HISTORICAL BACKGROUND

There has long been a notion in psychiatry that the most severe psychopathological disorders can—or should—be subdivided. It has been argued that some disorders run a chronic debilitating course, whereas others tend more toward fluctuation with periods of complete remission. In the 19th century, several authorities tried to distinguish between affective disorders with mood swings on the one hand, and more debilitating abnormalities with emotional blunting and poor psychosocial outcome on the other.

In 1896 Kraepelin discriminated *dementia preacox* from a larger group of pathological mental states. Kraepelin declared this condition to be a relatively discrete entity with a uniform etiology and a common, inevitably chronic course. He used the word "dementia" to highlight the trend toward progressive deterioration. "Praecox" referred to the early onset (during adolescence). DeSanctis (1906), in referring to "dementia praecocissima," noted that "Kraepelin's syndrome" sometimes had its onset in childhood.

Bleuler (1911) coined the term schizophrenia from the Greek "roots" *schizein* (= split), and *phren* (= mind, soul). Unlike Kraepelin, he felt that a hopeless attitude to prognosis was not always justified. Bleuler believed that the egocentric ("autistic") thinking that was the clinical hallmark of his patients, was caused by a "split" in several important aspects of psychological functioning [associative thoughts, thought and feeling, feeling and its expression, ambivalence (split between intention and action) and subjective experience (the conviction of being "split" and manipulated)]. It is of considerable interest that Bleuler also coined the term autism from the Greek word *autos* (self). He used this term to describe the nonempathic, egocentric quality of thought and feeling that characterized his patients. To him, autism was but a symptom of schizophrenia. In later years it has come to be used most often in connection with the severe childhood developmental disorder usually referred to as infantile autism, autistic disorder, or autistic syndrome.

Bleuler's concept of schizophrenia was broader than that of Kreapelin's. It was embraced particularly in the United States, where a gradual widening of schizophrenia's boundaries led to "overdiagnosis" as compared with the UK and Scandinavia, for example (Leff, 1977). Schneider reacted against overinclusive concepts of schizophrenia and suggested the introduction of relatively narrow, operationalized, phenomenological diagnostic criteria (Schneider, 1971). His suggested criteria for schizophrenia were close to the Scandinavian and British traditions. Schneider's position strongly influenced the development of the schizophrenia section in the *Diagnostic and Statistical Manual of Mental Disorders* (DSM), both in its third, third revised, and fourth editions (APA 1980, 1987, 1994). This has probably led to a more restrictive use of the schizophrenia diagnosis in the US.

SCHIZOPHRENIA AS A SYNDROME

Even after the rather considerable narrowing of the diagnostic concept of schizophrenia that has occurred over the last three decades, problems remain concerning the delineation of a syndrome. There is no clear consensus as to which symptoms are necessary and sufficient for a diagnosis to be made. Even though there is overlap between the schizophrenic syndrome as it emerges in the DSM-IV and the International Classification of Diseases (ICD-10) (WHO 1992, 1993), agreement is by no means complete. In fact, very few studies have critically examined the issue of whether the symptoms believed to be characteristic of schizophrenia cooccur reliably enough to warrant their clinical clustering as a "syndrome."

Characteristic symptoms of schizophrenia fall into two broad categories—positive and negative. Positive symptoms (e.g., hallucinations, delusions, and disorganized speech) are seen to reflect an exaggeration or distortion of normal functions. Negative symptoms (e.g., affective blunting, muteness, and lack of volition) are taken to mirror a diminution or loss of normal functions. There is usually a mixture of both positive and negative symptoms, but in certain subtypes, only one type of symptom may dominate the clinical picture (e.g., delusions in paranoid schizophrenia). Symptoms must have been present for at least a month (or at some time during most of the days). Many authorities require a considerable degree of social or occupational dysfunction for a diagnosis to be established. Most clinicians (but not the DSM-III-R or the ICD-10), in addition, require that there be no decrease in the individual's overall level of consciousness and that there be no "primary" mood disorder (mania or depression)—even though secondary depressive reactions are not uncommon.

Schizophrenia is usually grouped within the general category of psychosis. Given that psychosis has come to be used as a term for conditions in which there is a decrease in or breakdown of reality testing, however, some disorders classified as schizophrenia (e.g., dementia simplex) would not qualify as "psychotic." Many authorities use the term "regressive" schizophrenic syndromes when referring to schizophrenia with psychotic features and "nonregressive" syndromes when inferring schizophrenia without loss of reality testing. The DSM-IV takes for granted schizophrenia as a variant of psychotic disorders, whereas the ICD-10 has adopted a more neutral stance in referring to "schizophrenia, schizotypal, and delusional disorders."

CURRENT DIAGNOSTIC CRITERIA

Tables 2.1, 2.2, 2.3, and 2.4 outline the diagnostic criteria for schizophrenia as they appear in the DSM-III (APA, 1980), DSM-III-R (APA, 1987), DSM-IV (APA, 1994) and the ICD-10 (WHO, 1993).

In the case of the ICD, the operationalized criteria for research are shown because the outline of schizophrenia that appears in the diagnostic guidelines for clinicians is too vague for representation in a table.

DSM

The publication of the DSM-III in 1980 was a major step toward a unified view of schizophrenia. For the first time, operationalized criteria for the disorder were listed in a diagnostic manual intended for clinicians and researchers alike.

Changes in the diagnostic criteria for schizophrenia in the DSM-III-R were superficially minor, but substantial enough to cause potential diagnostic confusion. For instance, in the DSM-III, having "nonbizarre" delusions as the only active symptom would be sufficient for a diagnosis from the symptomatic point of view. According to the DSM-III-R, delusions would have to be combined with a least one other major active symptom for a diagnosis to be made. This difference would seem to make the DSM-III-R schizophrenia concept more restrictive in scope. The DSM-III-R allows the diagnosis in cases showing only the two symptoms "catatonic behavior" and "flat affect," however, a combination that would be insufficient for a DSM-III-diagnosis. Thus, it would seem that the DSM-III-R may be slightly broader in some instances and more restrictive in others. It is unclear how this would affect the prevalence of schizophrenia in clinical and epidemiological samples of individuals with severe psychopathology, and, to our knowledge, no study has examined these, or similar, validity aspects of the diagnosis in any detail. Theoretically, it is clear that there is room for diagnostic discrepancies in studies using the DSM-III criteria on the one hand and those employing the DSM-III-R criteria on the other.

The appearance of the DSM-IV meant little change in the symptom criteria as compared with the DSM-III-R. The wording of the E. and F. criteria (referring to the relationship of schizophrenia to organic/medical conditions and autism/autisticlike conditions), however, is sufficiently different across the two manuals to introduce the risk of considerable change in diagnostic practice. For instance, the DSM-III-R specifies that only if there is

TABLE 2.1 Diagnostic Criteria for Schizophrenia According to the DSM-III

A. At least one of the following during a phase of the illness:
   (1) bizarre delusions (content is patently absurd and has *no* possible basis in fact), such as delusions of being controlled, thought broadcasting, thought insertion, or thought withdrawal;
   (2) somatic, grandiose, religious, nihilistic, or other delusions without persecutory or jealous content;
   (3) delusions with persecutory or jealous content if accompanied by hallucinations of any type;
   (4) auditory hallucinations in which either a voice keeps up a running commentary on the individual's behavior or thoughts, or two or more voices converse with each other;
   (5) auditory hallucinations on several occasions with content of more than one or two words, having no apparent relation to depression or elation;
   (6) incoherence, marked loosening of associations, markedly illogical thinking, or marked poverty of content of speech if associated with at least one of the following:
      (a) blunted, flat, or inappropriate affect;
      (b) delusions or hallucinations;
      (d) catatonic or other grossly disorganized behavior.
B. Deterioration from a previous level of functioning in such areas as work, social relations, and self-care.
C. Duration: Continuous signs of the illness for at least 6 months at some time during the person's life, with some signs of the illness at present. The 6- month period must include an active phase during which there were symptoms from A, with or without a prodromal or residual phase, as defined below.
   Prodromal phase: A clear deterioration in functioning before the active phase of the illness not due to a disturbance in mood or to a Substance Use Disorder and involving at least *two* of the symptoms noted below.
   Residual phase: Persistence, following the active phase of the illness, of at least *two* of the symptoms noted below, not due to a disturbance in mood or to a Substance Use Disorder.
   Prodromal or Residual Symptoms
   (1) social isolation or withdrawal;
   (2) marked impairment in role functioning as wage-earner, student, or homemaker;
   (3) markedly peculiar behavior (e.g., collecting garbage, talking to self in public, or hoarding food);
   (4) marked impairment in personal hygiene and grooming;
   (5) blunted, flat, or inappropriate affect;
   (6) digressive, vague, overelaborate, circumstantial, or metaphorical speech;
   (7) odd or bizarre ideation, or magical thinking, for example, superstitiousness, clairvoyance, telepathy, "Sixth sense," "others can feel my feeling," overvalued ideas, ideas of reference;

(8) unusual perceptual experiences, for example, recurrent illusions, sensing the presence of a force or person not actually present.

Examples: Six months of prodromal symptoms with 1 week of symptoms from A; no prodromal symptoms with 6 months of symptoms from A; no prodromal symptoms with 2 weeks of symptoms from A and 6 months of residual symptoms; 6 months of symptoms from A, apparently followed by several years of complete remission, with 1 week of symptoms in A in current episode.

D. The full depressive or manic syndrome (criteria A and B of major depressive or manic episode), if present, developed after any psychotic symptoms, or was brief in duration relative to the duration of the psychotic symptoms in A.

E. Onset of prodromal or active phase of the illness before age 45.

F. Not due to any Organic Mental Disorder or Mental Retardation.

TABLE 2.2 Diagnostic Criteria for Schizophrenia According to the DSM-III-R

A. Presence of characteristic psychotic symptoms in the active phase; either (1), (2), or (3) for at least 1 week (unless the symptoms are successfully treated):

(1) two of the following:

(a) delusions,

(b) prominent hallucinations (throughout the day for several days or several times a week for several weeks, each hallucinatory experience not being limited to a few brief moments),

(c) incoherence or marked loosening of associations,

(d) catatonic behavior,

(e) flat or grossly inappropriate affect;

(2) bizarre delusions (e.g., involving a phenomenon that the person's culture would regard as totally implausible, for example, thought broadcasting, being controlled by a dead person;

(3) prominent hallucinations [as defined in (1)(b) above] of a voice with content having no apparent relation to depression or elation, or a voice keeping up a running commentary on the person's behavior or thoughts, or two or more voices conversing with each other.

B. During the course of the disturbance, functioning in such areas was work, social relations, and self-care is markedly below the highest level achieved before onset of the disturbance (or, when the onset is in childhood or adolescence, failure to achieve expected level of social development).

C. Schizoaffective Disorder and Mood Disorder with Psychotic Feature have been ruled out, that is, if a Major Depressive or Manic Syndrome has even been present during an active phase of the disturbance, the total duration of all episodes of a mood syndrome has been brief relative to the total duration of the active and residual phases of the disturbance.

Table 2.2 *(cont.)*

D. Continuous signs of the disturbance for at least 6 months. The 6-month period must include an active phase (of at least 1 week, or less if symptoms have been successfully treated) during which there were psychotic symptoms characteristic of Schizophrenia (symptoms in A), with or without a prodromal or residual phase, as defined below.

Prodromal phase: A clear deterioration in functioning before the active phase or the disturbance that is not due to a disturbance in mood or to a Psychoactive Substance Use Disorder and that involves at least two of the symptoms listed below.

Residual phase: Following the active phase of the disturbance, persistence of at least two of the symptoms noted below, these not being due to a disturbance in mood or to a Psychoactive Substance Use Disorder.

Prodromal or Residual Symptoms

(1) marked social isolation or withdrawal;

(2) marked impairment in role functioning as wage-earner, student, or home-maker;

(3) markedly peculiar behavior (e.g., collecting garbage, talking to self in public, hoarding food);

(4) marked impairment in personal hygiene and grooming;

(5) blunted or inappropriate affect;

(6) digressive, vague, overelaborate, or circumstantial speech, or poverty of speech, or poverty of content of speech;

(7) odd beliefs or magical thinking, influencing behavior and inconsistent with cultural norms, for example, superstitiousness, belief in clairvoyance, telepathy, "sixth sense," "others can feel my feeling," overvalued ideas, ideas of reference;

(8) unusual perceptual experiences, for example, recurrent illusions, sensing the presence of a force or person not actually present;

(9) marked lack of initiative, interests, or energy. *Examples:* Six months of prodromal symptoms with 1 week of symptoms from A; no prodromal symptoms with 6 months of symptoms from A; no prodromal symptoms with 1 week of symptoms from A and 6 months of residual symptoms.

E. It cannot be established that an organic factor initiated and maintained the disturbance.

F. If there is a history of Autistic Disorder, the additional diagnosis of schizophrenia is made only if prominent delusions or hallucinations are also present.

Classification of course. The course of the disturbance is coded in the fifth digit:

1—Subchronic. The time from the beginning of the disturbance, when the person first began to show signs of the disturbance (including prodromal, active, and residual phases) more or less continuously, is less than 2 years, but at least 6 months.

2—Chronic. Same as above, but more than 2 years.

3—Subchronic with Acute Exacerbation. Reemergence of prominent psychotic symptoms in a person with a subchronic course who has been in the residual phase of the disturbance.

4—Chronic with Acute Exacerbation. Reemergence of prominent psychotic symptoms in a person with a chronic course who has been in the residual phase of the disturbance.

5—In Remission. When a person with a history of schizophrenia is free of all signs of the disturbance (whether or not on medication), "in Remission" should be coded.
Differentiating Schizophrenia in Remission from No Mental Disorder requires consideration of overall level of functioning, length of time since the last episode of disturbance, total duration of the disturbance, and whether prophylactic treatment is being given.

0—Unspecified.

a history of *autistic disorder* (our italics) should a diagnosis of schizophrenia be reserved for those who, in addition, have prominent delusions or hallucinations. The DSM-IV, on the other hand, refers to the use of this criterion if there is a history of either *autistic disorder or another pervasive developmental disorder* (our italics). Thus, with the DSM-III-R, an individual with Asperger syndrome (one variant of the so-called pervasive developmental disorders) might well receive an additional diagnosis of schizophrenia without showing signs of delusions or hallucinations, whereas with the DSM-IV, the Asperger individual would be exempt from a diagnosis of schizophrenia unless he or she showed prominent delusions or hallucinations. Given that Asperger syndrome is a relatively common condition (Ehlers & Gillberg, 1993), this seemingly minor change in the criteria could, theoretically, affect prevalence rates of schizophrenia in epidemiological samples.

ICD

The ICD-10 research criteria for schizophrenia differ in both major and minor ways from those of the DSM-IV. First of all, the presence of characteristic schizophrenic thought-disorder symptoms (thought echo, insertion, or broadcasting) is sufficient for diagnosis according to the ICD-10. Such symptoms are not even mentioned in the list of DSM criteria. Even though "formal thought disorder" has long been argued (perhaps particularly by Bleuler and his followers) to be the single most important feature of

TABLE 2.3 Diagnostic Criteria for Schizophrenia According to the DSM-IV

A. *Characteristic symptoms:* Two (or more) of the following, each present for a significant portion of time during a 1-month period (or less if successfully treated):

  (1) delusions;

  (2) hallucinations;

  (3) disorganized speech (e.g., frequent derailment or incoherence);

  (4) grossly disorganized or catatonic behavior;

  (5) negative symptoms, i.e., affective flattening, alogia, or avolition.

  Note: Only one Criterion A symptom is required if delusions are bizarre or hallucinations consist of a voice keeping up a running commentary on the person's behavior or thoughts, or two or more voices conversing with each other.

B. *Social/occupational dysfunction:* For a significant portion of the time since the onset of the disturbance, one or more major areas of functioning such as work, interpersonal relations, or self-care are markedly below the level achieved prior to the onset (or when the onset is in childhood or adolescence, failure to achieve expected level of interpersonal, academic, or occupational achievement).

C. *Duration:* Continuous signs of the disturbance persist for at least 6 month. This 6-month period must include at least 1 month of symptoms (or less if successfully treated) that meet Criterion A (i.e., active-phase symptoms) and may include periods of prodromal or residual symptoms. During these prodromal or residual periods, the signs of the disturbance may be manifested by only negative symptoms or two or more symptoms listed in Criterion A present in an attenuated form (e.g., odd beliefs, unusual perceptual experiences).

D. *Schizoaffective and Mood Disorder exclusion:* Schizoaffective disorder and Mood Disorder with Psychotic Features have been ruled out because either (1) no Major Depressive, Manic, or Mixed Episodes have occurred concurrently with the active-phase symptoms; or (2) if mood episodes have occurred during active-phase symptoms, their total duration has been brief relative to the duration of the active and residual periods

E. *Substance/general medical condition exclusion:* The disturbance is not due to the direct physiological effects of a substance (e.g., drug abuse, medication) or a general medical condition.

F. *Relationship to a Pervasive Developmental Disorder:* If there is a history of Autistic Disorder or another Pervasive Developmental Disorder, the additional diagnosis of Schizophrenia is made only if prominent delusions or hallucinations are also present for a least a month (or less if successfully treated).

Classification of longitudinal course (can be applied only after at least 1 year has elapsed since the initial onset of active-phase symptoms):

  Episodic with Interepisode Residual Symptoms (episodes are defined by the reemergence of prominent psychotic symptoms); *also specify if:*

With Prominent Negative Symptoms
Episodic with No Interepisode Residual Symptoms
Continuous (prominent psychotic symptoms are present throughout the period of observation); *also specify if* **with Prominent Negative Symptoms**
Single Episode in Partial Remission; *also specify if* **with Prominent Negative Symptoms**
Single Episode in Full Remission
Other or Unspecified Pattern

---

schizophrenia, the developers of the DSM-IV felt that thought disorder is notoriously difficult to define and therefore emphasized its surmised outward symptom, disorganized speech, instead. Second, the specific combinations of symptoms that qualify an individual for a diagnosis of schizophrenia according to the ICD-10 are different from those of the DSM manuals. Finally, there is no requirement to take account of a possible previous history of autism when making the diagnosis of schizophrenia using the ICD-10.

THE CLASSICAL SCHIZOPHRENIA SUBTYPES

The subtypes of schizophrenia that are most often referred to are hebephrenia, paranoid schizophrenia, catatonia, and residual schizophrenia. These four "variants" are often referred to as the "classical" subtypes of schizophrenia.

For any of the subtypes to be diagnosed, the common criteria for schizophrenia (as shown in Tables 2.1–2.4) have to be met first. In the case of catatonic schizophrenia, these common schizophrenia criteria will have to be met eventually, although this may not be possible initially if the patient is uncommunicative.

Hebephrenia

Hebephrenia often commences in adolescence and early adult life (around ages 15–25 years). Premorbid personality may be characterized by oddities of social style and interaction, attention

**TABLE 2.4 Diagnostic Criteria for Schizophrenia
According to the ICD-10**

(a) Thought echo, thought insertion or withdrawal, and thought broadcasting;

(b) Delusions of control, influence, or passivity, clearly referred to body or limb movements or specific thoughts, actions, or sensations, delusional perception;

(c) Hallucinatory voices giving a running commentary on the patient's behavior, or discussing the patient among themselves, or other types of hallucinatory voices coming from some part of the body;

(d) Persistent delusions of other kinds that are culturally inappropriate and completely impossible, such as religious or political identity, or superhuman powers and abilities (e.g., being able to control the weather, or being in communication with aliens from another world);

(e) Persistent hallucinations in any modality, when accompanied with fleeting or half-formed delusions without clear affective content, or by persistent over-valued ideas, or when occurring every day for weeks or months on end;

(f) Breaks or interpolations in the train of thought, resulting in incoherence or irrelevant speech, or neologisms;

(g) Catatonic behavior, such as excitement, posturing, or waxy flexibility, negativism, mutism, and stupor;

(h) "Negative" symptoms such as marked apathy, paucity of speech, and blunting or incongruity of emotional responses, usually resulting in social withdrawal and lowering of social performance; it must be clear that these are not due to depression or to neuroleptic medication;

(i) A significant and consistent change in the overall quality of some aspects of personal behavior, manifest as loss of interest, aimlessness, idleness, a self-absorbed attitude, and social withdrawal.

deficits, and learning problems. What may at first appear to be nonalarming attentional problems, a slight decrease in academic performance, hypochondriasis, and an infatuation with a more or less extreme philosophical or religious movement may develop into hebephrenia.

This type of schizophrenia (roughly equivalent to "disorganized type" in the DSM editions) is characterized by disorganized speech (believed to be reflective of thought disorder), disorganized behavior (aimless and disjointed rather than goal-directed and usually leading to disruption in the ability to perform activities of daily life, such as showering, dressing, or preparing meals) and flat or inappropriate affect. Silliness and laughter, not closely connected with the content of speech, may be associated with the symptom of disorganized speech. Delusions and hallucinations are not prominent. Although they may be present they do not usually center around a coherent theme. In summary, onset of this subtype of schizophrenia is often insidious, and it tends to run a continuous course without significant remissions.

There may be significant impairment on neuropsychological tests, but it is unclear to what extent such dysfunction is specific to hebephrenia or relates more clearly to severity of disorder (McGlashan & Fenton, 1992). Hebephrenia is usually associated with poor outcome and, as a group, may be regarded as one of the most severe subtypes of schizophrenia.

Catatonia

"Catatonia" and "catatonic schizophrenia" (schizophrenia, catatonic type) represent relatively clear-cut syndromes from the symptomatic point of view. Their grouping with the schizophrenias in the current systems is problematic in that so many individuals with catatonia have associated brain disorders or other diagnosable psychiatric conditions/developmental disorders (Gelenberg, 1976; Gelenberg & Mandel, 1977). The catatonic syndromes may be acute, chronic, or periodic. In the latter case, there is sometimes associated nitrogen retention and a diet low in protein plus medication with thyroxine (to augment metabolism) can prevent the appearance of attacks of catatonia (Gjessing & Gjessing, 1961).

The essential feature of the catatonic type of schizophrenia is a marked psychomotor disturbance. The symptoms of catatonic schizophrenia may be any, some, or all of the following: motoric immobility (catalepsy—including "waxy flexibility," or stupor), extreme negativism with resistance to all demands, and maintenance of a rigid posture against attempts to be moved, mutism, excessive purposeless motor activity, posturing (including "voluntary" assumption of inappropriate or bizarre postures), rigidity, command automatisms (i.e., automatic compliance with instructions), prominent mannerisms, grimacing, echolalia, or echopraxia.

Paranoid Schizophrenia

Paranoid schizophrenia is considered to be the most common type of schizophrenia in most parts of the world. Onset is often later than in the other variants of schizophrenia and the age at first psychiatric admission is higher (Winokur et al., 1974; Zigler & Levine, 1981).

Its essential feature is the presence of prominent delusions (such as delusions of persecution, reference, exalted birth, special mission, bodily change, or jealousy) and auditory (and sometimes other) hallucinations in the context of a relatively well-preserved personality without major cognitive or affective dysfunction. Some affective incongruity is usually present, however, and mood disturbances such as irritability, fearfulness, and sudden anger are not infrequent. Suspiciousness, of course, is a typical concomitant in many cases. Disturbances of volition and speech are not prominent and catatonia is not a feature of this subtype of schizophrenia.

Paranoid schizophrenia often has a relatively acute (sometimes seemingly reactive) onset with either an intermittent and "distinct" course (McGlashan & Fenton, 1992), or it may (more rarely) run a chronic course with florid symptoms persisting for several years without discrete episodes. Outcome in the longer term may be considerably better than for the other types of schizophrenia, particularly with respect to educational/occupational functioning and capacity for independent living (Kendler et al., 1984; McGlashan & Fenton, 1992). There is usually little or no evidence of impairment on neuropsychological (or other cognitive) testing (Zigler & Glick, 1984).

Paranoid schizophrenia is differentiated from "delusional (paranoid) disorder" in the DSM-IV and "delusional disorder" in the ICD-10. The essential feature of this disorder is the presence of a persistent "nonbizarre" (i.e., *other than* completely impossible or culturally inappropriate) delusion in the context of a disorder that does not meet criteria for schizophrenia. This type of delusional disorder, which is probably relative uncommon (with a lifetime prevalence of less than 0.1%) is often of even later onset than paranoid schizophrenia (around ages 40–55 years).

Residual Schizophrenia

This type of schizophrenia is diagnosed when there has been at least one episode of disorder meeting full criteria for schizophrenia, but the current clinical picture is without prominent delusions, hallucinations, disorganized speech, or behavioral abnormality. The course of residual schizophrenia may some-times represent a transition between a full-blown episode and complete remission. Sometimes it is present for many years, with or without acute exacerbations.

Dementia Simplex (Simple Schizophrenia)

This variant of schizophrenia is not included in the DSM editions. It is one of the "classical" subtypes, however. It is sometimes included in the group of "nonregressive" schizophrenias together with "pseudoneurotic schizophrenia" (Nyman, 1978) (Figure 2.1). The ICD-10 refers to it as "simple schizophrenia."

In dementia simplex, there is often adolescent onset with rapid decline in academic and social functioning, a gradual appearance and deepening of negative symptoms, such as apathy, hypoactivity, blunting of affect and initiative, decrease in nonverbal communication, and finally the appearance of a self-absorbed attitude and complete social withdrawal. The individual has not previously met criteria for any of the other subtypes of schizophrenia. The pervasiveness of this disorder and the profound effects it has on the personality of the affected individual are not perceived by him or her as severe enough to warrant consultation. For this reason and because of the complete absence of positive symptoms, many of those affected are not known to psychiatric services.

SCHIZOPHRENIFORM DISORDER

According to the DSM-IV, the essential features of schizophreniform disorder are identical to those of schizophrenia except for

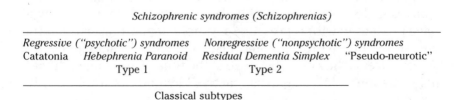

Schizophrenic syndromes (Schizophrenias)

Regressive ("psychotic") syndromes	Nonregressive ("nonpsychotic") syndromes	
Catatonia Hebephrenia Paranoid	Residual Dementia Simplex	"Pseudo-neurotic"
Type 1	Type 2	

Classical subtypes

Figure 2.1. Relationship of subgroups and diagnostic concepts in schizophrenia.

two differences: the total duration of the illness (prodromal, active, and residual phase included) is at least 1 month but less than 6 months and impairment in social or occupational functioning is not a requirement. According to the DSM-IV (APA, 1994), approximately one-third of individuals given a diagnosis of schizophreniform disorder will recover within the 6-month period. The other two-thirds go on to meet criteria for schizophrenia or schizoaffective disorder. Community studies are reported by the DSM-IV to have found a prevalence (lifetime) of 0.2% for schizophreniform disorder.

The ICD-10 refers to "acute schizophrenia-like psychotic disorder" when symptomatic, but not duration, criteria for schizophrenia are met. Because the ICD-10 requires "only" 1-month duration for a diagnosis of schizophrenia, acute schizophrenia-like psychotic disorder is made only if the total duration of the disorder is less than 1 month.

SCHIZOPHRENIA: TYPES 1 AND 2

Crow (1980) suggested that schizophrenia might best be subdivided according to the presence or absence of so-called productive symptoms. He suggested the term Type 1 schizophrenia for variants of the condition that comprised "active" ("productive," "positive") symptoms such as hallucinations and delusional phenomena. Type 2 schizophrenia, according to this model, comprises variants with emotional blunting and other "negative" symptoms. In more "dynamic" terms, Type 1 schizophrenia encompasses "regressive" or "psychotic" variants of schizophrenia, whereas Type 2 schizophrenia refers to "nonregressive" or "nonpsychotic" variants of schizophrenia, of which dementia simplex is the prototype. Residual schizophrenia, which may well have presented with regressive/psychotic symptoms early in the course of the disorder, would also be included among Type 2 schizophrenia; however, because at the time of assigning a "residual schizophrenia" diagnosis, "active" symptoms would not be present.

The relationship between various diagnostic subgroups and concepts are shown in Figure 2.1.

SCHIZOTYPAL (PERSONALITY) DISORDER

This diagnostic category has a controversial status as being either a disorder on the "schizophrenia spectrum" or a "personality disorder" (belonging, according to the DSM-IV, in the cluster A personality disorder group, i.e., those personality disorders that are characterized by oddness and eccentricity). It is also clear (Szatmari, 1992) that there is overlap of this concept with that of Asperger syndrome and other "autism spectrum disorders."

Schizotypal disorder is considered to be characterized by eccentric behavior and anomalies of thinking and affect that may resemble those seen in schizophrenia, though there are "no definite and characteristic schizophrenic anomalies . . . at any stage" (WHO, 1992, p. 95). No typical disturbance is always present, but several of the following are usually present: (1) inappropriate or constricted affect ("coldness," "aloofness"); (2) odd, eccentric, or peculiar behavior; (3) social withdrawal (lack of close friends and social anxiety that does not diminish with familiarity and tends to be associated with paranoid ideas rather than self-depreciation); (4) odd beliefs or magical thinking; (5) suspiciousness or paranoid ideation; (6) unusual perceptual experiences including bodily illusions, depersonalization, or derealization; (7) odd thinking and speech without gross incoherence; and (8) ruminations without inner resistance, often with dysmorphophobic, sexual, or aggressive content. Occasional periods of intense illusions or even hallucinations and "delusionlike" ideas are accepted for this diagnostic category by the ICD-10.

Symptoms of schizotypal personality disorder are usually evident in childhood or adolescence. It may be more common among males, but population data is largely lacking.

According to the DSM-IV (APA, 1994), this disorder may occur in 3% of the population. In a recent Swedish study schizotypal personality disorder was diagnosed in 4% of 16–17 year olds without attention deficits and in 18% of those with such problems (Hellgren et al., 1994). According to the DSM-IV, schizotypal personality disorder has a relatively stable (usually chronic) course, and only a small minority of individuals with this diagnosis go on to develop schizophrenia or another psychotic disorder. The disorder appears to aggregate familially and is also more prevalent among the relatives of individuals diagnosed as suffering from schizophrenia than among the general population.

SCHIZOID AND PARANOID PERSONALITY DISORDERS

The diagnostic categories of schizoid and paranoid personality disorders share many features with schizotypal disorder, but cognitive and perceptual distortions, common in the latter, are usually not encountered in the former. Both personality disorders are characterized by eccentric and odd or introspective ideas, but paranoid personality disorder is hallmarked by prominent suspiciousness, and paranoid ideation, whereas schizoid personality disorder is dominated more by flat affect, solitariness, and "emotional coldness."

Both these personality disorders appear to be more common and to cause more social impairment in men. From the clinical point of view, it is clear that they overlap (schizoid personality disorder in particular) to a considerable extent with Asperger syndrome (Wolff, 1992; Gillberg, 1992). They usually have their onset in childhood or adolescence. Paranoid personality disorder is believed to be relatively common, occurring in 0.5%–4% of the general population (APA, 1994; Hellgren et al., 1994), whereas schizoid personality disorder is considered to be much rarer. There is probably an overrepresentation of these personality disorders in the relatives of individuals with schizophrenia (and, in the case of schizoid personality disorder, in the relatives of individuals with schizotypal disorder).

SUMMARY OF DIFFERENCES IN DIAGNOSTIC CRITERIA CURRENTLY USED

Obviously, the boundaries of schizophrenia have changed many times since the days of Kraepelin and Bleuler. Much additional work is required in order to examine the validity of the syndrome(s) against external criteria, such as medical conditions, familial aggregation, and clinical course.

Although the various editions of the DSM and the ICD-10, currently the most widely used manuals for diagnosis in the field, employ relatively narrow definitions of schizophrenia, there are several major, and minor, points of disagreement. Some of the most important of these are (1) thought disorder is not specifically mentioned in the DSM-IV (although implicitly suggested by disorganized speech) but is a sufficient symptom for diagnosis in the ICD; (2) the constellation of symptoms that is required for a diagnosis differs from one manual to another; (3) the requirement for duration of active symptoms (and for the "psychotic illness") differs across all four of the DSM, DSM-III-R, DSM-IV, and ICD-10; (4) the various DSM editions all refer to some (albeit slightly variable) criteria of impairment/deterioration, whereas the ICD-10 makes no mention of such criteria; (5) the subtyping according to course and "class of schizophrenia" differs across all the currently used systems; and (6) the definition and weighting of positive and negative symptoms are done somewhat differently by the different manuals.

SCHIZOAFFECTIVE DISORDER

Schizoaffective disorder according to the DSM-IV (and the ICD-10) is characterized on the one hand by meeting criteria for major depression, mania, or both (Table 2.5) and, on the other hand, concurrently meeting symptomatic criteria for schizophrenia. Symptoms must not be due to the direct physiological effects of a substance or a general medical condition. The problem with this added criterion is illustrated by case reports of females with the fragile X syndrome who develop a characteristic clinical picture of schizoaffective disorder (Steffenburg, 1991; Gillberg et al., 1992). Onset is often in early adult life, but the disorder can present for the first time in adolescence as well as late in life.

The course is often episodic with some degree of occupational and social deterioration. Most authors agree, however, that outcome is better than in schizophrenia although it is considerably worse than the outcome for mood disorders. Schizoaffective disorder is believed to be less common than schizophrenia, but

TABLE 2.5 Diagnostic Criteria for Schizoaffective Disorder According to the DSM-IV

A. An uniterrupted period of illness during which there is either a Major Depressive Episode, a Manic Episode, or a Mixed Episode concurrent with symptoms that meet Criterion A for Schizophrenia.
Note: The Major Depressive Episode must include Criterion A1: depressed mood.
B. During the same period of illness, there have been delusions or hallucinations for at least 2 weeks in the absence of prominent mood symptoms.
C. Symptoms that meet criteria for a mood episode are present for a substantial portion of the total duration of the active and residual periods of the illness.
D. The disturbance is not due to the direct physiological effects of a substance (e.g., drug abuse, medication) or a general medical condition.
Specify type:
Bipolar Type: if the disturbance includes a Manic or a Mixed Episode (or a Manic or a Mixed Episode and Major Depressive Episodes)
Depressive Type: if the disturbance only includes Major Depressive Episodes

reliable epidemiological data is largely lacking. There is substantial evidence that an increased risk schizophrenia and mood disorders exists in the biological relatives of individuals who suffer from schizoaffective disorder.

ARE SCHIZOPHRENIA AND AFFECTIVE DISORDERS RELATED?

Ever since the early days of separation of schizophrenia from affective disorders, there has been a debate about whether or not the two conditions are related. Most of the research currently undertaken in the field of severe psychopathology accepts the Kraepelinian notion that schizophrenia and affective disorders are biologically distinct. The suggestion that "the psychoses" may be on a continuum of liability is a prominent feature in the work by some groups, however. It has been suggested that schizophrenia and affective disorders may represent opposite ends of a continuum on which schizophrenia is the most severe form and schizoaffective disorder is intermediate (Crow, 1990). Others have proposed that schizophrenia and affective disorder may be two independent conditions but that unipolar and schizo-affective disorder may be expressed in the relatives of individuals in both categories (Gershon et al., 1988). Taylor (1992) recently reviewed the evidence that schizophrenia and affective disorder may be related and concluded that investigators in the field should not presume a dichotomy or continuum, but should examine pure and mixed pedigrees and look for state-related and trait-related endophenotypes.

Even in the early writings of Rüdin (one of Kraepelin's co-workers) equal numbers of relatives with affective disorder and relatives with schizophrenia were found in the families of probands with schizophrenia (Rüdin, 1916). Odegaard found about three- quarters of psychotic relatives of "severe defect schizophrenia" probands had schizophrenia and one-quarter had affective disorders (Odegaard, 1972). Among psychotic relatives of manic-depressive probands, almost one-fifth had been diagnosed as suffering from schizophrenia. In the study by Tsuang et al. (1980), data supported "the distinction between schizophrenia and affective disorders, although the distinction between schizophrenia and mania was not clear." In the study of the Maudsley schizophrenia twin series, Farmer et al. (1987) found that of 24 identical twins with schizophrenia, 6 had a co-twin with schizophrenia and 7 had a co-twin with an affective disorder.

If the Krapelinian dichotomy is valid, intermediate forms, such as schizoaffective disorder, should be rare. However, Brockington and Leff (1979) and Surtees and Sashidharan (1986) found similar rates of schizoaffective disorder and schizophrenia in their samples of hospitalized psychosis patients on the one hand, and community-based cohorts on the other.

Some studies have tried to discriminate affective disorder from schizophrenia on the basis of various features thought to be characteristic of each disorder. Studies of symptoms have found a unimodal, rather than bimodal distribution (Kendell & Gourlay, 1970; Ni Bhrolchain et al., 1979). Soft neurological signs are as common in both types of disorder (Nasrallah et al., 1983), as are structural brain abnormalities (Andreasen, 1988), and neurotransmitter dysfunction (Carlsson, 1988). In summary, it would seem that it is yet not clear to what extent schizophrenia and affective disorders overlap. It seems that Taylor's recommendation to keep an open mind in this respect is valid.

CLINICAL DIFFERENTIAL DIAGNOSIS

The differential diagnosis of a hard-to-define condition such as schizophrenia is a difficult task. There are no pathognomonic symptoms and no biological marker and the diagnosis is based purely on the appropriate grouping of behaviors believed to reflect some underlying core, but as yet unknown, deficit.

Distinguishing schizophrenia from *mood disorders with psychotic features* and, perhaps particularly, from *schizoaffective disorder*, is rendered difficult by the fact that mood disturbance is a very common concomitant of schizophrenia, especially in the prodromal phase and during exacerbations.

In children and young adults there may be a problem separating *autism and autisticlike conditions ("pervasive developmental disorders")* in some instances. In classic autism, schizophrenic symptoms are rare (Wing, 1989) and differential diagnosis is usually relatively straightforward, but in Asperger syndrome (Wing, 1981; Gillberg, 1991) major problems can occur (see Chapter 3).

Young people with attention deficit hyperactivity disorder (ADHD) may occasionally be so hyperactive as to appear incoherent and the suspicion might be raised that schizophrenic symptoms may be present. Many individuals with schizophrenia have severe attentional dysfunction. According to one study (Hellgren et al., 1987), ADHD and the closely related diagnosis of DAMP (deficits in attention, motor control, and perception) occurred in the histories of a majority of cases with adolescent-onset schizophrenia.

Perhaps the most difficult aspect of differential diagnosis in schizophrenia is its distinction from *psychotic disorder due to a general medical condition, delirium, and dementia* (DSM-IV), or *organic delusional (schizophrenialike) disorder* (ICD-10). The current diagnostic systems exclude the diagnosis of schizophrenia when there is a general medical (or organic brain) condition that is believed to have caused the psychiatric syndrome. This line of reasoning is similar to old concepts of infantile autism: if a medical condition was found, "secondary autism" was inferred, if not, "primary autism" was diagnosed. Correspondingly, in psychotic disorders, if symptomatic diagnostic criteria for schizophrenia are met and no general medical condition is diagnosed (e.g., in individuals who do not receive a full medical work-up but who may well have an undiagnosed medical disorder), then the diagnosis of schizophrenia is assigned. If symptomatic criteria for schizophrenia are met and a general medical condition is found, however (e.g., in an individual who does receive a full medical work-up), a diagnosis of psychotic disorder due to a general medical condition/organic schizophrenialike disorder may be made instead. "Classic" autism cases without a demonstrable organic cause at the time of diagnosis were sometimes diagnosed later with a general medical condition (such as the fragile X syndrome or tuberous sclerosis). From this evidence came the conceptualization of autism as a behavioral syndrome regardless of underlying etiology. We believe that this would be a reasonable strategy in schizophrenia also. In the following sections we therefore do not consider psychotic disorder due to a general medical condition to be a differential diagnosis if symptomatic criteria for schizophrenia are met. Schizophrenia will be considered to be present when other criteria for this disorder are met regardless of whether there is an associated medical condition or not. The psychiatric (behavioral) syndrome would be coded on axis I of the multiaxial classification system, whereas the associated medical condition would be coded on axis III.

Incidentally, we have problems with the criterion relating to a general medical condition for other reasons than those already outlined. For instance, the DSM-IV specifier in this regard reads: "The disturbance is *not due to* (our italics) the direct physiological effects of a substance (e.g., a drug of abuse, a medication) or a general medical condition" (APA, 1994, p. 286). We fail to see how, in the individual case, if there is an associated general medical condition, a decision can always be reliably made regarding the *etiological* role of this condition for the development of the schizophrenic disorder.

According to the DSM-IV, psychotic disorder due to a general medical condition is characterized by prominent hallucinations or delusions. Hallucinations can occur in any sensory modality, but some etiological factors are known to evoke specific hallucinatory phenomena. Temporal lobe epilepsy is suggested by the appearance of olfactory hallucinations, particularly when these involve the smell of burning rubber or other unpleasant smells. Religious delusions are also suggestive of temporal lobe epilepsy in some cases. Individuals with right parietal brain damage/dysfunction sometimes develop a contralateral neglect syndrome in which they may disown parts of their body to a delusional extent. The problem with the distinction of psychotic disorder due to a general medical condition from schizophrenia is that exactly the same phenomena may occur without any clear evidence that a general medical condition is present. The clinical picture may be strongly suggestive of a specific kind of brain disorder, and yet, even after extensive investigation, no evidence to prove its presence can be demonstrated. Should such an individual be diagnosed as suffering from schizophrenia or from psychotic disorder *probably* due to a general medical condition?

EPIDEMIOLOGY

Schizophrenia is not an uncommon problem. The lifetime risk has been estimated at 1% of the general population. Prevalence among adults is on the order of 0.2%–0.5% (Jablensky & Sartorius, 1975), and appears to be relatively stable across cultures. This is somewhat surprising given the variability of diagnostic criteria that have been used over the latest 30-year period. The relatively high prevalence rate as compared with the lifetime risk of disorder reflects the chronicity of the disorder. The prevalence in adolescence is around 0.2% according to one study (Gillberg et al., 1986). Definite conclusions for this age group are not warranted because only one study has been published specifically addressing the prevalence of schizophrenia in adolescence.

SEX RATIOS AND AGE OF ONSET

The lifetime risk of schizophrenia appears to be equal for men and women. According to most studies, however, men have an earlier age of onset with a peak risk around 20 years of age. Women, on the other hand, have a peak incidence around age 30 years and a much higher risk than men of developing the disorder after age 50 years (Kay, 1975). Conclusions regarding male:female ratios and age of onset rely on the assumption that schizophrenia can be regarded as a single disorder. The available data could also be interpreted as showing the heterogeneity of the schizophrenic syndromes. Adolescent-onset schizophrenia may be more common in males than in females (Gillberg et al., 1986), but onset may actually be earlier in females in this variant of the disorder (Galdos & van Os, 1995). Mid-life schizophrenia may represent a different condition and may be considerably more common in females who may or may not have a different age of onset as compared with males with this variant of the disorder.

COURSE AND OUTCOME

The course and outcome of schizophrenia can be roughly predicted to fall into one of the following three categories: (1) episodic course with no deterioration, (2) episodic course with deterioration, and (3) steady downhill course to deterioration. Some patients have an episodic course without deterioration but later change to follow a trajectory to deterioration after all (Vaillant, 1978). Episodes are usually briefer than 6 months. Longer duration usually implies that some degree of deterioration will occur. Progressive deterioration after the first 5 years from diagnosis is uncommon. Once this stage has been reached, it is usually a question of a chronic condition with considerable loss of psychosocial functions. Nevertheless, even in this chronic state, rehabilitation measures can have some success in improving social functioning (Bleuler, 1974).

With older US schizophrenia concepts, outcome was often reported to belong to the first of the above-mentioned three categories. Nowadays, with the use of more narrow criteria, differences between the United States and Europe with respect to schizophrenia outcome are probably minor. Bleuler's own follow-up study found about 20% of patients were free of symptoms many years after diagnosis (Bleuler, 1974). A Swedish follow-up study performed before the modern treatment era found 1% of patients to be free of symptoms; 10% of patients had such mild symptoms that they were functioning socially 10 years after onset (Johansson, 1958). A later Swedish study, performed after the advent of neuroleptic treatment and social rehabilitation, yielded a slightly more positive result with 6% completely recovered and another 26% showing only mild symptoms and no deterioration (Nyman & Johnson, 1983). This study included "regressive" as well as "nonregressive" variants of schizophrenia, however, and the results of the two studies may not be readily comparable. Even so, the outcome of nonregressive schizophrenia appears to be as poor as in regressive variants of the disorder (Nyman, 1975).

The rate of suicide is very high in schizophrenia. According to two Swedish studies, 11%–12% had committed suicide 6–17 years after first admission for schizophrenia (Nyman & Johnson, 1983; Allebeck & Wistedt, 1986).

REFERENCES

Allebeck, P., & Wistedt, B. (1986). Mortality in schizophrenia. A ten-year follow-up based on the Stockholm County inpatient register. *Archives of General Psychiatry, 43*, 650–653.

American Psychiatric Association. (1980). *Diagnostic and statistical manual of mental disorders*, third edition. Washington, DC: American Psychiatric Press.

American Psychiatric Association. (1987). *Diagnostic and statistical manual of mental disorders*, third edition - Revised. Washington, DC: American Psychiatric Press.

American Psychiatric Association. (1994). *Diagnostic and statistical manual of mental disorders*, fourth edition. Washington, DC: American Psychiatric Press.

Andreasen, N. C. (1988). Evaluation of brain imaging techniques in mental illness. *Annual Review of Medicine, 39*, 335–345.

Bleuler, E. (1911). *Dementia praecox and the group of schizophrenias*, J. Zinkin, trans. New York: International Universities Press.

Bleuler, M. (1974). The offspring of schizophrenias. *Schizophrenia Bulletin,* 93–107.

Boyle, M. (1990). Is schizophrenia what it was? A re-analysis of Kraepelin's and Bleuler's population. *Journal of the History of the Behavioral Sciences, 26*, 323–333.

Brockington, I. F., & Leff, J. P. (1979). Schizo-affective psychosis: Definitions and incidence. *Psychological Medicine, 9,* 91–99.

Carlson, A. (1988). The current status of the dopamine hypothesis of schizophrenia. *Neuropsychopharmacology, 1,* 179–186.

Crow, T. J. (1980). Molecular pathology of schizophrenia: More than one desease process? *British Medical Journal, 280,* 66–68.

Crow, T. J. (1990). The continuum of psychosis and its genetic origins. The sixty-fifth Maudsley lecture. *British Journal of Psychiatry, 156,* 788–797.

De Sanctis, S. (1906). Sopra alcune varietà della demenza precoce. *Revista Sperimentale di Freniatria e di Medicina Legale delle Alienazioni Mentale, 32,* 141–165.

Ehlers, S., & Gillberg, C. (1993). The epidemiology of Asperger syndrome. A total population study. *Journal of Child Psychology and Psychiatry, 34,* 1327–1350.

Farmer, A., McGuffin, P., & Gottesman, I. I. (1987). Twin concordance for DSM-III schizophrenia. Scrutinizing the validity of the definition. *Archives of General Psychiatry, 44,* 634–641.

Galdos, P. M., & van Os, J. J. (1995). Gender, psychopathology, and development: From puberty to early adulthood. *Schizophernia Research, 14,* 105–112.

Gelenberg, A .J. (1976). The catatonic syndrome. *Lancet, 1,* 1339–1341.

Gelenberg, A. J., & Mandel, M. R. (1977). Catatonic reactions to high-potency neuroleptic drugs. *Archives of General Psychiatry, 34,* 947–950.

Gershon, E. S., DeLisi, L. E., Hamovit, J., Nurnberger, J. I. J., Maxwell, M. E., Schreiber, J., Dauphinais, D., Dingman, C. W. D., & Guroff, J. J. (1988). A controlled family study of chronic psychoses. Schizophrenia and schizoaffective disorder. *Archives of General Psychiatry, 45,* 328–336.

Gillberg, C. (1991). Clinical and neurobiological aspects of Asperger syndrome in six family studies. In U. Frith, (Ed.), *Autism and Asperger syndrome.* (pp. 122–146). Cambridge: Cambridge University Press.

Gillberg, C. (1992). The Emanuel Miller Memorial Lecture 1991: Autism and autistic-like conditions: subclasses among disorders of empathy. *Journal of Child Psychology and Psychiatry, 33,* 813–842.

Gillberg, C., Persson, E., Grufman, M., & Themnér, U. (1986). Psychiatric disorders, in mildly and severely retarded urban children and adolescents: Epidemiological aspects. *British Journal of Psychiatry, 149,* 68–74.

Gillberg, C., Gillberg, I. C., & Steffenburg, S. (1992). Siblings and parents of children with autism. A controlled population based study. *Developmental Medicine and Child Neurology, 34,* 389–398.

Gjessing, R., & Gjessing, L. (1961). Some main trends in the clinical aspects of periodical catatonia. *Acta Psychiatrica Scandinavica, 37,* 1–13.

Hellgren, L., Gillberg, C., & Enerskog, I. (1987). Antecedents of adolescent psychoses: A population-based study of school health problems in children who develop psychosis in adolescence. *Journal of the American Academy of Child and Adolescent Psychiatry, 26,* 351–355.

Hellgren, L., Gillberg, I. C., Bågenholm, A., & Gillberg, C. (1994). Children with Deficits in Attention, Motor control and Perception (DAMP). almost grown up: Psychiatric and personality disorders at age 16 years. *Journal of Child Psychology and Psychiatry, 35,* 1255–1271.

Jablensky, A., & Sartorius, N. (1975). Culture and schizophrenia. In H. M. Van Praag, (Eds.), *On the origin of schizophrenic psychoses.* Amsterdam: De Erven Bohn BV.

Johansson, E. (1958). A study of schizophrenia in the male. A psychiatric and social study based on 138 cases with follow-up. *Acta Psychiatrica Neurlogica Scandinavica, 33,* (Suppl.) 125.

Kay, D. W. K. (1975). Schizophrenia and schizophrenic-like states in the elderly. In T. Silverstone, & B. Barraclough (Eds.), *Contemporary psychiatry. Selected reviews from the British Journal of Hospitals and Medicine.* Ashford, Kent: Headley Brothers. *British Journal of Psychiatry,* Publ. 9, 18–24.

Kendell, R. E., & Gouraly, J. (1970). The clinical distinction between the affective psychoses and schizophrenia. *British Journal of Psychiatry, 117,* 261–266.

Kendler, K. S., Gruenberg, A. M., & Tsuang, M. T. (1984) Outcome of schizophrenic subtypes defined by four diagnostic systems. *Archives of General Psychiatry, 41,* 149–154.

Leff, J. (1977). International variations in the diagnosis of psychiatric illness. *British Journal of Psychiatry, 51,* 25–31.

McGlashan, T. H., & Fenton, W. S. (1992). The positive-negative distinction in schizophrenia: Review of natural history validators. *Archives of General Psychiatry, 49,* 63–72.

Nasrallah, H. A., Tippin, J., & McCalley-Whitters, M. (1983). Neurological soft signs in manic patients. A comparison with schizophrenic and control groups. *Journal of Affective Disorders, 51,* 45–50.

Ni Bhrolchain, M., Brown, G. W., & Harris, T. O. (1979). Psychotic and neurotic depression: 2. Clinical characteristics. *British Journal of Psychiatry, 134,* 94–107.

Nyman, A., & Jonsson, H. (1986). Patterns of self-destruction behaviour in schizophrenia. *Acta Psychiatrica Scandinavica, 73,* 252–262.

Nyman, A. K. (1978). Non-regressive schizophrenia. Clinical course and outcome. *Acta Psychiatrica Scandinavica, Suppl. 272,* 143.

Nyman, G. E. (1975). The clinical picture of non-regressive schizophrenia. *Nordisk Psykiatrisk Tidskrft, 75*, 249–258.

Odegaard, O. (1972). The multifactorial theory in predisposition to schizophrenia. In A. R. Kaplan (Ed.), *Genetic factors in schizophrenia.* Springfield, IL: Charles. C. Thomas.

Rüdin, E. (1916). *Zur Verebung und Neuentslehung der Demntia Praecox.* Berlin: Springer.

Schneider, K. (1971). *Klinische psychopathologie.* Stuttgart: Georg Thieme Verlag.

Steffenburg, S. (1991). Neuropsychiatric assessment of children with autism: A population-based study. *Developmental Medicine and Child Neurology, 33*, 495–511.

Surtees, P. G., & Sashidharan, S.P. (1986). Psychiatric morbidity in two matched community samples: a comparison of rates and risks in Edinburgh and St. Louis. *Journal of Affective Disorders, 10*, 101–113.

Szatmari, P. (1992). The validity of autistic spectrum disorders: A literature review. *Journal of Autism and Developmental Disorders, 22*, 583–600.

Taylor, M. A. (1992). Are schizophrenia and affective disorder related? A selective literature review. *American Journal of Psychiatry, 149*, 22–32.

Tsuang, M. T., Winokur, G., & Crowe, R. R. (1980). Morbidity risks of schizophrenia and affective disorders among first degree relatives of patients with schizophrenia, mania, depression and surgical conditions. *British Journal of Psychiatry, 137*, 497–504.

Vaillant, G. E. (1978). Prognosis and the course of schizophrenia. *Schizophrenia Bulletin, 4*, 20–24.

WHO (1992). *The ICD-10 classification of mental and behavioural disorders. Clinical descriptions and guidelines.* Geneva: Author.

WHO (1993). *The ICD-10 classification of mental and behavioural disorders. Diagnostic Criteria for Research.* Geneva: Author.

Wing, L. (1981). Asperger's syndrome: A clinical account. *Psychological Medicine, 11*, 115–129.

Wing, L. (1989). The diagnosis of autism. In C. Gillberg, (Ed.), *Diagnosis and treatment of autism.* New York: Plenum Press.

Winokur, G., Morrison, J., Clancy, J., & Crowe, R. (1974). Iowa 500: The clinical course and genetic distinction of hebephrenic and paranoid schizophrenia. *Journal of Nervous and Mental Diseases, 159*, 12–19.

Wolff, S. (1992). Psychiatric morbidity and criminality in "schizoid" children grown-up: A records survey. *European Child & Adolescent Psychiatry, 1*, 214–221.

Zigler, E., & Glick, M. (1984). Paranoid schizophrenia: An unorthodox view. *American Journal of Orthopsychiatry, 54*, 43–70.

Zigler, E., & Levine, J. (1981). Age on first hospitalization of schizophrenics: A developmental approach. *Journal of Abnormal Psychology, 90,* 458–467.

CHAPTER 3

Childhood-Onset Schizophrenia

Ever since the days of Kraepelin and De Sanctis it has been widely recognized that schizophrenia may have its onset in childhood. The concept of childhood schizophrenia has held variable attraction for clinicians and researchers over the past 50 years. Just recently (Asarnow, 1994) it has come to the forefront as one of the most intensive areas of scientific inquiry in child and adolescent psychiatry.

HISTORICAL BACKGROUND

Kraepelin stated that at least 3.5% of his cases of dementia praecox had onsets prior to 10 years of age, with another 2.7% commencing between 10 and 15 years (Kraepelin, 1913, 1919). Bleuler (1911) and Lutz (1937) estimated that 4% of schizophrenia cases had onset prior to age 15 years.

As early as 1867, Maudsley, the noted British psychiatrist, had included in his textbook *The Physiology and Pathology of Mind*, a 34-page chapter on "Insanity of Early Life." In it he identified seven different varieties of mental derangement in children. By 1883, Clevenger had compiled 55 references to mental illness in childhood. Spitzka, in the same year, referred to "infantile psychosis" and said that it was rare and caused by heredity, fright, change of temperature or masturbation [see Kanner (1971) for a more detailed historical overview].

De Sanctis made a distinction between intellectually retarded children with psychotic behavior on the one hand, and normally intelligent children with "dementia praecocissima" on the other, acknowledging the existence of very early onset cases of "Kraepelin's disorder," dementia praecox (de Sanctis, 1906).

Heller (1908) described the condition now known as disintegrative disorder, Kanner (1943) delineated infantile autism, and Asperger (1944) described "autistic psychopathy," of late referred to as Asperger syndrome or Asperger's disorder (American Psychiatric Association, 1994). All of these three conditions have previously been included under the rubric of "childhood schizophrenia" or "childhood psychosis." Since the 1980s they have usually been grouped under separate headings, such as "pervasive developmental disorders" (APA, 1987) or "autism and autisticlike conditions" (Steffenburg & Gillberg, 1986).

Homburger (1926), Potter (1933, cited in Kanner 1971), Lutz (1937), Bender (1947, 1959, 1969) and Goldfarb (1961) were early proponents of a syndrome of child schizophrenia that shares many features of the childhood schizophrenia condition as it is conceptualized today. Nevertheless, in retrospect, it appears that their view of the condition may have been considerably more inclusive than the one currently most favored.

SCHIZOPHRENIA AS A SYNDROME IN CHILDHOOD

Up until the mid-1970s, childhood "psychosis"/schizophrenia was considered by many to be a rather broad band type of diagnosis, comprising several different variants of disorders involving severe and early onset psychopathology in childhood. Infantile autism, for example, was seen as one subtype of childhood psychosis. The leading scientific journal in the field changed its name from *Journal of Autism and Childhood Schizophrenia* to *Journal of Autism and Developmental Disorders* in 1978. This marked the end of an era during which psychosis, schizophrenia, and autism had often been used as synonyms or, at least, as partly overlapping concepts. After Kolvin's studies, it had become clear that autism and "later onset psychoses" could usually be reliably separated both by age of presenting symptoms and on the basis of separate sets of background factors (Kolvin, 1971).

There are obvious problems with the concept of childhood schizophrenia or, rather, childhood-onset schizophrenia. Very young children cannot communicate verbally at the level of an adolescent or adult. For the adequate reporting of some of the symptoms of schizophrenia (notably thought disorder, hallucinations, and delusions), a certain degree of intellectual and language development is required. Literature reviews suggest that the diagnosis has not been made in anyone under age 4.75 years (Campbell, Kafantaris, Malone, Kowalik, & Locascio, 1991; Russell, 1994). Almost all the 300 plus patients reported in 12 studies (Campbell et al., 1991; Remschmidt, Schulz, Martin, & Fleischhaker, 1994) were aged 6 years or older at the time of diagnosis. Two thirds of all patients have been 8 years or older at the time of first admission for onset of psychosis. "Nonpsychotic" symptoms, however, may have been present from a much younger age (Russell, 1994).

CURRENT DIAGNOSTIC CRITERIA AND SUBTYPING

Almost all researchers in the field now seem to agree that childhood-onset schizophrenia should be diagnosed only in cases meeting currently accepted criteria for schizophrenia as diagnosed in adults. Thus, the criteria for schizophrenia of the DSM or ICD should be used when assigning a diagnosis of childhood-onset schizophrenia. "Childhood-onset" has been variably defined. Many authors (Makita, 1966; Kydd & Werry, 1982; Volkmar et al., 1988) have included cases with teenage onset. We would favor the position of Green, Padron-Gayol, Hardesty, and Bassiri (1992) who have included only subjects aged 12 or under in their series of "schizophrenia with childhood onset." Perhaps in the future the most reasonable approach would be to refer to "prepubertal" schizophrenia and include only children who have not reached Tanner stage II of genital pubertal development.

There is some evidence (Werry, 1992) that schizophrenia can be reliably diagnosed in children using the same criteria as for adults. A small number of studies of schizophrenia in middle childhood have used semi-structured diagnostic interviews to

elicit diagnostic information and have employed operational diagnostic criteria (Russell, Bott, & Sammons, 1989; Spencer, Kafantaris, Padron-Gayol, Rosenberg, & Campbell, 1992; Asarnow,
Tompson, Hamilton, Goldstein, & Guthrie, 1994; Gordon et al.,
1994). These studies suggest that there may exist a syndrome of
middle childhood that bears very strong resemblances to schizophrenia as diagnosed in adults.

No study has systematically compared the types of symptoms
that characterize childhood-onset schizophrenia with those that
occur in adult-onset variants of the disorder. However, results
from different studies suggest that symptomatology, at least in
certain respects, may be similar in the very young and older
patients. Auditory hallucinations were present in 80% of the sample reported by Russell et al. (1989), 84% of that reported by
Green et al. (1992), 100% in the young schizophrenia cases in the
Spencer et al. (1994) series, and in 70% of adults reported by
Andreasen (1987). Delusions occurred in 63%, 55%, 100%, and
84%, respectively.

Very few studies have attempted subtyping in accordance
with currently accepted criteria for adult schizophrenia. Remschmidt et al. (1994) found paranoid schizophrenia to be the most
common variant, accounting for about two-thirds of all cases.
Hebephrenia (disorganized subtype) was found in about one in
five of all cases of early-onset schizophrenia.

CLINICAL COURSE AND OUTCOME

The course of childhood-onset schizophrenia is variable. Onset
usually appears to be quite insidious rather than acute. A small
number of children experience dramatic onset of hallucinations
or delusions without a prior history of major psychopathology.
Nevertheless, the majority of children appear to have been chronically impaired or to show insidious onset patterns (Kolvin, 1977;
Fish, 1977; Green et al., 1992). Children with early-onset schizophrenia appear to have poorer peer relationships, few interests,
and lower levels of scholastic achievement than children with
depressive disorders (Asarnow, Goldstein, & Ben-Meir, 1988).

There is a paucity of studies investigating the outcome of childhood-onset schizophrenia. The long-term outcome studies that are available rely on samples collected during the pre-DSM-III era when more modern assessment and diagnostic procedures were not available. Nevertheless, it seems that overall outcome may be poor for childhood-onset schizophrenia (Fish, 1987; Werry, McClellan, & Chard, 1991) with only a few percent experiencing remission after follow-up for at least 5 years. The vast majority develop chronic schizophrenia or have at least two more schizophrenic episodes. Mortality is probably much raised with suicides and delusion-driven accidents being common causes of death. Eggers (1989) reported a somewhat better outcome for patients diagnosed as suffering from schizophrenia prior to 14 years of age. At follow-up 6–14 years later, 27% were described as in remission, 24% had a mild defect, and 49% a severe defect.

DIFFERENTIAL DIAGNOSIS AND COMORBIDITY

Many children diagnosed as suffering from schizophrenia meet criteria for additional diagnoses. Russell et al. (1989) found that two-thirds of their sample of childhood-onset schizophrenia met criteria for at least one other psychiatric diagnosis, the most common of which were affective disorders (atypical depression and dysthymic disorder) and conduct disorder. Carlson and Strober (1978) conducted a retrospective review of six individuals diagnosed as suffering from schizophrenia at ages 12–16 years. All six met criteria for mania or depression but not Feighner et al.'s (1972) or Spitzer, Endicott, and Robins's (1978) research diagnostic criteria for schizophrenia.

Alaghband-Rad, McKenna, and Gordon (1995) analyzed the premorbid histories of 23 children with schizophrenia with onset prior to age 12 and compared them with cases with later onset. Specific developmental disabilities and transient early symptoms of autism, particularly motor stereotypies were common. Watkins, Asarnow, and Tanguay (1988) reported that children with early-onset schizophrenia often had a history of early language delay and abnormality, motor delays, hypotonia, lack of social responsiveness during infancy and bizarre responses to the environment. These problems are very similar to those encountered in children who receive a diagnosis of autism, typical or atypical. In early childhood, the most conspicuous symptoms were often hyperactivity, mood lability, inappropriate clinging, and rage reactions. These types of problems are often encountered in children diagnosed in Scandinavia as suffering from deficits in attention, motor control, and perception (DAMP) (Gillberg, 1983; Hellgren, Gillberg, Bågenholm, & Gillberg, 1994). Severe instances of DAMP are often associated with early-onset autistic symptoms. DAMP also overlaps with the US diagnostic concept of attention deficit hyperactivity disorder (ADHD) (Landgren, Kjellman, & Gillberg, 1996). Later, thought disorder, flattening of affect (after age 6), and hallucinations and delusions (after age 9) developed.

The course of symptom development described by Watkins et al. (1988) in children with early-onset schizophrenia would be exceedingly rare in children prospectively followed for autism or DAMP. In a large series of children with autism followed from early childhood, classical instances of schizophrenia/hallucinations/delusions have been reported in no more than a few percent (Gillberg, 1991). In the one major follow-up study of children with DAMP, not 1 out of 42 individuals developed hallucinations or delusions before age 16 years, but 4 (10%) met criteria for bipolar disorder or mania (Hellgren et al., 1994).

Russell et al. (1989) found that 9 out of 35 children (26%) with early-onset schizophrenia had shown various autistic-type symptoms prior to the onset of schizophrenia. However, none of them had met full criteria for autism. Typical symptoms included echolalia and hand flapping. Kolvin (1971) reported that about half of his group of "late-onset" child psychosis (possibly equivalent to the US concept of childhood schizophrenia) had developmental retardation and speech delay and 6% had echolalia.

One of the authors of this book has examined a number of the patients diagnosed as suffering from psychosis (including schizophrenia) by Spencer et al. (1994). A majority of these met criteria for DAMP or were of low normal or subnormal intelligence. Some of them would have been diagnosed as suffering from DAMP with autistic features in Scandinavia. Several also met criteria for additional diagnoses (mostly affective disorders and conduct disorder).

Gordon et al. (1994) in their study of childhood-onset schizophrenia subdivided a group of 49 individuals meeting DSM-III-R criteria for schizophrenia into one group of "schizophrenia" ($n=28$) and another one of "multidimensionally impaired" ($n=21$). The latter group comprised children with multiple impairments in many areas of cognitive functioning. They felt that the DSM-IV concept of borderline personality disorder came closest to describing this group.

EPIDEMIOLOGY

Childhood-onset schizophrenia is generally agreed to be extremely rare. It has been estimated to occur 50 times less frequently than adult-onset schizophrenia (Karno & Norquist, 1989).

According to a US study (from North Dakota), the point prevalence of childhood-onset schizophrenia (among 2–12 year olds) was 0.19 in 10,000. This prevalence figure was based on two individuals with the disorder.

According to a study from Göteborg, Sweden (Gillberg & Steffenburg, 1987), the point prevalence of schizophrenia among 4–18 year olds was 0.17 in 10,000. This prevalence figure was also based on two individuals with the disorder. These two cases (both boys, one of normal intelligence and one with an IQ of about 65) plus one more (a girl with an IQ of about 80), seen recently, represent all the instances of schizophrenia in prepubertal Swedish children seen by one of the authors of this book over a period of 21 years. This author has personally examined well over 1000 children with severe psychopathology (including autism and autisticlike conditions). He has also personally examined at least a dozen Swedish individuals with schizophrenia diagnosed at age 13–15 years, reflecting the increase in prevalence that occurs with the onset of puberty.

In the Dunedin (New Zealand) longitudinal study, no case of schizophrenia was reported in a sample of 792 carefully evaluated children at the age of 11 years (Anderson et al., 1987).

INTELLECTUAL FUNCTIONING

IQ is usually somewhat below average, with means of about 85–90 in several samples (Campbell, Kafantaris, Malone, Kowalik, & Locascio, 1991). Occasionally it may be much higher, however, and at least one study included an individual with early-onset schizophrenia and an IQ above 120 (Green et al., 1992). According to Campbell et al. (1991), the clinical picture becomes more similar to adult-onset schizophrenia in those childhood cases with the highest IQs. Some published series (Kolvin, 1971; Green et al., 1992; Werry & McClellan, 1992) report that 15%–25% of all childhood-onset schizophrenia cases have IQs under 70–80.

GENDER RATIOS

The male:female ratio is typically reported to be around 2:1 in schizophrenia cases with onset under age 16 years. The lowest ratio (0.9:1) was reported by Werry, McClellan, Andrews, & Ham (1994). The subjects of that study had a mean age at onset of about 14 years. Almost all the studies including subjects with a younger age at onset report much higher male:female ratios. For instance, the study by Green et al. (1992) in which mean age at onset was 9.6 years, showed a male:female ratio of 2.2:1. Those who had been diagnosed with schizophrenia under age 10 years had an even higher ratio (2.7:1). These findings are compatible with the overall finding that severe psychopathology in prepubertal children is 2 to 3 times more frequent in males than in females (Gillberg, 1995).

IS CHILDHOOD-ONSET SCHIZOPHRENIA DIFFERENT FROM ADULT SCHIZOPHRENIA?

Asarnow (1994) recently surveyed the literature and concluded that childhood-onset schizophrenia as compared with schizophrenia with onset at an adult age may be a more familial and severe variant of the disorder. It is similar to adult schizophrenia in several aspects pertaining to symptomatology and neuropsychology (attentional dysfunction and information-processing deficits seem to be common to both variants). Premorbid adjustment seems to be particularly poor, insidious onset more frequent, and outcome even worse than for adult-onset schizophrenia. Jacobsen et al. (1995) found more smooth-pursuit eye-movement impairment in cases of schizophrenia with childhood onset than in children with ADHD and normal children. Neurologic signs were correlated with frequency-mean saccadic amplitude product of anticipatory saccades. The latter measure yielded more abnormal results in the childhood-onset group than in comparable samples of adult-onset schizophrenia.

All these findings, combined with the advantages of studying the very early-onset variants of a disorder (in which features intrinsic to the disorder may not be severely confounded by consequences of it), suggest that children with schizophrenia should be intensively studied so as to provide clues for the understanding of the etiology in this devastating syndrome. The rarity of the disorder calls for collaborative research efforts in the field.

REFERENCES

Alaghband-Rad, J., McKenna, K., & Gordon, C. T. (1995). Childhood-onset schizophrenia: The severity of premorbid course. *Biological Psychiatry, 37*, 625.

American Psychiatric Association. (1987). *Diagnostic and statistical manual of mental disorders*, 3rd ed., rev. Washington, DC: American Psychiatric Press.

American Psychiatric Association. (1994). *Diagnostic and statistical manual of mental disorders*. 4th ed. Washington, DC: American Psychiatric Press.

Anderson, J. C., Williams, S., McGee, R., & Silva, P. A. (1987). DSM-III disorders in preadolescent children. Prevalence in a large sample from the general population. *Archives of General Psychiatry, 44*, 69–76.

Andreasen, N. C. (1987). The diagnosis of schizophrenia. *Schizophrenia Bulletin, 13*, 9–22.

Asarnow, J. R. (1994). Annotation: Childhood-onset schizophrenia. *Journal of Child Psychology and Psychiatry, 35*, 1345–1371.

Asarnow, J. R., Tompson, M., Hamilton, E. B., Goldstein, M. J., & Guthrie, D. (1994). Family-expressed emotion, childhood-onset depression, and childhood-onset schizophrenia spectrum disorders: Is expressed emotion a nonspecific correlate of child psychopathology or a specific risk factor for depression. *Journal of Abnormal Child Psychology, 22,* 129–146.

Asarnow, J. W., Goldstein, M. J., & Ben-Meir, S. (1988). Parental communication deviance in childhood onset schizophrenia spectrum and depressive disorders. *Journal of Child Psychology and Psychiatry, 29,* 825–838.

Asperger, H. (1944). Die autistischen Psychopathen im Kindesalter. *Archiv für Psychiatrie und Nervenkrankheiten, 117,* 76–136.

Bender, L. (1947). One hundred cases of childhood schizophrenia treated with electric shock. *Transcript of the American Neurological Association, 72,* 165 17, 40–56.

Bender, L. (1959). Emerging pattern in child psychiatry. *Bulletin of the New York Academy of Sciences, 34,* 794–810.

Bender, L. (1969). A longitudinal study of schizophrenic children with autism. *Hospital and Community Psychiatry, 20,* 230–237.

Bleuler, E. (1911). *Dementia praecox or the group of schizophrenias.* Vienna: Translated by J. Zinkin. New York: International University Press.

Campbell, M., Kafantaris, V., Malone, R. P., Kowalik, S. C., & Locascio, J. J. (1991). Diagnostic and assessment issues related to pharmacotherapy for children and adolescents with autism. *Behaviour Modification, 15,* 326–354.

Carlson, G. A., Strober, M. (1978). Manic-depressive illness in early adolescence. A study of clinical and diagnostic characteristics in six cases. *Journal of the American Academy of Child and Adolescent Psychiatry, 17,* 138–153.

Clevenger, S. V. (1883). Report on the recent appearances observed post-mortem in a case of delirium grave. *American Journal of Neurology and Psychiatry, 2,* 486–489.

De Sanctis, S. (1906). Sopra alcune varietà della demenza precoce. *Revista Sperimentale di Freniatria e di Medicina Legale delle Alienazioni Mentale, 32,* 141–165.

Eggers, C. (1989). Schizo-affective psychoses in childhood: A follow-up study. *Journal of Autism and Developmental Disorders, 19,* 327–342.

Feighner, J. P., Robins, E., Guze, S. B., Wodduff, R. A., Winokur, G., & Munoz, R. (1972). Diagnostic criteria for use in psychiatric research. *Archives of General Psychiatry, 26,* 57–93.

Fish, B. (1977). Neurobiologic antecedents of schizophrenia in children. Evidence for an inherited, congenital neurointegrative defect. *Archives of General Psychiatry, 34*, 1297–1313.

Fish, B. (1987). Infant predictors of the longitudinal course of schizophrenic development. *Schizophrenia Bulletin, 13*, 395–410.

Gillberg, C. (1983). Perceptual, motor and attentional deficits in Swedish primary school children. Some child psychiatric aspects. *Journal of Child Psychology and Psychiatry, 24*, 377–403.

Gillberg, C. (1991). Clinical and neurobiological aspects of Asperger syndrome in six family studies. In U. Frith, (Ed.), *Autism and Asperger syndrome* (pp. 122–146). Cambridge: Cambridge University Press.

Gillberg, C. (1995). *Clinical child neuropsychiatry.* Cambridge: Cambridge University Press.

Gillberg, C., & Steffenburg, S. (1987). Outcome and prognostic factors in infantile autism and similar conditions: A population-based study of 46 cases followed through puberty. *Journal of Autism and Developmental Disorders, 17*, 273–287.

Goldfarb, W. (1970). A follow-up investigation of schizophrenic children treated in residence. *Psychosocial Process, 1*, 9–64.

Gordon, C. T., Frazier, J. A., McKenna, K., Giedd, J., Zametkin, A., Zahn, T., Hommer, D., Hong, W., Kaysen, D., Albus, K. E., & Rapoport, J. L. (1994). Childhood onset schizophrenia: An NIMH study in progress. *Schizophrenia Bulletin, 20*, 697–712.

Green, W. H., Padron-Gayol, M., Hardesty, A. S., & Bassiri, M. (1992). Schizophrenia with childhood onset: A phenomenological study of 38 cases. *Journal of the American Academy of Child and Adolescent Psychiatry, 31*, 968–976.

Heller, T. (1908). Dementia infantilis. *Zeitschrift für die Erforschung und Behandlung des jugendlichen Schwachsinns (Journal for Research and Treatment of Juvenile Feeblemindedness), 2*, 17–28.

Hellgren, L., Gillberg, I. C., Bågenholm, A., Gillberg, C. (1994). Children with Deficits in Attention, Motor control and Perception (DAMP) almost grown up: psychiatric and personality disorders at age 16 years. *Journal of Child Psychology and Psychiatry, 35*, 1255–1271.

Homburger, A. (1926). *Vorselungen über Psychopathologies des Kindesalters.* Berlin: Springer-Verlag.

Jacobsen, L. K, Hong, W., Hommer, D. W., Castellanos, F. X., Frazier, J. A., Giedd, J. N., Gordon, C. T., Karp, B. I., McKenna, K., & Rapoport, J. L. (1995). Smooth pursuit eye movements in childhood onset schizophrenia. *Biological Psychiatry, 37*, 625.

Kanner, L. (1943). Autistic disturbances of affective contact. *Nervous Child, 2*, 217–250.

Kanner, L. (1971). Follow- up study of eleven children originally reported in 1943. *Journal of Autism and Childhood Schizophrenia, 1*, 119–145.

Karno, M., & Norquist, G. S. (1989). Epidemiology. In H. I. Kaplan & B. J. Sadock (Eds.), *Comprehensive textbook of psychiatry* (Vol. I, pp. 699–704). Baltimore, MD: Williams & Wilkins.

Kolvin, I. (1971). Studies in the childhood psychoses. *British Journal of Psychiatry, 118*, 381–419.

Kraepelin, E. (1913). *Lectures on clinical psychiatry*. Bailliére, Tindall & Cox.

Kraepelin, E. (1919). *Dementia praecox and paraphrenia*. Edinburgh: Livingstone.

Kydd, R. R., & Werry, J. S. (1982). Schizophrenia in children under 16 years. *Journal of Autism and Developmental Disorders, 12*, 343–357.

Landgren, M., Kjellman, B., & Gillberg, C. (1996). ADHD, DAMP and other neurodevelopmental/neuropsychiatric disorders in six-year-old children. Epidemiology and comorbidity. *Developmental Medicine and Child Neurology*. In press.

Lutz, J. (1937). Über schizophrenie im kindesalter. *Schweizer Archiv für Neurologie und Psychiatrie* (Zurich), *39*, 335–372.

Makita, K. (1966). The age of onset of childhood schizophrenia. *Folia Psychiatrica Neurologica Japonica, 10*, 111–121.

Maudsley, H. (1867). *The physiology and pathology of the mind*. London: Macmillan.

Potter, H. W. (1933). Schizophrenia in children. *American Journal of Psychiatry, 89*, 1253–1270.

Remschmidt, H., Schulz, E., Martin, M., Fleischhaker, C., & Trott, G. E. (1994). Frühmanifestation schizophrener Psychosen (Early manifestations of schizophrenic psychoses). *Zeitschrift Kinder und Jugendpsychiatrie, 22*, 239–252.

Russell, A. T. (1994). The clinical presentation of chilhood-onset schizophrenia. *Schizophrenia Bulletin, 20*, 529–538.

Russell, A. T., Bott, L., & Sammons, C. (1989). The phenomenology of schizophrenia occurring in childhood. *Journal of the American Academy of Child and Adolescent Psychiatry, 28*, 399–407.

Spencer, E. K., Alpert, M., & Pouge, T. E. (1994). Scales for the assessment of neuroleptic response in schizophrenic children: Specific measurers derived from the CPRS. *Psychopharmacology Bulletin, 30*, 199–202.

Spitzka, E. C. (1883). *Insanity, its classification, diagnosis and treatment. A manual for students and practitioners of medicine*. New York: Birmingham & Co.

Spitzer, R. L., Endicott, J., & Robins, E. (1978). Research diagnostic criteria: Rationale and reliability. *Archives of General Psychiatry, 35*, 773–782.

Steffenburg, S., & Gillberg, C. (1986). Autism and autistic-like conditions in Swedish rural and urban areas: A population study. *British Journal of Psychiatry, 149*, 81–87.

Volkmar, F. R., Cohen, D. J., Hoshino, Y., et al. (1988). Phenomenology and classification of the childhood psychoses. *Psychological Medicine, 18*, 191–201.

Watkins, J. M., Asarnow, R. F., & Tanguay, P. E. (1988). Symptom development in childhood onset schizophrenia. *Journal of Child Psychology and Psychiatry, 29*, 865–878.

Werry, J. S. (1992). Child and adolescent (early onset) schizophrenia: A review in light of DSM-III-R. *Journal of Autism and Developmental Disorders, 22*, 601–624.

Werry, J. S., & McClellan, J. M. (1992). Predicting outcome in child and adolescent (early onset) schizophrenia and bipolar disorder. *Journal of the American Academy of Child Adolescent Psychiatry, 31*, 147–150.

Werry, J. S., McClellan, J. M., & Chard, L. (1991). Childhood and adolescent schizophrenic, bipolar, and schizoaffective disorders: A clinical and outcome study. *Journal of the American Academy of Child and Adolescent Psychiatry, 30*, 457–465.

Werry, J. S., McClellan, J. M., Andrews, L. K., & Ham, M. (1994). Clinical features and outcome of child and adolescent schizophrenia. *Schizophrenia Bulletin, 20*, 619–630.

CHAPTER 4

The Heterogeneous Etiologies
of Schizophrenia

IS SCHIZOPHRENIA ONE DISEASE?

This book provides another demonstration of the thesis that schizophrenia is not a single disease but rather a syndrome of many different etiologies. As noted before, this reality probably was understood by Bleuler more than 80 years ago when he spoke of "the group of schizophrenias" in 1911 (Bleuler, 1911). One of the Menningers used the term "syndrome" when he was studying the possible infectious etiologies of schizophrenia; the title of a 1925 paper was "The Schizophrenic Syndrome As a Product of Acute Infectious Disease" (Menninger, 1925).

One could argue that it is hard to squeeze the signs and symptoms of schizophrenia into one disease. To take just one example, if schizophrenia were truly only one disease, what is one to make of the abnormal movements described in such different body areas? Some psychiatrists consider motor disturbance as a hallmark of schizophrenia (Manschreck et al., 1990). In one study of 94 neuroleptic-naive patients with schizophrenia, the percentages of adventitious movements were found as follows: face or mouth—19%; eyes and periorbital areas—7%, neck—3%, arm—11%, leg—2%, gait—6%, and trunk—3% (Fenton, Wyatt, & McGlashan, 1994).

Exactly what the symptoms are that characterize schizophrenia was discussed in the last two chapters. The clinical precision and calibration of the diagnosis of schizophrenia has changed back and forth since the time of Bleuler. Sometimes, the definition has expanded; at other times it has contracted. In many of the earlier papers discussed in this book, the term schizophrenia was used in a somewhat different sense than it might be used today. [For additional reviews of these expansions and contractions of the definition of schizophrenia, see N.C.A. (1994).]

DISINTEREST IN THE HETEROGENEITY OF SCHIZOPHRENIA

It is more than an intellectual exercise to demonstrate that there may be many different disease entities underlying the clinical presentation called schizophrenia. There are two major consequences of the disinterest in the heterogeneity of schizophrenia. One directly affects patients because any truly effective treatment for any disease in medicine is always based on an accurate, exact diagnosis. As can be seen in some of the patients described in Appendix A, specific treatments often can be more successful in reversing the symptoms of schizophrenia than nonspecific treatments directed at that indistinct concept of a single disease called schizophrenia. Although successful for many individuals with schizophrenia, these nonspecific treatments also can cause debilitating side effects, such as tardive dyskinesia or pseudo-Parkinsonism, blood toxicity or neutropenia, enhanced negative symptoms, lethargy, or dizziness. The other consequence of the disinterest in the heterogeneity of schizophrenia affects research; as summarized in 1993 by a thoughtful neuropsychologist "The failure to achieve a rigorous grasp of the heterogeneity problem has created an uncertainty that hinders schizophrenia research at all levels" (Heinrichs, 1993, p. 230).

THE MEDICAL SUBGROUPS OF THE SCHIZOPHRENIAS

The underlying etiology of schizophrenia in many patients remains unknown; we call those cases idiopathic schizophrenia. Each year brings information about new etiologies. This book marks a point in time in the history of schizophrenia. As Davison

**TABLE 4.1 Treatable or Preventable Disease Entities that
Can Present with Schizophrenic Symptoms**

Addison's disease—Chapter 8
Cerebral cysts and abscesses—Chapter 5
Cushing's syndrome—Chapter 8
Hartnup disease—Chapter 6
Homocystinuria—MTHFR reductase deficiency—Chapter 6
Hydrocephalus, late onset—treatable—Chapter 12
Hyperparathyroidism—Chapter 8
Hyperthyroidism—Chapter 8
Hypoparathyroidism, postsurgical—Chapter 8
Hypothyroidism—Chapter 8
Neurosyphilis—Chapter 5
Pellegra—Chapter 7
Pernicious anemia—Chapter 7
Porphyrias—Chapter 6
Rheumatic chorea—Chapter 9
Systemic lupus erythematosus—Chapter 9
Toxicity (drugs and heavy metals)—Chapter 14
Tumors of the brain, treatable—see Chapter 12
Wilson's disease—Chapter 6

Candidate diseases under investigation for TABLE 4.1*

Vitamin A deficiency—Chapter 7
Vitamin D deficiency—Chapter 7
Fabry's disease—Chapter 6
Hypopituitarism—Chapter 8
Zinc deficiency—Chapter 7

---

* These disease entities are candidate diseases for Table 4.1 but cannot be added at this
time because their candidacy is based, so far, on too few cases. They are candidate
diseases because there were clear-cut, often crossover, therapeutic results following
accurate diagnosis and treatment. To enter this table in future editions, additional cases
must be reported.

has pointed out, the association of many organic cerebral disorders with schizophrenia exceeds chance expectation (Davison, 1983).

The disease entities associated with schizophrenia discussed in this monograph are divided into three groups for clinical and practical reasons. Table 4.1 lists the disease entities in which the possibility exists that the mechanisms of the diseases themselves have produced symptoms of schizophrenia. In order to be listed in Table 4.1, a disease entity also has to have established or research treatments that—at a minimum—prevent the disease, stop further deterioration or—at a maximum—reverse the symptoms of schizophrenia. In evaluating case histories regarding treatment that reverses a disease entity, it is important to keep in mind that "occasionally, a schizophrenic patient with a psychotic episode will recover and not have subsequent psychotic episodes" (Carpenter, Kirkpatrick, & Buchanan, 1990). In fact in a Scandinavian series, one out of every four patients recovered after a single schizophrenic episode and did not experience a recurrence (Bland & Orn, 1978). This is a factor that makes evaluation of treatment in schizophrenia so difficult and which has driven the field into its tangled love affair with statistics. The prognosis in schizophrenia was described in DMS III (APA, 1980) as follows: "The most common course is one of acute exacerbation with increasing residual impairment between episodes." This is considered by many psychiatrists today to be too pessimistic.

Chapter 16, the chapter on clinical and laboratory diagnostic studies, is focused on the disease entities found in Table 4.1. It is the goal of this book to help physicians be sure that every patient with a potentially treatable form of schizophrenia has had an accurate diagnosis and a subsequent opportunity for a trial of therapy. Tables 4.1 and 4.2 may well have Type I Errors (when a claim is made that an exposure is associated with a disease when it is not). However, other patients with the diagnosis of schizophrenia show Type II Errors (when an assumption is made that an exposure is not associated with a disease when, in fact, it is). Some of the patients documented in Appendix A were suffering from Type II Errors for many years—one individual for 45 years (Hunter, 1968). That person lived through four diagnostic eras (dementia praecox, dementia paranoides, delusional insanity, and finally schizophrenia) before the underlying etiology of the schizophrenic symptoms—a frontal-lobe meningioma—was identified. Improved technology, such as magnetic resonance imaging (MRI) scans, should cut down on the number of Type II Errors in the future if used appropriately. When one considers how few physicians publish their mistakes, it is a tribute to the psychiatric profession that so many Type II Errors were published in the medical literature. However, there remains the inevitable question—for each one published, how many went unpublished?

TABLE 4.2 Disease Entities That May Present with Schizophrenic Symptoms in Which There Currently Is No Successful Long-Term Treatment Individualized for That Disease

Adrenomyeloneuropathy—Chapter 2
Cerebral malaria—Chapter 5
Cerebrovascular lesions—Chapter 12
Chromosomal disorders—in some cases, the karyotype is relevant to the patient's psychiatric symptoms, see Chapter 10
Cranial trauma—Chapter 12
Encephalitis and the sequelae of encephalitis—Chapter 5
Familial basal ganglia calcification—Chapter 11
GM2 gangliosidosis—Chapter 6
Huntington's disease—Chapter 11
Hydrocephalus, late onset—not treatable—Chapter 12
Kartagerer's syndrome—Chapter 11
Klinefelter syndrome—Chapter 10
Metachromatic leukodystrophy, adult type—Chapter 6
Narcolepsy—Chapter 15
Oculocutaneous albinism—Chapter 11
Occult hydrocephalus—Chapter 12
Pick's disease—Chapter 15
Porphyrias (hepatic type)—Chapter 6
Prenatal static encephalopathy—Chapter 12
Schilder's cerebral sclerosis—Chapter 11
Tourette syndrome—Chapter 11
Toxicity (drugs, heavy metals)—Chapter 14
Tuberous sclerosis—Chapter 11
Tumors of the brain, not successfully treatable—Chapter 12
Velo-cardio-facial syndrome—Chapter 10

Because a patient with a mistaken diagnosis of a Type I Error usually can be disproven by laboratory testing whereas a patient suffering from a Type II Error often has *no chance at all of being tested in the first place*, if this monograph errs, it is on the side of Type I Errors.

Table 4.2 lists the disease entities in which it is reasonable to speculate that, in some patients, the mechanism of the disease could underlie the symptoms of schizophrenia but for which no specific medical treatments are currently established. In some of these disease entities, research therapies are in process and it

TABLE 4.3   Disease Entities for Which the Reported Case of Schizophrenia May Be a Coincidental Second Disease

Ataxia, dominant type—A paranoid psychosis has been described in a mother and two sons with hereditary ataxia of probably the Menzel type (Keddie, 1969).

Chromosomal disorders—In many cases their presence in an individual with schizophrenia may be irrelevant; for discussion see Chapter 10.

Congenital adrenal hyperplasia—(Rashkis & Harris, 1964).

Cowden disease—A man with chronic schizophrenia and Cowden disease had a mentally normal sister also with Cowden disease (King, Coyne, Spearritt, & Boyle 1992).

Erthropoietic porphyria—There is one case of schizophrenia reported with this rare form of porphyria that is likely to be a coincidence (Gibney, Jones, & Meek, 1972).

Fredreich's ataxia—Although a subgroup of patients with Fredreich's ataxia have paranoid delusions, nocturnal hallucinations and aggressive, excited, impulsive behavior (these outbreaks have been labeled "Fredreich's psychosis"), a careful review did not conclusively show that these are related to the neurological disorder (Davison & Bagley, 1969b). For discussion, see Chapter 11.

Gaucher's disease, adult type—There is an "atypical psychosis" in one family (Neil, Glew, & Peters, 1979). This disease may be a candidate for Table 4.1 if the hypothesis by Goodman (1994a) regarding the alleles of the Gaucher's gene is verified.

G-6-PD deficiency—There are two case reports of an acute paranoid psychosis provoked by fava beans (Nasr, 1976) and typhoid fever (Forrest, Lee, Tsang, & Yu, 1969).

Hemochromatosis—There is a single case report of a paranoid psychosis (Ott, 1957).

Hyperasparaginemia—There is a single case report of chronic schizophrenia (Perry, Wright, & Hansen, 1983).

Ichthyosis vulgaris (autosomal dominant type)—Two siblings with ichthyosis and a schizophrenialike psychosis have been described (Mochizuki, Tobo, & Itoi, 1980).

Laurence–Moon–Biedl syndrome—There are two case reports, one with a schizophrenialike psychosis (Weiss, Meshulam, & Wijsenbeek, 1981) and one with a paranoid psychosis (Todd, 1955).

Leber's hereditary optic atrophy—Psychotic patients with diagnoses such as as chronic undifferentiated schizophrenia are recorded in the medical literature (Androp, 1941; Walsh, 1957; Bates, 1964). When details are available, these patients appear to have visual hallucinations (in addition to the more classical symptoms) as might be expected in a disease that affects the visual pathway.

Marchiafava-Bignami disease—(Freeman, 1980). This disease, which causes demyelination of the corpus callosum, optic tracts, and cerebellar peduncles, usually presents with slowly progressive dementia and paralysis but the symptoms of schizophrenia have been recorded.

Table 4.3 *(cont.)*

Marfan syndrome—(Melissari et al., 1995). This single case report includes cardiac and pulmonary disease.

Multiple sclerosis—Although there can be evidence of lesions in the temporal lobe in individuals with schizophrenia and multiple sclerosis, the evidence at this time is not strong enough to assume a direct relationship; this may be reconsidered in the future. For discussion of these considerations, see Chapter 9.

Myasthenia gravis—Because the symptoms of myasthenia gravis can mimic both conversion symptoms and psychotic symptoms during acute attacks, this disease entity is hard to pin down. See discussion in Chapter 9.

Niemann-Pick's disease, late type—There is a single case report of schizophrenia (Fox & Kane, 1967).

Oculocutaneous albinism—For discussion of the cases in the medical literature, see Chapter 11.

Phenylketonuria, adult type—For discussion of this controversial subject, see Chapter 6.

Sarcoidosis—For discussion of cases in the medical literature, see Chapter 15.

Scleroderma—Three case reports of scleroderma and possible schizophrenia exist. In one patient there was (Muller, Gizycki-Nienhaus, Botschev, & Meurer, 1993) and the second patient there was not (Wise & Ginzler, 1975) evidence of cerebral involvement by immunological studies in the cerebral spinal fluid (CSF). The third individual also had hypothyroidism, confusing the diagnostic picture (Schmid & Meltzer, 1994). For discussion see Chapter 9.

Uremia—Both catatonic (Baker & Knutson, 1946) and paranoid (Menninger, 1924) forms of schizophrenia (Schreiner, 1959) have been diagnosed in the past in patients with uremia. For discussion, see Chapter 15.

---

will be a pleasure to change these diseases from Table 4.2 to Table 4.1 someday. The decisions on which table to enter a particular disease are made based on experimental, epidemiological, theoretical, and therapeutic crossover data and are not fixed in concrete.

There are also many case reports in the medical literature of a disease entity that has affected one or more patients who also have schizophrenia and for which, as yet, no significant evidence exists linking the two problems, even if they happen to be in the same patient. Because schizophrenia occurs in such a high frequency (close to 7:1000 individuals), often it is very hard to know if the schizophrenia is related to the disease entity or if the patient unfortunately has two separate diseases—a disease causing schizophrenia and a second disease that has been detected. Disease entities that appear to these authors to have such case histories are listed in Table 4.3. Judging by the history of medicine, it is likely that in the future some of the disease entities in each these tables eventually will be moved to other tables.

It also should be noted that because schizophrenia occurs in such a high frequency, decompensation of almost every organ system in the body has at least one reported case of schizophrenia associated with its failure in the medical literature—hepatic disease (Read, Sherlock, Laidlaw, & Walder, 1967); hypoglycemia (Nash, 1983); hyponatremia (Burnell & Foster, 1972); and the hypercalcemia of malignancy (Weizman et al., 1979).

How was it decided in which table to put the disease entities that had a subgroup of patients who were also schizophrenic? Reasonable investigators may disagree about the choices made. For example, there are five disease entities that are candidates for Table 4.1 that have various types of evidence suggesting involvement of that disease with schizophrenia yet only one or two patients with schizophrenia are so far recorded in the medical literature who meet the criterion of a successful medical therapy reversing the symptoms of schizophrenia as demonstrated by crossover trials. Because the spontaneous remission of schizophrenia is well documented, caution must always be kept in mind regarding the interpretation of a therapy achieving successful reversal of psychiatric symptoms. These five diseases—listed separately—are the exceptions to the principle of reasonable frequency of good therapeutic results. If, as a result of the publication of this book, these disease entities will be tested for in significant numbers, then one of two things will happen. The next edition of this book may include many more patients with these five diseases because they have been systematically tested for and uncovered, or these case histories will turn out to be anomalies and one, two, or all of these disease entities might move to Table 4.3.

Why some of the more common diseases listed in Tables 4.1 and 4.2 have a small subgroup of patients with schizophrenia is beginning to be understood. In the metabolic diseases in which the majority of patients usually do not have schizophrenia, enzymology and molecular biology are beginning to identify a difference in enzyme levels or alleles themselves between the children who present with neurological disease and adult patients who present with schizophrenia (see Chapter 6).

IS THERE MORE THAN ONE GENE INVOLVED IN THE INHERITED TYPES OF SCHIZOPHRENIA?

As one reviews the Tables, it seems clear that there is overwhelming evidence that schizophrenia is a syndrome caused by a number of separate distinct diseases all presenting with a somewhat similar set of clinical symptoms, rather than that all patients with schizophrenia have a single disease entity. However, there is an active debate about whether it is necessary for a patient to have *two or more* etiologies, instead of one, in order to have the symptoms of schizophrenia. These speculations show up in the theory of "polygenic predisposition" (Davison & Bagley, 1969; Propping, 1983), which was reinforced by the case of the man with schizophrenia with a folate-sensitive form of homocystinuria who had a nonschizophrenic sister with the same enzyme defect (Freeman, Finkelstein, & Mudd, 1975). They also are discussed in the "two-hit" hypothesis about the second trimester gestational type of schizophrenia (Mednick, Cannon, Barr, & Lyon, 1991). They also are examined in the work on monozygotic twins discordant for schizophrenia (Torrey, Bowler, Taylor, & Gottesman, 1994). Regarding the identical twins discordant for schizophrenia, a sophisticated analysis by Torrey et al. goes over these concepts (Torrey et al., 1994). The fact that sometimes one of the twin pair, even a monozygotic pair, probably has nongenetic etiology of schizophrenia (such as an infection) is explored (Davis & Phelps, 1995). Also, in the subset of discordant twin pairs with likely genetic etiologies, the increased incidence of schizophrenia among the children of the well twin supports the assumption of an underlying genetic etiology in the well twin modified by nongenetic secondary factors (Gottesman & Bertelsen, 1989).

It is already clear that some familial diseases that can present with schizophrenia are single gene diseases, such as Huntington disease (see Chapter 10). With the new sophistication of molecular genetics, however, some geneticists believe that in some of the families with inherited patterns of schizophrenia that do not follow straightforward Mendelian patterns, single genes may not be found to underlie the disease entity. Instead in such families there may be multiple genes of varying effect size that cause the psychiatric symptoms (Plomin, Owin, & McGuffin, 1994). Genes that contribute to genetic variance in quantitative traits are called quantitative trait loci (QTL) (Lander & Botstein, 1989). In such a multigene system, any single gene is neither necessary nor sufficient to cause a disorder. Such a genetic pattern possibly could account for some of the false-positive linkage studies for schizophrenia discussed in Chapter 10. These "multiple-hit" hypotheses, however, are yet to be fully worked out for a group of familial patients with the complex behaviors of schizophrenia. Thus this hypothesis does not mean that it is not very important to struggle hard at this time to try to identify a single underlying "hit" in each individual patient—the primary etiology—the "hit" that will respond to a specific therapy because many, many patients (genetic, infectious, endocrine, etc.) have primary, often treatable, underlying etiologies of their psychotic symptoms.

An attempt to pull out the information on the primary identification of each underlying disease that causes schizophrenia in each patient from the background noise is the purpose of this book.

THE NEED FOR A ONE-TIME EXTENSIVE COMPLETE WORK-UP IN EVERY INDIVIDUAL WITH SCHIZOPHRENIA

There is simply no substitute for the painstaking, extensive medical work-up (see Chapter 16) needed for each patient who presents with the symptoms of schizophrenia. Every patient deserves that opportunity. Sometimes, during the the first stage of the work- up—the individual and family history, as well as the physical and neurological examinations—an etiological diagnosis can be made and confirmed by a single laboratory test. In many patients for whom the first stage does not suggest a specific etiological diagnosis, however, the entire battery of laboratory tests often is indicated. As reported throughout this book, there are innumerable cases in which the laboratory diagnosis came as a surprise to the physician handling the patient. Schizophrenia does not easily yield its secrets.

Only by exact diagnosis of the primary illness in each individual with the symptoms of schizophrenia is there the best chance for a permanent healing therapy likely to be found for that person. Such a therapy may exist today or is yet to be developed in the future.

REFERENCES

American Psychiatric Association. (1980). *Diagnostic and statistical manual of mental disorders*. Washington, DC: American Psychiatric Press.

Androp, S. (1941). *Psychiatric Quarterly*, 15, 215.

Baker, A. B., & Knutson, J. (1946). Psychiatric aspects of uremia. *American Journal of Psychiatry, 102*, 683–687.

Bates, G. R. (1964). Leber's disease and schizophrenia. *American Journal of Psychiatry, 120*, 1017–1019.

Bland, R. C., & Orn, H. (1978). 14-year outcome in early schizophrenia. *Acta Psychiatrica Scandinavica, 58*, 327–338.

Bleuler, E. (1911). *Dementia precox*. New York: International University Press.

Burnell, G. M., & Foster, T. A. (1972). Psychosis with low sodium syndrome. *American Journal of Psychiatry, 128*, 133.

Carpenter, W. T., Kirkpatrick, B., & Buchanan, R. W. (1990). Conceptual approaches to the study of schizophrenia. In A. Kales, C. N. Stefanis, & J. A. Talbott (Eds.), *Recent advances in schizophrenia*. New York: Springer-Verlag.

Davis, J. O., & Phelps, J. A. (1995). Twins with schizophrenia: Genes or germs? *Schizophrenia Bulletin, 21*, 13–18.

Davison, K. (1983). Schizophrenia-like psychoses associated with organic cerebral disorders: Review. *Psychiatric Developments, 1*, 1–34.

Davison, K., & Bagley, C. R. (1969a). Schizophrenia-like psychoses associated with organic disorders of the central nervous system: A review of the medical literature. In R. N. Herrington (Ed.), *British Journal of Psychiatry Special Publication No. 4*.

Davison, K., & Bagley, C. R. (1969b). Schizophrenia-like psychoses associated with organic disorders of the central nervous system: A review of the literature. In R. N. Herrrington (Ed.), *Current problems in neuropsychiatry: Schizophrenia, epilepsy, the temporal lobe*. Ashford Kent: Headley Brothers Ltd.

Fenton, W. S., Wyatt, R. J., & McGlashan, T. H. (1994). Risk factors for spontaneous dyskinesia in schizophrenia. *Archives of General Psychiatry, 51*, 643–650.

Forrest, C. R., Lee, T. T. Y., Tsang W. K., & Yu, S. Y. (1969). Typhoid fever in Hong Kong Junk family. *British Medical Journal, 4*, 279.

Fox, J. T., & Kane, F. J. (1967). Niemann-Pick's disease manifesting as schizophrenia. *Diseases of the Nervous System, 28*, 194.

Freeman, A. M. III. (1980). Delusions, depersonalization and unusual psychopathological symptoms. In R. C. W. Hall (Ed.), *Psychiatric presentations of medical illness.* New York: SP Medical and Scientific Books.

Freeman, J. M., Finkelstein, M. D., & Mudd, S. H. (1975). Folate-responsive homocystinuria and "schizophrenia." A defect in methylation due to deficient 5, 10-methylenetetrahydrofolate reductase activity. *New England Journal of Medicine, 292*, 491–496.

Gibney, G. N., Jones, I. H., & Meek, J. H. (1972). Schizophrenia in association with erthropoietic porphyria. *British Journal of Psychiatry, 121*, 79–81.

Goodman, A. B. (1994a). Medical conditions in ashkenazi schizophrenic pedigrees. *Schizophrenia Bulletin, 20*, 507–517.

Goodman, A. B. (1994b). A family history study of schizophrenia spectrum disorders suggests new candidate genes in schizophrenia and autism. *Psychiatric Quarterly, 65*, 287–297.

Gottesman, I. I., & Bertelsen, A. (1989). Confirming unexpressed genotypes for schizophrenia. *Archives of General Psychiatry, 46*, 867–872.

Heinrichs, R. W. (1993). Schizophrenia and the brain: Conditions for a neuropsychology of madness. *American Psychologist, 48*, 221–233.

Hunter, R., Blackwood, W., & Bull, J. (1968). Three cases of frontal meningiomas presenting psychiatrically. *British Medical Journal, 3*, 9–16.

Keddie, K. M. (1969). Hereditary ataxia, presumed to be the Menzel type, complicated by paranoid psychosis, in a mother and two sons. *Journal of Neurology, Neurosurgery, Psychiatry, 32*, 82.

King, M. A., Coyne, T. J., Spearritt, D. J., & Boyle, R. S. (1992). Lhermitte-Duclos disease and Cowden disease: A third case. (letter) *Annals of Neurology, 32*, 112–113.

Lauder, E. S., & Botstein, D. (1989). Mapping Mendelian factors underlying quantitative traits using RFLP linkage maps. *Genetics, 121*, 185.

Manschreck, T. C., Keuthen, N. J., Schneyer, M. L., Celada, M. T., Laughery, J., & Collins, P. (1990). Abnormal involuntary movements and chronic schizophrenic disorders. *Biological Psychiatry, 27*, 150–158.

Mednick, S. A., Cannon, T. D., Barr, C. E., & Lyon, M. (Eds.). (1991). *Fetal neural development and adult schizophrenia.* Cambridge, UK: Cambridge University Press.

Melissari, M., Giordano, G., Crafa, P., Martella, E. M., & Ricci, R. (1995). Mitral valve prolapse in a case of Marfan syndrome with congenital cardiac disease, chronic obstructive pulmonary disease and schizophrenia. *Pathologica, 87,* 78–81.

Menninger, K. A. (1924). Paranoid psychosis with uremia. *Journal of Nervous and Mental Disease, 60,* 26–34.

Menninger, K. A. (1925). The schizophrenic syndrome as a product of acute infectious disease. *Association of Research on Nervous and Mental Disorders Proceedings, 5,* 182. [Published 1928]

Mochizuki, H., Tobo, M., & Itoi, K. (1980). A case of ichthyosis vulgaris associated with schizophrenia-like psychosis and spike-wave stupor. *Folia Psychiatrica et Neurologica Japonica, 34,* 392–393.

Muller, N., Gizycki-Nienhaus, B., Botschev, C., & Meurer, M. (1993). Cerebral involvement of scleroderma presenting as schizophrenia. *Schizophrenia Research, 10,* 179–181.

N.C.A. (1994). Changing concepts of schizophrenia and the ahistorical fallacy. *American Journal of Psychiatry, 151,* 1405–1407 (editorial).

Nash, J. L. (1983). Delusions. In J. O. Cavenar, Jr. & H. K. H. Brodie (Eds.), *Signs and symptoms in psychiatry.* Philadelphia: Lippincott.

Nasr, S. J. (1976). Glucose-6-phosphate dehydrogenase deficiency with psychosis. *Archives of General Psychiatry, 33,* 1202–1203.

Neil, J. F., Glew, R. H., & Peters, S. P. (1979). Familial psychosis and diverse neurologic abnormalities in adult-onset Gaucher's disease. *Archives of Neurology, 36,* 95–99.

Ott, B. (1957). Uber psychische veranderungen bei hamochromatose. *Nervenarzt, 28,* 356–360.

Perry, T. L., Wright, J. M., & Hansen, S. (1983). Hyperasparaginemia in a schizophrenic patient. *Biological Psychiatry, 18,* 89–97.

Plomin, R., Owen, M. J., & McGuffin, P. (1994). The genetic basis of complex human behaviors. *Science, 264,* 1733–1739.

Propping, P. (1983). Genetic disorders presenting as "schizophrenia." Karl Bonhoeffer's early view of the pscyhoses in the light of medical genetics. *Human Genetics, 65,* 1–10.

Rashkis, H. A., & Harris, C. (1964). Schizophrenia and adrenal hypercorticolism. *Diseases of the Nervous System, 25,* 624.

Read, A. E., Sherlock, S., Laidlaw, J., & Walder, J. G. (1967). The neuropsychiatric syndromes associated with chronic liver disease and extensive portal-systemic collateral circulation. *Quarterly Journal of Medicine, 36,* 135.

Schmid, A. H., & Meltzer, B. R. (1994). Psychotic episodes in an elderly woman with scleroderma, IgA deficiency and hypothyroidism. *Journal of Geriatric Psychiatry and Neurology*, 7, 93–98.

Schreiner, G. E. (1959). Mental and personality changes in the uremic syndrome. *Medical Annals of the District of Columbia*, 28, 316.

Todd, J. (1955). A case of the Laurence-Moon-Biedl syndrome with paranoid psychosis. *American Journal of Mental Deficiency*, 60, 331–334.

Torrey, E. F., Bowler, A. E., Taylor, E. H., & Gottesman, I. I. (1994). *Schizophrenia and manic-depressive disorder*. New York: Basic Books.

Walsh, F. B. (1957). *Clinical neuroophthalmology*. Baltimore: Williams and Wilkins.

Weiss, M., Meshulam, B., & Wijsenbeek, H. (1981). The possible relationship between Laurence–Moon–Biedl syndrome and a schizophrenia-like psychosis. *Nervous and Mental Diseases*, 169, 259–260.

Weizman, A., Elder, M., Shoenfeld, Y., Hirschorn, M., Wijsenbeck, H., & Pinkhas, J. (1979). Hypercalcaemia-induced psychopathology in malignant disease. *British Journal of Psychiatry*, 135, 363.

Wise, T., Ginzler, E. M. (1975). Scleroderma cerebritis, an unusual manifestation of progressive system sclerosis. *Diseases of the Nervous System*, 36, 60–62.

CHAPTER 5

Infections and Schizophrenia

There is evidence suggestive of infectious etiologies of schizophrenia that can be found in prenatal, childhood, and adult infections. Almost from the beginning of defining this disease entity, before the availability of antibiotics, major figures in psychiatry were suggesting that there may be an etiologic relationship between certain infections and some cases of schizophrenia (Menniger, 1925; Sagel, 1934; Rosenfeld, 1935). More recent data suggests the acuity of their observations although, fortunately today, some of those presumed etiologies (rheumatic fever/schizophrenia) are extremely rare thanks to modern therapies. Yolken and Torrey (1995) recently reviewed the body of literature on this subject.

PRENATAL INFECTIONS

The concept that an infection prior to birth could actually cause a major lifelong disease that doesn't start until 20 years later seems counterintuitive. Yet evidence from epidemiology, neuropathology, and studies of physical anomalies have suggested just such a scenario. For example, a study of monozygotic twins discordant for schizophrenia has led to the conclusion that some cases of adult-onset schizophrenia are likely to be associated with prenatal events (Torrey et al., 1994). In this study, the twin who became schizophrenic had significantly different physical anomaly scores and total finger-ridge counts compared to the other twin (who had exactly the same genetic material) but remained well. Something must have happened in utero to differentiate the twins.

Neuropathology also contributes to this concept by the post-mortem studies of some individuals with schizophrenia who have evidence of damage to brain cells as early as the gestational period. Cannon and Mednick (1991) note that the three findings most directly linked to a prenatal pathogenesis are (1) disturbances of pyramidal-cell orientation in the anterior and medial portions of the hippocampus (Kovelman & Scheibel, 1984), (2) heterotopic displacement of pre-alpha cell groups in the rostral entorhinal region of the parahippocampal gyrus (Jakob & Beckmann, 1986; Falkai, Bogerts, Roberts, & Crowe, 1988), and (3) reduced depth of the granule cell layer in the dentate gyrus (McLardy, 1974). On the other hand, an abnormally high neuronal density has been reported in prefrontal area 9 and occipital area 17 (Selemon, Rajkowska, & Goldman-Rakic, 1995).

There are several possible etiologies of this kind of disturbance of brain development; it can be genetic, structural, or infectious. One etiology identified in other types of brain dysfunctions traced to the middle trimester (such as lissencephaly) is a viral infection that occurs during critical time periods of gestation (Chan, Egbert, Herrick, & Urich, 1980).

Infections are more likely to occur in utero if there is immune-system dysfunction in the fetus, and there is some evidence that schizophrenic patients may have reduced immune function (King & Cooper, 1989) (also see Chapter 9). In animal studies, the interesting observation has been made that autosomal mutations at the gene level that are known to produce immune-system dysfunctions in the fetus also have pleiotropic effects on neuronal migration during the development of the nervous system (Nowakowski, 1988). Two of these mutants cause similar disorders in the hippocampal formation and the cerebellar cortex—the presence of ectopic granule cells.

If prenatal infections might cause the kind of brain damage that leads to adult-onset schizophrenia, which infectious agents are likely to be responsible? A modest winter–spring seasonality of excess births of individuals who later develop schizophrenia is one of the most consistently replicated finding in psychiatry—there are at least 44 separate studies in 18 countries (Torrey, Bowler, Rawlings, & Terrazas, 1993; Aschauer et al., 1994; O'Callaghan et al., 1995; Takei, Sham, O'Callaghan, Glover, & Murray,

1995). Zipursky and Schultz 2(1987) studied ventricle size by computed tomography (CT) correlated with season of birth; they report that schizophrenic patients born in the last third of the year (fall, winter months) had larger ventricle sizes. They note that in their study fewer patients with a positive family history were born in the winter months. Franzek and Beckmann (1992) interpret their own study to reveal the existence of etiologically different groups of schizophrenia; they suggest that what they call the "seasonal exogenic noxious influences" (p. 378) during only the fifth and sixth month of gestation contribute to the etiology of a subgroup of schizophrenia that is not genetic.

There is probably more than one gestational infection that can interfere with brain development at a critical stage, such as the second trimester of pregnancy. At this moment in the medical literature, influenza A appears to be the most investigated candidate yet its episodic pattern of infection usually does not produce winter births except during epidemic years. Another candidate is the recent discovery in twins nonconcordant for schizophrenia of antibodies to the group of viruses called pestiviruses in the plasma of the individuals with schizophrenia (Yolken et al., 1994). This virus group is of particular interest because some of its members are strongly neurotrophic and have a special affinity for neurons in the hippocampus (Fernandez, Hewicker, Trautwein, Pohlenz, & Liess, 1989). A study of retroviruses as an etiology of schizophrenia was declared negative based on 17 cases (Feenstra, Kirch, Bracha, & Wyatt, 1989). Other infectious agents yet to be identified may contribute to the seasonality pattern.

Also there may be noninfectious factors (Cooper, 1992); one hypothesis targets cytokines, generated during the maternal, fetal, or placental immune response to infection, as possibly altering normal neuronal development in a genetically vulnerable fetus (Gilmore, Wilkie, Xiaol, & Lauder, 1995). Another hypothesis has suggested the release of seasonal preovulatory overripe ovum (SPrOO) (Pallast, Jongbloet, Straatmen, & Zielhuis, 1994).

Influenza

There is epidemiological evidence that influenza during the sixth month of gestation may place some individuals at risk for adult schizophrenia (Barr, Mednick, & Munk-Jorgensen, 1990). In the annals of scientific research, this painstaking study by Barr, Mednick and Munk-Jorgensen (1990) must be regarded as a remarkable achievement. The investigators looked at data from over 40 years by months, of (1) the number of live births for Denmark, 2) the number of those born who were eventually diagnosed as schizophrenics (*over 7500(!)*), and (3) the number of cases of influenza reported to the Danish Ministry of Health. These investigators did not examine any one specific epidemic but all the influenza that occurred between 1911 and 1950. They found that unusually high levels of maternal influenza during the sixth month of fetal development were related to unusually high levels of births of individuals who later became adult schizophrenics. Because they had such a large database, these authors were able to make statistical calculations; they calculated that 4% of all cases of schizophrenia in Denmark could be accounted for by the association that they found between influenza and schizophrenia.

This very large study by Barr et al. was undertaken as a follow-up to a study published in 1988 of the children of mothers infected during a specific epidemic of severe Type A2 influenza in Finland. Mednick et al. examined the children when they reached 26 years of age. Examination of psychiatric hospital records from each of the hospitals in the Helsinki area revealed that rates of adult schizophrenia were elevated for those exposed to the epidemic in utero during their second trimester of fetal development (Mednick, Machon, Huttunen, & Bonett, 1988). First- and third-trimester exposure was not associated with an elevation (Mednick, Huttenen, & Machon, 1994). A repeat study of the same group when the patients were 29.7 years of age confirmed the previous report of elevated rates in patients exposed during their second trimester (Machon, Mednick, & Huttunen, 1990).

A Japanese follow-up study based on the psychiatric hospitals around the Tokyo metropolitan area studied the effect of the A2 influenza pandemic in 1957 (Kunugi et al., 1993). These studies compared the number of births of individuals who later became schizophrenic in each month of the index year with the average number of births in the corresponding month of the 2 years before and 2 years after the index year. The data was complicated because in Japan during 1957 there were multiple waves of the influenza epidemics—there was an A/B mixed type epidemic(Jan/Feb) and two other waves of the A2 influenza epidemic(June/July and November/December). Nevertheless analysis of the data showed an excess (63%) of schizophrenic births 5 months after the peak of the A/B mixed-type epidemic and another excess (49%) of schizophrenic births 5 months after the November/December epidemic. No excess births were found after the June/July epidemic. In the two sets with excess births, however, again the second trimester was implicated. A reevaluation of the 1957 influenza epidemics in Japan confirmed the finding of excessive births but found them limited to females (Kunugi et al., 1995).

A study of maternal influenza and subsequent schizophrenia in England and Wales also found evidence of increased risk for schizophrenia at the fifth or sixth month of gestation but the results were statistically significant for women only, not for men (O'Callaghan et al., 1991a; 1991b; Sham et al., 1992; Takei et al., 1994). This study was quickly challenged by another team of British investigators who, using a different approach, found no association between births from pregnancies that were exposed to the same 1957 influenza epidemic (Crow, Done, & Johnstone, 1991; Crow & Done, 1992). The same gender difference emerged in a study of data sets from Scotland, England and Wales, and Denmark (Adams et al., 1993) as well as for the 1957 epidemic in the southern hemisphere (McGrath et al., 1994). The Australia group, however, found an excess of *male* births for the epidemic of 1954 (McGrath et al., 1994).

Two other studies by sophisticated investigators also have failed to confirm the relationship between influenza and schizophrenia, although these studies were hampered by the inability of finding the place of birth of a large number of the patients in the study (Kendell & Kemp 1989; Bowler & Torrey, 1990). There were two earlier American studies that showed a trend, but not of statistical significance, toward the association (Watson, Kucala, Tilleskjor, & Jacob, 1984; Torrey, Rawlings, & Waldman, 1988). Two recent studies from Holland failed to confirm a risk of schizophrenia to a prenatal exposure to the 1957 A2 influenza epidemic in that country (Selten & Slaets, 1994; Susser, Shang, Brown, Lumey, & Erlenmeyer-Kimling, 1994). A study from Croatia of prenatal exposure during the 1957 A2 influenza epidemic also failed to confirm a relationship with schizophrenia (Erlenmeyer-Kimling et al., 1994). In the southern hemisphere, the 1959 influenza epidemic was not associated with an excess of births of future people with schizophrenia (McGrath et al., 1994). Some investigators now believe that it is unlikely that maternal influenza is a risk factor for schizophrenia (Crow, 1994).

Influenza is one of a very small number of orthomyxoviruses that possess the enzyme capsular neuraminidase, which affects sialic acid. Because the cell-binding properties of NCAMs depend to a great extent on the presence of sialic acid moieties (N-acetyl-neuraminic acid)(Crossin et al., 1984), a possible link has been postulated to exist between the presence of a neuraminidase-bearing virus and cell migration problems during neurogenesis (Scheibel & Conrad, 1993). Whatever the eventual interpretation of the studies linked to a specific A2 influenza epidemic, it is reasonable to assume that further research needs to continue on the effect of midtrimester influenza infections.

A viral infection in utero that damaged the central nervous system at a critical developmental stage could then lead to a static encephalopathy, which is present for the rest of the individual's life. Such a static condition is one possible explanation for some of the findings from imaging studies (reviewed in Chapter 12). Both CT and MRI studies in some patients with schizophrenia suggest that their disease process is static (Breslin & Weinberger, 1991). The basis on which these authors give this interpretation to these studies is the failure of correlation between the patients' ventriculomegaly and ventricular size with the duration of their illnesses.

INFECTIONS OF CHILDHOOD

Before the invention of penicillin, a progressive obliterating cerebral endarteritis was sometimes found in patients with schizophrenia who died from long-term complications of rheumatic cardiac disease, which often starts in childhood. In one autopsy series from an institution in 1940, 9% of the patients with dementia praecox had definite signs of chronic rheumatic endocarditis although none of the patients were known to have gone through an acute attack of rheumatic fever while a resident of the institution (Bruetsch, 1940). [Fessel and Solomon (1960) have raised the possibility that some of Breutsch's cases may have been examples of systemic lupus erythematosus with psychosis rather than rheumatic fever.] For further information, see Chapter 9.

It is possible that encephalitis in children still can be a risk factor for the development of psychosis in adulthood (Greenbaum & Lurie, 1948). Malamud (1975) reports a case of lethargic encephalitis in a 3 year old who was later diagnosed as schizophrenic at age 20 who was diagnosed with postencephalitic Parkinsonism at 36 years.

A recent study has raised the question of whether middle ear disease (otitis media) could be an aetiological factor in some cases of schizophrenia (Mason & Winston, 1995); otitis media is more common in children.

ADULT INFECTIONS

Acute Infections

In the initial stages of the disease, viral infections with a high affinity for the medial temporal lobe (herpes simplex encephalitis, rabies) often produce severe emotional symptoms, including paranoia and hallucinations. These patients may be diagnosed as schizophrenic (Greenwood, Bhalla, Gordon, & Roberts, 1983). In addition, according to Nasrallah (1986), a great variety of infectious agents have been associated with the later development of schizophrenic-like psychosis. These include meningococcal, Japanese B, Vilyuisk, subacute sclerosing, measles, typhus, toxoplasma, crytococcal, trypanosoma, and even tuberculosis (Nasrallah, 1986). There also is an hypothesis that schizophrenia may be an encephalitis caused by the spirochete, *Borrelia burgdorferi*, which causes Lyme disease (Brown, 1994).

Encephalitis, especially herpes simplex encephalitis

Encephalitis, a seasonal illness, usually presents acutely with headache, considerable fatigue, irritability, vomiting, and low-grade pyrexia; these symptoms make the diagnosis readily apparent. Sometimes impairment of consciousness and headache is missing, however, and there may be negative findings on lumbar puncture in the initial stages in patients who actually have acute encephalitis. In the medical literature there are a number of cases of such individuals admitted to a psychiatric unit of a hospital with the diagnosis of schizophrenia due to delusions and vivid and colorful hallucinations (Sands, 1928; Misra & Hays, 1971; Wilson, 1976; Crow, 1978; Steadman, 1992). In contrast to the many kinds of chronic disease entities that present with schizophrenic symptoms that are detailed throughout this book and are some-times discovered too late or even at autopsy, patients with acute encephalitis who present with schizophrenic symptoms usually develop additional clues (fever, neurological signs, epilepsy, drowsiness, coma) that tend to reveal the underlying infection within days or weeks.

It is not unusual for these patients, who present primarily with psychiatric symptoms, to have a herpes simplex encephalitis (Drachman & Adams, 1962), although psychiatric symptoms also have been recorded in many other types of encephalitis. Herpes simplex encephalitis is usually a severe disease with a high mor-tality rate. Psychiatric symptoms, such as olfactory and gustatory hallucinations, as well as anosmia, are suggestive of a more focal encephalititis. The lesions in the brain tend to be asymmetrical and especially involve the medial temporal and orbital regions. Brain biopsy may reveal the type A inclusion bodies characteristic of the disease but a negative result is not conclusive. A more accurate test is PCR (polymerase chain reaction of small quanti-ties of deoxyribose nucleic acid—DNA—or ribonucleic acid—RNA—in cerebrospinal fluid), which has become the single most important test for rapid diagnosis of herpes simplex virus (HSV) encephalitis (Aurelius, 1993). In spite of the capacity of this virus to become latent, the HSV genome is not detectable in the cerebro-spinal fluid of HSV-seropositive individuals without neurological disease (Tyler, 1994), and thus PCR testing is clinically invaluable.

Cerebral cyst and abscess

Cerebral cysticercosis has been described in a medical graduate in England who was brought up in India (Johnstone, MacMillan, & Crow, 1987). Presenting with the symptoms of schizophrenia, a

CT scan revealed a cerebral cyst. Cysts can also be of probable noninfectious origin as in the right sylvian fissure arachnoid cyst described in a 63 year old (Lesser et al., 1992).

Headache, a neurological symptom, is the most likely presenting symptom in cerebral abscesses. However, it is surprising to note that psychiatric symptoms (rather than other neurological symptoms) are second in frequency of presentation (Gates, Kernohan, & Craig, 1950). Psychiatric symptoms can be present from the start in almost a quarter of the cases. A marked personality change may herald a brain abscess. One explanation of this may be that a common site of abscess in the brain is the temporal lobe, where the focus of the infection is from the middle ear. The organisms chiefly responsible are streptococcus, staphylococcus, pneumococcus, or *E. coli.*

Cerebral malaria

In areas where malaria is endemic, psychoses of acute onset may be the initial sign of cerebral malaria. In one survey, half of the patients admitted to a Sudanese psychiatric hospital with a mental illness precipitated by a physical disease were found to have malaria (Lishman, 1987).

Chronic Infections

Neurosyphilis (general paresis)

Neurosyphilis, infection of the brain by the spirochete treponema pallidum, can so closely resemble schizophrenia that Froshaug and Ytrehus wrote "In some cases the symptoms may be so characteristic of schizophrenia that the signs of general paresis detected in the CSF come as a great surprise" (Froshaug & Ytrehus, 1956, p. 36).

Neurosyphilis was the first major mental illness to respond to medical treatment (pyrexia therapy with malaria), the discovery of which earned the Nobel prize for Wagner-Jauregg in 1927 (Lishman, 1987). With the later introduction of penicillin, syphilitic infections of the central nervous system showed a very marked decrease and neurosyphilis looked like it was heading toward becoming an historical disease. Unfortunately, in 1987 Lishman stated "It can still be said that syphilis represents the most important infection of the nervous system which is encountered in psychiatric practice" (p. 277) (Lishman, 1987; Dewhurst, 1969). Syphilis has made a comeback and thus still has to be considered in the differential diagnosis of infectious causes of schizophreniclike symptoms. Partial or incomplete suppression of syphilitic infection by inadequate doses of drugs given for other reasons can lead to neurosyphilis appearing later in atypical and attenuated forms with consequent difficulty in diagnosis; the classical presentation of general paresis is rare nowadays (Lishman, 1987). Neurological signs may be missing (Joffe, Black, & Floyd, 1968). No organic features were noted in the three cases of schizophrenia reported by Johnstone et al. (1987).

Although syphilis classically presents in four stages—the last one being neurosyphilis—these divisions do not always hold. Even with primary infections (the appearance of the local lesion at the site of inoculation), the nervous system is sometimes involved ("early asymptomatic neurosyphilis") and meningovascular syphilis can appear in the secondary or tertiary stages. Walton (1977) has suggested that of every 12 patients with neurosyphilis approximately 5 have general paresis, 4 meningovascular syphilis, and 3 tabes dorsalis. General paresis is the most important manifestation of syphilis in psychiatric practice.

General paresis is a dementing process of insidious onset that affects males approximately three times more than females. The peak age of onset is between 30 and 50 years of age, but paresis has been described in every age group from early childhood (congenital general paresis) to extreme old age. In one series of 3,889 cases considered in the older literature, 19% of the cases developed schizophrenia (Cheney, 1935).

Grandiose delusions have been reported in one series in 58% of the patients (Varma, 1952); expansive or manic symptoms in 72% in another series (Liu, 1960). There may occasionally be a picture of true manic elation accompanied by a flight of ideas. When the presentation is primarily with schizophrenic features, paranoid delusions are then common, together with ideas of influence, passivity phenomena, and auditory hallucinations of an abusing or threatening nature (the "paranoid" or "paraphrenic" form of general paresis) (Lishman, 1987).

Serological testing in the blood, used in the past to diagnose syphilis, may be falsely negative if penicillin has been given for some other infection or a previous course of treatment has been carried out. Modern testing with TPI (Treponema Pallidum Immobilization test), TPHA (Treponema Pallidum Hemagglutination test) or FTA-ABS (Fluorescent Treponemal Antibody Absorption Test) are generally more reliable. For greater certainty of diagnosis, testing of the cerebral spinal fluid is indicated. In a recent discovery of human-immunodeficiency-virus (HIV)-seropositive individuals, even the standard cerebrospinal fluid (CSF) serological tests for neurosyphilis may be nonreactive even in the presence of viable T. pallidum (Davis, 1990). In such cases, we are back to clinical judgment as the cornerstone in establishing this diagnosis. Penicillin is the only proven therapy for neurosyphilis (Davis, 1990).

HIV-associated psychosis

Most victims of acquired immunodeficiency syndrome (AIDS) will eventually be afflicted with brain disease. In up to 60% of this patient group, the most common problem will be dementia (Wortis, 1986). An evaluation of 20 human immunodeficiency virus (HIV)-infected individuals with psychosis, an uncommon but serious complication of HIV, raised more questions than it answered (Sewell et al., 1994). Three of the autopsied brains had no detectable HIV virus present nor was there good evidence for other "opportunistic" infections underlying the psychosis. There was no significant increase in family history of schizophrenia compared to controls. The only significant finding was that the psychotic patients had a more frequent past history of stimulant and sedative/hypnotic abuse prior to the HIV infection. Studies of the neuropsychiatric effects of AIDS in five geographic areas predominantly affected by the HIV-1 epidemic has suggested that previous studies on predominantly middle-class Americans may underestimate the mental disorders accompanying AIDS (Maj et al., 1994). Also, Hart, Heath, Sautter, Garry, and Beilke (1995) have raised the possibility of a novel human retrovirus related to HIV-1 being involved in some schizoid disorders in these patients.

Slow viruses / Prions

In 1973 a question was raised by Torrey and Peterson (1973) about the possibility of "slow viruses" underlying some cases of schizophrenia. Since that time evidence has shown that so-called slow viruses are not viruses at all but instead appear to be rogue protein molecules labeled prions, possibly a new class of infectious agents that cause disease by aberrations of the protein conformation (Cohen et al., 1994). These fascinating molecules can be either infectious or genetic in origin. Whether prions will be relevant to schizophrenia is unknown at this time; the human prion diseases identified to date (kuru, Gerstmann-Straussler-Scheinker disease, Creutzfeldt-Jakob disease, and fatal familial insomnia) are invariably fatal (Prusiner & Hsiao, 1994). As we go to press, British patients afflicted with a new variant of bovine spongiform encephalopathy "initially fooled doctors into thinking they had a psychiatric disturbance" as early symptoms included paranoia, withdrawal, and fearfulness (Altman, 1996). This new disease is fatal and falls into the category of a human prion disease.

REFERENCES

Adams, W., Kendell, R. P., Hare, E. H., et al. (1993). Epidemiological evidence that maternal influenza contributes to the etiology of schizophrenia. An analysis of Scotish, English and Danish data. *British Journal of Psychiatry, 143*, 1522–534.

Altman, L. K. (1996). British study says brain patients had psychiatric symptoms. *New York Times*, April 5.

Aschauer, H. N., Meszavos, K., Willinger, U., Reiter, E., Heiden, M., Lenzinger, E., Beran, H., & Resinger, E. (1994). The season of birth of schizophrenics and schizoaffectives. *Psychopathology, 27*, 298–302.

Aurelius, E. (1993). Herpes simplex encephalitis. Early diagnosis and immune activation in the acute stage and during long-term followup. *Scandinavian Journal of Infectious Diseases (Suppl.), 89*, 3–62.

Barr, C. E., Mednick, S. A., & Munk-Jorgensen, P. (1990). Exposure to influenza epidemics during gestation and adult schizophrenia: A 40 year study. *Archives of General Psychiatry, 47*, 869–874.

Bowler, A. E., Torrey, E. F. (1990). Influenza and schizophrenia: Helsinki vs Edinburgh. *Archives of General Psychiatry, 47*, 876–877.

Breslin, N. A., & Weinberger, D. R. (1991). Brain imaging studies of schizophrenia. In S. A. Medncik, T. D. Cannon, C. E. Barr, & M. Lyon (Eds.), *Fetal neural development and adult schizophrenia.* Cambridge, UK: Cambridge University Press.

Brown, J. S. (1994). Geographic correlation of schizophrenia to ticks and tick-borne encephalitis. *Schizophrenia Bulletin, 20,* 755–775.

Breutsch, W. L. (1940). Chronic rheumatic brain disease as a possible factor in the causation in some cases of dementia praecox. *American Journal of Psychiatry, 97,* 276–296.

Cannon, T. D., & Mednick, S. A. (1991). Fetal neural development and adult schizophrenia: an elaboration of the paradigm. In S. A. Mednick, T. D. Cannon, C. E. Barr, & M. Lyon, (Eds.), *Fetal neural development and adult schizophrenia.* Cambridge, UK: Cambridge University Press.

Chan, C. C., Egbert, P. B., Herrick, M. K., & Urich, H. (1980). Oculocerebral malformations: A reappraisal of Walker's "lisssencephaly." *Archives of Neurology, 37,* 104.

Cheney, C. O. (1935). Clinical data on general paresis. *Psychiatric Quarterly, 9,* 467–485.

Cohen, F. E., Pan, K-M., Huang, Z., Baldwin, M., Fletterick, R. J., & Prusiner, S. B. (1994). Structural clues to prion replication. *Science, 264,* 520–531.

Cooper, S. J. (1992). Schizophrenia after prenatal exposure to 1957 A2 influenza epidemic. *British Journal of Psychiatry, 161,* 394–396.

Crossin, K. L., Edelman, G. M., & Cunningham, B. A. (1984). Mapping of three carbohydrate attachment sites in embryonic and adult forms of the neural cell adhesion molecule. *Journal of Cell Biology, 99,* 1848–1855.

Crow, T. J. (1978). Viral causes of psychiatric disease. *Postgraduate Medical Journal, 54,* 763–767.

Crow, T. J. (1994). Prenatal exposure to schizophrenia. There are inconsistencies and contradictions in the evidence. [editorial] *British Journal of Psychiatry, 164,* 588–592.

Crow, T. J., & Done, D. J. (1992). Prenatal exposure to influenza does not cause schizophrenia. *British Journal of Psychiatry, 161,* 390–393.

Crow, T. J., & Done, D. J., & Johstone, E. C. (1991). Schizophrenia and influenza. *Lancet, 338,* 116–117.

Davis, L. E. (1990). Neurosyphilis in the patient infected with human immunodeficiency virus. *Annals of Neurology, 27,* 211–212.

Dewhurst, K. L. (1969). The neurosyphilitic psychoses today. *British Journal of Psychiatry, 115,* 31.

Drachman, D. A., & Adams, R. D. (1962). Herpes simplex and acute inclusion-body encephalitis. *Archives of Neurology, 7,* 45–63.

Erlenmeyer-Kimling, L., Folnegovic, Z., Hrabak-Zerjavic, V., Borcic, B., Folnegovic-Smalc, V., & Susser, E. (1994). Schizophrenia and prenatal exposure to the 1957 A2 influenza epidemic in Croatia. *American Journal of Psychiatry, 151,* 1496–1498.

Falkai, P., Bogerts, B., Roberts, G. W., & Crowe, T. J. (1988). Measurement of the alpha-cell- migration in the entorhinal region: A marker for developmental disturbance in schizophrenia? *Schizophrenia Research, 1,* 157–158.

Feenstra, A., Kirch, D. G., Bracha, H. S., & Wyatt, R. J. (1989). Lack of evidence for a role of T-cell-associated retroviruses as an etiology of schizophrenia. *Biological Psychiatry, 25,* 421–430.

Fernandez, A., Hewicker, M., Trautwein, G., Pohlenz, J., & Liess, B. (1989). Viral antigen distribution in the central nervoius system of cattle persistently infected with bovine viral diarrhea virus. *Veterinary Pathology, 26,* 26–32.

Fessel, W. J., & Solomon, G. F. (1960). Psychosis and systemic lupus erythematosus: A review of the literature and case report. *California Medicine, 92,* 266–270.

Franzek, E., & Beckmann, H. (1992). Season-of-birth effect reveals the existence of etiologically different groups of schziophrenia. *Biological Psychiatry, 32,* 375–378.

Froshaug, H., & Ytrehus, A. (1956). A study of general paresis with special reference to the reasons for the admission of these patients to hospital. *Acta Psychiatrica Neurologica Scandinavica, 31,* 35–60.

Gates, E. M., Kernohan, J. W., & Craig, W. M. (1950). Metastatic brain abscess. *Medicine, 29,* 71–98.

Gilmore, J. H., Wilkie, M. B., Xiaol, H., & Lauder, J. M. (1995). Cytokine regulation of fetal neuronal survival: A role in schizophrenia? *Biological Psychiatry, 37,* 665. (abstract)

Greenbaum, J. V., & Lurie, L. A. (1948). Encephalitis as a causative factor in behaviour disorders of children. *Journal of the American Medical Association, 136,* 923.

Greenwood, R., Bhalla, A., Gordon, A., & Roberts, J. (1983). Behavior disturbances during recovery from herpes simplex encephalitis. *Journal of Neurology, Neurosurgery and Psychiatry, 46,* 809–817.

Hart, D. J., Heath, R. G., Sautter, Jr., F. J., Garry, R. F., & Beilke, M. A. (1995). Detection of retroviral serum antibodies in schizophrenics. *Biological Psychiatry, 37,* 593–683.

Jakob, J., & Beckmann, H. (1986). Prenatal developmental disturbances in the limbic allocortex in schizophrenics. *Journal of Neural Transmission, 65,* 303–326.

Joffe, R., Black, M. M., & Floyd, M. (1968). Changing clincial picture of neurosyphilis; report of seven unusual cases. *British Medical Journal, 1*, 211–212.

Johnstone, E. C., MacMillan, J. F., & Crow, T. J. (1987). The occurrence of organic disease of possible or probable etilogical significance in a population of 268 cases of first episode schizophrenia. *Psychological Medicine, 17*, 371–379.

Kendell, R. E., & Kemp, I. W. (1989). Maternal influenza in the aetiology of schizophrenia. *Archives of General Psychiatry, 46*, 878–882.

King, D. J., & Cooper, S. J. (1989). Viruses, immunity and mental disorder. *British Journal of Psychiatry, 154*, 1–7.

Kovelman, J. A., & Scheibel, A. B. (1984). A neurohistological correlate of schizophrenia. *Biological Psychiatry, 19*, 1601–1621.

Kunugi, H., Nanko, S., Takei, N., Saito, K., Hayashi, N., Kikumoto, K., Hirai, T., & Kazamatsuri, H. (1993). Schizophrenia following prenatal exposure to influenza during the second trimester. *Seishin Shinkei-gaku Zasshi, 95*, 453–462.

Kunugi, H., Nanko, S., Takei, N., Saito, K., Hayashi, N., & Kazamatsuri, H. (1995). Schizophrenia following in utero exposure to the 1957 influenza epidemics in Japan. *American Journal of Psychiatry, 152*, 450–452.

Lesser, I. M., Jeste, D. V., Boone, K. B., Harris, M. J., Miller, B. L., Heaton, R. K., & Hill-Gutierrez, E. (1992). Late-onset psychotic disorder, not otherwise specified: Clinical and neuroimaging findings. *Biological Psychiatry, 31*, 419–423.

Lishman, W. A. (1987). *Organic psychiatry*, second edition. Oxford: Blackwell Scientific.

Liu, M. C. (1960). General paralysis of the insane in Peking between 1933 and 1943. *Journal of Mental Science, 106*, 1082–1092.

Machon, R. A., Mednick, S. A., & Huttunen, M. O. (1990). An update on the Helsinki influenza project. *Archives of General Psychiatry, 47*, 292.

Maj, M., Janssen, R., Starace, F., Zaudig, M., Satz, P., Sughondhabirom, B., Luabeya, M-K., Riedel, R., Ndetei, D., Calil, H. M., Bing, E. G., St Louis, M., & Satorius, N. (1994). WHO neuropsychiatric AIDS study, cross-sectional phase I. *Archives of General Psychiatry, 51*, 39–49.

Malamud, N. (1975). Organic brain disease mistaken for psychiatric disorder. In D. F. Benson & D. Blumer (Eds.), *Psychiatric aspects of neurologic disease* (pp. 287–307). New York: Grune & Stratton.

Mason, P. R., & Winston, F. E. (1995). Ear disease and schizophrenia: A case-controlled study. *Acta Psychiatrica Scandinavica, 91*, 217–221.

McGrath, J. J., Pemberton, M. R., Welhan, J. L., & Murray, R. M. (1994). Schizophrenia and the influenza epidemics of 1954, 1957 and 1959: A southern hemisphere study. *Schizophrenia Research, 14*, 1–8.

McLardy, T. (1974). Hippocampal zinc and structural deficit in brains from chronic alcoholics and some schizophrenics. *Journal of Orthmolecular Psychiatry, 4*, 32–36.

Mednick, S. A., Machon, R. A., Huttunen, M. O., & Bonett, D. (1988). Adult schizophrenia following prenatal exposure to an influenza epidemic. *Archives of General Psychiatry, 45*, 189–192.

Mednick, S. A., Huttenen, M. O., & Machon, R. A. (1994). Prenatal influenza infections and adult schizophrenia. *Schizophrenia Bulletin, 20*, 263–267.

Menniger, K. A. (1925). The schizophrenic syndrome as a product of acute infectious disease. *Association of Research on Nervous and Mental Disorders Proceedings, 5*, 182.

Misra, P. C., & Hays, G. G. (1971). Encephalitis presenting as acute schizophrenia. *British Medical Journal, 1*, 532–533.

Nasrallah, H. A. (1986). The differential diagnosis of schizophrenia: Genetic, perinatal, neurological, pharmacological and psychiatric factors. In H. A. Nasrallah & D. R. Weinberger (Eds.), *The neurology of schizophrenia*. Amsterdam: Elsevier.

Nowakowski, R. S. (1988). Development of the hippocampal formation in mutant mice. *Drug Development Research, 15*, 316–336.

O'Callaghan, E., Sham, P., Takei, N. et al. (1991a). Schizophrenia after prenatal exposure to 1957 A2 influenza epidemic. *Lancet, 337*, 1248–1250.

O'Callaghan, E., Sham, P., Takei, N. et al. (1991b). Schizophrenia and influenza. *Lancet, 338*, 118–119.

O'Callaghan, E., Cotter, D., Colgan, K., Larkin, C., Walsh, D., & Waddington, J. L. (1995). Confinement of winter birth excess in schizophrenia to the urban-born and its gender specificity. *British Journal of Psychiatry, 166*, 51–54.

Pallast, E. G. M., Jongbloet, P. H., Straatmen, H. M., & Zielhuis, G. A. (1994). Excess seasonality of births among patients with schizophrenia and seasonal ovopathy. *Schizophrenia Bulletin, 20*, 269–276.

Prusiner, S. B., & Hsiao, K. K. (1994). Human prion diseases. *Annals Neurology, 35*, 385–395.

Rosenfeld, M. (1935). Zur Frage nach den infeksen Ursachen schizophrener Psychosen. *37* (Aug 31), 417.

Sagel, B. (1934). Beitrag zur Klarung der Frage nach zusammenhangen von Schizophreien mit Veranlagungen und Infektionen. Grundlagen einer Kausaltherapie. *Psychiatrisch Neurologische Wochenschrift, 36* (Feb 24), 85.

Sands, I. J. (1928). The acute psychiatric type of epidemic encephalitis. *American Journal of Psychiatry, 7,* 975–987.

Scheibel, A. B., & Conrad, A. S. (1993). Hippocampal dysgenesis in mutant mouse and schizophrenic man: Is there a relationship? *Schizophrenia Bulletin, 19,* 21–33.

Selemon, L. D., Rajowska, G., & Goldman-Rakic, P. S. (1995). Abnormally high neuronal density on the schizophrenic cortex. A morphological analysis of prefrontal area 9 and occipital area 17. *Archives of General Psychiatry, 52,* 805–818.

Selten, J-P. C. J., & Slaets, J. P. J. (1994). Evidence against maternal influenza as a risk factor in schizophrenia. *British Journal of Psychiatry, 164,* 674–676.

Sewell, D. D., Jeste, D. V., Atkinson, J. H., Heaton, R. K., Hesselink, J. R., Wiley, C., Thal, L., Chandler, J. L., Grant, I., & the San Diego HIV Neurobehavioral Research Group Center. (1994). HIV-associated psychosis: A study of 20 cases. *American Journal of Psychiatry, 151,* 237–242.

Sham, P. C., O'Callaghan, E., Takei, N., Murray, G. K., Hare, E. H., & Murray, R. M. (1992). Schiozphrenia following pre-natal exposure to influenza epidemics between 1939 and 1960. *British Journal of Psychiatry, 160,* 461–466.

Steadman, P. (1992). Herpes simplex mimicking functional psychosis. *Biological Psychiatry, 32,* 207–213.

Susser, E., Shang, P. L., Brown, A. S., Lumey, L. H., & Erlenmeyer-Kimling, L. (1994). No relation between risk of schizophrenia and prenatal exposure to influenza in Holland. *American Journal of Psychiatry, 151,* 922–924.

Takei, N., Sham, R., O'Callaghan, E., Murray, G. K., Glover, G., & Murray, R. M. (1994). Prenatal exposure to influenza and the development of schizophrenia. Is this effect confined to females? *American Journal of Psychiatry, 151,* 117–119.

Takei, N., Sham, P. C., O'Callaghan, E., Glover, G., & Murray, R. M. (1995). Schizophrenia: Increased risk associated with winter and city births—A case-control study in 12 regions within England and Wales. *Journal of Epidemiology and Community Health, 49,* 106–107.

Torrey, E. F., & Peterson, M. R. (1973). Slow and latent viruses in schizophrenia. *Lancet, ii,* 22.

Torrey, E. F., Rawlings, R., & Waldman, I. N. (1988). Schizophrenic births and viral diseases in two states. *Schizophrenia Research, 1,* 73–77.

Torrey, E. F., Bowler, A. E., Rawlings, R., & Terrazas, A. (1993). Seasonality of schizophrenia and stillbirths. *Schizophrenia Bulletin, 19,* 557–562.

Torrey, E. F., Taylor, E. H., Bracha, H. S., Bowler, A. E., McNeil, T. F., Rawlings, R. R., Quinn, P. O., Bigelow, L. B., Rickler, K., Sjostrom, K., Higgins, E. S., & Gottesman, I. I. (1994). Prenatal origin of schizophrenia in a subgroup of discordant monozygotic twins. *Schizophrenia Bulletin, 20,* 423–432.

Tyler, K. L. (1994). Polymerase chain reaction and the diagnosis of viral central nervous system diseases. *Annals of Neurology, 36,* 809–811. (editorial)

Varma, L. P. (1952). The incidence and clinical features of general paresis. *Indian Journal of Neurology and Psychiatry, 3,* 141–163.

Walton, J. N. (1977). *Brain's diseases of the nervous system,* 8th edition. Oxford: Oxford University Press.

Watson, C. G., Kucala, T., Tilleskjor, C., & Jacob, L. (1984). Schizophrenic birth seasonality in relation to the incidence of infectious diseases and temperature extremes. *Archives of General Psychiatry, 41,* 85–90.

Wilson, L. G. (1976). Viral encephalopathy mimicking functional psychosis. *American Journal of Psychiatry, 133,* 165–170.

Wortis, J. (1986). Neuropsychiatry of acquired immune deficiency syndrome. (editorial) *Biological Psychiatry, 21,* 1357–1359.

Yolken, R. H., & Torrey, E. F. (1995). Viruses, schizophrenia and bipolar disorder. *Clinical Microbiology Reviews, 8,* 131–145.

Yolken, R. H., Collett, M., Petric, M., Yao, L., Sun, Y., & Torrey, E. F. (1994). *Antibodies to pestivirus in identical twins discordant for schizophrenia.* (Abstract). Seventh Biennial Winter Workshop on Schizophrenia, January 23–28, Switzerland.

Zipursky, R. B., & Schultz, S. C. (1987). Seasonality of birth and CT findings in schizophrenia. *Biological Psychiatry, 22,* 1288–1292.

Chapter 6

Metabolic Diseases

Abnormal levels of enzymes or variations in the structure of enzymes can result in major diseases of the central nervous system called metabolic disease entities. Usually hereditary and often recessive in genetic pattern, these diseases also sometimes occur sporadically. In Chapter 10, the molecular biological errors underlying each of these diseases is discussed in greater detail if they are known. The diseases discussed in this chapter have a subgroup of patients who have symptoms associated with schizophrenia.

This book as a whole is focused on individuals with normal intelligence who present with the symptoms of schizophrenia. Individuals with known etiologies of mental retardation also can develop the symptoms associated with schizophrenia, however, usually as adults. Several diseases in which psychiatric symptoms developed in persons with mental retardation (argininosuccinic aciduria) (phenylketonuria) are discussed in this chapter as possible examples of this phenomenon. Professionals dealing with populations of developmentally delayed individuals will be aware of many other disease entities and of their special diagnostic and therapeutic problems (Ryan, 1994; Swiezy et al., 1995).

In a number of the disease entities listed in this chapter, the majority of patients present in early childhood with neurological symptoms, and late-onset or adult-onset cases are rarer. Of the diseases that usually present in childhood (adrenoleukodystrophy-X-linked and metachromatic leukodystrophy are examples), however, if the presentation occurs in adulthood, the first symptoms of the disease can be psychiatric, even presenting as schizophrenia.

ADRENOLEUKODYSTROPHY-X-LINKED/
ADRENOMYELONEUROPATHY

Adrenoleukodystrophy (ALD) consists of intellectual, memory, and behavioral deterioration and is usually seen in children. This devastating disease is characterized by upper motor unit involvement with gait disturbances caused by spasticity and ataxia with continuing progression to quadriplegia until death occurs. ALD may present at any age as a psychiatric disorder, however (Powell et al., 1975; Moser, 1992). One review of 109 cases of ALD revealed that 17% presented exclusively as a psychiatric problem, whereas 39% included some psychiatric sign or symptoms in their overall presentation (Kitchen, Cohen-Cole, & Mickel, 1987). In this group, although there were other patients with hallucinations or unspecified psychosis, three had been diagnosed only with schizophrenia.

A clinical subgroup of ALD is adrenomyeloneuropathy (AMN), which is seen in adults; the mean age of onset is 27.6 years and it is slowly progressive over the years (Moser, 1993). In one recent study, AMN was the phenotype of 66 (33%) of the 202 patients with the biochemistry of X-linked ALD (Aubourg et al., 1992). In many instances these men present in their 20's or 30's with symptoms that may resemble schizophrenia, sometimes with dementia or a specific cerebral defect (Moser & Moser, 1989). When a peripheral neuropathy becomes apparent, the underlying diagnosis becomes more evident. Although it is a severely disabling disease, it is compatible with survival into the seventh decade.

In the nervous system, ALD mainly affects the white matter. ALD and its subtypes are associated with the abnormal accumulation of saturated, very long chain fatty acids (VLCFA). The functional enzyme defect (VLCFA Co A synthetase) involves an impaired capacity to catalyze VLCFAs.

Diagnosis is made measuring abnormally high levels of saturated VLCFA in accessible tissues of body fluids. Tissues that can be used are white blood cells (Molzer, Bernheimer, Heller, Toifu, & Vetterlein, 1982), red blood cells (Antoku, Sakai, Gotto, Iwashita, & Kuroway, 1984), plasma (Alberghina, Fiumara, Pavone, & Guiffrida, 1984), cultured muscle (Askanas, McLaughlin, Engel, &

Adornato, 1979) and cultured skin fibroblasts (Tonshoff, Lehnert, & Ropers, 1982). The analytic procedures used are capillary gas liquid chromatography, which may be combined with mass spectrometry or high-performance liquid chromatography. The pattern of VLCFAs produced in these procedures is distinctive although a similar pattern may be seen in children on a ketogenic diet. One recent study recommended that testing for VLCFA levels be performed on all patients who present with Addison's disease as 25% of the men with Addison's disease in that study had elevated concentrations and half of those patients already had symptoms of adrenomyeloneuropathy (Schafer et al., 1994). For a full clinical and laboratory differential diagnosis of adrenomyeloneuropathy, see Moser and Moser (1989). This disease entity is known to be an X-linked disorder and the primary gene defect has been mapped to chromosome X q28. A candidate gene has been isolated (see Chapter 10). This raises the possibility of future gene therapy (Moser, 1993). In the meantime, other research therapy is now available. There have been some attempts at bone marrow transplants, which show promise only in the early stages of the disease (Aubourg et al., 1990, 1992). A new experimental dietary therapy has been tried with Lorenzo's oil (a 4:1 mixture of glycerol trioleate and glycerol triucate), which is combined with a diet that restricts the intake of saturated VLCFAs; this therapy is reported to increase the levels of erucic acid in both the total lipid and triglyceride fractions isolated from the brain (Rizzo et al., 1989). There has been a report of clinical and magnetic resonance imaging (MRI) improvement in one patient who had been treated with Lorenzo's oil (Maeda et al., 1992). The postmortem studies of another patient who had the Lorenzo's oil therapy showed, however, that although moderating effects could be detected in plasma and liver, the treatment was of limited value in correcting the accumulation of VLCFAs in the brain, suggesting that very little erucic acid crossed the blood–brain barrier (Poulos, Gibson, Sharp, Beckman, & Grattan-Smith, 1994). By now, there is agreement that Lorenzo's oil does not have a significant effect on the rate of progress of the childhood cerebral form of ALD and the answer for older patients is "suggestive at best" (Moser, 1993). There is a side effect, however, which is a reduction in the platelet count.

ARGININOSUCCINIC ACIDURIA

Argininosuccinic aciduria is an autosomal recessive disorder of the urea cycle caused by a deficiency of the enzyme L-argininosuccinic acid lyase. The onset of the disease varies from the fetal, neonatal period usually leading to an early death up to a late-onset type with neurological abnormalities and varying degrees of mental retardation. Patients with the late-onset type of disease are characterized by retarded intellectual and motor development, incoordination and intermittent ataxia, and unusual tufting and friability of the hair (trichorrhexis nodosa).

A brother and sister, with late-onset disease, are described who developed a paranoid psychosis as older adults. The brother, with an 1.Q. of 40–50, was a 63 year old who had thrown his refrigerator out of the window because he thought his food was poisoned (Lagas & Ruokonen, 1991). Other cases of psychotic behavior in adults with late-onset disease are described in the literature (von Wendt, Simila, Roukonen, & Puukka, 1982; Odent et al., 1989); approximately 20% of the adult-onset cases become psychotic. Diagnosis is usually made from the increased concentration of argininosuccinic acid in the urine. Increased levels of argininosuccinic acid and citrulline are found in the serum.

FABRY DISEASE

Fabry disease (angiokeratoma corporis diffusum) is an X-linked glycosphingolipid storage disease due to a deficiency of the enzyme alpha-galactosidase A. In this disease, there is excess lyosomal storage of glycosphingolipids in both the blood vessels and the neurons. The lesions in the central nervous system present as diffuse cerebral atrophy, especially of the frontal regions, and premature atherosclerosis of the cerebral vasculature; stroke can also be a symptom.

Clinical manifestations of Fabry's disease include a characteristic rash of the skin and conjunctivae (skin angiectasia), acroparesthesia, peripheral edema, pain in the extremities, febrile crises, renal failure, and episodes of severe abdominal pain.

Liston, Martin, and Philippart (1973) described a patient with Fabry disease and severe paranoid schizophrenia. The authors were pleasantly surprised that the treatment for the Fabry disease (phenoxybenzamine—10 mg qid) resulted in dramatic reversal of the symptoms of paranoid schizophrenia and he was sent home on that maintenance therapy. Six months after discharge from the hospital, the patient discontinued his phenoxybenzamine for several weeks and the severe paranoid schizophrenia reoccurred. After 3 weeks in the hospital where he received only supportive therapy, the patient remained psychotic, so phenoxybenzamine was restarted; the schizophrenia again abated. The authors, from a major academic medical center, state "If it were not for the known existence of Fabry disease, the diagnosis of paranoid schizophrenia would have been made without equivocation" (Liston et al., 1973, p. 403).

Skin biopsy is helpful in the diagnosis. Exact diagnosis for each family can be made by molecular biology; a number of different mutations in the alpha-galactosidase A gene of Fabry disease have been described and can be used to confirm diagnoses in both homozygotes and heterozygotes (Sakuraba, 1989; Ishii et al., 1991) (see Chapter 10).

GM2 GANGLIOSIDOSIS

Gangliosides, like other glycosphingolipids, are typical components of the outer leaflet of plasma membranes of animal cells and are particularly abundant in the neuron. The term GM2 gangliosidosis was coined by Suzuki and Chen (1967) to refer to disorders characterized by the accumulation of GM2 ganglioside in the brain and peripheral neurons usually due to an abnormality of the lysomal enzyme called hexosaminidase (Hex). In 1969 Okada and O'Brien (1969) discovered the absence of Hex A activity in Tay-Sachs disease and a combined deficiency of Hex A and Hex B was described by Sandhoff (1969). Hex A is composed of alpha and beta subunits, whereas Hex B is composed of beta subunits only. A deficiency of the GM2 activator protein also has been reported to cause increased neuronal storage of the ganglioside; it is sometimes called the AB-variant form. All these diseases are genetically distinct but share a biochemical deficiency in the hydrolysis of GM2 ganglioside in the lysosomes of the cells of the central and peripheral nervous system (Neote, Mahuran, & Gravel, 1991).

GM2 gangliosidosis in the adult form is a very rare autosomal recessive disorder in which a deficiency of Hex A leads to the accumulation of lysosomal GM2 gangliosides. Mutations in the alpha-subunit that give rise to some residual level of Hex A result in juvenile and adult-onset gangliosidoses, whereas the mutation that results in complete absence of the enzyme give rise to the infantile Tay-Sachs disease (Navon, 1991). It has been shown that fibroblasts of adult patients synthesize the alpha-subunit precursor, but not the mature enzyme (Frisch, Baran, & Navon, 1984). In contrast to the severe infantile mutations that produce no or highly unstable messenger ribose nucleic acid (mRNA), the late-onset forms are due to point mutations within the protein coding region, which generate stable mRNA. Adult GM2 gangliosidosis is caused by the deficiency, but not total absence, of Hex A due to a single base change in the alpha-subunit of Hex, resulting in a substitution of Ser for Gly at position 269 in the alpha-subunit of the enzyme (Navon, 1991).

Like Tay-Sachs, adult-onset GM2 gangliosidosis mainly affects Ashkenazi Jews. Fewer than 100 patients with adult GM2 gangliosidosis have been described in the literature. Neurological manifestations usually dominate the clinical picture including spinocerebellar, cerebellar, and lower and/or upper motor neuron syndromes which reveal the diagnosis (Neote et al., 1991).

Psychiatrically, both psychotic and affective symptoms have been noted in as many as 35% of reported patients (Navron, Argor, & Frisch, 1986; Streifler, Golomb, & Gaduth, 1989; Federico et al., 1991). In some patients psychosis precedes other neurologic manifestations (Navon, 1991). The patient described by Renshaw et al. developed chronic auditory hallucinations and intermittent paranoid delusions at the age of 19 years; later he had episodes of catatonia (Renshaw, Stern, Welch, Schouten, & Kolodny, 1992).

A computed tomography (CT) and MRI study of 10 patients with late-onset GM2 gangliosidosis, six of whom had recurrent psychosis, showed several interesting features (Streifler, Gornish,

Hadar, & Gadoth, 1993). Although both the gray and white matter of the cerebral hemispheres had no areas of abnormal signal intensity, half of the patients had some thinning of the corpus callosum including three of the patients with recurrent psychosis. All patients had some degree of cerebellar vermian atrophy.

HARTNUP DISEASE

Hartnup disease, which was first described by Baron and colleagues (1956), is a recessive hereditary disorder of tryptophan metabolism. The disease is characterized by a pellagralike skin rash, temporary cerebellar ataxia, neuropsychiatric symptoms and is associated with a diagnostic type of aminoaciduria.

The medical literature has a number of cases of withdrawn individuals with bizarre delusions, hallucinations, feelings of depersonalization and meaningless talk (Hersov, 1955; Hersov & Rodnight, 1960; Halvorsen & Halvorsen, 1963; Oyanagi, Takagi, Kitabatake, & Nakao, 1967; Navab & Asatoor, 1970; Hartelheimer, Gruttner, & Simon, 1971). Many of these cases were reported to recover from their neuropsychiatric symptoms with treatment.

Hartnup disease can be suspected by the presence of a sun-sensitive red, scaly rash and a severe (but reversible) cerebellar ataxia in a young person with psychiatric symptoms. There is often a positive family history. The disease can present intermittently and is precipitated by exposure to sunlight, fever, poor diet, or sulfonamides. The age of onset is either late childhood, adolescence, or occasionally, adulthood. There is a case in the literature with "autistic behavior with stereotyped movements and vocalizations" that presented at 11 months of age; the child also had a fatal seizure disorder (Schmidtke et al., 1992, p. 900).

HOMOCYSTINURIA

Homocystinuria results from interruptions of the degradative bio-synthetic pathways of the amino acid methionine. Classically, homocystinuria due to cystathionine beta synthetase (CBS) deficiency was associated with mental retardation, dislocated lenses, tall stature, osteoporosis, and arterial and venous thrombosis (Clarke et al., 1991). Today it is now known that there are numerous genetic and environmental causes of homocystinuria (see Table 6.1) although the most common genetic disease resulting in homocystinuria remains cystathionine beta synthase deficiency.

The question of whether schizophrenia is related to homocystinuria historically has been a troubling one. Psychiatric disorders can be common in patients with classical homocystinuria (CBS deficiency). In a report of 63 classic homocystinuric patients, however, 51% had significant psychiatric disorders, none of which were schizophrenia (Abbott, Folstein, Abbey, & Pyeritz, 1987). This careful study helped correct an impression in the earlier literature in which case reports had suggested that schizophrenia was a fairly common manifestation of homocystinuria (Bracken & Coll, 1985) and that there was a high incidence of relatives who also had schizophrenia. In fact this early impression about homocystinuria boosted one hypothesis about the cause of schizophrenia—the transmethylation hypothesis—which was partly based on the "methionine effect," an effect demonstrated by Kety and his co-workers that 40% of chronic schizophrenics react to 20 g/day of L-methionine with an acute psychotic reaction (Park, Baldessarini, & Kety, 1965).

How many of those early diagnoses of schizophrenia and homocystinuria were correct? Abbott et at. (1987) reported that probably many of the early diagnoses of schizophrenia in patients with homocystinuria were incorrect; their literature review revealed only three well-documented cases of schizophrenia. Many psychotic patients with homocystinuria have had this diagnosis considered and eventually rejected. Schimke et al. studied 38 individuals with homocystinuria and found only one with a diagnosis of acute schizophrenia. Looking at the problem the other way around, there were a few cases of supposedly well-established schizophrenia who were later found to have homocystinuria (Spiro, Schimke, & Welch, 1965; Kaeser, Rodnight, & Ellis, 1969). In view of contemporary knowledge, these patients may have had a form of homocystinuria other than CBS, possibly a transmethylation defect (see Table 6.1). Mudd, Levy, and Skovby (1989, p. 707) summed up the situation as follows: "Although antidotal reports have suggested that schizophrenia might be

TABLE 6.1 Homocystinuria

I. *Transsulfuration Defect*
  A. Cystathionine beta synthase deficiency ("classical homocystinuria")
II. *Transmethylation Defects*
  A. Methylenetetrahydrofolate reductase deficiency
  B. cblC, cblD, cblF (failure to form Me Cbl and Ad Cbl)
  C. cblE, cblG (failure to form Me Cbl)
III. *Other*
  A. Vitamin B_{12} deficiency
    1. Disorder of absorption or transport
    2. Nutritional disorder
  B. Folate deficiency
  C. Drugs
    1. 6-azauridine triacetate
    2. isonicotinic acid hydrazide
  D. Artifactual, due to bacterial metabolism of urinary cystathionine

Table courtesy of David S. Rosenblatt, M.D.

common among cystathionine beta synthase deficiency patients, it may, in fact, be uncommon." The gene that codes for the enzyme cystathionine-beta-synthase is located on chromosome 21 (see Chapter 10).

Methylenetetrahydrofolate reductase deficiency (MTHFR deficiency), first discovered in 1972 (Mudd et al., 1972), can present from birth to adult life. In the older group of patients, psychiatric manifestations have been reported. The question of the diagnosis of schizophrenia has been raised with some of these patients, including some whose psychiatric symptoms appeared to respond to therapy (Freeman, Finkelstein, Mudd, & Uhlendorf, 1972; Freeman, Finkelstein, & Mudd, 1975; Pasquier, Lebert, Pett, Zittoun, & Marquet, 1994). One distinguishing characteristic of this form of homocystinuria is the presence of concomitant neuropathies with the schizophrenic symptoms. Although homocystinuria is consistently seen in patients with MTHFR deficiency, and indeed usually is the clinical clue by which the diagnosis is made, the level of homocystinuria is less than that which is found in cystathionine beta synthase deficiency (Rosenblatt, 1995).

The molecular information to create the enzyme, methylenetetrahydrofolate reductase, has been localized on chromosome 1p36.3 (Goyette et al., 1994) (see Chapter 10). A common mutation in MTHFR, at a frequency of 38% of unselected chromosomes, is associated with significantly elevated plasma homocysteine levels, which in turn can be associated with risk for vascular complications (Frosst et al., 1995). Other symptoms of MTHFR deficiency described include seizures, motor and gait disturbances and, in small children, developmental delay.

This biochemical disorder is resistant to treatment but a number of different therapies have been reported to be helpful to this patient group. They include folic acid (Freeman et al., 1975), vitamin B12 (Rosenblatt, 1989), riboflavin (Fowler, Whitehouse, & Rensma, 1990) and betaine (Wendel & Bremer, 1984; Holme, Kjellman, & Ronge, 1989).

There is a very interesting recent finding about MTHFR deficiency that conceivably could help shed light on why these patients sometimes present with the symptoms of schizophrenia. Apparently patients with MTHFR deficiency may have MRI findings characteristic of leukodystrophy (Walk, Soo-Sang, & Horwitz, 1994; Brown et al., 1995). The authors point out the similarity of the findings to adrenoleukodystrophy and metachromatic leukodystrophy. Both of these diseases are described in this chapter and they have a known pattern of lesions in postpuberty patients that sometimes results in the symptoms of schizophrenia. How an aminoaciduria could result in an MRI pattern reminiscent of the leukodystrophies needs to be worked out in the future through biochemical research.

Undoubtedly there will continue to be controversy about the relationship of the diagnosis of schizophrenia in patients with homocystinuria. Because the diagnosis has been seriously considered in so many of these patients and because therapy may be of some value to patients who have a combination of schizophrenia and one of the biochemical subtypes (MTHFR deficiency), clinicians should remain informed about this disease entity.

METACHROMATIC LEUKODYSTROPHY, ADULT TYPE

Metachromatic leukodystrophy is a progressive neurological disorder, usually presenting in childhood, caused by an inherited lysosomal storage disorder with a marked deficiency of the enzyme, arylsulfatase A (ASA). This enzyme is involved in the degradation of cerebroside sulfate, an important constituent of myelin in the brain. Deficiency of ASA results in the accumulation of cerebroside sulfate (Kolodny, 1989). The storage of the sulfatide mainly affects the nervous system, where it is associated with progressive demyelination and loss of white matter.

Three forms of the disease can be distinguished according to severity of symptoms and age of onset: late infantile (1–2 years), juvenile (3–16 years), and adult (> 16 years). In the late infantile form, the child invariably progresses to being a bedridden quadriplegic without speech or comprehension. In the adult form, it is rare for the first signs or symptoms to be neurological; rather the disease begins with emotional instability leading to psychosis or a gradual onset of dementia (Prensky, 1982). About 10% of all metachromatic leukodystrophy patients have the adult form.

In a review of 129 published case reports of metachromatic leukodystrophy, it was found that 53% of the adolescent and early adult-onset patients had either hallucinations, delusions, and/ or a diagnosis of schizophrenia or psychosis (Hyde, Ziegler, & Weinberger, 1992). These authors noted that the frequency of auditory hallucinations in adolescent and early adult-onset metachromatic leukodystrophy was particularly noteworthy; auditory hallucinations were reported in every case in which hallucinations were mentioned. These hallucinations usually were described as hearing voices. The hearing of multiple voices, making complex and usually denigrating observations about the patient, is considered a classic feature of schizophrenia. Hyde et al. (1992) also noted references to thought fragmentation, catatonic posturing, bizarre gesturing, talking to oneself, and poor insight.

Thus perhaps it is not surprising that many patients with metachromatic leukodystrophy have been diagnosed as schizophrenic or having a schizophrenic reaction (Wicke, 1938; Peiffer, 1959; Sourander & Svennerhom, 1962; Sakai & Tano, 1965; Kothbauer, Jellinger, Gross, Molzer, & Bernheimer, 1977; Manowitz, Kling, & Kohn, 1978; Besson, 1980; Mahon-Haft, Stone, Johnson, & Shah, 1981; Manowitz, Goldstein, & Nora, 1981; Finelli, 1985; Schaffer, Oepen, & Ott, 1988). In one of these studies, determination of ASA in a study of 18 schizophrenics led to the detection of three new cases of metachromatic leukodystrophy in just that one study (Mahon-Haft et al., 1981).

An interesting study by Manowitz, Goldstein, and Nora (1981) obtained blood samples from 90 adult, male schizophrenic subjects who were inpatients in a VA Hospital. The two of these individuals who had schizophrenia also had ASA levels that were at an intermediate level between those of symptomatic patients homozygous for metachromatic leukodystrophy and asymptomatic individuals who are obligatory heterozygotes. The gene for ASA is on the long arm of chromosome 22. This paper raised the question of whether there could be evidence of different alleles that may account for delay until adult life of enough storage of sulfatides to cause symptoms? Did the Manowitz et al. (1981) intermediate levels of ASA correlate with particular alleles suggesting that patients with such alleles are more likely to present in adult life with schizophrenia?

In a seminal paper, Polten et al. (1991) used molecular biological techniques to analyze the alleles of ASA associated with metachromatic leukodystrophy. They studied two alleles—allele I and allele A. They found that allele I was associated with the late-infantile form. Any patient with a combination of allele I and allele A had the juvenile form. Homozygosity (two identical alleles) for allele A was associated with the adult form (5 cases) or juvenile form (3 cases). Allele A found in combination with another, unidentified metachromatic leukodystrophy allele resulted in either juvenile (7 cases) or adult (3 cases) forms.

In other words, Polten et al. (1991) found evidence that the difference in the presentation of clinical symptoms in metachromatic leukodystrophy related to age—neurologic in young ages and often psychiatric in older ages—appeared to have a relationship to the heterogeneity of ASA alleles. Allele I was associated with the earlier and more severe form of the disease, whereas allele A was associated with clinical subtypes that present at a later age. Other studies of alleles that are thought to provide some residual activity in metachromatic leukodystrophy include studies by Fluharty, Fluharty, Bohne, von Figura, and Gieselmann (1991), Kappler, von Figura, and Gieselmann (1992), and Hasegawa, Kawame, Ida, Ohashi, and Eto (1994).

Keefe and Harvey point out that metachromatic leukodystrophy could be a model of connectivity dysfunction for schizophrenia because the lesions are found in the connections between different brain areas, particularly the neural circuits leading to the frontal cortex (Keefe & Harvey, 1994). The same demylination also occurs in the early infantile cases but is much more extensive. A certain developmental stage and age of the brain along with a more limited demyelination appears to be necessary for symptoms of schizophrenia to appear.

Diagnosis of metachromatic leukodystrophy can be made by sulfatase levels in the urine (Baum, Dodgson, & Spencer, 1959) and/or enzyme activity in the leukocytes or cultured fibroblasts (Kudoh & Wenger, 1982). In the future, exact genetic mutations for each patient also may become standard (Ben-Yoseph & Mitchell, 1994). The diagnosis is complicated by the existence of an ASA pseudodeficiency allele present in approximately 1% of the normal population, which has no apparent clinical sequelae (Nelson, Carey, & Morris, 1991). (On the basis of a mathematical model, Conzelmann and Sandhoff (1983–1984) have calculated that very low lysosomal enzyme activity often is sufficient to sustain normal catabolism thus making pseudodeficiency alleles benign.)

Bone marrow transplantation has been proposed as a treatment for metachromatic leukodystrophy and some early reports have shown some stabilization of the degenerative process (Krivit et al., 1994; Shapiro & Lipton, 1992). There is evidence that the low levels of enzyme delivered to the brain by microglial cells derived from the donor's bone marrow might be sufficient to alter the course of the disease; it has been postulated that patients with the juvenile or adult forms would be the best candidates for the bone marrow transplantation (Polten et al., 1991).

PHENYLKETONURIA (PKU) SCHIZOPHRENIA

There are a number of case reports of schizophrenia or psychosis in adults with phenylketonuria (PKU). Most but not all had some degree of mental retardation (Bjornson, 1964; Dorninger & Plochl, 1969; Pitt, 1971; Perry, Hansen, Tischler, Richards, & Sokol, 1973; Fisch, Hosfield, Chang, Barranger, & Hastings, 1979). In the two cases described by Pitt, the ages of onset of major psychotic illnesses labeled schizophrenia were adolescence in the first patient and 49 years of age in the second.

In such cases of homozygous PKU and schizophrenia, there is the question of either the coincidence of two diseases in one individual or a relationship between the metabolic disorder and the psychiatric symptoms. In a paper entitled "Unrecognized Adult Phenylketonuria," Perry and colleagues wrote that "Two of the adults with phenylketonuria have suffered major psychotic illnesses resulting in their admission to a mental hospital where they were inappropriately given electroshock and antipsychotic drugs" (Perry et al., 1973). They make the point that the fact that a patient with untreated PKU has escaped serious mental defect in childhood may not guarantee that other manifestations of cerebral malfunction will not appear in later life.

Because the error in patients with PKU directly effects the catecholamine (dopamine-norepinephrine-epinephrine) pathway and perhaps because the disease was identified as early as 1934 and, when diagnosed in infancy, produces a preventable form of mental retardation/autism, there is greater interest in the medical literature of the hypothesis of a direct relationship between PKU and schizophrenia than might usually be found in such a very rare disease. Reveley and Reveley (1982) took up the challenge of testing the hypothesis by performing the simple screening test (Phenistix) for PKU on consecutive, unselected admissions to two mental health facilities—a state-supported psychiatric hospital and a psychiatric unit of a private hospital. Among the admissions were 262 patients diagnosed as schizophrenic all of whom were negative for PKU. (In this study, there were a total of 786 consecutive admissions of all known forms of mental illness and, unfortunately, this larger figure made its way into the medical literature and is the figure quoted in secondary sources when referring to the number of schizophrenics tested in this study. An example of using the 786 figure is the otherwise reliable paper by Sweetman and Haas, 1992.)

When dealing with rare possible causes (PKU) of a common disease entity (schizophrenia), there is an element of chance that screening studies of populations will pick up cases unless these screens are very large indeed. Another approach might come from cases of schizophrenia identified from families already at risk for PKU, as is described in a number of the previously listed papers. It would really be meaningful if the initiation of specific therapy (low phenylalanine diet for PKU) reversed some of the symptoms of schizophrenia in an individual who had both PKU and schizophrenia. The only example of dietary therapy we could find in the literature, however, was a 22-year-old diagnosed as "a classic hebephrenic schizophrenic" who was demonstrated to have PKU (Fisch, Hosfield, Chang, Barranger, & Hastings, 1979, p. 244). This young man had no relief from his hallucinations, no change in his abnormal electroencephalographic findings or any other brain abnormalities on either the low phenylalanine diet or, for that matter, on many of the drug therapies for schizophrenia. This case may reinforce the maxim that irreversibility is a finding of advanced degenerative diseases of the brain. Considering all relevant factors, we consider PKU to be on the list of diseases to be tested for in schizophrenia if there is any family history (no matter how remote) of PKU.

THE PORPHYRIAS

The porphyrias are a group of clinically heterogeneous diseases associated with disturbances in heme biosynthesis (see Figure 6.1). Porphyrins are pigments that serve as intermediates in this pathway formed from the precursors delta-aminolevulinic acid (ALA) and porphobilinogen (PBG). Porphyrias are classified as either hepatic or erythroid, depending on the principle site of expression of the specific enzyme defect in each disorder. The acute hepatic porphyrias (acute intermittent porphyria, porphyria variegata, hereditary coproporphyria) result from approximately 50% deficiencies of specific enzyme levels. Only 10% of the subjects who inherit a prophyrin enzyme deficiency develop the corresponding acute porphyria (Hindmarsh, 1993).

The porphyria that is most likely to have symptoms diagnosed as schizophrenia is *acute intermittent porphyria* (Peters, 1962; Matiar-Vahr & Lungershausen, 1967; Roth, 1968). Expression of the disease is highly variable, determined in part by environmental, metabolic, and hormonal factors that induce hepatic

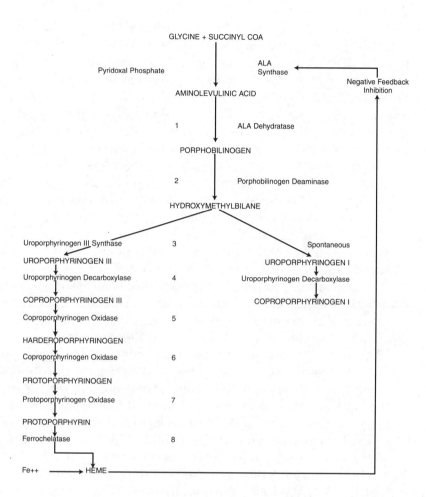

Figure 6.1 The pathway of heme biosynthesis.
The pathway of heme synthesis including sites of enzyme insufficiency in the porphyrias.
1. ALA dehydratase deficiency, tyrosinemia, lead poisoning. 2. Acute intermittent porphyria. 3. Congenital erythropoietic porphyria. 4. Porphyria cutanea tarda, hepatoerythropoietic porphyria, toxic porphyria - commonest site. 5. Hereditary coproporphyria, lead poisoning. 6. Harderophorphyria. 7. Porphyria variegata. 8. Erythropoietic protoporphyria, lead poisoning.

Reprinted with permission from Hindmarsh, J. T. (1993). Variable phenotypic expression of genotypic abnormalities in the porphyrias. *Clinica Chimica Acta*, *217*, 29–38.

delta-aminolevulinic acid synthase activity (ALA synthase), the first and rate-limiting enzyme of heme biosynthesis (see Figure 6.1). Its discoverer, Waldenström (1939), described the various psychiatric symptoms of acute intermittent porphyria. Surveys of hospitalized psychiatric patients have turned up between a low of 2 cases to a high of 21 cases of porphyria in each patient population studied (Hadlik & Rodova, 1960; Kaelbing, Craig, & Pasamanick, 1961; Wetterberg, 1967). Lishman reports that "Psychotic developments may resemble schizophrenia and paranoid reactions are not uncommon. . . . Clouding of consciousness and confusion may progress to delirium, with hallucinations, delusions and noisy disturbed behavior" (Lishman, 1987, p. 483).

Porphyria is of historical interest because the disease has been traced back to Mary Queen of Scots through the royal houses of Stuart, Hanover, and Prussia; there is evidence that England's George III's puzzling mental illness may have been associated with porphyria (Miller, 1993). The prevalence of acute intermittent porphyria in the general population was estimated as 1.5–7.7 in 100,000 for Sweden (Kappas, Sassa, & Anderson, 1983).

Three of the hepatic porphyrias—intermittent acute porphyria, hereditary coproporphyria, and variagate porphyria—have many features in common. They all may present with disease of the central nervous system and they all follow an autosomal dominant genetic pattern. Acute attacks of a life-threatening neuropsychological syndrome are precipitated by a variety of drugs as well as by hormones and other agents. During acute attacks excessive urinary excretion of the porphyrin precursors aminolevulinic acid (ALA) and porphobilinogen (PBG) occurs in all three, but the patterns of porphyrin excreted in urine and feces differ. Some of the features of these porphyrias follow.

1. The type most likely to include hallucinations and paranoia is *acute intermittent porphyria*. The clinical features begin at any age after puberty, most often in the third decade. The individual becomes emotionally disturbed—either violent, agitated, or severely depressed. Marked emotional lability is common with histrionic, noisy, disturbed behavior. Sometimes there is little clouding of consciousness and the patients are thought to be schizophrenic. Clouding of consciousness combined with headaches and confusion is the more common pattern of symptoms

and may progress to delirium with hallucinations and delusions. In severe cases, coma may develop; fatalities sometimes occur. Twenty percent of the patients develop a seizure disorder; status epilepticus has been reported. Multiple reversible cerebral lesions have been reported by MRI during hallucinations and seizures (King & Bragdon, 1991).

Classical nonpsychiatric symptoms of acute intermittent porphyria are acute abdominal pain with nausea, vomiting, and constipation. Weakness, numbness, paresthesiae, and pain in the extremities or in the back may indicate that a peripheral neuropathy is developing; the acute presentation of a neuropathy is usually motor, but sensory components can be seen. Cases have been reported of severe paralysis with compromise of the respiratory system. Photosensitivity does not occur.

Attacks of acute intermittent porphyria can be precipitated by alcohol, infection, and certain drugs. See Table 6.2 for lists of unsafe, potentially unsafe, probably safe, and safe drugs for this patient group (Kappas, Sassa, Galbraith, & Nordmann, 1989). In some clinically asymptomatic family members, only the biochemical or enzymatic abnormalities are found. This emphasizes the role of outside precipitating agents as particularly important in this group of diseases. Because barbiturates often are given to sedate agitated patients, it is important to note that they may aggravate this disorder. In spite of a great deal of controversy on this subject, the role of emotional stress in precipitating attacks has not been confirmed (Ackner, Cooper, Gray, Kelly, & Nicholson, 1962). The mechanism of porphyrinogenicity induced by drugs is multifaceted and complex; in each case, the final step appears to be the induction of hepatic ALA synthase, an enzyme that normally has a regulating, repressor effect on heme synthesis (Hindmarsh, 1993). (see Figure 6.1).

A defect in the function of the enzyme, porphobilinogen deaminase [also called hydroxymethylbilane synthase (Chen, Astrin, Lee, Anderson, & Desnick, 1994)], is responsible for acute intermittent porphyria. There is increased formation and excretion of ALA and PBG in the urine. The gene for porphobilinogen deaminase is located on the long arm of chromosome 11 (see Chapter 10).

TABLE 6.2 Reported Drug Experience in Acute Porphyrias

1. Unsafe	2. Potentially unsafe	3. Probably safe	4. Safe
Antipyrine	Alfadolone acetate	Adrenaline	Acetaminophen
Amidopyrine	Alfaxolone	Chloramphenicol	Amitryptyline
Aminoglutethimide	Alkylating agents	Chlordiazepoxide	Aspirin
Barbiturates	2-Allyloxy-3-methylbenzamide	Colchicine	Atropine
Carbamazepine	Bemegride	Diazepam	Bromides
Carbromal	Clonidine	Dicumarol	Chloral hydrate
Chlorpropramide	Chloroform	Digoxin	EDTA
Danazol	Chloroquine	Diphenhydramine	Ether
Dapsone	Colistin	Guanethidine	Glucocorticoids
Diclophenac	Etomidate	Hyoscine	Insulin
Diphenylhydantoin	Erythromycin	Ibuprofin	Narcotic analgesics
Ergot preparations	Fluroxene	Imipramine	Penicillin and derivatives
Ethclorvynol	Food additives	Indocid	Phenothiazines
Ethinamate	Heavy metals	Labetalol	Propranolol
Glutethimide	Hydralazine	Lithium	Steptomycin
Griseofulvin	Ketamine	Mandelamine	Succinylcholine
Isopropylmeprobamate	Methyldopa	Mefanamic acid	Tetracycline
Mephenytoin	Metoclopramide	Methylphenidate	
Meprobamate	Metyrapone	Naproxen	
Methylprylon	Nalidixic acid	Neostigmine	
N-butyl-scopolammonium bromide	Nikethamide	Nitrofurantoin	
Novobiocin	Nitrazepam	Nitrous oxide	
Phenylbutazone	Nortryptyline	Paracetamol	
Primadone	o,p'-DDD	Penicillamine	
Pyrazolone preparations	Pargyline	Procaine	
Succinimides	Pentazocine	Propanid	
Sulfonamide antibiotics	Pentylenetetrazole	Propoxyphene	
Sulfonethylmethane	Phenoxybenzamine	Prostigmin	
Sulfonmethane	Pyrazinamide	Rauwolfia alkaloids	

Table 6.2 *(cont.)*

1. Unsafe	2. Potentially unsafe	3. Probably safe	4. Safe
Synthetic estrogens, progestins	Rifampicin	Thiouracil	
Tolazamide	Spironolactone	Thyroxine	
Tolbutamide	Theophylline	Tubocurarine	
Trimethadione	Tolazamide	Vitamin B	
Valproic acid	Tranylcypromine	Vitamin C	

Reprinted with permission from Kappas, A., Sassa, S., Galbraith, R. A., Nordmann, Y. (1989). The porphyrias. In C. R. Scriver, A. L. Beaudet, W. S. Sly, & D. Valle (Eds.), *The metabolic basis of inherited disease*. New York: McGraw Hill, p. 1327.

2. *Porphyria variegata* presents with light-sensitive skin lesions and/or the symptoms of acute intermittent porphyria. The disease is particularly common among the white population of South Africa, where its incidence is estimated at 1 in 400. Acute attacks of neuropsychiatric dysfunction are indistinguishable from those of intermittent acute porphyria. There is a report in the literature of serine loading producing a schizophrenialike psychosis in a patient with porphyria variegata (Pepplinkhuizen, Bruinvels, Blom, & Moleman, 1980).

The enzymatic lesion, a defect in protoporphyrinogen oxidase, leads to the excretion of large amounts of protoporphyrin in bile and feces and to markedly increased excretion of ALA, PBG, and coproporphyrin in the urine during acute attacks. The gene for protoporphyrinogen oxidase is found on the long arm of the 14th chromosome (see Chapter 10).

3. *Hereditary corpoporphyria* is characterized by acute attacks of neuropsychiatric dysfunction identical to those of intermittent acute porphyria and porphyria variegata; in addition, photosensitivity sometimes occurs. The primary genetic defect is a deficiency of coproporphyrinogen oxidase. Large amounts of coproporphyrinogen III, mainly in the feces but also in the urine, are excreted. Excretion of ALA and PBG in the urine is increased during acute attacks.

Regarding the other porphyrias, *porphyria cutanea tarda* is the only hepatic porphyria not associated with any neuropsychiatric disorders. Neither are *protoporphyria* or *erythropoietic porphyria*. Probably in the exception that proves the rule, however, one case of erythropoietic porphyria—a disease with skin lesions and hemolytic anemia—has been reported with a clinical diagnosis of schizophrenia in the medical literature (Gibney, Jones, & Meek, 1972).

The laboratory diagnosis of the porphyrias can be difficult. Porphyrins are intermediates in the production of heme. Levels of PBG and ALA are measured in the urine in acute intermittent porphyria and in the stool in porphyria variegata, but there is not always a clear relationship between these levels and the presence or absence of symptoms. Paper chromatographic measures to identify carriers of the gene or measurements in the erythrocytes by a test for porphobilinogen deaminase are preferable (Schumaker, Tishler, & Knighton, 1976; McColl, Moore, Thomson, & Goldberg, 1982). Some carriers of the gene remain asymptomatic. A simple and unique method of identification of acute intermittent porphyria has been recently proposed—molecular diagnosis of porphobilinogen deaminase by analysis of deoxyribose nucleic acid (DNA) extracted from hair roots; it requires five hairs with intact roots (Schreiber, Fong, & Jamani, 1994).

More than 40 genetic mutations have been described in porphobilinogen deaminase (PBGD), the enzyme malfunctioning in acute intermittent porphyria (Lee et al., 1988). In molecular biology, a population association between a restriction fragment length polymorphism allele at the PBGD locus and idiopathic schizophrenia has been reported (Sanders, Hamilton, Fann, & Patel, 1991). As a result of these findings, it has been postulated that investigations of other sites around thc PBGD locus may lead to the discovery of additional diseases that cause schizophrenia.

Treatment remains prophylactic—prevention of attacks is the main therapeutic stratagem. Any infection should be identified and treated immediately, alcohol must be avoided, and the patient should be educated about avoiding the drugs in Table 6.2. When an attack does occur, the treatment consists of the administration of glucose and heme. Hematin, ferric heme, at a maximal dosage of 4 mg/kg can be infused over a period of 2 hours. Standard treatments for psychiatric symptoms, vomiting, and seizures may be needed. If vomiting is persistent, correction of electrolyte imbalance may be indicated. In the cases with peripheral neuropathies, a watch must be kept regarding possible embarrassment of the respiratory system. The majority of attacks subside completely without sequelae. Some patients remain psychotic for long periods of time, however (Lishman, 1987).

WILSON'S DISEASE (HEPATOLENTICULAR DEGENERATION)

Wilson's disease, first described by him in 1912, is an autosomal recessive disorder that affects both the central nervous system and the liver; in this metabolic disease, ingested copper is improperly handled by the body and becomes toxic. Psychiatric symptoms were prominent in eight of Wilson's 12 original patients and his cases 2 and 3 presented with schizophrenialike psychoses (Wilson, 1912). Later series found the same high percentage of mental illness, in fact, all 12 of Walker's patients developed psychiatric symptoms (two with acute schizophrenia) before the first neurological signs; all the patients had psychiatric treatment with drugs, psychotherapy, or electroconvulsive therapy (Walker, 1969). A literature review in 1969 found 11 acceptable and 11 doubtful cases of Wilson's disease with schizophrenia (Davison & Bagley, 1969). Walshe (1972) wrote that on some occasions, severe psychiatric disturbances can precede the onset of other signs of nervous system disease.

The patients who present with schizophrenic symptoms usually show paranoid symptoms in adults and hebephrenic or catatonic symptoms in adolescents and younger children (Lishman, 1987). There are quite a number of serious psychiatric cases in the medical literature—a case study of a catatonic syndrome in the course of a schizophreniform psychosis (Modai, Karp, Liberman, & Munitz, 1985); a case study of a catatonic syndrome without delusions or hallucinations (Davis & Borde, 1993); a review of 30 cases with psychiatric disturbances that included manic states, delusions, and paranoid ideas among 30 patients

(Scheinberg, Sternlieb, & Richman, 1968); and autopsy studies of three brains of young adults with the diagnosis of schizophrenia who actually had Wilson's disease (Malamud, 1975). There also are studies documenting improvement of psychiatric symptoms with specific therapy for Wilson's disease (Goldstein, Ewert, Randall, & Gross, 1968; Modai et al., 1985).

However, there is controversy whether the full DSM-III-R (APA, 1987) criteria of schizophrenia occur in patients with Wilson disease or, if these criteria do occur, is it just a coincidence? Patients with severe untreated Wilson's disease can be mute, drooling, rigid, akinetic with abnormal postures and catatonic waxy flexibility (Davis & Borde, 1993). Such cases can be easily mistaken for a catatonic psychosis even if there is no evidence of delusions or hallucinations. In 1959, Beard reviewed the literature and felt that in the majority of cases the diagnosis of schizophrenia was incorrect; nevertheless, in a patient in his own practice a typical schizophrenic illness developed with olfactory and auditory hallucinations and paranoid delusions (Beard, 1959).

The most impressive and extensive review has been done by Dening (1985, 1991), who reviewed nearly 650 cases of Wilson's disease reported since 1959. He reported that the occasional patient with Wilson's disease who did meet DSM-III-R criteria for schizophrenia occurred at a frequency similar to the general population and thus these individuals had two diseases simultaneously—schizophrenia and Wilson's disease (Dening & Berrios, 1989). [Wilson's disease has a worldwide frequency of between 1 in 35,000 and 1 in 100,000 live births (Danks, 1989).] In the 1990 paper in which Dening and Berrios followed 129 cases of Wilson's disease through two follow-up periods, there were only two cases with a schizophrenialike psychosis; the authors point out it was unlikely to be due to selection bias because some cases were referred from psychiatric institutions (Dening & Berrios, 1990). Dening's review contradicted an earlier study of 520 case reports of Wilson's disease by Davison (1983) who reported that the association of schizophrenia with Wilson's disease exceeded chance expectation.

It is possible that Beard and Dening may well be correct that classic schizophrenia is not one of the presenting symptoms of Wilson's disease; Dening's work in particular seems outstanding.

Nevertheless, we have chosen to include Wilson's disease in this book because

- not all scientific reviewers agree with Beard and Dening and the new knowledge of a minimum of 22 mutations to the Wilson's disease gene may eventually sort out which, if any, of the alleles is associated with schizophrenia;
- in reality numbers of clinicians have, mistakenly or not, seen patients with Wilson's disease and called them schizophrenic or schizophreniformlike;
- there are cases in which the therapy for Wilson's disease appeared to ameliorate the symptoms thought to be schizophrenic (Goldstein et al., 1968; Modai et al., 1985), and
- because Wilson's disease is an entity that can be modified by therapy and has a potentially lethal outcome if not correctly identified and treated, it would be remiss to leave it out of the differential diagnosis for schizophrenia until the issue is fully settled.

In addition to psychiatric symptoms, neurological symptoms, such as a wing-beating tremor, dysarthria, dystonia, ataxia, and rigidity (sometimes mimicking catatonia) can be present. MRI and evoked potential studies can be used to document brain abnormalities (Selwa et al., 1993). Another major organ involved in Wilson's disease is the liver: signs of hepatic involvement such as jaundice or hepatosplenomegaly can be the presenting feature and later there may be ascites, ankle swelling or hematemesis from rupture of esophageal varices. Aminoaciduria has been reported suggesting renal involvement. An invaluable diagnostic sign is the Kaiser-Fleischer ring—a brown or greyish-green ring at the margin of the cornea. It can be sometimes seen by the naked eye and is readily detectable on slit-lamp examination.

Ceruloplasmin, a copper-containing alpha$_2$-glycoprotein, is reduced in Wilson disease and can be used, along with serum copper levels, for diagnostic purposes. In spite of its value for diagnosis, the disease is not directly linked to a molecular defect in ceruloplasmin (Bull, Thomas, Rommens, Forbes, & Cox, 1993; Petrukin et al., 1993). Wilson's disease is an autosomal recessive disorder; the Wilson's disease gene has been mapped to chromosome 13q14.3 (Bull et al., 1993; Petrukin et al., 1993) (see Chapter 10). A number of mutations have already been identified (Thomas, Forbes, Roberts, Walshe, & Cox, 1995).

Treatment is focused on eliminating excessive copper from the body. This can be achieved with chelating agents such as D-penicillamine or trithylene tetramine or with blockers of copper absorption from the bowel, such as zinc sulfate or tetrathiomolybdate. These treatments are usually combined with a low-copper diet. In at least one case, however, an attempt to lower copper by giving zinc appeared to cause fatal deterioration (Lang, Rabas-Kolominsky, Engelhardt, Kabras, & Konig, 1993). There is evidence that the chelating treatment can help brain functioning in the sense that severity of neurological deficits improve after therapy; in one series treated with penicillamine all six patients improved and four became asymptomatic (Medalia & Scheinberg, 1991).

CONCLUSIONS

The metabolic diseases that can present with schizophrenic symptoms are interesting when viewed as a group. In a number of them, they are the adult forms of disease entities that usually present as childhood neurological disorders. Why do some adults with the same enzyme deficiency as children with a classical neurological disease present at a later age and with a different, more psychiatric set of symptoms? Possibilities include hypotheses that the enzyme level may not be at such a low level as is usually seen in the child full homozygote (Manowitz et al., 1981) or that the enzyme is a structural variant (Farrell, MacMartin, & Clark, 1979). This latter possibility has already been demonstrated regarding the allelles in metachromatic leukodystrophy (see Chapter 10). As the nucleotide sequences of the genes underlying the enzyme errors are worked out by molecular biology in the future, the reasons for each of these unusual presentations in adult age may become clearer.

There is another interesting pattern that is beginning to appear among the metabolic diseases that present with schizophrenic symptoms. Two of them (adrenoleukodystrophy and metachromatic leukodystrophy) are diseases that mainly affect the myelin of white matter. Walk et al. (1994) have pointed out that one of the aminoacidurias discussed in this chapter (methylenetrahydrofolate reductase deficiency) also may have MRI pictures similar to the findings of the leukodystrophies.

It is well established that individuals with schizophrenia usually have less overall brain tissue and concomitant larger ventricles (see Chapter 12). The question is exactly what tissue is diminished. A recent MRI computerized summary study created an "average" schizophrenic brain image and an "average" control image (Andreasen et al., 1994). These investigators confirmed less overall brain volume, larger ventricles, a smaller lateral thalamus and smaller areas of white matter in the frontal, parietal, and temporal lobes of persons with schizophrenia. The anatomical study of the brain in schizophrenia mostly has been focused on specific lobes, such as the temporal or frontal lobes; there is much literature on this. It has been reported that the layers of the prefrontal cortex (cortical layers III and V) affected in the brains of some individuals with schizophrenia are the layers known to give rise to association projections to other cortical areas (Rajkowska, Selemon, Goldman-Rakic, & Halaris, 1995). A recent MRI study (Wible, Shenton, Kikinis, Jolesz, & McCarley, 1995) has suggested that prefrontal and temporal areas may be affected *in a parallel manner* (emphasis ours).

The leukodystrophies that present with schizophrenia raise the question of whether the association areas and the communicating pathways between the lobes might not be one major site of damage that could lead to schizophrenic symptoms. There is evidence of smaller neuron size in schizophrenia in hippocampal subfields that mediate cortical–hippocampal interactions (Arnold et al., 1995) as well as alterations in the hippocampal mossy fiber pathway in schizophrenia (Goldsmith & Joyce, 1995). Keefe and Harvey (1994) have emphasized that the neural circuits leading to the frontal cortex may be particularly vulnerable in metachromatic leukodystrophy. Thus, a not unreasonable hypothesis may be that in some of these metabolic diseases, symptoms—such as hallucinations—may arise from neural circuit damage.

REFERENCES

Abbott, M. H., Folstein, S. E., Abbey, H., & Pyeritz, R. E. (1987). Psychiatric manifestations of homocystinuria due to cystathionine-B-synthase deficiency; prevalence, natural history and relationship to neurologic impairment and vitamin B6-responsiveness. *American Journal of Medical Genetics, 26,* 959–969.

Ackner, B., Cooper, J. E., Gray, C. H., Kelly, M., & Nicholson, D. C. (1962). Acute porphyria: A neuropsychiatric and biochemical study. *Journal of Psychosomatic Research, 6,* 1–24.

Alberghina, M., Fiumara, A., Pavone, L., & Giuffrida, A. M. (1984). Determination of C20-C30 fatty acids by reversed-phase chromatographic techniques: An efficient method to quantitate minor fatty acids in serum of patients with adrenoleukodystrophy. *Neurochemical Research, 9,* 1719–1727.

American Psychiatric Association. (1987). *Diagnostic and statistical manual of mental disorders.* Third ed., revised. Washington, DC: American Psychiatric Press.

Andreasen, N. C. et al. (1994). Thalamic abnormalities in schizophrenia visualized through magnetic resonance image averaging. *Science, 266,* 294–298.

Antoku, Y., Sakai, T., Gotto, I., Iwashita, H., & Kuroway, Y. (1984). Adrenoleukodystrophy: Abnormality of very long chain fatty acids in erythrocyte membrane phospholipids. *Neurology, 35,* 1499–1501.

Arnold, S. E., Franz, E. R., Gur, R. C., Gur, R. E., Shapiro, R. M., Moberg, P. J., & Trojanowski, J. (1995). Smaller neuron size in schizophrenia in hippocampal subfields that mediate cortical-hippocampal interactions. *American Journal of Psychiatry, 152,* 738–748.

Askanas, V., McLaughlin, J., Engel, K. W., & Adornato, B. T. (1979). Abnormalities in cultured muscle and peripheral nerve of a patient with adrenomeyloneuropathy. *New England Journal of Medicine, 301,* 588–590.

Aubourg, P., Adamsbaum, C., Lavallard-Rousseau, M. C., Lemaitre, A., Boureau, F., Mayer, M., & Kalifa, G. (1992). Brain MRI and electrophysiologic abnormalities in preclinical and clinical adrenomyeloneuropathy. *Neurology, 42,* 85–91.

Aubourg, P., Blanche, S., Jambaque, I. et al. (1990). Reversal of early neurologic and neuroradiologic manisfestations of X-linked adrenoleukodystrophy by bone marrow transplantation. *New England Journal of Medicine, 322,* 1860–1866.

Baron, D. N., Dent, C. E., Harris, H., Hart, E. W., & Jepson, J. B. (1956). Hereditary pellegra-like skin rash with temporary cerebellar ataxia.

Constant renal amino-acidura and other bizarre features. *Lancet*, *ii*, 421.

Baum, H., Dodgson, K. S., & Spencer, B. (1959). The assay of arylsulfatases A and B in human urine. *Clinica Chimica Acta*, *4*, 453–455.

Beard, A. W. (1959). The association of hepatolenticular degeneration with schizophrenia. *Acta Psychiatrica et Neurologica Scandinavica*, *34*, 411–467.

Ben-Yoseph, Y., & Mitchell, D. (1994). Rapid detection of common metachromatic leukodystrophy mutations by restriction analysis of arylsulfatase A gene amplimers. *Clinica Chimica Acta*, *226*, 77–82.

Besson, J. A. O. (1980). A diagnostic pointer to adult metachromatic leucodystrophy. *British Journal of Psychiatry*, *137*, 186–187.

Bjornson, J. (1964). Behavior in phenylketonuria. Case with schizophrenia. *Archives of General Psychiatry*, *10*, 65–70.

Bracken, M. G., & Coll, P. (1985). Homocystinuria and schizophrenia. Literature review and case report. *Journal of Nervous and Mental Diseases*, *173*, 51–55.

Brown, F. W., Lewine, R. R., & Hudgins, P. A. (1995). White matter hyperintensity signal associated with vascular risk factors in schizophrenia. *Progress in Neuro-Psychopharmacology & Biological Psychiatry*, *19*, 39–45.

Bull, P. C., Thomas, G. R., Rommens, J. M., Forbes, J. R., & Cox, D. W. (1993). The Wilson disease gene is a putative copper transporting P-type ATPase similar to the Menkes disease gene. *Nature Genetics*, *5*, 327–337.

Chen, C-H., Astrin, K. H., Lee, G., Anderson, K. E., & Desnick, R. J. (1994). Acute intermittent porphyria: Identification and expression of exonic mutations in the hydroxymethylbilane synthase gene. *Journal of Clinical Investigations*, *94*, 1927–1937.

Clarke, R., Daly, L., Robinson, K., Naughten, E., Cahalane, S., Fowler, B., & Graham, I. (1991). Hyperhomocysteinemia: An individual risk factor for vascular disease. *New England Journal of Medicine*, *423*, 1149–1155.

Conzelmann, E., & Sandhoff, K. (1983–1984). Partial enzyme deficiencies: Residual activities and the development of neurological disorders. *Developmental Neuroscience*, *6*, 58–71.

Danks, D. M. (1989). Disorders of copper transport. In A. I. Beaudet, W. S. Sly, & D. Valle (Eds.), *Metabolic basis of inherited diseases* (pp. 1411–1431). New York: McGraw Hill.

Davis, E. J. B., & Borde, M. (1993). Wilson's disease and catatonia. *British Journal of Psychiatry*, *162*, 256–259.

Davison, K., & Bagley, C. R. (1969). Schizophrenia-like psychoses associated with organic disorders of the central nervous system: A review of the literature. In R. N. Herrington (Ed.), *British Journal of Psychiatry Special Publication No. 4*. Ashford, Kent: Headley Brothers.

Davison, K. (1983). Schizophrenia-like psychoses associated with organic cerebral disorders: A review. *Psychiatric Developments, 1*, 1–34.

Dening, T. R., & Berrios, G. E. (1989). Wilson's disease: Psychiatric symptoms in 195 cases. *Archives of General Psychiatry, 46*, 1126–1134.

Dening, T. R., & Berrios, G. E. (1990). Psychiatric symptoms in Wilson's disease. *Biological Psychiatry, 28*, 255–265.

Dening, T. R. (1985). Psychiatric aspects of Wilson's disease. *British Journal of Psychiatry, 147*, 677–682.

Dening, T. R. (1991). The neuropsychiatry of Wilson's disease: A review. *International Journal of Psychiatry in Medicine, 21*, 135–148.

Dorninger, F., & Plochl, E. (1969). Patientin mit hebephrener verlaufsform der schizophrenie und spater diagnostizierter phenylketonurie. *Weiner Z Nervenheilk, 27*, 328–337.

Farrell, D. F., MacMartin, M. P., & Clark, A. F. (1979). Multiple molecular forms of arylsulfatase A in different forms of metachromatic leukodystrophy (MLD). *Neurology, 29*, 16.

Federico, A., Palmeri, S., Malandrini, A., Fabrizi, G., Mondelli, M., & Guazzi, G. C. (1991). The clinical aspects of adult hexosaminidase deficiencies. *Developments in Neuroscience, 13*, 280–287.

Finelli, P. F. (1985). Metachromatic leukodystrophy manifesting as a schizophrenic disorder: Computed tomography. *Archives of Neurology, 18*, 94–95.

Fisch, R. O., Hosfield, W. B., Chang, P. N., Barranger, J., & Hastings, D. W. (1979). An adult phenylketonuric with schizophrenia. *Minnesota Medicine, 62*, 243–246.

Fluharty, A. L., Fluharty, C. B., Bohne, W., von Figura, K., & Gieselmann, V. (1991). Two new arylsufatase A (ARSA) mutations in a juvenile metachromatic leukodystrophy patient. *American Journal of Human Genetics, 49*, 1340–1350.

Fowler, B., Whitehouse, C., & Rensma, P. L. (1990). Homocystinuria due to methylene THF reductase deficiency: A new form responsive to riboflavin. *Proceedings of the Vth International Congress of Inborn Errors of Metabolism*, Monterey, CA, June 1-5, 1990.

Freeman, J. M., Finkelstein, J. D., Mudd, S. H., & Uhlendorf, B. (1972). Homocystinuria presenting as reversible "schizophrenia": A new defect in methionine metabolism with reduced methylene-tetrahydro-reductase activity. *Pediatric Research, 6*, 423.

Freeman, J. M., Finkelstein, J. D., & Mudd, S. H. (1975). Folate-responsive homocystinuria and "schizophrenia." *New England Journal of Medicine, 292*, 491–496.

Frisch, A., Baram, D., & Navon, R. (1984). Hexosaminidase A deficient adults: Presence of a alpha-chain precursor in cultured skin fibroblasts. *Biochemical and Biophysical Research Communication, 119,* 101–107.

Frosst, P., Blom, H. J., Mathews, R. G., Boers, G. J. H., den Heijer, M., Kluijtmans, L. A. J., van den Heuvel, L. P., & Rozen, R. (1995). A candidate genetic risk factor for vascular disease: A common mutation in methylenetetrahydrofolate reductase. *Nature Genetics, 10,* 111.

Gibney, G. N., Jones, I. H., & Meek, J. H. (1972). Schizophrenia in association with erythropoietic protoporphyria. Report of a case. *British Journal of Psychiatry, 121,* 79–81.

Goldsmith, S. K., & Joyce, J. N. (1995). Alterations in hippocampal mossy fiber pathway in schizophrenia and Alzheimer's disease. *Biological Psychiatry, 37,* 122–126.

Goldstein, N. P., Ewert, J. C., Randall, R. V., & Gross, J. B. (1968). Psychiatric aspects of Wilson's disease: Results of psychometric tests during long-term therapy. *Birth Defects Original Article Series, 4,* 77–84.

Goyette, P., Sumner, J. S., Milos, R., Duncan, A. M. V., Rosenblatt, D. S., Mathews, R. G., & Rozen, R. (1994). Human methylenetetrahydrofolate reductase: Isolation of cDNA, mapping and mutation identification. *Nature Genetics, 7,* 195–200.

Hádlik, J., & Rodová, A. (1960). Porphyrie in aetiopathogenese der psychischen störungen. *Psychiatr Neurol Med Psychol, 12,* 341–343.

Halvorsen, K., & Halvorsen, S. (1963). Hartnup disease. *Pediatrics, 31,* 29.

Hartelheimer, H. K., Gruttner, K., & Simon, H. A. (1971). Das Hartnup-syndrome. 1. Diagnose, therapies und klinischer verlauf. *Monatsschrift fur Kinderheilkunde, 119,* 52.

Hasegawa, Y., Kawame, H., Ida, H., Ohashi, T., & Eto, Y. (1994). Single exon mutation in arylsulfatase A gene has two effects: Loss of enzyme activity and aberrant splicing. *Human Genetics, 93,* 415–420.

Hersov, L. A., & Rodnight, R. (1960). Hartnup disease in psychiatric practice: Clinical and biochemical features of three cases. *Journal of Neurology, Neurosurgery, and Psychiatry, 23,* 40.

Hersov, L. A. (1955). A case of childhood pellagra with psychosis. *Journal of Mental Science, 101,* 878.

Hindmarsh, J. T. (1993). Variable phenotypic expression of genotypic abnormalities in the porphyrias. *Clinica Chemica Acta, 217,* 29–38.

Holme, E., Kjellman, B., & Ronge, E. (1989). Betaine for treatment of homocystinuria caused by methylenetetrahydrofolate reductase deficiency. *Archives of the Diseases of Childhood, 64,* 1061–1064.

Hyde, T. M., Ziegler, J. C., & Weinberger, D. R. (1992). Psychiatric disturbances in metachromatic leukodystrophy. *Archives in Neurology*,
49, 401–406.
Ishii, S., Sakuraba, H., Shimmoto, M., Minamikawa-Tachino, R., Suzuki,
T., & Suzuki, Y. (1991). Fabry disease: Detection of 13-bp deletion
in alpha-galactosidase A gene and its application to gene diagnosis
of heterozygotes. *Annals of Neurology*, *29*, 560–564.
Kaelbing, R., Craig, J. B., & Pasamanick, B. (1961). Urinary prophobilinogen: results of screening 2500 psychiatric patients. *Archives of General Psychiatry*, *5*, 494–508.
Kaeser, A. C., Rodnight, R., & Ellis, B. A. (1969). Psychiatric and biochemical aspects of a case of homocystinuria. *Journal of Neurology, Neuro-
surgery and Psychiatry*, *32*, 88.
Kappas, A., Sassa, S., & Anderson, K. E. (1983). The porphyrias. In J. B.
Stanbury, J. B. Wyngaarden, D. S. Fredrickson, J. L. Goldstein, &
M. S. Brown (Eds.), *The metabolic basis of inherited disease* (pp.
1301–1384). New York: McGraw-Hill.
Kappas, A., Sassa, S., Gailbraith, R. A., & Nordmann, Y. (1989). The
porphyrias. In C. R. Scriver, A. L. Beaudet, W. S. Sly, & D. Valle
(Eds.), *The metabolic basis of inherited disease* (p. 1327). New York:
McGraw-Hill.
Kappler, J., von Figura, K., & Gieselmann, V. (1992). Late-onset metachro-
matic leukodystrophy: Molecular pathology in two siblings. *Annals
of Neurology*, *31*, 256–261.
Keefe, R. S. E., & Harvey, P. D. (1994). *Understanding schizophrenia*. New
York: Free Press.
King, P. H., & Bragdon, A. C. (1991). MRI reveals multiple reversible
cerebral lesions in an attack of acute intermittent porphyria. *Neurol-
ogy*, *41*, 1300–1302.
Kitchen, W., Cohen-Cole, S. A., & Mickel, S. F. (1987). Adrenoleukodystrophy: Frequency of presentation as a psychiatric disorder. *Biological
Psychiatry*, *22*, 1375–1387.
Kolodny, E. H. (1989). Metachromatic leukodystrophy and multiple sul-
fatse deficiency: Sulfatide lipidosis. In C. R. Scriver, A. L. Beaudet,
W. S. Sly, & D. Valle (Eds.), *The metabolic basis of inherited disease*,
6th edition, vol. 2 (pp. 1721–1750). New York: McGraw-Hill.
Kothbauer, P., Jellinger, K., Gross, H., Molzer, B., & Bernheimer, H.
(1977). Adulte metachromatische leukodystrophie unter dem bild
einer schizophrenen psychose. *Archiv fur Psychiatrie und Nervenkrankheiten*, *224*, 379–387.
Krivit, W., Shapiro, E., Kennedy, W. et al. (1994). Treatment of late
infantile metachromatic leukodystrophy by bone marrow transplantation. *New England Journal of Medicine*, *322*, 28–32.

Kudoh, T., & Wenger, D. A. (1982). Diagnosis of metachromatic leukodystrophy, Krabbe disease and Farber disease after the uptake of fatty acid-labeled cerebroside sulfate into cultured skin fibroblasts. *Journal of Clinical Investigation, 70*, 89–97.

Lagas, P. A., & Ruokonen, A. (1991). Late onset argininosuccinic aciduria in a paranoid retardate. *Biological Psychiatry, 30*, 1229–1232.

Lang, C. J., Rabas-Kolominsky, P., Engelhardt, A., Kabras, G., & Konig, H. J. (1993). Comment. *Archives of Neurology, 50*, 1007–1008.

Lee, J-S., Anvert, M., Floderus, Y., Gellerfors, P., Lannfelt, L., Linsten, J., Thunell, S., & Wetterberg, L. (1988). DNA polymorphism within the porphobilinogen deaminase gene in two Swedish families with acute intermittent porphyria. *Human Genetics, 79*, 379–381.

Lishman, W. A. (1987). *Organic psychiatry: The psychological consequences of cerebral disorder.* Oxford: Blackwell Scientific.

Liston, E. H., Martin, D. L., & Philippart, M. (1973). Psychosis in Fabry disease and treatment with phenoxybenzamine. *Archives of General Psychiatry, 29*, 402–403.

Maeda, K., Suzuki, Y., Yajima, S. et al. (1992). Improvement of clinical and MRI findings in a boy with adrenoleukodystrophy by dietary eruric acid therapy. *Brain Development, 14*, 409–412.

Mahon-Haft, H., Stone, R. K., Johnson, R., & Shah, S. (1981). Biochemical abnormalities of metachromatic leukodystrophy in an adult psychiatric population. *American Journal of Psychiatry, 138*, 1372–1374.

Malamud, N. (1975). Organic brain disease mistaken for psychiatric disorder: A clinicopathologic study. In D. F. Benson & D. Blumer (1975). *Psychiatric aspects of neurologic disease.* New York: Grune & Stratton.

Manowitz, P., Kling, A., & Kohn, H. (1978). Clinical course of adult metachromatic leucodystrophy presenting as schizophrenia. *Journal of Nervous and Mental Diseases, 166*, 500–506.

Manowitz, P., Goldstein, I., & Nora, R. (1981). An arylsulfatase variant in schizophrenic patients: Preliminary report. *Biological Psychiatry, 16*, 1107–1114.

Matiar-Vahr, H., & Lungershausen, E. (1967). Zur symptomatologie der akuten intermittierenden porphyrie. *Deutsche Medizinische Wochenschrift, 92*, 1809–1816.

McColl, K. E. L., Moore, M. R., Thomson, G. G., & Goldberg, A. (1982). Screening for latent acute intermittent porphyria—The value of measuring both leucocyte deltaaminolaevulinic acid synthase and erythrocyte uroporphyrinogen-1-synthase activities. *Journal of Medical Genetics, 19*, 271–276.

Medalia, A., & Scheinberg, I. H. (1991). Intellectual functioning in treated Wilson's disease. *Annals of Neurology, 29*, 573–574.

Miller, J. M. (1993). Vignette of medical history: Porphyria in royalty. *Maryland Medical Journal, 42,* 1015–1017.

Modai, I., Karp, L., Liberman, V. A., & Munitz, H. (1985). Penicillamine therapy for schizophreniform psychosis in Wilson's disease. *Journal of Nervous and Mental Disease, 173,* 698–701.

Molzer, B., Bernheimer, H., Heller, R., Toifu, K., & Vetterlein, M. (1982). Detection of adrenoleukodystrophy by increased C26:0 fatty acid levels in leukocytes. *Clinica Chemica Acta, 125,* 299–305.

Moser, H. W. (1992). Adrenoleukodystrophy. *Biological Psychiatry, 31,* 76A (Abstract).

Moser, H. W. (1993). Lorenzo oil therapy for adrenoleukodystrophy: A prematurely amplified hope (Editorial) *Annals of Neurology, 34,* 121–122.

Moser, H., & Moser, A. (1989). Adrenoleukodystrophy-X-linked. In Stanbury et al. (Eds.), *The metabolic basis of inherited disease,* sixth edition. New York: McGraw Hill.

Mudd, S. H., Uhlendorf, W., Freeman, J. M., Finkelstein, J. D., & Shih, V. E. (1972). Homocystinuria associated with decreased methylene tetrahydrofolate reductase activity. *Biochemical Biophysical Research Communications, 46,* 905.

Mudd, S. H., Levy, H. L., & Skovby, F. (1989). Disorders of transsulfuration. In C. R. Scriver, A. L. Beaudet, W. S. Sly, & D. Valle (Eds.), *The metabolic basis of inherited disease* (pp. 701–720). New York: McGraw-Hill.

Navab, F., & Asatoor, A. M. (1970). Studies on intestinal absorption of amino acids and a dipeptide in a case of Hartnup disease. *Gut, 11,* 373–379.

Navon, R. (1991). Molecular and clinical heterogeneity of adult GM2 gangliosidosis. *Developments in Neuroscience, 13,* 295–298.

Navron, R., Argov, Z., & Frisch, A. (1986). Hexosaminidase A deficiency in adults. *American Journal of Medical Genetics, 24,* 179–196.

Nelson, P. V., Carey, W. F., & Morris, C. P. (1991). Population frequency of a rylsulfatase A pseudodeficiency allele. *Human Genetics, 87,* 87–88.

Neote, K., Mahuran, D. J., & Gravel, R. A. (1991). Molecular genetics of beta-hexosaminidase deficiencies. In L. P. Rowland (Ed.), *Advances in neurology, vol 56: Amyotrophic lateral sclerosis and other motor disorders.* New York: Raven Press.

Odent, S., Roussey, M., Journal, H., Betremieux, P., David, V., & Le Marec, B. (1989). Lacidurie argininosucccinique: A propos dun nouveau cas revele par des troubles psychiatriques. *Journal of Genetique Humaine* (Geneva), *37,* 39–42.

Okada, S., & O'Brien, J. S. (1969). Tay-Sachs disease. Generalized absence of B-D-N-acetylhexosaminadase compound. *Science, 165,* 698–700.

Oyanagi, K., Takagi, M., Kitabatake, M., & Nakao, T. (1967). Hartnup disease. *Tohuku Journal of Experimental Medicine*, *91*, 383.

Park, L. L., Baldessarini, R. J., & Kety, S. S. (1995). Methionine effects in chronic schizophrenia. *Archives of General Psychiatry*, *2*, 346–351.

Pasquier, F., Lebert, F., Pett, H., Zittoun, J., & Marquet, J. (1994). Methylenetetrahydrofolate reductase deficiency revealed by a neuropathy in a psychotic adult. *Journal of Neurology, Neurosurgery and Psychiatry*, *57*, 765–766.

Peiffer, J. (1959). Metachromatic leukodystrophies (Scholz type). *Arch Psychiatr Z Ges Neurol*, *199*, 386–416.

Pepplinkhuizen, L., Bruinvels, J., Blom, W., & Moleman, P. (1980). Schizophrenia-like psychosis caused by a metabolic disorder. *Lancet, i,* 454–456

Perry, T. L., Hansen, S., Tischler, B., Richards, F. M., & Sokol, M. (1973). Unrecognized adult phenylketonuria: Implications for obstetrics and psychiatry. *New England Journal of Medicine*, *289*, 395–398.

Peters, H. A. (1962). Porphyric psychosis and chelation therapy. *Research Advances in Biological Psychiatry*, *4*, 204–217.

Petrukin, K., Fisher, S. G., Pirastu, M., Tanzi, R. E., Chernov, I., Devoto, M., Brzustowski, L. M., Cayanis, E., Vitale, E., Russo, J. J., Matseoane, D., Boukhgalter, B., Wasco, W., Figus, A. L., Loudianos, J., Cao, A., Sternlieb, I., Evgrafov, O., Parano, E., Pavone, L., Warburton, D., Ott, J., Penchaszadeh, G. K., Scheinberg, I. H., & Gilliam, T. C. (1993). Mapping, cloning and genetic characterization of the region containing the Wilson disease gene. *Nature Genetics*, *5*, 338.

Pitt, D. (1971). The natural history of untreated phenylketonuria. *Medical Journal of Australia*, *1*, 378–383.

Polten, A., Fluharty, A. L., Fluharty, C. B., Kappler, J., von Figura, K., & Gieselmann, V. (1991). Molecular basis of different forms of metachromatic leukodystrophy. *New England Journal of Medicine*, *324*, 18–22.

Poulos, A., Gibson, R., Sharp, P., Beckman, K., & Grattan-Smith, P. (1994). Very long chain fatty acids in X-linked adrenoleukodystrophy brain after treatment with Lorenzo's oil. *Annals of Neurology*, *36*, 741–746.

Powell, H., Tindall, R., Schultz, P., Paa, D., O'Brien, J., & Lambert, P. (1975). Adrenoleukodystrophy. *Archives of Neurology*, *32*, 250.

Prensky, A. L. (1982). Metachromatic leukodystrophy, multiple sulfatase deficiency and Farber disease. In K. F. Swaiman & F. S. Wright (Eds.), *The practice of pediatric neurology* (pp. 532–542). St. Louis: Mosby.

Rajkowska, G., Selemon, L. D., Goldman-Rakic, P. S., & Halaris, A. (1995). Morphometric changes in prefrontal cortex of schizophrenic postmortem brain. *Biological Psychiatry*, *37*:667 (abstract).

Renshaw, P. F., Stern, T. A., Welch, C., Schouten, R., & Kolodny, E. H. (1992). Electroconvulsive therapy treatment of depression in a patient with adult GM2 gangliosidosis. *Annals of Neurology, 31*, 342–344.

Reveley, A. M., & Reveley, M. A. (1982). Screening for adult phenylketonuria in psychiatric inpatients. *Biological Psychiatry, 17*, 1343–1345.

Rizzo, W. B., Leshner, R. T., Odone, A. et al. (1989). Dietary erucic acid therapy for X-linked adrenoleukodystrophy. *Neurology, 39*, 1415–1422.

Rosenblatt, D. S. (1989). Inherited disorders of folate transport and metabolism. In C. R. Scriver, A. L. Beaudet, W. S. Sly, & D. Valle (Eds.), *The metabolic basis of inherited disease* (pp. 2053–2055). New York: McGraw-Hill.

Roth, N. (1968). Psychiatric syndromes of porphyria. *International Journal of Neuropsychiatry, 4*, 32–44.

Ryan, R. M. (1994). Recognizing psychosis in persons with developmental disabilities who do not use spoken communication. In R. J. Ancill, S. Holliday, & J. Higenbottam (Eds.), *Schizophrenia: Exploring the spectrum of psychosis*. Chichester: Wiley.

Sakai, M., & Tano, T. (1965). Biochemical analysis of the brains of metachromatic leucodystrophy. *Yokohama Medical Bulletin, 16*, 57–64.

Sakuraba, H. (1989). Molecular genetics of Fabry disease. *Seikagaku, 61*, 294–299.

Sanders, A. R., Hamilton, J. D., Fann, W. E., & Patel, P. I. (1991). Association of genetic variation at the porphobilinogen deaminase gene with schizophrenia. *American Journal of Human Genetics*, (Suppl.) *49*, 358. Abstract.

Sandhoff, K. (1969). Variation of the B-N-acetylhexosaminidase-pattern in Tay-Sachs disease. *FEBS Letters, 4*, 351–354.

Schafer, J. R., Ehlenz, K., Steinmetz, A., Pilz, C., Hunneman, D. H., Baerwald, C., von Wichert, P., & Kaffarnik, H. (1994). Adrenomyeloneuropathy, a common cause of Addison's disease. *Deutsche Medizinische Wochenschrift, 119*, 327–331.

Schaffer, S., Oepen, G., & Ott, D. (1988). Adulte Form der metachromatischen Leukodystrophie mit vorwiegend psychotischem Erscheinungsbild. *Nervenarzt, 59*, 731–733.

Scheinberg, I. H., Sternlieb, I., & Richman, J. (1968). Psychiatric manifestations in patients with Wilson's disease. *Birth Defects Original Article Series, 4*, 85–87.

Schimke, R. N., McKusic, V. A., Huang, T., & Pollack, A. D. (1965). Homocystinuria; Studies of 20 families with 38 affected members. *Journal of the American Medical Association, 193*, 87–95.

Schmidtke, K., Endres, W., Roscher, A., Ibel, H., Herschkowitz, N., Bachmann, C., Plochl, E., & Hadorn, H. B. (1992). Hartnup disease, progressive encephalopathy and allo-albuminaemia. *European Journal of Pediatrics*, *151*, 899–903.

Schreiber, W. E., Fong, F., & Jamani, A. (1994). Molecular analysis of acute intermittent porphyria by analysis of DNA extracted from hair roots. *Clinica Chemica Acta*, *40*, 1744–1748.

Schumaker, H. M., Tishler, P. V., & Knighton, D. J. (1976). A spot test for uroporphyrinogen I synthase, the enzyme that is deficient in intermittent acute porphyria. *Clinica Chemica Acta*, *22*, 1991–1994.

Selwa, L. M., Vanderzant, C. W., Brunberg, J. A., Brewer, G. J., Druray, I., & Beydoun, A. (1993). Correlation of evoked potential and MRI findings in Wilson's disease. *Neurology*, *43*, 2059–2064.

Shapiro, E. G., & Lipton, M. E. (1992). White matter dysfunction and its neuropsychological correlates: A longitudinal study of a case of metachromatic leukodystrophy treated with bone marrow transplant. *Journal of Clinical & Experimental Neuropsychology*, *14*, 610–624.

Sourander, P., & Svennerhom, L. (1962). Sulphatide lipidosis in the adult with the clinical picture of progressive organic dementia with epileptic seizures. *Acta Neuropathologica*, *1*, 384–396.

Spiro, H. R., Schimke, R. N., & Welch, J. P. (1965). Schizophrenia in a patient with a defect in methionine metabolism. *Journal of Nervous and Mental Diseases*, *141*, 285–290.

Streifler, J., Golomb, H., & Gaduth, N. (1989). Psychiatric features of adult GM2 gangliosidosis. *British Journal of Psychiatry*, *153*, 387–389.

Streifler, J. Y., Gornish, M., Hadar, H., & Gadoth, N. (1993). Brain imaging in late-onset GM2 gangliosidosis. *Neurology*, *43*, 2055–2058.

Suzuki, K., & Chen, G. C. (1967). Brain ceramide hexosides in Tay-Sachs disease and generalized gangliosides. *Journal of Lipid Research*, *8*, 105–113.

Sweetman, L., & Haas, R. H. (1992). Abnormalities of amino-acid metabolism. In B. O. Berg (Ed.), *Neurologic aspects of pediatrics*. Boston: Butterworth-Heinemann.

Swiezy, N. B., Matson, J. L., Kirkpatrick-Sanchez, S., & Williams, D. E. (1995). A criterion validity study of the schizophrenia subscale of the Psychopathology Instrument for Mentally Retarded Adults. *Research in Developmental Disabilities*, *16*, 75–80.

Thomas, G. R., Forbes, J. R., Roberts, E. A., Walshe, J. M., & Cox, D. W. (1995). The Wilson disease gene: spectrum of mutations and their consequences. *Nature Genetics*, *9*, 210–217.

Tonshoff, B., Lehnert, W., & Ropers, H. H. (1982). Adrenoleukodystrophy: Diagnosis and carrier detection by determination of long-chain fatty acids in cultured fibroblasts. *Clinical Genetics, 22,* 25.

von Wendt, L., Simila, S., Ruokonen, A., & Puukka, M. (1982). Argininosuccinic aciduria in a Finnish woman presenting with psychosis and mental retardation. *Annals of Clinical Research (Helsinki), 14,* 145–147.

Waldenström, J. (1939). Neurological symptoms caused by so-called acute porphyria. *Acta Psychiatrica Scandinavica, 14,* 375–379.

Walk, D., Soo-Sang, K., & Horwitz, A. (1994). Intermittent encephalopathy, reversible nerve conduction slowing and MRI evidence of cerebral white matter disease in methylenetetrahydrofolate deficiency. *Neurology, 44,* 344–347.

Walker, S. (1969). The psychiatric presentation of Wilson's disease (hepatolenticular degeneration) with an etiologic explanation. *Behavioral Neuropsychiatry, 1,* 38–43.

Walshe, J. M. (1972). The biochemistry of copper in man and its role in the pathogenesis of Wilson's disease (hepatolenticular degeneration). In J. N. Cumings (Ed.), *Biochemical aspects of nervous disease.* London: Plenum Press.

Wendel, U., & Bremer, H. J. (1984). Betaine in the treatment of homocystinuria due to 5, 10 methylenetetrahydrofolate reductase deficiency. *European Journal of Pediatrics, 142,* 147–150.

Wetterberg, L. (1967). *A neuropsychiatric and genetical investigation of acute intermittent porphyria.* Norstedts: Svenska Bokförlaget.

Wible, C. G., Shenton, M. E., Kikinis, R., Jolesz, F., & McCarley, R. W. (1995). Prefrontal subdivisions, temporal lobe, and schizophrenia: An MRI study. *Biological Psychiatry, 37,* 683. (abstract)

Wicke, R. (1938). A contribution to the question of the familial diffuse sclerosis including Pelizaeus-Merzbacher disease and its relation to amaurotic idiocy. *Zhurnal Neuropatalogii i Psikiatrii, 162,* 741–766.

Wilson, S. A. K. (1912). Progressive lenticular degeneration; a familial disease associated with cirrhosis of the liver. *Brain, 34,* 295–509.

CHAPTER 7

Vitamin and Mineral Deficiencies

T he use of vitamins as a treatment for a psychiatric disorder is still considered very controversial even though vitamin treatments are as old as medicine itself—the Mesopotamians recorded the curative effect of liver on night blindness over 4000 years ago (Köcher, 1963, 1980). In the twentieth century, the central nervous system symptoms of beriberi were first identified as caused by vitamin deficiency in 1912, and the dementia of pellagra was discovered in 1937. Since then, knowledge of the role of vitamins and minerals in many crucial pathways in the central nervous system has increased.

Today it is documented in the medical literature that disease entities can exist either due to inadequate amounts of vitamins (vitamin/mineral deficiencies) or the need for extraordinarily large amounts of a vitamin due to low levels of an enzyme (vitamin/mineral dependencies). These latter disease entities are covered in Chapter 6 on metabolic diseases. This chapter focuses on vitamin-and-mineral-deficiency diseases (inadequate amounts of the vitamin or mineral in the diet or inadequate absorption of them), which can present with schizophreniclike illnesses. Also discussed in this chapter are vitamin and mineral supplements in which patients with schizophrenia are reported in the medical literature to have responded to the therapy even though the mechanism of the pathology or the biochemistry is not fully worked out.

It is important to remember that if a vitamin deficiency is found in a patient with schizophrenia, it is not necessarily proof of the etiology of the disorder in that particular person. The poor eating habits of many delusional persons, particularly homeless individuals, can lead to vitamin deficiencies. The correction of such deficiencies, however, particularly those listed in this chapter that have been associated with schizophreniclike symptoms, is essential for the well-being of the patient.

A source of controversy in the field of psychiatry is the question of whether any patients with schizophrenic symptoms could have developed those symptoms because of particular foods they ingested that interfere with absorption of nutrients. The greatest controversy centers on celiac disease; gluten-containing cereals are known to cause a syndrome called celiac disease in some individuals. Thought to be a malabsorption syndrome, gluten causes inflammatory effects on the bowel of some individuals. It can be a factor in a neurological seizure syndrome (Gobbi et al., 1992).

A number of investigators have suggested that a relationship exists between celiac disease and schizophrenia (Ashkenazi et al., 1979; Reichelt & Landmark, 1995). Using epidemiological studies, case histories, and eventually a double-blind study, Dohan became convinced that a diet containing cereal could be a factor in the expression of schizophrenia in patients (Dohan, 1969; Dohan, 1983). More recently, others have also raised this possibility (De Palma, Sandri, Mazzetti, Di Pietrlata, & Bersani, 1995). However, Stevens et al. (1977) studied 380 individuals with schizophrenia and was unable to demonstrate celiac disease in any of them. Also Hallert (1995) who studied patients with celiac disease using the Minnesota Multiphasic Personality Inventory (MMPI) found evidence for depression, not schizophrenia. In autistic children with symptoms suggestive of gluten intolerance, two studies also have failed to confirm celiac disease (Walker-Smith, 1973; McCarthy & Coleman, 1979). With modern methods, this controversy should be able to be resolved by future controlled studies in individuals with schizophrenia because celiac disease can now be diagnosed by relatively easy blood tests (antiendomysial autoantibodies, antigliadin antibodies, HLA allele testing) instead of the more difficult jejunal biopsy after gluten loading.

VITAMINS

Vitamin A

Vitamin A (retinoid) is an essential nutrient for mammalian development and survival. According to Goodman (1994, 1995) minor physical anomalies (see Chapter 12) and chromosomal locations with their modes of actions in the retinoid system support their involvement in the etiology of schizophrenia. These findings raise the possibility of retinoid disregulation as a fetal neurodevelopmental mechanism resulting in later schizophrenia. Alterations in the functioning of the retinoid cascade may have profound implications for neurodevelopmental and/or neurodegenerative disorders like schizophrenia (Goodman, 1995).

There are two known cases of individuals with chronic schizophrenia (Olver, 1986; Coleman, Appendix A) who were found to have vitamin-A deficiency. In the Olver case, the patient also had bilateral keratomalacia and presented with the perforation of his right cornea. Both individuals were treated vitamin A with subsequent improvement. In the Coleman case where the patient had been hospitalized for 10 years, the classical symptoms of schizophrenia disappeared although the patient remained—outside the psychiatric hospital—as a neurotic loner. The difficulties of using serum retinol levels to monitor treatment in disturbed individuals is described in the Olver case. It is relevent to keep in mind that even patients hospitalized in well-functioning psychiatric placements may still manage to create bizarre diets for themselves.

Vitamin A is a fat-soluable vitamin that should be prescribed only in doses necessary to correct an *established laboratory deficiency*. Overdoses of fat-soluable vitamins can cause serious or fatal side-effects.

Vitamin B₃ (Nicotinamide)

Pellegra

The classic triad of symptoms in pellegra are psychiatric disturbance, gastrointestinal disorders, and skin lesions. Multiple vitamin deficiencies may be a problem in pellegra; however, the lack of nicotinic acid is apparently the most crucial as administration of nicotinic acid can rapidly relieve symptoms.

Pellegra often develops gradually. Sometimes the florid psychiatric disturbances of pellegra can present abruptly and dominate the clinical picture even though they may be associated with gastrointestinal and skin changes (Spivak & Jackson, 1977). The gastrointestinal disturbances include stomatitis and glossitis. Skin changes include roughening and reddening of the dorsum of the hands and pigmentation over bony prominences. Although the most common mental pattern in pellegra is disorientation, confusion, and impairment of memory, in some of patients the symptoms of mania or outbursts of violent behavior or paranoia may be the presenting symptoms. In the paranoid presentation, there are hallucinations and delusions of persecution (Lishman, 1987). If there is no clouding of consciousness, the symptoms may mimic schizophrenia.

The acute psychotic picture responds to nicotinic acid in a short period of time—between 10–48 hours (Spies, Aring, Gelperin, & Bean, 1938). Discontinuance of treatment without the patient's knowledge caused reoccurrence of the symptoms (Lishman, 1987). However, in the case of chronic pellagra with long-term mental dysfunction, less success can be expected. Presumably these treatment failures are due to structural changes in the neurons of the cortex, brain stem, and spinal cord observed in autopsies of pellagra victims (Spillane, 1947).

Acute nicotinic acid deficiency encephalopathy

An acute psychotic syndrome that responds promptly to nicotinic acid therapy can rarely occur in connection with alcoholism or after surgery related to the gastrointestinal tract (Lishman, 1987). Fifty years ago a number of cases of this syndrome were described [in 1942 Slater described a case in which "the picture simulated schizophrenia" (Slater, 1942, p. 257)] but now such reports have virtually disappeared from the medical literature. One of the authors of this volume saw one such case in 1985, however, in Washington, D.C. which occurred to a previously normal 27-year-old woman after gastrointestinal surgery. The addition of nicotinic acid to her intravenous fluid resulted in rapid, total remission of her auditory hallucinations and delusions.

LSD-precipitated psychosis

Nicotinic acid or niacin appears to be an antidote for the acute psychedelic psychosis induced by lysergic acid diethylamide

(LSD). During the 1950s when Hoffer and Osmond (1967) were experimenting with LSD, they routinely terminated their sessions with intravenous nicotinic acid. This reported effect of vitamin B_3 on psychedelic psychosis was duplicated by Goldstein (1973).

Vitamin B_6 (Pyridoxine)

Although vitamin B_6 is used to treat homocystinuria, it is far from proven that the vitamin B_6-responsive form of homocystinuria, cystathionine beta-synthase, is related to schizophrenia (see Chapter 6). In a case of zinc deficiency (see below), vitamin B_6 was given with the zinc supplement.

Vitamin B_{12}

Pernicious anemia

Pernicious anemia is known primarily because of the neurological complication of subacute combined degeneration of the cord. However, pernicious anemia sometimes can present first with a schizophrenialike psychosis or a paranoid state that antedates the anemia or spinal cord disease by months or even years (Davidson & Bagley, 1969; Huber, 1972; Lishman, 1987).

Methylenetetrahydrofolate (MTHFR) reductase deficiency

Methylenetetrahydrofolate (MTHFR) reductase deficiency is one of the etiologies of homocystine in the urine that has documented cases with the symptoms of schizophrenia. It is a form of homocystinuria that is difficult to treat. However, Rosenblatt reports that vitamin B_{12} is one of the therapies that may be helpful (Rosenblatt, 1989). Other therapies that have been tried in this patient group include folic acid, riboflavin, and betaine (see Chapter 6).

Vitamin D and Calcium

The role of vitamin D is to bring calcium into the body; low levels of calcium may be associated with seizure disorders, sometimes secondary to the long-term side effects of anticonvulsants. Clinically, the action of vitamin D on the brain is seen in the reduction of seizures after vitamin D treatment, without a measurable effect on serum calcium and magnesium levels (Christiansen, Rodbro, & Sjo, 1974). On the other hand, when calcium is measured in 24-hour urine, the rationale for the use of vitamin D is clearer if hypocalcinuria is discovered. In one such case in which the seizures were accompanied by delusions and hallucinations, supplementation with oral vitamin D corrected the patient's hypocalcinuria, brought the seizures to an abrupt halt, and also restored the patient to a normal psychiatric state (Coleman & Brown, 1976). Vitamin D is a fat-soluable vitamin that must be given only in doses adequate to correct an *established deficiency.*

Folic Acid

Folic acid is one of the treatments used in the MTHFR reductase deficiency form of homocystinuria (Freeman, Finkelstein, & Mudd, 1975) (see Chapter 6).

Riboflavin

Riboflavin is one of the treatments used in the MTHFR reductase deficiency form of homocystinuria (Fowler, Whitehouse, & Rensma, 1990) (see Chapter 6).

MINERALS

Magnesium

A negative magnesium balance occurs when magnesium is mobilized along with calcium from the bones during a state of hyperparathyroidism; there is an increased excretion of magnesium the urine. Although discussion of parathyroid disease with psychosis is focused on changes in the level of calcium (see Chapter 8), the complicated interrelationship between calcium and magnesium, particularly in this disease entity needs to be taken into consideration.

The medical literature has reports of abnormalities of magnesium in patients diagnosed as schizophrenia (Ueno et al., 1961; Cade, 1964; Seal & Eist, 1967; Chugh, Ohingra, & Gulati, 1973; Pandey et al., 1973; Hall & Joffe, 1973). There is a case in which correction of a recorded magnesium deficiency due to hyperparathyroidism was followed by clearing of psychiatric symptoms (Jacob & Merritt, 1966). Also, in the temporary psychosis that occasionally follows parathyroidectomy, magnesium infusions have been used until psychiatric symptoms subside (Potts & Roberts, 1958; Bergeron, Murphy, & Warner, 1961).

Selenium

Medical geology, the application of trace-element geography to epidemiology, is used to compare the geographic distribution of trace elements in soil and food to the geographic distribution of disease entities. Out of such a comparison came the selenium theory of schizophrenia following a study by Foster (1988) that found the highest correlation coefficient (0.58) for high rates of schizophrenia was associated with low-selenium crops (Foster, 1988). Because some of the enzymes that are theorized to be important in the pathogenesis of schizophrenia involve selenium, Brown (1994) has written a paper suggesting the experimental data that needs to be generated to prove or disprove the selenium theory of schizophrenia.

Evidence against this theory includes a study of serum and blood selenium levels in a group of Norwegians with schizophrenia that was no different from control subjects (Alertsen, Aukrust, & Skaug, 1986) and the fact that neither of the two selenium-deficiency diseases known in humans (Kaschin-Beck disease, Keshan disease) are associated with psychiatric symptoms.

Zinc

Both the research literature (Henkin, Patten, Re, & Bronzert, 1975) and the clinical literature (Staton, Donald, & Green, 1976) raise the question of whether zinc deficiency can cause symptoms of schizophrenia. Staton reported the case of a young man with loose associations, blunted affect, auditory and visual hallucinations, disorientation in time and place, drooling, and catatonic postures who had been diagnosed as having catatonic schizophrenia. Phenothiazines were ineffective and caused severe extrapyramidal disturbance. After some months electroconvulsive therapy was tried and produced only transient improvement. A low-serum zinc and high-serum copper was discovered and oral zinc sulfate and pyridoxine was prescribed. The patient soon began a major improvement and remained well a year later (Staton et al., 1976).

Henkin et al. (1975) monitored the lowering serum zinc produced by histadine in the treatment of six patients with progressive systemic sclerosis. At first the patients had the symptoms of dysfunction of taste and smell—the classic signs of zinc deficiency—but ultimately developed symptoms of central nervous system dysfunction. These included auditory and visual hallucinations and pronounced emotional lability. The authors reported the disturbances correlated with the degree of lowering of serum zinc; fortunately the psychiatric symptoms were quickly reversed following the administration of zinc sulfate.

Zinc deficiency also has been associated with anorexia, loss of libido, and fatigue, all of which apparently responded to zinc replacement (Tasman-Jones, 1980). In one study, six of nine zinc-deficient patients were either endogenously or psychotically depressed; this is thought to be a more usual presentation than schizophrenia (Little, Castellanos, Humphries, & Austin, 1989).

Zinc deficiency is rare but can be found in third world countries (malnourishment from lack of food); in people with unusual diets (bread with a high phytate content); a few disease entities (regional enteritis and other malabsorption syndromes, liver disease, diabetes and some renal diseases); and certain drugs (Lancet, 1973). Zinc deficiency, if it exists as a cause of schizophrenia in a first world country, is likely to be rare. In a study from Germany of the regional distribution of zinc in the postmortem brain of schizophrenic patients compared to that of matched controls, in none of the brain regions investigated were significant differences observed (Kornhuber et al., 1994). As the Staton case suggests, however, functional zinc deficiency for whatever reason is not unknown.

Zinc is known to be necessary for normal brain development. It is well established that zinc deprivation in pregnant animals at a critical stage in gestation may result in severe congenital malfunctions of the neural tube (Hurley, 1981). Later in gestation zinc deprivation is postulated to have profound effects on subsequent brain development and behavior (Sandstead, 1985). Zinc is more concentrated in the hippocampus than in any other structure within the mammalian brain (Crawford, 1983). A number of studies have associated zinc levels with structural and functional properties of the mossy fiber boutons of the hippocampus.

There is a medical hypothesis that gestational zinc deficiency is the primary etiology of some cases of schizophrenia (Andrews, 1990, 1992). It is known from animal studies that zinc is essential for the synthesis of nucleic acids and protein during gestation (Sandstead, Gillespie, & Brady, 1972). Andrew points out that his hypothesis is concordant with several details that are known about a schizophrenic population—that low birthweight is common, that males are more severely affected, and that there is hippocampal damage. The hypothesis also could fit with some current thinking about the possibility of second-trimester damage to the central nervous system in a subgroup of patients (see Chapter 12). Because zinc is usually adequate in the diet of first world countries, however, this hypothesis has little support.

Zinc provides a perfect example of the necessity of fully understanding a metabolic pathway or of establishing a laboratory deficiency of a vitamin or a mineral before treating a patient. Although zinc greatly helped the Stanton case, patients with Wilson's disease (see Chapter 6) may have a fatal deterioration if placed on zinc supplements (Lang, Rabas-Kolowinsky, Engelhardt, Kabros, & Konig, 1993).

It can be stated that there has never been a systematic monitoring of serum zinc levels in any large population of schizophrenics or their families, so very little information is available. Accurate estimation of zinc in human populations is unusually difficult. Because of the Stanton case and the research data, for the time being, serum zinc will remain on the list of tests indicated when trying to detect treatable forms of schizophrenia. Zinc deficiency usually can be successfully treated by oral zinc sulfate.

REFERENCES

Alertsen, A. R., Aukrust, A., & Skaug, O. E. (1986). Selenium concentration in blood and serum from patients with mental diseases. *Acta Psychiatrica Scandinavica, 74*, 217–219.

Andrews, R. C. R. (1990). Unification of the findings in schizophrenia to the effects of gestational zinc deficiency. *Medical Hypothesis, 31*, 141–153.

Andrews, R. C. R. (1992). An update of the zinc deficiency theory of schizophrenia. Identification of the sex determining system as the site of action of reproductive zinc deficiency. *Medical Hypothesis, 38*, 284–291.

Ashkenazi, A., Krasilowsky, D., Levin, S., Idar, D., Kalian, M., Hyala, O., Ginat, Y., & Halperin, B. (1979). Immunological reaction of psychotic patients to fractions of gluten. *American Journal of Psychiatry, 136*, 1306–1309.

Bergeron, R., Murphy, R., & Warner, K. (1961). Acute pancreatitis, acute hyperthyroidsim and low magnesium syndrome: A case report. *Lahey Clinic Bulletin, 12*, 181–191, 1961.

Brown, J. S. (1994). Role of selenium and other trace elements in the geography of schizophrenia. *Schizophrenia Bulletin, 20*, 387–398.

Cade, J. A. (1964). Significant elevation of plasma magnesium levels in schizophrenia and depressive states. *Medical Journal of Australia, 1*, 195.

Christiansen, C., Rodbro, P., & Sjo, O. (1974). "Anticonvulsant action" of vitamin D in epileptic patients? A controlled pilot study. *British Medical Journal, 2*, 258–259.

Chugh, T., Ohingra, R., & Gulati, R. (1973). Magnesium in schizophrenia. *Indian Journal of Medical Research, 61*, 762–764.

Coleman, M., Brown, W. M. (1976). Apparent reversal of a familial syndrome of seizures and later dementia by administration of vitamin D. In D. V. Siva Sankar (Ed.), *Psychopharmacology of childhood*. Westbury, NY: PJD Publications.

Crawford, I. L. (1983). Zinc and the hippocampus: Histology, neurochemistry, pharmacology and putative functional relevance. In I. E. Dreosti & R. M. Smith (Eds.), *Neurobiology of the trace elements. Vol. 1. Trace element neurobiology and deficiencies*. Clifton, NJ: Humana Press.

Davison, K., & Bagley, C. R. (1969). Schizophrenia-like psychoses associated with organic disorders of the central nervous system: a review of the literature. In R. N. Herrington (Ed.), *Current problems in neuropsychiatry: Schizophrenia, epilepsy, the temporal lobe* (pp. 113–184). Ashford, Kent: Headley Brothers Ltd.

De Palma, F., Sandri, G., Mazzetti, M., Di Pietrlata, L., & Bersani, G. (1995). *Malattia celiaca e schizofrenia: ipotesi si una possibile associazione*. Paper presented at the meeting for Epilepsy and other Neurological Disorders in Coeliac disease. San Marino, April 1995.

Dohan, F. C. (1969). Is celiac diseae a clue to the pathogenesis of schizophrenia? *Mental Hygiene, 53*, 525–529.

Dohan, F. C. (1983). More on celiac disease as a model for schizophrenia. *Biological Psychiatry, 18*, 501–564.

Foster, H. D. (1988). The geography of schizophrenia: Possible links with selenium and calcium deficiencies, inadequate exposure to sunlight and industrialization. *Journal of Orthomolecular Medicine, 3*, 135–140.

Fowler, B., Whitehouse, C., & Rensma, P. L. (1990). Homocystinuria due to methylene THF reductase deficiency: A new form responsive to riboflavin. *Proceedings of the Vth International Congress of Inborn Errors of Metabolism*, Monterrey, CA, June 1–5.

Freeman, J. M., Finkelstein, J. D., & Mudd, S. H. (1975). Folate-responsive homocystinuria and "schizophrenia." *New England Journal of Medicine, 292*, 491.

Gobbi, G., Bouquet, F., Greco, L., Lambertini, A., Tassinari, C. A., Zentura, A., & Zanboni, M. G. (1992). Coeliac disease, epilepsy and cerebral calcifications. *The Lancet, 340*, 439–443.

Goodman, A. B. (1994). Retinoid disregulation in schizophrenia. Letter to the Editor. *American Journal of Psychiatry, 151*, 452–453.

Goodman, A. B. (1995). Chromosonal locations and modes of action of genes of the retinoid (vitamin A) system support their involvement in the etiology of schizophrenia. *American Journal of Medical Genetics, 60*, 335–348.

Goldstein, J. A. (1973). Treatment for a trip. *Emergency Medicine, 5*, 13.

Hall, R. C. W., & Joffe, J. R. (1973). Hypomagnesemia. Physical and psychiatric symptoms. *Journal of the American Medical Association, 224*, 1749–1751.

Hallert, C. (1995). *Depression in coeliac disease*. Paper presented at the meeting of Epilepsy and Other Neurological Disorders in Coeliac Disease. San Marino, April 1995.

Henkin, R. I., Patten, B. M., Re, P. K., & Bronzert, D. A. (1975). A syndrome of acute zinc loss. Cerebellar dysfunction, mental changes, anorexia and taste and smell dysfunction. *Archives of Neurology, 32*, 745–751.

Hoffer, A., & Osmond, H. (1967). *The hallucinogens*. New York: Academic Press.

Huber, G. (1972). Klinik und psychopathologie der organischen pscyhosen. In K. P. Kisker, J. E. Meyer, & C. Muller (Eds.), *Psychiatrie der Gegenwart*, Vol. 2/2 (pp. 71–146). Berlin: Springer Verlag.

Hurley, L. S. (1981). Tetratogenic aspects of manganese, zinc and copper nutrition. *Physiology Reviews, 61,* 249–295.

Jacobs, J. K., & Merrit, C. R. (1966). Magnesium deficiency in hyperparathyroidism: Case report of a toxic psychosis. *Annals of Surgery, 162,* 260–262.

Köcher, F. (1963, 1980). *Die babylonisch-assyriche Medizin in Texten und Untersuchungen.* Berlin: Walter de Gruyter.

Kornhuber, J., Lange, K. W., Kruzik, P., Rausch, W-D., Gabriel, E., Jellinger, K., & Riederer, P. (1994). Iron, copper, zinc, magnesium and calcium in postmortem brain tissue from schizophrenic patients. *Biological Psychiatry, 36,* 21–30.

Lancet (1973). Zinc deficiency in man. *Lancet, I,* 299–300.

Lang, C. J., Rabas-Kolowinsky, P., Engelhardt, A., Kabros, G., & Konig, H. J. (1993). Comment. *Archives of Neurology, 50:* 1007–1008.

Lishman, W. A. (1987). *Organic psychiatry,* second edition. Oxford: Blackwell Scientific.

Little, K. Y., Castellanos, X., Humphries, L. L., & Austin, J. (1989). Altered zinc metabolism in mood disorder patients. *Biological Psychiatry, 26,* 646–648.

McCarthy, D. M., & Coleman, M. (1979). Response of intestinal mucosa to gluten challenge in autistic subjects. *Lancet, ii,* 877–878.

Olver, J. (1986). Keratomalacia on a "healthy diet." *British Journal of Opthalmology, 70,* 357–360.

Pandey, S., Devpura, J., & Bedi, H. et al. (1973). An estimation of magneisum and calcium in the serum and CSF in schizophrenia. *Journal of the Association of Physicians of India, 21,* 203–205.

Potts, J., & Roberts, B. (1958). Clinical significance of magnesium deficiency and its relation to parathyroid disease. *American Journal of Medical Science, 235,* 206–219.

Reichelt, K. L., & Landmark, J. (1995). Specific IgA antibody increases in schizophrenia. *Biological Psychiatry, 37,* 410–413.

Rosenblatt, D. S. (1989). Inherited disorders of folate transport and metabolism. In C. R. Scriver, A. L. Beaudet, W. S. Sly, & D. Valle (Eds.), *The metabolic basis of inherited disease* (pp. 2053–2055). New York: McGraw-Hill.

Standstead, H. S. (1985). Zinc: Essentiality for brain development and function. *Nutritional Review, 43,* 129–137.

Sandstead, H. H., Gillespie, D. D., & Brady, R. N. (1972). Zinc deficiency; Effect on brain of the suckling rat. *Pediatric Research, 6,* 119–125.

Seal, V., & Eist, H. (1967). Serum magnesium concentration in schizophrenia and epilepsy. *Clinical Chemistry, 13,* 1021.

Slater, E. (1942). Psychosis associated with vitamin B deficiency. *British Medical Journal, 1,* 257–258.

Spies, T. D., Aring, C. D., Gelperin, J. & Bean, W. B. (1938). The mental symptoms of pellegra: Their relief with nicotinic acid. *American Journal of the Medical Sciences, 196*, 461–475.

Spillane, J. D. (1947). *Nutritional disorders of the nervous system.* Edinburgh: Livingstone.

Spivak, J. L., & Jackson, D. L. (1977). Pellagra: An analysis of 18 patients and a review of the literature. *Johns Hopkins Medical Journal, 140*, 295.

Staton, M. A., Donald, A. G., & Green, G. B. (1976). Zinc deficiency presenting as schizophrenia. *Current Concepts in Psychiatry, 2*, 11–14.

Stevens, F. M., Lloyd, R. S., Geraghty, S. M., Reynolds, M. T., Sarsfield, M. J., McNicholl, B., Fottrell, P. F., Wright, R., & McCarthy, C. F. (1997). Schiozophrenia and coeliac disease—the nature of the relationship. *Psychological Medicine, 7*, 259–263.

Tasman-Jones, C. (1980). Zinc deficiency states. *Advances in Internal Medicine, 26*, 97–114.

Ueno, Y., Aoki, N., Yabuki, T. et al. (1961). Electrolyte metabolism in blood and cerebrospinal fluid in psychoses. *Folia Psychiatrica et Neurologica Japonica* (Tokyo), *15*, 304–326.

Walker-Smith, J. (1973). Gastrointestinal disesae and autism—the results of a survey. *Symposium on Autism.* Sydney, Australia: Abbott Laboratories.

CHAPTER 8

Endocrine Disorders

M ost of the patients with the endocrine disorders described in this chapter do not develop psychotic episodes. As discussed elsewhere, schizophrenia is such a common disease entity in adults that it could always be a coincidence when two disease entities appear in any particular patient. For the small subgroup of individuals with endocrine disorders that do become psychotic, however, often there is evidence that correction of the endocrine dysfunction also corrects the schizophreniclike psychoses, suggesting that hormonal abnormalities were the major factor in the induction of the mental aberration.

ADDISON'S DISEASE

Addison's disease, which results from a low output of all adrenal steroids, is associated with some kind of psychiatric abnormalities in almost all patients. Only approximately 5% of these individuals have symptoms, however, such as acute and chronic paranoia, hallucinations or delusions, which are characteristic of schizophrenia. Cleghorn (1951, 1965) reported on patients with what he called schizophreniform psychoses and commented that he thought that the incidence of psychosis in Addison's disease is much higher than an estimate based on the described cases in the medical literarture would indicate. McFarland (1963) reviewed reports of 10 patients with classical schizophrenia, 6 with affective psychosis, and 1 with organic psychosis, and concluded that the

134

exact form of psychotic development is not predictable in this disease entity. One of McFarland's patients developed hypomania, which masked the endocrine disorder until the patient lapsed into a coma after electroconvulsive treatment. At that point, severe hyponatremia was found leading to the medical diagnosis of Addison's disease.

Addison's disease results from atrophy of the adrenal cortices and the output from all adrenal steriods is low—cortisol, aldosterone, corticosterone, and androgens. Often the disease presents slowly, incrementally, and starts with weight loss, loss of appetite, and a feeling of generalized weakness. On exposed skin surfaces, pigmentation develops. There is a pronounced intolerance of cold and the body temperature may be subnormal. The immune system becomes weakened. Female amenorrhea and male impotence may occur. Syncope is usually accompanied by hypotension. There is an increased incidence of seizure disorders.

Sometimes the disease presents itself with a severe "Addisonian crisis." The crisis may consist of pyrexia, vomiting, epigastric pain, and dehydration in the presence of severe hypotension. The crisis may occur spontaneously or in response to infection, chilling or drugs, such as morphine or anesthetic agents.

According to Cleghorn (1951), of the 11 cases described by Addison in 1855, only some would now be considered bona fide examples of his syndrome. It is now known that Addison's disease can present secondary to many disease processes that injure the adrenal cortex. This includes adrenomyeloneuropathy (Schafer et al., 1994), pituitary adenoma (Kubota et al., 1992), non-Hodgkin's lymphoma, amyloid disease, hemachromatosis, tuberculosis, and paracoccidodioidomycosis. There is also an autoimmune form of Addison's disease that occurs sporadically or as a component of an autoimmune polyglandular syndrome (APS). Patients with autoimmune Addison's disease typically have serum autoantibodies to adrenocortical microsomal fractions. Recent studies have shown that the enzyme active sites and autoantibody sites on steroid 21-hydroxylase are closely related (Wedlock et al., 1993). In Addison's disease autoimmune destruction of the adrenal cortex is probably due mainly to cellular mechanisms, but it appears the autoantibodies also have the potential of inhibiting 21-hydroxylase enzyme activity (Furmaniak et al., 1994).

Replacement therapy of the depressed hormonal levels is usually highly successful in alleviating both physical and mental disturbances (Lishman, 1987). Glucocorticoids appear to be more important than mineralcorticoids for reversing the mental symptoms, indicating that these do not rest entirely on disturbances of electrolyte and water balance. Overdosing with corticosteroids can precipitate manic symptoms, even in some normal individulas (Ur, Turner, Goodwin, Grossman, & Besser, 1992). Although adrenal steroids have acquired a bad reputation from their ability to promote immunosuppression and destruction of neurons in the hippocampus, they are important adaptive and protective agents that mediate the effects of the environment on the brain and the rest of the body (McEwen et al., 1992). Patients with Addison's disease remind us of the essential functions of adrenal hormones.

CUSHING'S SYNDROME

Cushing's syndrome is primarily an endocrine disorder and the majority of patients who suffer from it are correctly diagnosed. Some patients with Cushing's syndrome may present with psychotic features so early in their illness, however, that it dominates the clinical picture to such an extent that the endocrine disorder itself goes unnoticed at first or even for many years (Spillane, 1951; Trethowan & Cobb, 1952; Hertz, Nadas, Wojtkowski, 1955; Johnson, 1975; Lishman, 1987). This is a most unfortunate situation as treatment of the underlying endocrine disorder is, by far, the most effective therapy for the psychiatric symptoms. Lishman (1987) states that psychotic pictures of a schizophrenic nature are more common in Cushing's disease than in Addison's disease.

The literature reports symptoms that are classic for schizophreniclike psychoses (Hickman, Atkinson, Flint, & Hurxthal, 1961; Huber, 1972). The severe psychoses accompanying Cushing's syndrome often are depressive in character with delusions and auditory hallucinations; paranoid symptoms may accompany the most florid maninfestations. The patients sometimes appear to be so slowed down that they are bordering on stupor; others have an anxious agitation. There may be marked fluctuations in the psychiatric symptoms.

About one-third of patients with chronic elevations of corticorsteroids due to spontaneous Cushing's syndrome manifest variable degrees of impairment on neuropsychologic testing (Whelan, Schteingart, Storkman, & Smith, 1980). The hippocampal formation contains the highest concentration of corticosteroid binding sites in the entire brain and glucocorticoid excess is associated with hippocampal damage in animals (Sapolsky, Uno, Rebert, & Finch, 1990). Using magnetic resonance studies, Starkman, Gebarski, Berent, and Schteingart (1992) have shown an inverse relationship in patients with Cushing's syndrome between hippocampal volume and plasma corticol levels.

Cushing's syndrome is more common in women than men and begins in adult life at any time from puberty onward. In most cases, Cushing's syndrome is due to pituitary overproduction of adrenocorticotrophic hormone (ACTH) resulting in secondary bilateral hyperplasia of the adrenal cortices. The physical symptoms of Cushing's syndrome are a moon face, buffalo hump, and purple striae on the abdomen and thighs. The patients are usually obese and insidious weight gain may be the earliest sign. The skin may also become hirsute and easily bruised, and a "plethoric complexion" is described.

A serious complication of Cushing's disease is severe hypertension. Also amenorrhea is usual in the female and impotence, testicular atrophy, or gynecomastia in the male. Some patients describe a feeling of weakness; others suffer multiple infections. Osteoporosis leading to backache or vertebral collapse has been reported.

When the endocrine disorder is successfully treated, the psychiatric symptoms can be expected to disappear (Jeffcoate, Silverstone, Edwards, & Besser, 1979; Cohen, 1980; Kelly, Checkley, Bender, & Mashiter, 1983). The remission may occur within days or weeks; very occasionally the symptoms may take as long as a year to completely clear.

HYPERPARATHYROIDISM

There are many case histories published of highly disturbed patients with apparent psychiatric manifestations of hyperparathyroidism; affective symptoms are most commonly reported. There are relatively few cases in which the symptoms are limited to those associated only with classic schizophrenia (Agras & Oliveau, 1964; Reilly & Wilson, 1965; Gatewood, Organ, & Mead, 1975).

In cases in which long-standing psychiatric symptoms did not respond well to neuroleptics, however, but cleared completely with parathyroidectomy, a not unreasonable assumption is that the psychiatric symptoms were brought on by the effect on the patient's ion metabolism of the parathyroid adenomas. In the case reported by Alarcon and Francheschini (1984), the authors report that, if anything, the patient's delusions were exacerbated with doses of trifluoperazine even when it was increased to 5 mg three times daily; however, her mental status cleared after the excision of a left inferior parathyroid adenoma.

Another psychotic state associated with hyperparathyroidism is the temporary psychosis that occasionally occurs after surgery, probably involving the rapid changes in ions in the immediate postoperative period (Karpati & Frame, 1964; Mikkelsen & Reider, 1979). These cases are not a diagnostic problem and the prognosis for recovery from the psychiatric manifestations is excellent, usually occurring within days or weeks after the surgery.

Most of the medical literature suggests that the psychiatric manifestations in hyperparathyroidism are the result of the level or rate of change of the hypercalcemia rather than of the high levels of parathyroid hormone per se. Another possible etiology of psychiatric symptomology in a few cases may be the magnesium imbalance that also occurs in this disease entity (Potts & Roberts, 1958; Jacobs & Merrit, 1966) (see Chapter 7).

HYPERTHYROIDISM

Hyperthyroidism, the result of thyroid overactivity, is commonly accompanied by psychological disturbances (MacCrimmon et al., 1979). These problems are generally of a neurotic rather than a psychotic nature, but around 1% of inpatients in psychiatric hospitals have been found to have hyperthyroidism. In a survey of psychiatric hosptials that found 8 such patients, the hyperthyroidism was unsuspected in 6 prior to the survey (McLarty, Ratcliff, Ratcliffe, Shimmins, & Goldberg, 1978). After it was uncovered in these 6 patients, it was determined that the hyperthyroidism seemed to be contributing to their mental illness in 5 of 6 of the patients.

Schizophrenic illnesses of all types have been reported—hebephrenic, catatonic, and paranoid—and sometimes have been found to outnumber the affective psychoses in this patient group even though mania is more frequent than depression (Bursten, 1961; Greer & Parsons, 1968). Hypomania can be a presenting symptom. Lishman (1987) describes a case in which a patient with hypomanaia was in and out of a psychiatric hospital three times, each time responding satisfactorily to the most common treatment for schizophrenia at that time—chlorpromazine. On the third admission, an enlarged thyroid gland was noticed and a diagnosis of hyperthyroidism led to specific and successful therapy. The admission note on the two previous admissions had shown a tachcardia that had been overlooked at the time. Lishman reports, however, that some specialists no longer believe that a specific "thyroid psychosis" exists, but that it is generally agreed that a distinctive coloring may be lent by the hyperthyroidism: "Thus a manic component may accompany otherwise typical schizophrenic symptomology, and agitation is often profound in the presence of depression. Most observers are also agreed that paranoid features are especially common whatever form the psychosis may take" (Lishman, 1987, p. 430).

Hyperthyroidism is most commonly seen in the second and third decades of life but can begin at any age. Females are affected more than males by a ratio of 6:1. Symptoms of hyperthyroidism include sensitivity to heat and preference for cold, increased appetite, loss of weight, sweating, palpitations, tiredness, and dyspnea on effort. The signs of hyperthyroidism are cardiac dysrhythmias (chiefly auricular fibrillation), hyperkinetic movements, tachycardia exceeding 90 beats per minute, a palpable thyroid gland, a bruit audible over the thyroid, exophthalmos, lid retraction, hot hands, lid-lag, and fine finger tremor.

Often the thyroid gland is diffusely overactive but the cause also may lie in a hyperplastic nodule or a secreting adenoma. A goiter may or may not be present. Grave's disease—patients with exophthalmic goiter—is now known to be an autoimmune disease entity. A patient with an episode of schizophrenia due to iatrogenic biochemical thyrotoxicosis has even been reported (Johnstone, MacMillan, & Crow, 1987). In this case the psychotic features receded when the thyroxine dosage was reduced; neuroleptics were also given.

Diagnosis of hyperthyroidism is standard; it can be made by laboratory testing of the thyroid hormones in the serum, radioactive iodine uptake testing, and serum protein-bound iodine tests. Both medical and surgical therapies are available for patients with hyperthyroidism. Occasionally, during treatment with antithyroid drugs, symptoms of schizophrenia may make a temporary appearance, possibly due to the rapid alteration of the level of circulating thyroxine (Bewsher, Gardiner, Hedley, & Maclean, 1971). The result of treatment is generally satisfactory, however, with the resolution of the the emotional disorder as the patient is rendered euthyroid (Lishman, 1987).

HYPOPARATHYROIDISM

Psychotic illnesses of the schizophrenic type may rarely be seen due to rapid rates of decreases in calcium, particularly in cases following surgery (Lishman, 1987; Mikkelson & Reider, 1979). These post-parathyroidectomy psychoses clear rapidly so their etiology is clear; the longest period seen in the medical literature was a recovery 18 days after surgery (Potts & Roberts, 1958).

HYPOPITUITARISM (SHEEHAN'S SYNDROME)

There is a case in the medical literature in which psychotic symptoms (paranoid delusions and auditory hallucinations) gradually worsened for 2 years until the patient received a diagnosis of hypopituitarism (Hanna, 1970). When initially admitted to a psychiatric hospital, she also was disoriented and her memory was impaired. She was started on thioridazine but then developed a grand mal seizure 1 week after admission and began deteriorating to a semi-conscious state. A specialist—noting her dry skin, lack of axillary and pubic hair, and precomatose condition—made a diagnosis of hypopituitarism leading to a course of cortisone and thyroxine. There was a dramatic response and within 8 weeks the patient had lost all her mental symptoms, including delusions and hallucinations and was physically well.

This 55-year-old woman had received an admitting diagnosis of a paranoid state with an organic dementia. Although she could repeat four digits forward and three backward, her age and her muddled and inaccurate account of recent events led to the diagnosis of dementia rather than schizophrenia. However because of the dramatic nature of her psychotic symptoms that lasted for 2 years and that overshadowed any memory loss, this case is included in this textbook.

There is another case in the literature that also describes a patient who had psychotic symptoms due to hypopituitarism that were relieved by replacement therapy (Blau & Hinton, 1960). However, this case differs in that the dementia was the presenting symptom and the psychotic symptoms did not present until after the coma.

HYPOTHYROIDISM

Hypothyroidism is of great importance in psychiatric practice and notorious for leading to mistakes in diagnosis—it is liable to be overlooked on account of its insidious development and the minor and diffuse nature of early complaints (Lishman, 1987). Although the typical mental picture is of lethargy and slowing of all cognitive functions, irritability, agitation, and even outright psychosis do develop in some patients (Sanders, 1962; Tonks, 1964).

The concept of "myxedema madness" is based on Asher's (1949) paper of that name, which described a series of patients with hypothyroidism—in this classical paper five of his patients showed the picture of typical schizophrenia with a marked paranoid coloring. In patients with the severe psychiatric sequelae of hypothyroidism, florid delusions of persecution may be gross and bizarre. Auditory hallucinations appear to be particularly common (Lishman, 1987). The condition may run a fluctutating course; the schizophrenic psychoses will in general be colored by mental slowing.

Hypothyroidism is commoner in females compared to males at a ratio of 8:1. The age of presentation most frequently is middle age although the age range is wide. Adult hypothyroidism is frequently called "myxedema" because of the nonpitting edematous appearance over the face and limbs and in the supraclavicular fossae. The skin is dry, rough, often with a pale puffy complexion, and baggy eyelids. The patient tends to be sluggish and inert with a slow pulse and may have experienced increased loss of hair. Menorrhagia is common in females and impotence in males. Vague generalized aches and pains are a common complaint.The neurological examination shows a slowed ankle reflex with a marked delay in the relaxation phase. Diagnosis is confirmed by laboratory tests of thryoid hormones.

The treatment of hypothyroidism can be highly rewarding if it occurs within a year or two of the onset of the illness. The patients gradually regain vitality and the mental symptoms melt away. The exception to these good results occurs when the patient has been undiagnosed for a long period of time and then may be left with permanent defects of intellect and memory in spite of adequate treatment (Jellinek, 1962). Tonks (1964) who surveyed hypothyroid patients in a psychiatric hospital during a period of treatment with thyroid preparations found that no patient with a mental illnesses exceeding 2 years had a completely satisfactory reponse.

REFERENCES

Agras, S., & Oliveau, D. C. (1964). Primary hyperparathyroidism and psychosis. *Canadian Medical Association Journal, 91*, 1366–1367.

Alarcon, R. D., & Franceschini, J. A. (1984). Hyperparathyroidism and paranoid psychosis: case report and review of the literature. *British Journal of Psychiatry, 145*, 477.

Asher, R. (1949). Myxoedematous madness. *British Medical Journal, 2*, 555–562.

Bewsher, P. D., Gardiner, A. Q., Hedley, A. J., & Maclean, H. C. S. (1971). Psychosis after acute alteration of thyroid status. *Psychological Medicine 1*, 260–62.

Blau, J. N., & Hinton, J. M. (1960). Hypopituitary coma and psychosis. *Lancet, i*, 408–409.

Bursten, B. (1961). Psychoses associated with thyrotoxicosis. *Archives of General Psychiatry, 4*, 267–273.

Cleghorn, R. A. (1951). Adrenal cortical insufficiency: Psychological and neurological observations. *Canadian Medical Association Journal, 65*, 449–454.

Cleghorn, R. A. (1965). Hormones and humors. In L. Martini & A. Pecile (Eds.), *Hormonal steroids. Biochemistry, pharmacology and therapeutics*, vol 2. New York: Academic Press.

Cohen, S. I. (1980). Cushing's syndrome: A psychiatric study of 29 patients. *British Journal of Psychiatry, 136*, 120–124.

Furmaniak, J., Kominami, S., Asawa, T., Wedlock, N., Colls, J., & Rees Smith, B. (1994). Autoimmune Addison's disease—Evidence for a role of steroid 21-hydroxylase autoantibodies in adrenal insufficiency. *Journal of Clinical Endocrinology and Metabolism, 79*, 1519–1521.

Gatewood, J. W., Organ, C. H., & Mead, B. T. (1975). Mental changes associated with hyperthyroidism. *American Journal of Psychiatry, 132*, 129–132.

Greer, S., & Parsons, V. (1968). Schizophrenia-like psychosis in thyroid crisis. *British Journal of Psychiatry, 114*, 1357–1362.

Hanna, S. M. (1970). Hypopituitarism (Sheehan's syndrome) presenting with organic psychosis. *Journal of Neurology, Neurosurgery, Psychiatry, 33*, 192–103.

Hertz, P. E., Nadas, E., & Wojtkowski, H. (1955). Cushing's syndrome and its management. *American Journal of Psychiatry, 112*, 144–145.

Hickman, J. W., Atkinson, R. P., Flint, L. D., & Hurxthal, L. M. (1961). Transient schizophrenic reaction as a major symptom of Cushing's syndrome. *New England Journal of Medicine, 264*, 797–800.

Huber, G. (1972). Klinik und psychopathologie der organischen psychosen. In K. P. Kisker, J. E. Meyer, & C. Muller (Hrsg.), *Psychiatrie der Gegenwart*, Vol 2/2 (pp. 71–146). Berlin: Springer.

Jacobs, J. K., & Merrit, C. R. (1966). Magnesium deficiency in hyperparathyroidism: Case report of toxic psychosis. *Annals of Surgery, 162*, 260–262.

Jeffcoate, W. J., Silverstone, J. T., Edwards, C. R. W., & Besser, G. M. (1979). Psychiatric manifestations of Cushing's syndrome: Response to lowering plasma cortisol. *Quarterly Journal of Medicine, 191*, 465–472.

Jellinek, E. H. (1962). Fits, faints, coma and dementia in myxedema. *Lancet, 2*, 1010–1012.

Johnson, J. (1975). Schizophrenia and Cushing's syndrome cured by adrenalectomy. *Psychological Medicine, 5*, 165–168.

Johnstone, E. C., MacMillan, J. F., & Crow, T. J. (1987). The occurrence of organic disease of possible or probable aetiological significance in a population of 268 cases of first episode schizophrenia. *Psychological Medicine, 17*, 371–379.

Karpati, G., & Frame, B. (1964). Neuropsychiatric disorders in primary hyperparathyroidism. *Archives of Neurology, 10*, 387–397.

Kelly, W. F., Checkley, S. A., Bender, D. A., & Mashiter, K. (1983). Cushing's syndrome and depression—a prospective study of 26 patients. *British Journal of Psychiatry, 142*, 16–19.

Kubota, T., Hayashi, M., Kabuto, M., Shirasaki, N., Aradachi, H., Miyanaga, K., & Miyabo, S. (1992). Corticotroph cell hyperplasia in a patient with Addison disease: Case report. *Surgical Neurology, 37*, 441–447.

Lishman, W. A. (1987). *Organic psychiatry; The psychological consequences of cerebral disorder.* Oxford: Blackwell Scientific.

MacCrimmon, D. J., Wallace, J. E., Goldberg, W. et al. (1979). Emotional disturbance and cognitive deficits in hyperthyroidism. *Psychosomatic Medicine, 41*, 331.

McEwen, B. S., Angulo, J., Cameron, H., Chao, H. M., Daniels, D., Gannon, M. N., Gould, E., Mendelson, S., Sakai, R., Spencer, R., & Woolley, C. (1992). Paradoxical effects of adrenal steroids on the brain: protection vs degeneration. *Biological Psychiatry, 31*, 177–199.

McFarland, H. R. (1963). Addison's disease and related psychoses. *Comprehensive Psychiatry, 4*, 90–95.

McLarty, D. G., Ratcliffe, W. A., Ratcliffe, J. G., Shimmins, J. G., & Goldberg, A. (1978). A study of thyroid function in psychiatric in-patients. *British Journal of Psychiatry, 133*, 211–218.

Mikkelsen, E. J., & Reider, A. A. (1979). Post-parathyroidectomy psychosis: Clinical and research implications. *Journal of Clinical Psychiatry, 40*, 352–358.

Potts, J., & Roberts, B. (1958). Clinical significance of magnesium deficiency and its relation to parathyroid disease. *American Journal of Medical Science, 235*, 206–219.

Reilly, E. L., & Wilson, W. P. (1965). Mental symptoms in hyperparathyroidism (A report of three cases). *Diseases of the Nervous System, 26*, 361–363.

Sanders, V. (1962). Neurologic manifestations of myxedema. *New England Journal of Medicine, 266*, 547.

Sapolsky, R. M., Uno, H., Rebert, C. S., & Finch, C. E. (1990). Hippocampal damage associated with prolonged glucocorticoid exposure in primates. *Journal of Neuroscience, 10*, 2897–2902.

Schafer, J. R., Ehlenz, K., Steinmetz, A., Pilz, C., Hunneman, D. H., Baerwald, C., von Wichert, P., & Kaffarnik, H. (1994). Eine Haufige Ursache des Morbus Addison. *Deutsche Medizinische Wochenschrift, 119,* 327–331.

Spillane, J. D. (1951). Nervous and mental disorders in Cushing's syndrome. *Brain, 74,* 72–94.

Starkman, M. N., Gebarski, S. S., Berent, S., & Schteingart, D. E. (1992). Hippocampal formation volume, memory dysfunction and corticol levels in patients with Cushing's syndrome. *Biological Psychiatry, 32,* 756–765.

Tonks, C. M. (1964). Mental illness in hypothyroid patients. *British Journal of Psychiatry, 110,* 706–710.

Trethowan, W. H., & Cobb, S. (1952). Neuropsychiatric aspects of Cushing's syndrome. *Archives of Neurology and Psychiatry, 67,* 283–309.

Ur, E., Turner, T. H., Goodwin, T. J., Grossman, A., & Besser, G. M. (1992). Mania in association with hydrocortisone replacement for Addison's disease. *Postgraduate Medical Journal, 68,* 41–43.

Wedlock, N., Asawa, T., Baumann-Antczak, A., Rees Smith, B., & Furmaniak, J. (1993). Autoimmune Addison's disease: Analysis of autoantibody binding sites on human steroid 21-hydroxlase. *FEBS Letters, 332*: 123–126.

Whelan, T., Schteingart, D. E., Starkman, M. N., & Smith, A. (1980). Neuropsychological deficits in Cushing's syndrome. *Journal of Nervous and Mental Disorders, 168,* 753–757.

CHAPTER 9

Autoimmune Disorders

The possible role of the autoimmune process in the pathogenesis of schizophrenia, which has been been discussed for decades, is now becoming a major focus (Knight, Knight, & Ungvari, 1992; Kessler & Shinitzky, 1993; Kirch, 1993; Ganguli et al., 1993; Noy, Achiron, & Laor, 1994). There are two approaches to determine whether a disease has an autoimmune pathology (Rose, 1991). The direct approach, as exemplified by myasthenia gravis and Graves' disease (see Chapter 8), is the detection of antigen-specific autoantibodies with pathophysiological significance. In most other diseases such as systemic lupus erythematosus and multiple sclerosis there is only indirect evidence of autoimmunity at this time, such as nonorgan specific autoantibodies and so on.

In an effort to unravel some of the puzzling and contradictory information, a new field of research called psychoimmunology has emerged. As a result, many experiments have shown abnormal immune responses, including those that are autoimmune, in some individuals with schizophrenia (Pandey, Gupta, & Chaturvedi, 1981; DeLisi, Weber, & Pert, 1985; Muller, Ackenheil, Eckstein, Hofschuster, & Mempel, 1987; Honer, Hurwitz, Li, Palmer, & Paty, 1989; McAllister et al., 1989; Rapaport, McAllister, Pickar, Nelson, & Paul, 1989; Ganguli & Rabin, 1989; Yannitsi et al., 1990; Muller, Ackenheil, Hofschuster, Mempel, & Eckstein, 1987; Shima, Yano, Sugiura, & Tokunaga, 1991; Ganguli, Brar, Solomon, Chengappa, & Rabin, 1992; Hochtlen & Muller, 1992; Kilidireas et al., 1992; Achiron et al., 1994; Sasaki et al., 1994; Maes, Meltzer, & Bosmans, 1994). For those who consider schizophrenia one disease entity and are looking for proof of autoimmunity as an etiological underpinning to that putative single disease, however, research has been disappointing; Kirch (1993) states "no research evidence to date irrefutably indicates an autoimmune etiologic process in schizophrenia" (p. 355).

There is a paper that reports that patients who do not respond to neuroleptic treatments have lower levels of polyreactive natural autoantibodies than schizophrenic individuals who do respond to neuroleptics (Levy-Soussan et al., 1994). On the one hand, a rationale for immunostimulants as a nonneuroleptic treatment for schizophrenia has been advanced (Levine, Susnovski, Handzel, Leykin, & Shinizky, 1994); on the other hand, it has been pointed out that neuroleptics exhibit immunosuppressive effects (Maes et al., 1994). It has even been suggested that there might be a relationship between cerebrospinal fluid immunoglobulin G and the expression of negative symptoms in schizophrenia (Muller & Ackenheil, 1993).

Several disorders, currently classified as probably autoimmune in origin, show an involvement of the central nervous system, which can include the symptoms of schizophrenia. In some of these disease entities, there is small group of patients who present with schizophrenia before the underlying disease is yet apparent. In many disorders in which the patients have evidence of autoimmunity, it is not known if the autoimmune features are the result of an unknown disease with which the symptoms started or if the autoimmune phenomena are the actual basis of the pathology. The disease entities listed in this chapter are those in which autoimmunity is a prominent part of the laboratory presentation of the disease. In some of these disease entities, there appears to be evidence that the brain has lost its status as an immunologically privileged and protected compartment of the body.

In any individual disease, of course, it may be difficult to tell whether the schizophrenia occurred as an independent second illness in the patients or was, in fact, the first manifestation of a disease classified as autoimmune. However, there is enough medical literature now published to raise a concern about the likelihood of psychiatric presentations of some of the autoimmune disorders. This chapter discusses the reports in the medical literature of patients with schizophrenia and a disease likely to be autoimmune. As more specific treatments are developed for this group of disorders, this will further increase the importance of exact identification of the underlying pathology.

ADDISON'S DISEASE

Addison's disease, which is characterized by diminished function of the adrenal cortex, is a syndrome of multiple etiologies. It appears likely that so-called idiopathic Addison's disease is autoimmune in origin and there are predictions of an immunodiagnostic tool for this form of Addison's disease (Song et al., 1994). See Chapter 8 for a full discussion of Addison's disease and its relationship to schizophrenia.

MULTIPLE SCLEROSIS

Multiple sclerosis is a neurological disease with probable autoimmune pathogenesis in which cerebral pathology occurs in almost all cases (Ormerod et al., 1987). Thus perhaps it is no surprise that the medical literature on multiple sclerosis includes cases in which patients have symptoms of schizophrenia as a predominant symptomatology (Piessiur-Strelow, Power, & Felgenhauer, 1988; Bandelow & Muller, 1990; Felgenhauer, 1990; Zarranz, Antiguedad, & Barcena, 1995). In fact, in some cases described in the literature, the patients may initially present with schizophrenia or other psychiatric symptoms and then, only later, a diagnosis of multiple sclerosis is made during the clinical course (Geocaris, 1957; Mur, Kumpel, & Dostal, 1966; Mathews, 1979; Schiffer & Babigian, 1984; Stenager & Jensen, 1988) or at autopsy (Parker, 1956).

In 1969 Davison and Bagley investigated 39 cases of schizophrenia in patients with multiple sclerosis from the medical literature and made the contribution that neurological symptoms such as paresthesiae were sometimes incorporated into the paranoid delusional systems (Davison & Bagley, 1969). These authors noted that in their series the psychiatric symptoms appeared early in the disease, tending to cluster around the time of the first appearance of neurological abnormalities (36% of cases) or within 2 years before or after the first appearance of neurological signs (25%). In their series there was no statistical indication that the overall incidence of schizophrenia in patients with multiple sclerosis exceeded chance expectation, however; but they noted that the clustering of the onset of the psychosis around the time of the first appearance of neurological signs suggested that the two disorders were not independent.

Several investigators, using magnetic resonance imaging (MRI), have found that patients with multiple sclerosis and psychiatric symptoms have a greater chance of having lesions in and around the temporal lobe than those patients with multiple sclerosis who are without psychotic symptoms (Honer, Hurwitz, Li, Palmer, & Paty, 1987; Feinstein, du Boulay, & Ron, 1992; Fontaine, 1994). In fact, in one series the results from the initial scans showed 91% of the MRI-detected lesions were found in the cerebral hemispheres in contrast to the 5% localized to the spinal cord; 96% of the hemispheric lesions were less than 1 cm in diameter (Wiebe et al., 1992). When evaluating this work, however, it is important to keep in mind that in one MRI study of multiple sclerosis, MRI abnormalities indistinguishable from multiple sclerosis were also detected among a small number of normal control subjects (Ron & Logsdail, 1989).

In an attempt to cut through controversy about the relationship of multiple sclerosis and schizophrenic symptoms, Skegg (1993) performed a population-based study but was unable to give a definitive answer; the author recommended that a larger population-based study with controls was needed to settle this question. In trying to decide whether an individual has schizophrenia independently of his/her multiple sclerosis, it is relevant to keep in mind that multiple sclerosis is a relatively common disease; for example, a recent estimate showed that there were between 250,000 to 350,000 persons in the United States with physician-diagnosed multiple sclerosis (Anderson et al., 1992).

It is interesting that the question has been raised if there may be a genetic component in some cases of multiple sclerosis. In a twin study, the monozygotic concordance rate was 25.9%, whereas in the dizygotic twins, it was only 2.3% (Ebers et al., 1986).

Thus it is unclear at this time if a patient presenting with schizophrenia could actually have an underlying multiple sclerotic lesion of the central nervous system (CNS) (perhaps in or around the temporal lobe) as a primary etiology; if so, presumably the lesion would be detected by the CNS-imaging studies that are part of the standard initial work-up of any patient presenting with the symptoms of schizophrenia (see Chapter 16). Recently, an immunologic response to a herpes virus (see Chapter 5) has been postulated as a cause of multiple sclerosis (Challoner, 1995).

Because of the intermittent presentation of multiple sclerosis and the frequency of remissions, it has been difficult to evaluate medical therapies for this disease entity. Besides the standard steroid-based therapies, new therapies such as human recombinant interferon beta-1b, Copolymer-1 (Cop 1), IVIg and plasmapheresis hold a yet-to-be-verified promise. At the present time, many investigators feel that no known treatment can significantly alter the progression of multiple sclerosis (Bansil, Cook, & Rohowsky-Kochan, 1995).

MYASTHENIA GRAVIS

Myasthenia gravis is a disorder that appears to be secondary to an antibody-mediated autoimmune reaction directed against the postsynaptic nicotinic acetylcholine receptors of the neuromuscular junction (Drachman, 1994). Antibodies to these receptors are detected in the serum of 85% to 90% of myasthenic patients (Steck, 1990). Other immunological disorders may coexist in such a patient—thymoma, thymic hyperplasia, and lupus erythematosus. Myasthenia gravis is not a completely rare disease; there is a prevalence of 50 to 125 cases per million population.

The relationship of myasthenia gravis and schizophrenia in the same individual is extremely complex to interpret. The symptoms of myasthenia gravis, often dramatic and even life threatening, can produce overwhelming stress on the individual and may resemble those in conversions reactions and in schizophrenia. It should, be noted however, that the psychiatric symptoms often precede the myasthenia, as in the case of paranoid schizophrenia reported by Dorrell (1973).

In a review of the literature of myasthenia and psychiatric disease included in a case report, the incidence of psychosis in myasthenia gravis was described as 12.8% but the incidence of schizophrenia as only 0.035% (Ananth, Davies, & Kerner, 1984). Gittleson and Richardson (1973) described their case of myasthenia gravis and schizophrenia as a "rare combination." Musha, Tanaka, and Ohuti (1993) have proposed what they call "a para-neoplastic autoimmune neuropsychiatric syndrome" (p. 336) based on three patients that they had with thymomas.

There is a single childhood case of schizophrenia in which the psychiatric symptoms improved with the drug treatment (ne-ostigmine bromide) of the myasthenia (Schnackberg & Holmes, 1977) prompting the authors to speculate whether there is a central component as well as a peripheral one in this disease entity. They note that the odds against childhood schizophrenia and myasthenia gravis occurring in a 12-year-old boy are approxi-mately 200,000,000 to 1. This is not a totally clear-cut therapeutic case, however, as the boy also received thyroid supplements. Evidence to support the view of central nervous system involve-ment in myasthenia has been found in reports of antibodies to cholinergic receptors identified in the cerebrospinal fluid (Ful-pius, 1977; Lefvert & Pirskanen, 1977; Vincent, Newsom-Davis, Newton, & Beck, 1983).

In the adult-onset cases in the literature with both disease entities, authors write that the patient's schizophrenic symptoms appear to respond to neuroleptics rather than specific treatment for myasthenia (Gittleson & Richardson, 1973; Burkitt & Khan, 1973). In some cases, however, medications suspected of ex-acerbating or even precipitating myasthenia include some of the classic psychiatric drugs, such as chlorpromazine (McGuillen, Gross, & Jones, 1963) and lithium (Neil, Himmelhock, & Licata, 1976). Care has to be exercised because in most of the cases in the literature, the psychosis preceded the myasthenia (Ananth et al., 1984). Regarding the therapy of the myasthenia gravis part of the symptoms of a patient, with the use of modern immunother-apy nearly all patients are able to lead full, productive lives (Drachman, 1994).

At this time, there is insufficient evidence to prove a central component in myasthenia gravis as suggested by Schnackberg and Holmes (1977). The fact that the symptoms of adult patients respond to neuroleptics rather than immunotherapy argues against a central autoimmune problem. Considering the prevalence of both schizophrenia and myasthenia gravis, there is the likelihood that patients with both diseases in fact have two separate diseases although there is a great deal yet to be learned about both disease entities.

RHEUMATIC FEVER/RHEUMATIC CHOREA

Rheumatic chorea, which occurs in 10%–15% of the patients with rheumatic fever, has sometimes been regarded as a form of "rheumatic encephalitis" (Lees, 1970). Rheumatic fever and rheumatic chorea may occur together or rheumatic chorea may occur in the absence of joint, skin, or cardiac manifestations. Sydenham's chorea, which is a specific form of rheumatic encephalitis in children, has been shown to produce a schizophreniclike disorder in adolescence (Wertheimer, 1963; Casanova et al., 1995). In adults psychotic features are not uncommon, such as bizarre beliefs, ideas of reference, auditory and/or visual hallucinations, delusion of persecution and high excitement (maniacal chorea) (Lewis & Minski, 1955; Lishman, 1987).

The relationship between rheumatic disease and schizophrenia has been the subject of interest to a number of investigators. The symptom of grimacing occurs in both rheumatic chorea and some types of schizophrenia. It was reported that a history of chorea was twice as common in patients with schizophrenia as in patients with manic-depressive psychosis (Guttman, 1936). Breutsch (1940) reported that a small group of schizophrenics had progressive obliterating cerebral endarteritis at autopsy, together with rheumatic valvular disease of the heart, even though none had had a recent attack of rheumatic fever. [Fessel and Solomon have raised the possibility that some of Breutsch's cases may have been examples of systemic lupus erythematosus with psychosis rather than rheumatic fever (Fessel & Solomon, 1960).]

Krauss (1957) investigated 20 patients with schizophrenialike psychoses following various forms of brain insult and found that 6 had had rheumatic fever with cerebral involvement.

Wertheimer (1963) did a very large follow-up study of 663 cases of rheumatic fever and 279 cases of Sydenhan's chorea and found that children first showing rheumatic symptoms during puberty (peak ages of 12 or 13 years) were found to have subsequent "functional" psychiatric records four times as often compared to children with rheumatic disease at other ages or with nonrheumatic disease at any age. The excess of cases was significant at the 0.001 level. The excess was in two clinical presentations—the chronic insidious schizophrenias and the psychiatric disorders with antisocial implications.

Group A streptocococcal infections of the upper respiratory tract are a prerequisite for the development of rheumatic fever. Streptococci are not always found on throat culture at the time of the acute rheumatic fever because the organisms often disappear from the pharynx during the 2–5 week latent period between the upper respiratory infection and the onset of rheumatic fever. How the streptococci located in the throat effect the heart, brain, and other organs is not fully understood but the most widely held theory is that rheumatic fever is an autoimmune disease with streptococcal antigens cross-reacting with human tissue antigens. Because streptococcal infections are treatable, in an ideal world rheumatic fever/chorea and its many complications, including the symptoms of schizophrenia, should be a disease of the past and, in fact, it is now much rarer than before antimicrobial therapy. If rheumatic fever does occur, continuous microbial prophylaxis should be started at once (Behrman & Vaughan, 1983).

SCLERODERMA

Systemic scleroderma is a rare autoimmune disease in which fewer than 20% of the patients have any neurological involvement (Gordon & Silverstein, 1970). There are several patients in the literature with scleroderma and the symptoms of schizophrenia. In one of the patients, the cerebrospinal fluid had no antinuclear antibodies (ANA) so the presence of two separate disease entities (scleroderma and schizophrenia) in this individual is a distinct possibility (Wise & Ginzler, 1975). Regarding another patient, however, the indirect immunoflourescence (IIF) analysis of the cerebrospinal fluid (CSF) showed high titers of ANA and anticentromere antibodies (ACA); by Western blot immunoprecipitation of the CSF, ACA, histon I-, and Ro-antibodies were detected (Muller, Gizycki-Nienhaus, Botschev, & Meurer, 1993). Because of the timing of symptoms and the laboratory results, the authors believe that their patient's psychiatric symptoms were a cerebral manifestation of the systemic scleroderma. A third older patient who had psychotic episodes was a complicated case involving hypothyroidism and immunoglobulin A (IgA) deficiency as well as scleroderma (Schmid & Meltzer, 1994).

SYSTEMIC LUPUS ERYTHEMATOSUS

Systemic lupus erythematosus is a multisystem inflammatory disease with the majority of its manifestations attributable to vascular lesions or more directly to disturbances of connective tissue. In the brain it has been postulated that arteritic lesions and/or cerebritis may lead to the psychiatric symptoms. These disease processes are most likely the result of an autologous autoimmune process although the etiology is far from being completely understood.

Neuropsychiatric manifestations are common (Lim et al., 1988); they may be seen in up to 50% (Bluestein, 1987) to 60% (Lishman, 1987) of the patients. Some clinicians believe that the central nervous system involvement may be more important than renal disease as the major clinical problem with this disorder (Hughes, 1974). Seizures can occur, particularly in the younger age groups; chorea and peripheral neuropathy are seen. Mental disorders are the most common of the neuropsychiatric manifestations; the majority of mental disturbances appear to be transient, often clearing within 6 weeks and usually over by 6 months, though the episodes are often recurrent (Gurland, Ganz, Fleiss, & Zubin, 1972).

The psychiatric features of systemic lupus erythematosis are varied as are other manifestations of the disease. Among the variations, schizophreniclike illnesses can occur (O'Connor, 1959; Fessel & Solomon, 1960; Lief, 1960; Guze, 1967; Hall & Stickney, 1983; Lishman, 1987; Johnstone, MacMillan, & Crow, 1987). The psychiatric illnesses show a tendency to appear in the later stages and to develop during relapse of the disorder. However, central nervous system involvement can sometimes be the primary manifestation, antedating other clear-cut evidence of the disease by months or years (Siekert & Clark, 1955). The percentage of patients who have symptoms of schizophrenia varies according to the series from 5% (Guze, 1967) to 16% (Estes & Christian, 1971). Paranoid delusions and hallucinations may be the most predominant symptoms in a patient leading to a diagnosis of schizophrenia (Guze, 1967). In patients with schizophrenia going into surgery, the presence or absence of lupus is relevant to anticoagulation (Minezaki & Ichikawa, 1993).

Systemic lupus erythematosus is nine times more common in females than males and the mean age of onset is 30 years, although there is a wide range including the adolescent age group. Lupus is an often misdiagnosed disease. The onset is usually insidious with the development of fatigue, malaise, muscle aching, and low-grade intermittent fever. The disease may be acute, subacute, or chronic; progression with repeated exacerbations and remissions is a common pattern.

There are 11 signs or symptoms that help distinguish lupus from other diseases; The American Rheumatism Association reports that a patient must have a minimum of four or more of these symptoms to make the diagnosis. They are (1) butterfly-rash across the cheeks and nose; (2) a discoid rash; (3) photosensitivity: (4) mouth or nose ulcers; (5) usually painless arthritis; (6) psychotic symptoms or convulsions; (7) pericarditis and/or pleurisy; and the following laboratory tests: (8) a positive lupus erythematosus (LE) cell test with repeated false-positive blood tests for syphilis or antibodies to deoxyribose nucleic acid (DNA) and/or antibodies to Sm; (9) excessive protein or cellular casts in the urine; (10) hemolytic anemia, low white count or low platelet count; and (11) antinuclear antibodies (ANA). Anorexia, nausea, vomiting, and abdominal pain also are described. Viseral involvement is most common with the kidneys and severe hypertension has been reported. The pleura, lungs, heart, and pericardium may also become involved. The migratory arthritis develops in the majority of cases. Other skin changes include edema, purpura, and alopecia. Raynaud's phenomenon and retinopathy may develop. Imaging studies of the central nervous system can be of value in cases that present with psychotic symptoms (Gonzalez-Scarano et al., 1979).

Corticosteroids are the mainstay of treatment; before their introduction, this was often a fatal disorder. Sometimes steroids aggravate the psychiatric symptoms, however, causing a steroid psychosis on their own. A psychotic episode due to systemic lupus erythematosus is most likely to occur during an acute exacerbation of the illness, whereas the steroid psychoses are most likely to occur shortly after steroids are instituted or the dose is increased (Hall & Stickney, 1983).

Nevertheless, despite the severe occurrence of acute psychiatric disturbances, the ultimate prognosis can be excellent (Sergent, Lockshin, Klempner, & Lipsky, 1975). Immunosuppressive drugs, such as certain monoclonal antibodies directed against various lymphocyte subpopulations, are an experimental alternative therapy. One extremely unlucky patient started out with paranoid schizophrenia at age 25 years, systemic lupus erythematosus at age 32, followed by hypothyroidism of unknown etiology. Both her positive and negative symptoms of schizophrenia responded to azathioprine, a drug used for autoimmune and inflammatory diseases; the authors reported that the drug acted "on a putative autoimmune arm of schizophrenia" rather than as an anti-lupus or a non-specific steroid effect (Levine et al., 1994, p. 60).

REFERENCES

Achiron, A., Noy, S., Pras, E., Lereya, J., Hermesh, H., & Laor, N. (1994). T-cell subsets in acute psychotic schizophrenic patients. *Biological Psychiatry, 35*, 22–26.

Ananth, J., Davies, R., & Kerner, B. (1984). Single case study: Psychosis associated with thymoma. *Journal of Nervous and Mental Diseases, 172*, 556–558.

Anderson, D. W., Ellenberg, J. H., Leventhal, C. M., Reingold, S. C., Rodriquez, M., & Silbergberg, D. H. (1992). Revised estimate of the prevalence of multiple sclerosis in the United States. *Annals of Neurology, 31*, 333–336.

Bandelow, B., & Muller, P. (1990). Paranoid-halluzininatorische syndrome bei multipler sklerose. *Nervenheilkunde, 9*, 18–21.

Bansil, S., Cook, S. D., & Rohowsky-Kochan, C. (1995). Multiple sclerosis: Immune mechanisms and update on current therapies. *Annals of Neurology, 37* (S1), S87–S101.

Behrman, R. E., & Vaughan, V. C. (1983). *Nelson textbook of pediatrics.* Philadelpia: W. B. Saunders.

Bluestein, H. G. (1987). Neuropsychiatric manifestations of systemic lupus erthythematosis. *New England Journal of Medicine, 317*, 309–311.

Bruetsch, W. L. (1940). Chronic rheumatic brain disease as a possible factor in the causation in some cases of dementia praecox. *American Journal of Psychiatry, 9*, 276–296.

Burkitt, E. A., & Khan, K. (1973). Myasthenia gravis and schizophrenia—A rare combination (Correspondence) *British Journal of Psychiatry, 122*, 735–736.

Casanova, M. F., Crapanzano, K. A., Mannheim, G., & Kruesi, M. (1995). Sydeham's chorea and schizophrenia: A case report. *Schizophrenia Research, 16*, 76–77.

Challoner, P. B. (1995). Plague-associated expression of human herpes virus 6 in multiple sclerosis. *Proceedings of the National Academy of Science USA, 92*, 7440–7444.

Davison, K., & Bagley, C. R. (1969). Schizophrenia-like psychoses associated with organic disorders of the central nervous system: A review of the literature. In R. N. Herrington (Ed.), *British journal of psychiatry special publication No. 4.* Ashford, Kent: Headley Brothers.

DeLisi, L. E., Weber, R. J., & Pert, C. B. (1985). Are there antibodies against the brain in sera from schizophrenic patients? *Biological Psychiatry, 20*, 94–119.

Dorrell, W. (1973). Myasthenia gravis and schizophrenia. *British Journal of Psychiatry, 123*, 249.

Drachman, D. B. (1994). Medical progress: Myasthenia gravis. *New England Journal of Medicine, 330*, 1797–1810.

Ebers, G. C., Bulman, D. E., Sadovnick, A. D. et al. (1986). A population based twin study in multiple sclerosis. *New England Journal of Medicine, 315*, 1638–1642.

Estes, D., & Christian, C. L. (1971). The natural history of systemic lupus erythematosus by prospective analysis. *Medicine, 50*, 85–95.

Feinstein, A., du Boulay, G., & Ron, M. A. (1992). Psychotic illness in multiple sclerosis: A clinical and MRI study. *British Journal of Psychiatry, 161,* 680–685.

Felgenhauer, K. (1990). Psychiatric disorders in the encephalitic form of multiple sclerosis. *Journal of Neurology, 736,* 11–18.

Fessel, W. J., & Solomon, G. F. (1960). Psychosis and systemic lupus erythematosus: A review of the literature and case reports. *California Medicine, 92,* 266–270.

Fontaine, B., Seilhean, D., Tourbah, A., Daumas-Dupont, C., Duyckaerts, C., Benoit, N., Devaux, B., Hauw, J-J., Rancurel, G., & Lyon-Caen, O. (1994). Dementia in two histologically confirmed cases of multiple sclerosis: One case with isolated dementia and one case associated with psychiatric symptoms. *Journal of Neurology, Neurosurgery, and Psychiatry, 57,* 353–359.

Fulpius, B. W., Fontan, A., & Cuenoud, S. (1977). Central nervous system involvement in experimental autoimmune myasthenia gravis. *Lancet, 2,* 350–351.

Ganguli, R., & Rabin, B. S. (1989). Increased serum interleukin 2 receptor concentration in schizophrenic and brain damaged subjects. *Archives of General Psychiatry, 46,* 292.

Ganguli, R., Brar, J. S., Solomon, W., Chengappa, K. N. R., & Rabin, B. S. (1992). Altered interleukin-2 production in schizophrenia: Association between clinical state and auto-antibody production. *Psychiatric Research, 44,* 113–123.

Ganguli, R., Brar, J. S., Chengappa, K. N. R. et al. (1993). Autoimmunity in schizophrenia: A review of recent findings. *Annals of New York Academy of Science, USA, 496,* 676–685.

Geocaris, K. (1957). Psychotic episodes heralding the diagnosis of multiple sclerosis. *Bulletin of the Menninger Clinic, 21,* 107–116.

Gittleson, N. L., & Richardson, T. D. E. (1973). Myasthenia gravis and schizophrenia—a rare combination. *British Journal of Psychiatry, 122,* 343–344.

Gonzalez- Scarano, F., Lisak, R. P., Bilaniuk, L. T., Zimmerman, R. A., Atkins, P.C., & Zweiman, B. (1979). Cranial computed tomography in the diagnosis of systemic lupus erythematosus. *Annals of Neurology, 5,* 158.

Gordon, R. M., & Silverstein, A. (1970). Neurologic manifestations in progressive systemic sclerosis. *Archives of Neurology, 24,* 126–134.

Gurland, B. J., Ganz, V. F., Fleiss, J. L., & Zubin, J. (1972). The study of the psychiatric symptoms of systemic lupus erythematosus: A critical review. *Psychosomatic Medicine, 34,* 199–206.

Guttman, E. (1936). On some constitutional aspects of chorea and its sequelae. *Journal of Neurology and Psychopathology, 17,* 16–26.

Guze, S. B. (1967). The occurrence of psychiatric illness in systemic lupus erythematosus. *American Journal of Psychiatry, 123,* 1562–1570.

Hall, R. C. W., & Stickney, S. K. (1983). Medical and psychiatric features of systemic lupus erythematosus. In R. C. W. Hall (Ed.), *Psychiatric medicine,* vol 1, no. 3. (pp. 287–301). New York: SP Medical & Scientific Books.

Hochtlen-Vollmar, W., & Muller, N. (1992). Autochthone masernantikorperbildung im liquor schizophrener patienten. *Nervenheilkunde, 11,* 339–343.

Honer, W. G., Hurwitz, T., Li, D. K. B., Palmer, M., & Paty, D. W. (1987). Temporal lobe involvement in multiple sclerosis patients with psychiatric disorders. *Archives of Neurology, 44,* 187–190.

Honer, W. G., Kaufmann, C. A., Kleinman, J. E., Casanova, M. F., & Davies, P. (1989). Monoclonal antibodies to study the brain in schizophrenia. *Brain Research, 500,* 379–383.

Hughes, G. V. (1974). Systemic lupus erhthematosus. *British Journal of Hospital Medicine, 12,* 309–319.

Johnstone, E. C., MacMillan, J. F., & Crow, T. J. (1987). The occurrence of organic disease of possible or probable aetiological significance in a population of 268 cases of first episode schizophrenia. *Psychological Medicine, 17,* 371–379.

Kessler, A., & Shinitzky, M. (1993). Platelets from schizophrenic patients bear autoimmune antibodies that inhibit dopamine uptake. *Psychobiology, 21,* 299–306.

Kilidireas, K., Latov, N., Strauss, D. H., Gorig, A. D., Hashim, G. A., Gorman, J. M., & Sadiq, S. A. (1992). Antibodies to the human 60 kDa heat-shock protein in patients with schizophrenia. *Lancet, II,* 340, 569–572.

Kirch, D. G. (1993). Infection and autoimmunity as etiologic factors in schizophrenia: A review and reappraisal. *Schizophrenia Bulletin, 19,* 355–370.

Knight, J., Knight, A., & Ungvari, G. (1992). Can autoimmune mechanisms account for the genetic predisposition to schizophrenia? *British Journal of Psychiatry, 160,* 533–540.

Krauss, S. (1957). Schizophreniform psychosis in the later lives of encephalopathic persons. *Report of the second international congress of psychiatry,* Zurich, vol 2, pp. 100–103.

Lees, F. (1970). *The diagnosis and treatment of disease affecting the nervous system.* London: Staples Press.

Lefvert, A. K., & Pirskanen, R. (1977). Acetylcholine receptor antibodies in cerebrospinal fluid of patients with myasthenia gravis. *Lancet, 2,* 351–352.

Levine, J., Susnovski, M., Handzel, Z. T., Leykin, I., & Shinizky, M. (1994). Treatment of schizophrenia with an immunosuppressant. *Lancet,* *344,* 59–60.

Levy-Soussan, P., Barbouche, R., Poirer, M-F., Galinowski, A., Loo, H., & Avrameas, S. (1994). A preliminary prospective study on natural autoantibodies and the response of untreated schizophrenic patients to neuroleptics. *Biological Psychiatry, 35,* 135–138.

Lewis, A. J., & Minski, L. (1935). Chorea and psychosis. *Lancet, I,* 536–538.

Lief, V. F. (1960). Psychosis associated with lupus erythematosus: A report of three cases. *Archives of General Psychiatry, 3,* 608–611.

Lim, I., Ron, M. A., Ormerod, I. E. et al. (1988). Psychiatric and neurological manifestations in systemic lupus erythematosus. *Quarterly Journal of Medicine, 66,* 27–38.

Lishman, W. A. (1987). *Organic psychiatry: The psychological consequences of cerebral disorder,* second ed. Oxford: Blackwell Scientific.

Maes, M., Meltzer, H. Y., & Bosmans, E. (1994). Immune-inflammatory markers in schizophrenia: Comparison to normal controls and effects of clozapine. *Acta Psychiatrica Scandinavica, 89,* 346–351.

Mathews, W. B. (1979). Multiple sclerosis presenting with acute remitting psychiatric symptoms. *Journal of Neurology, Neurosurgery and Psychiatry, 42,* 859–863.

McAllister, C. G., Rapaport, M. H., Pickar, D., Podruchny, T. A., Christison, G., Alphs, L. D., & Paul, S. M. (1989). Increased numbers of CD+-B Lymphocytes in schizophrenic patients. *Archives of General Psychiatry, 46,* 890–894.

McGuillen, M. P., Gross, M., & Jones, R. J. (1963). Chlorpromazine-induced weakness in myasthenia gravis. *Archives of Neurology, 8,* 286.

Minezaki, T., & Ichikawa, Y. (1993). Surgical experience on patients with serum lupus anticoagulants. A report of two cases. *Tokai Journal of Experimental & Clinical Medicine, 18,* 95–97.

Muller, N., & Ackenheil, M. (1993). Immunoglobulin and albumin contents of cerebrospinal fluid in schizophrenic patients: The relationship to negative symptomatology. *Schizophrenia Research, 4,* 223–227.

Muller, N., Ackenheil, M., Eckstein, R., Hofschuster, E., & Mempel, W. (1987). Reduced suppressor cell activity in psychiatric patients. *Annals of the New York Academy of Science, 496,* 686–690.

Muller, N., Ackenheil, M., Hofschuster, E., Mempel, W., & Eckstein, R. (199- 1). Cellular immunity in schizophrenic patients before and during neuroleptic treatment. *Psychiatry Research, 37,* 147–160.

Muller, N., Gizycki-Nienhaus, B., Botschev, C., & Meurer, M. (1993). Cerebral involvement of scleroderma presenting as schizophrenia-like psychosis. *Schizophrenia Research, 10,* 179–181.

Mur, J., Kumpel, G., & Dostal, S. (1966). An anergic phase of disseminated sclerosis with psychotic course. *Confinia Neurologica, 28,* 37–49.

Musha, M., Tanaka, F., & Ohuti, M. (1993). Psychoses in three cases of myasthenia gravis and thymoma—Proposal of a paraneoplastic autoimmune neuropsychiatric syndrome. *Tohoku Journal of Experimental Medicine, 169,* 335–344.

Neil, J. F., Himmelhock, J. M., & Licata, S. M. (1976). Emergency of myasthenia gravis during treatment with lithium carbonate. *Archives of General Psychiatry, 33,* 1090–1092.

Noy, S., Achiron, A., & Laor, N. (1994). Schiozphrenia and autoimmunity—a possible etiological mechanism? *Neuropsychobiology, 30,* 157–159.

O'Conner, J. F. (1959). Psychoses associated with systemic lupus erythematosus. *Annals of Internal Medicine, 51,* 526–536.

Ormerod, I. E. C., Miller, D. H., McDonald, W. I., du Boulay, G. H., Rudge, P., Kendall, B. F., Moseley, I. F., Johnson, G., Tofts, P. S., Halliday, A. M., Bronstem, A. M., Scaravilli, F., Harding, A. E., Barnes, D., & Zilkha, K. J. (1987). The role of NMR imaging in the assessment of multiple sclerosis and isolated neurological lesions. *Brain, 110,* 1579–1616.

Pandey, R. S., Gupta, A. K., & Chaturvedi, U. C. (1981). Autoimmune model of schizophrenia with special reference to antibrain antibodies. *Biological Psychiatry, 16,* 1123–1136.

Parker, N. (1956). Disseminated sclerosis presenting as schizophrenia. *Medical Journal of Australia, 1,* 405–407.

Piessiur-Strelow, B., Power, S., & Felgenhauer, K. (1988). Paranoid-halluzinatorische psychose als manifestation einer multiplen sklerose. *Nervenarzt, 59,* 621–623.

Rapaport, M. H., McAllister, C. G., Pickar, D., Nelson, D. L., & Paul, S. M. (1989). Elevated levels of soluable interleukin 2 receptors in schizophrenia. *Archives of General Psychiatry, 46,* 291–292.

Ron, M. A., & Logsdail, S. J. (1989). Psychiatric morbidity in multiple sclerosis: A clincial and MRI study. *Psychological Medicine, 19,* 887–895.

Rose, N. R. (1991). Characteristics of autoimmune disease. *Journal of Investigative Dermatology, 96,* 87S.

Sasaki, T., Nanko, S., Fukuda, R., Kawate, T., Kunugi, H., & Kazamatsuri, H. (1994). Changes of immunological functions after acute exacerbation in schizophrenia. *Biological Psychiatry, 35,* 173–178.

Schiffer, R. B., & Babigian, H. M. (1984). Behavioral disorders in multiple sclerosis, temporal lobe epilepsy and amyotrophic lateral sclerosis: An epidemiologic study. *Archives of Neurology, 41*, 1067–1069.

Schmid, A. H., & Meltzer, B. R. (1994). Psychotic episodes in an elderly woman with scleroderma, IgA deficiency and hypothyroidism. *Journal of Geriatric Psychiatry and Neurology, 7*, 93–98.

Schnackenberg, R. C., & Holmes, G. (1977). Co-exisiting childhood schizophrenia and myasthenia treated successfully with neostigmine bromide. *American Journal of Psychiatry, 134*, 1025.

Sergent, J. S., Lockshin, M. D., Klempner, M. S., & Lipsky, B. A. (1975). Central nervous system disease in systemic lupus erythematosus. *American Journal of Medicine, 58*, 644.

Shima, S., Yano, K., Sugiura, M., & Tokunaga, Y. (1991). Anticerebral antibodies in functional psychoses. *Biological Psychiatry, 29*, 322–328.

Siekert, R. G., & Clark, E. C. (1955). Neurological signs and symptoms as early manifestations of systemic lupus erythematosus. *Neurology, 5*, 84–88.

Skegg, K. (1993). Multiple sclerosis presenting as a pure psychiatric disorder. *Psychological Medicine, 23*, 909–914.

Song, Y-H., Conner, E. L., Muir, A., She, J. X., Zorovich, B., Derovanesian, D., & Maclaren, N. (1994). Autoantibody epitope mapping of the 21-hydroxlase antigen in autoimmune Addison's disease. *Journal of Clinical Endocrinology and Metabolism, 78*, 1108–1112.

Steck, A. J. (1990). Antibodies in the neurology clinic. *Neurology, 40*, 1489–1492.

Stenager, F. & Jensen, K. (1988). Multiple sclerosis: Correlation of psychatric admissions to onset of initial symptoms. *Acta Neurologica Scandinavica, 77*, 414–417.

Vincent, A., Newsom-Davis, J., Newton, P., & Beck, N. (1983). Acetylcholine receptor antibody and clincial response to thymectomy in myasthenia gravis. *Neurology, 33*, 1276–1282.

Wertheimer, N. M. (1963). A psychiatric follow-up of children with rheumatic fever and other chronic diseases. *Journal of Chronic Diseases, 16*, 223.

Wiebe, S., Lee, D. H., Karlik, S. J., Hopkins, M., Vandervoort, M. K., Wong, C. J., Hewitt, L., Rice, G. P. A., Ebers, G.C., & Noseworthy, J. H. (1992). Serial cranial and spinal cord magnetic resonance imaging in multiple sclerosis. *Annals of Neurology, 32*, 643–650.

Wise, T., & Ginzler, E. M. (1975). Scleroderma cerebritis, an unusual manifestation of progressive system sclerosis. *Diseases of the Nervous System, 36*, 60–62.

Yannitsi, S. G., Manoussakis, M. N., Mavridis, A. K., Tzioufas, A. G., Loukas, S. B., Plataris, G. K., Liakos, A. D., & Moutsopoulos, H. M. (1990). Factors related to the presence of autoantibodies in patients with chronic mental disorders. *Biological Psychiatry, 27,* 747–756.

Zarranz, J. J., Antiguedad, A. R., & Barcena, J. (1995). Psychotic crisis symptomatic of an outbreak of multiple sclerosis. [Spanish] *Neurologica, 10,* 205–208.

Chapter 10

The Chromosomes and
Their Genes

The ability to tease out chromosomes in human cells was discovered in the late 1950s and was followed shortly thereafter by the cracking of the genetic code. It then became clear that it was just a matter of time until the location of each gene was found on one of the chromosomes. In addition, work began on the elucidation of the mechanisms of protein synthesis directed by genes.

As often happens when science makes giant steps, principles found in earlier studies (i.e, that a single gene may determine a single trait regarding the color of flowers) were extrapolated over to a number of other fields. The possibility that even human behavior might have a genetic basis that could be demonstrated was considered. Enthusiasm became so great that lectures and papers were given entitled "From Gene to Behavior" (Benzer, 1971) and "The Genetics of Behavior" (Brenner, 1973).

However investigators of behavior in simple organisms, such as a fruit fly, began to discover that a multitude of genes, some acting quite subtly, contributed to even the most ritualistic of behaviors (Hall, 1994). As Greenspan points out, there is every reason to believe that the genetic influences on behavior will be at least as complicated in people as fruit flies; hence the notion of many, multipurpose genes making small contributions is likely to apply (Greenspan, 1995). With humans, it is a truly monumental task to try to sort out the effects on behavior of the genetic substrate interacting with both child rearing and culture.

The job ahead is very complex. In the past, Mendelian concepts provided the framework of genetic analysis. For example, in genetic diseases of the central nervous system in general, dominant diseases appear to be in the majority (Rosenberg, 1986). In these dominant diseases of the brain, however, often there is no known primary metabolic clue or primary storage product to indicate a potential molecular basis of the disease. (Fuller details of some of these dominant diseases as they relate to schizophrenia may be found in Chapter 11.) In contrast, in the recessive diseases of the brain—such as the mucopolysaccharidoses, the leukodystrophies, the aminoacidopathies, and the gangliosidoses—are all associated with the accumulation of a metabolite related to a well-established biochemical pathway (Rosenberg, 1981). (Fuller details of some of these recessive diseases as they relate to schizophrenia may be found in Chapter 6.)

This recent generation's work in molecular genetics has had a major impact on the study of diseases of the brain; for example, non-Mendelian forms of inheritance have now emerged; concepts of pathogenesis are on a more secure footing; and novel treatments are being explored (Rowland, 1992). Although what is called a Mendelian latent structure model has been hypothesized that predicts essential genetic homogeneity for schizophrenia (Levy, Holzman, Matthysse, & Mendell, 1993), in fact, familial schizophrenia is a complex phenotype that often fails to show Mendelian patterns of segregation. In some families, the pattern might be explained by genes with triplet repeats (Ross et al., 1993) including anticipation (Bassett & Honer, 1994) and/or imprinting; even then, a number of families cannot be squeezed into any established genetic pattern (Asherson et al., 1994).

Studies of family members have raised many questions. To quote only one paper from the very large field of neuropsychology, Cannon et al. (1994) have shown a similar spectrum of disease in some families with schizophrenic individuals. This paper reported that siblings of schizophrenics have a tendency toward certain neuropsychological deficiencies compared to controls. The pattern was even more marked in the siblings with a diagnosis of schizotypical personality (Cannon et al., 1994). What could account for such often subtle findings? One possibility among many is the pattern of expansion of trinucleotide repeats, now recognized as a major cause of many familial diseases of the central nervous system (La Spada, Paulson, & Fischbeck, 1994).

Such families have a spectrum of disease within the family with mildly affected members having a slight expansion of trinucleotide repeats (premutations), whereas the clinically impaired members of the families have the classical symptoms accompanied by quite long expansions of the trinucleotide repeats (full mutation). In some of these trinucleotide repeat disorders, the number of repeats in the mutated allele is inversely correlated with age at disease onset (Goldfarb et al., 1996). In one of the trinucleotide repeat expansion disorders so far identified that occasionally presents with schizophreniclike symptoms (Huntington's disease, see chromosome 4), it is interesting that even in the parents and siblings of the families of the apparently sporatic (nonfamilial) cases, a premutation has been identified (Davis et al., 1994).

That familial schizophrenia, which is the tendency of schizophrenia to occur in other members of the patient's family, exists is no longer disputed. It has long been documented. There has been a long history of discussion over whether this phenomenon reflected genetic (Gottesman, 1991) or environmental factors (Murray, Lewis, & Reveley, 1985) in these families. It has been argued that although the evidence for a genetic contribution to schizophrenia is now strong, environmental factors must play a role that will eventually be identified, as the pattern of inheritance in many families is so complex. Others argue that stochastic events affecting gene expression or structure, rather than environmental factors per se, will account for the complex pattern of inheritance (McGuffin, Asherson, Owen, & Farmer, 1994).

Historically, one way of trying to tease out whether genetic factors were relevant to schizophrenia was the adoption strategy studies. The ground-breaking Copenhagen study by Kety, Rosenthal, Wender, Schulsinger, and Jacobsen (1975) has now been extended to include the population of the rest of Denmark. In these combined studies of the Danish population, the authors found that "of adoptees with chronic schizophrenia, that disorder was found exclusively in their biological relatives and its prevalence overall was 10 times greater than that in the biological relatives of controls" (p. 442) (Kety et al., 1994; Kendler, Gruenberg, & Kinney, 1994). This finding adds additional weight to other studies addressing this problem (Heston, 1966; Karlsson, 1970; Tienari, 1991).

In this book, we have taken the evidence suggesting the genetic etiology of schizophrenia in many afflicted families and divided it into several chapters. In this chapter, the role of possible errors as evidenced by chromosomal and molecular biological laboratory methods is reviewed. In Chapter 6, metabolic diseases caused by known errors in a well-established metabolic pathway are featured. (The molecular biology for these enzyme diseases, when known, is briefly reviewed in this chapter.) Another chapter of other inherited diseases of less certain origin (Chapter 11) is also included.

Of course there are limitations to the soundest epidemiological reports of genetic inheritance predisposing to schizophrenia. Because there also are infectious, toxic, traumatic, space-occupying, and so many other factors that can apply in any individual case, the genetic cases remain a subgroup within the spectrum of schizophrenia. Keeping nongenetic factors in mind might help explain the fascinating studies by Torrey, Bowler, Taylor, and Gottresman (1994) that there could be identical twin studies where the twins, sharing the same genetic material, are discordant for schizophrenia. There is speculation at this time, however, that genetic etiologies account for quite a large subgroup of idiopathic schizophrenia.

A number of initial deoxyribose nucleic acid (DNA) studies in families with multiple members with schizophrenia did not produce evidence of the specific genes in these families underlying the psychiatric symptoms, (Aschauer et al., 1990; Wang, Black, Andreason, & Crowe, 1994). Previous reports of linkage for schizophrenia, originally greeted with excitement, so far have not been confirmed (Cloninger, 1994). Two recent genome scans published in 1994 failed to reveal any significant evidence of linkage (Coon et al., 1994; Barr et al., 1994).

In 1995, however, a large study investigating 186 multiplex schizophrenia families from Ireland found a susceptibility locus for schizophrenia on chromosome 6 (6p22-25) (Wang et al., 1995). At the time of publication of this book, there are reports totaling 430 families from different populations and 113 schizophrenics with unaffected parents from China that are focusing researchers on the 6p21–24 region, which may contain hundreds of genes (Peltomen, 1995). In view of a decade of linkage studies in schizophrenia that were unproductive, all reports await further confirmation.

Techniques such as locating unstable DNA sequences with tandem repeats or teasing out evidence of genomic imprinting may eventually be quite helpful in understanding the predisposition to schizophrenia that exists within some of the families. Genetic heterogeneity is highly likely; the answers may differ from one family to another. As you read this, there is much research going on in this arena.

It is already known that subgroups of patients with established genetic disease entities that usually present with neurological signs can sometimes present instead with symptoms diagnosed as schizophrenia by the initial examining clinician. In some genetic illnesses that present primarily in childhood, a small portion of the patients present instead in adult life; these older patients are the ones most likely to be diagnosed as schizophrenic. Examples described in Chapter 6 and in this chapter include the adult form of metachromatic leukodystrophy and the adult form of adrenoleukodystrophy—X-linked (adrenomyeloneuropathy).

Meanwhile what is one to make of the individual patients with schizophrenia who have been reported in the medical literature who have easy-to-spot chromosomal aberrations? Because both schizophrenia and chromosomal aberrations are relatively frequent in a human population, the chance of coincidental findings is a distinct probability in any individual person. Each case has to be evaluated on its own merits, however, in light of chromosomal studies in family members and also compared to other patients with identical or similar chromosomal aberrations. At this time, the relevance to brain dysfunction of these individual chromosomal sightings in persons with schizophrenia generally remains to be determined.

CHROMOSOME 1

A large Scottish pedigee has been described with a major mental illness, classified as a schizoaffective disorder, which was seen to segregate with a balanced translocation, t(1:11)(q43;q21)—see details of this family under chromosome 11. A patient with a childhood onset of schizophrenia who met DSM-III-R (APA, 1987) criteria has been reported with a presumably balanced rearrangement between chromosomes 1 and 7— 46,XY,t(1;7)(p22,q22) (Gordon, Krasnewich, White, Lenane, & Rapoport, 1994). However, three other nonschizophrenic members of the family carried the translocation which could mean that the cytogenetic abnormality was unrelated to the patient's diagnosis. Yet it was noted that the cytogenetically affected relatives did have other significant psychopathology, such as drug/ alcohol abuse and language delay.

Methylenetetrahydrofolate Reductase Deficiency (MTHFR Deficiency)

The human gene for methylenetetrahydrofolate reductase (MTHFR) has been localized to chromosome 1p36.3 (Goyette et al., 1994). A common mutation may be responsible for the genetic risk factor for vascular disease (Frosst et al., 1995). Also, novel mutations have been found in this gene (Goyette, Frosst, Rosenblatt, & Rozen, 1995) (see Chapter 6).

CHROMOSOME 2

A balanced translocation 2;18 (q21;q23) has been reported in a family with schizophrenic members in two generations (Genest, Dumas, & Genest, 1976). There were no physical abnormalities in the male proband, who also suffered from alcoholism. His wife and 3 out of 4 of the children were normal. One of the daughters had a major behavioral disturbance.

CHROMOSOME 3

Based on a sample of 57 families, 3p26-p24 was located as a potential site of susceptibility genes for schizophrenia (Pulver et al., 1995). A pericentric inversion of chromosome 3 (karyotype: inv(3) (p11;q11)QFQ) has been described on one of the chromosome 3s of a male with schizophrenia (Korner et al., 1993). A similar pericentric inversion on both chromosome 3s has been found in a female suffering from a bipolar affective disorder (Korner et al., 1993).

CHROMOSOME 4

Huntington's Disease
(Also Known As Huntington's Chorea)

After a decade-long collaborative effort to identify the genetic basis of Huntington's disease also known as Huntington's chorea, a novel 4p16.3 gene was found on chromosome 4 called the IT15 gene (Huntington's Disease Collaborative Research Group, 1993). Huntington's disease does not appear to have genetic heterogeneity; all of Huntington's disease seems to be the same worldwide; all families so far studied have been mapped to the same location on chromsome 4 (Conneally et al., 1989).

The gene has an expanded trinucleotide repeat sequence $(CAG)_n$. The run of CAGs in the gene encodes a polyglutamine tract. The length of the polyglutamine tract is 37 to 121 repeats in individuals with Huntington's disease. (The length in normal individuals is 11 to 34 repeats.) It is most likely that the trinucleotide repeat expansion causes the symptoms of Huntington's disease by its effect, either at the messenger ribose nucleic acid (mRNA) or protein level, on the expression and/or structure of the protein product of the IT15 gene named "huntingtin"; a novel protein with as yet no known function (Trottier et al., 1995) although researchers are studying HAP1, GAPDH, and other proteins that bind to it (Burke et al., 1996).

The expanded trinucleotide repeats are unstable. The largest trinucleotide repeat segments were found in juvenile cases (Huntington's Disease Collaborative Research Group, 1933). Thus, in some families with Huntington's disease, the phenomenon of anticipation—worsening of disease phenotype over successive generations—exists and may be associated with increasing expansion size of the trinucleotide repeat sequence (Andrew et al., 1993; Duyao et al., 1993; Snell et al., 1993; Novelletto et al., 1994). There also may be evidence of imprinting of the gene in a very small (less than 6%) number of the families studied so far. The gene has been identified in both familial and sporadic cases of Huntington's disease. In some sporadic cases, including some that were classified as "clinically doubtful," the presence of DNA studies made the specific diagnosis possible (Davis et al., 1994).

Huntington's disease is generally thought to occur with a prevalence of 4 cases per 100,000 (Brewis, Poskanzer, Rolland, & Miller, 1966) although in some areas (south Wales) it has been reported at twice that frequency (MacMillan & Harper, 1991). It usually presents with choreiform movements combined with dementia. However, psychotic features can appear early in the course of the disease in some patients and may proceed with the onset of the chorea and dementia. In fact, Bolt (1970) has described patients with a diagnosis of schizophrenia or paranoid psychosis carried throughout the individual's life and never revised; the diagnosis of Huntington's disease in this patient group was made on autopsy. Of 199 cases of Huntington's chorea reported from a study in Norway, 20% were discharged from their first admission to a psychiatric hospital with a diagnosis of schizophrenia (Saugstad & Odegard, 1986).

The schizophrenic picture of delusions of persecution with religiosity and sometimes grandiosity may occur early in the course of the disease process (Streletski, 1961). McHugh and Folstein (1975), who prefer the term "delusional-hallucinatory state" to describe these initial symptoms, nevertheless make this point: The terms given to these disorders and issues of what they resemble are of less practical importance than the fact that they can be hard to distinguish from the standard "functional psychosis" and can appear before any choreic movements signal the diagnosis (McHugh & Folstein, 1975).

The age of presentation of the disease process can vary widely even within members of the same family. If the disease presents at an earlier age in a succeeding generation (the phenomenon of anticipation), genetic testing may show an ever-increasing expansion of the trinucleotide sequence in patients with the earliest ages of onset (Duyao et al., 1993). There is evidence that the disease follows a more severe course when the onset is early; psychiatric disturbances in particular become more prominent as a premonitory feature (Lishman, 1987).

For patients presenting with psychiatric symptoms, McHugh and Folstein (1981) describe a typical progression as follows: the patient is overwhelmed by a vague impression of an uncanny change in reality that becomes laden with meaning of an uncertain nature. Delusions and hallucinations distill from this, often welling up suddenly and lasting for several months. These disturbances can be present for some time before the chorea or intellectual impairment become apparent. Paranoid developments may be the earliest stage accompanied by depression and anxiety; in other cases a florid schizophrenic illness may be the presenting symptom: Treatment with neuroleptics can lead to considerable improvement.

Diagnosis of Huntington's disease may be made throughout the lifespan by several techniques. The older approach used imaging techniques that showed a marked dilation of the ventricular system, especially the frontal horns combined with a striking atrophy of the caudate nuclei, which may be represented only by a rim of tissue along the ventrolateral edge of the dilated anterior horns. The more recent molecular biological approach involves DNA testing for the gene for Huntington's disease as described previously. For individuals "at risk" for Huntinton's disease, this new approach offers accurate preclinical testing. (For more information on Huntington's disease including its more classical presentations, see Chapter 11.)

CHROMOSOME 5

A man with a paranoid psychosis was identified in a survey of male patients in a psychiatric hospital (Axelsson & Wahlström, 1984). Also, the diagnosis of schizophrenia has been associated with trisomy of part of the long arm of the fifth chromosome in two related individuals; both showed trisomy for the 5q11.2-5q13.3 segment (Basset et al., 1988, p. 323).

When schizophrenics are studied as a single large group, linkage analysis has suggested that genes on chromosome 5 might somehow be involved in schizophrenia (Byerley et al., 1989). Such a finding raises the possibility that there may be genetic disease entities within schizophrenia with such a high frequency that, even mixing all the diseases that are inherited into one group, the disease(s) with a gene loci on chromosome 5 is so numerous as to effect overall genetic linkage analysis. In another careful review of the literature, 5q was identified as a "possibly relevant" chromosomal region for further study (Bassett, 1992). For example, linkage between two chromosome markers on the long arm of chromosome 5 and the presence of schizophrenia in five Icelandic and two English families have been reported (Sherrington et al., 1988). Studies of the location of these markers in other families with schizophrenia failed to find evidence for linkage, however (Kennedy et al., 1988; St Clair et al., 1989; Detera-Wadleigh et al., 1989; Aschauer et al., 1990). Linkage to the short arm of chromosome 5 (5p11.1-13.1) in one large pedigree has recently been described (Shihabuddin, Silverman, Buchsbaum, Metzger, & Davis, 1995).

CHROMOSOME 6

A weak association has been suggested for paranoid schizophrenia in seven of nine studies with the A9 allele of human leukocyte antigen (HLA), yielding a combined relative risk of 1.6, which could account for about 1% of the liability to the disorder (McGuffin & Stuart, 1986). In a study of 186 Irish multiplex families, Wang et al. (1995) have reported a susceptibility locus for schizophrenia on chromosome 6p22–25 (Wang et al., 1995). Since then, four other studies have reported locus heterogeneity for schizophrenia in the 6p21–24 area from different populations (Straub et al., 1995; Moises et al., 1995; Schwab et al., 1995; Antonarakis et al., 1995). Taken together, they describe results that at last provide firm evidence for one important locus that, according to Peltonen (1995), when perturbed in some way, predisposes carriers to schizophrenia.

CHROMOSOME 7

A chromosomal survey of male patients in maximum security hospitals lead to the finding of a man with a balanced transloca-

tion (7p12;8p23). He had a diagnosis of schizophrenia and antisocial behavior (Price et al., 1976). He had no physical abnormalities.
A boy with childhood-onset schizophrenia has been reported with
46,XY,t(1;7)(p22;q22) (Gordon et al., 1994). For further discussion,
see the Chromosome 1 heading.

CHROMOSOME 8

In addition to the patient described above with a balanced translocation (7p12;8p23), a woman with mosaic trisomy 8 (47,XX,8+) and
schizophrenia has been found. The patient also had a diagnosis of
"organic brain syndrome" and had multiple physical abnormalities (Sperber, 1975). Based on a sample of 57 families, 8p22-p24
was identified as a potential site of suspectibility genes for schizophrenia (Pulver et al., 1995).

CHROMOSOME 9

A woman with schizophrenia and a pericentric inversion of chromosome 9 has been reported (Nanko, 1993). A man with a paranoid psychosis and a chromosomal karyotype that included
inverted segments (9p11-9q11 or 9p11-9q12 or 9p11-9q13) was
found in a survey of male patients in a maximum security hospital
(Axelsson & Wahlström, 1984).

One of the genes causing tuberous sclerosis (TSC 1 gene)
is likely to be located on chromosome 9q34 but had not been
specifically identified as this book goes to press. For more on
tuberous sclerosis, see the chromosome 16 heading.

CHROMOSOME 10

A man with a paranoid psychosis and a chromosomal karyotype
that included an inverted segment (10p12-10q21) was found in a
survey of male patients in a maximum security hospital (Axelsson & Wahlström, 1984).

CHROMOSOME 11

The long arm of the eleventh chromosome has a number of associations with disease entities where schizophrenia can present. This has stimulated a lot of research on the long arm of this chromosome.

Acute Intermittent Porphyria

For example, the gene for porphobilinogen deaminase (PBGD) is located on the long arm of chromsome 11 near the breakpoint identified in the translocations reported in three separate families that cosegregated for schizophrenialike illnesses (Llewellyn et al., 1987) (see below). A population association between a restriction fragment length polymorphm allele at the PBGD locus and idiopathic schizophrenia has been reported (Sanders, Hamilton, Fann, & Patel, 1991). The mutation in PBGD causes acute intermittent porphyria, an autosomal dominant disease sometimes characterized by schizophreniclike symptoms (Lee et al., 1988). (For full details of this illness, see Chapter 6.)

Oculocutaneous Albinism

The gene for tyrosinase has been located on the long arm of chromosome 11; this gene conceivably might be implicated in the documented cases of schizophrenia in families with albino individuals (Baron, 1976; Clarke & Buckley, 1989). Although the overwhelming number of albino individuals do not suffer from psychiatric problems, in the pedigree reported by Baron (1976), five of the six albino individuals suffered from schizophrenia. The relevance of these sporadic clinical reports is unknown.

Neural Cell Adhesion Molecule

A neurodevelopmental etiology to schizophrenia has been proposed (see Chapter 12). Another candidate gene located on the long arm of chromosome 11 is the neural cell adhesion molecule

(NCAM) and there is speculation that an error in the application of this molecule regarding neural migration during the second trimester of pregnancy may be responsible for some cases of schizophrenia.

Other Studies Related to the Long Arm of Chromosome 11

The gene for the dopamine D2 receptor has also mapped to chromosome 11q (Seeman, Niznik, Guan, Booth, & Ulpian, 1989). In a study of 156 Japanese patients with schizophrenia compared to controls, Arinami et al. (1994) report they found an excess of a variant of the D2 gene in which cysteine replaces serine in the aminoacid sequence of the third intracytoplasmic loop of the receptor protein (Cys311). The authors found three schizophrenic patients homozygous and 11 schizophrenic patients heterozygous for Cys311; these patients, mostly classified either catatonic or paranoid, had an earlier age of onset of schizophrenia than of those without the variant.

In a large Scottish pedigree, a balanced translocation t(1:11)(q43,q21) was found to cosegregate tightly with a major mental illness, classifiable as a schizoaffective disorder (St. Clair et al., 1990). Two other, smaller families have been described with less clear-cut cosegregation of mental illness with two independent chromosome 11 q translocations—one with chromosome 9 (Smith et al., 1989) and one with chromosome 6 (Holland & Gosden, 1990). Although the breakpoints in the two smaller families have not yet been clearly defined, the existence of two other families with both mentally ill members and with 11 q translocations strengthened interest in the Scottish family. Using material from the Scottish family, genes for antigens mapped on either side of the 11q breakpoint have been reported, but the theoretical SCZD2 gene has yet to located (Fletcher et al., 1993). However, a study by Kalsi et al. (1995) has questioned both the D_2 receptor and the 11q translation sites studies.

A study of 12 multiplex pedigrees looking for a susceptibility locus for schizophrenia on chromosome 11q also was unsuccessful to date. The authors had tested more than 130 centimorgans on the q arm of chromosome 11 encompassing the reported translocation regions using both dominant and recessive models (Wang, Black, Andreasen, & Crowe, 1993). A study of 24 families multiply affected with schizophrenia using 12 polymorphic markers from the long arm of chromosome 11 also was unrevealing (Gill et al., 1993).

CHROMOSOME 12

Dentatorubal-Pallidoluysian Atrophy

The gene for hereditary dentatorubal-pallidoluysian atrophy (DRPLA), an autosomal dominant neurodegenerative disorder, has recently been found on chromosome 12p. It is identified as an unstable expansion of CAG repeats in the brain transcript B37. Normal chromosomes had 7–34 repeats, whereas DRPLA was associated with 49–75 repeats (Koide et al., 1994; Nagafuchi et al., 1994).

The clinical presentation of DRPLA is characterized by a varying combination of progressive myoclonus, epilepsy, ataxia, choreoathetosis, and dementia. There is a marked clinical heterogeneity of this condition, however. For example, Koide et al. (1994) reported that 2 out of the 22 patients that he studied had been diagnosed by psychiatrists as schizophrenic (Koide et al., 1994). These two patients had 57 repeats, near the lower end of the abnormal range. Because of the Koide report from Japan, Rubinsztein et al. (1994) examined 55 unrelated patients with schizophrenia from the USA, UK, and Italy for abnormal expansion of the CAG repeats in the brain transcipt B37, but did not identify any abnormal expansions of the B37 gene in the population that they studied. Warner et al. (1995) reported the disease in four European families with two members diagnosed as psychotic, however.

Neurotrophin-3

Because there are reports of atrophic or dystrophic changes without gliosis reported in the brains of patients with schizophrenia (see Chapter 12), there is a possibility of errors in neuronal migration during gestation; this has led to studies of the neuro-trophins responsible for development of the nervous system, such as the neural cell adhesion molecule discussed under chromosome 11. Neurotrophin-3 (NT-3) is another neurotrophin of importance for proliferation, migration, and differentiation of neural precursors in humans. The NT-3 gene has been assigned to the chromosomal region of 12p13 (Ozcelik, Rosenthal, & Francke, 1991).

A study of the allelic distribution of dinucleotide repeat polymorphism at the NT-3 gene locus in 70 patients with schizophrenia and 70 controls showed a significant difference at allele A3. Individuals either homozygous or heterozygous for the allele A3 had a 2.4-fold increased risk of schizophrenia (Nanko et al., 1994). Because the NT-3 polymorphism itself is not the direct sequence affecting protein structure or expression, this raises the question of whether there is another intragenic polymorphism on an allele 3 background that confers susceptibility to schizophrenia. This area of research will be followed with great interest.

CHROMOSOME 13

Wilson's Disease

The locus for Wilson's disease, an autosomal-recessive disorder of copper metabolism (see Chapter 6 for a full description), has been found on the long arm of chromosome 13—13(q14 band) (Bowcock et al., 1988). Several polymorphic DNA markers found to be closely linked to the locus can now be used for prenatal diagnosis (Cossu et al., 1992). The gene has been mapped to chromosome 13q14.3 (Petrukhin et al., 1993).

Robertsonian Translocations

Three patients with Robertsonian translocations on the 13th chromosome have been reported who have schizophrenia; in all three cases it was a translocation between the 13th and the 14th chromosome. A child with bilateral colobama of the iris had a diagnosis of schizophrenia and borderline mental retardation as well as a Robertsonian balanced translocation (13;14) (Escobar, 1976); it is not clear if such a young person would have been given a diagnosis of schizophrenia today. However two male adults with schizophrenia also have showed a Robertsonian translocation of chromosomes 13 and 14 (karyotype: 45, XY, t(13q14q)QFQ) (Korner et al., 1993) (13;14) (Price et al., 1976). The latter patient was detected in a survey of maximum security hospital patients. It should be noted that a translocation between the 13th and the 14th chromosome is the most common translocation found in a general population.

CHROMOSOME 14

Porphyria Variegata

One of the porphyrias that present with neuropsychiatric symptoms is porphyria variegata. The positional mapping of the error in the enzyme, protoporphyrinogen oxidase, is found on the long arm of the 14th chromsomes—14q32.1.

CHROMOSOME 15

GM2 Gangliosidosis

The location of the genetic defect that causes GM2 gangliosidosis is on the long arm of the 15th chromosome (15q22-15q25.1). GM2 in the adult form is a very rare disorder in which a deficiency of hexosaminidase A leads to an accumulation of lysosomal GM2 gangliosides. The mutation that results in the complete absence of the enzyme gives rise to the infantile Tay-Sachs disease. A residual level of hexosaminidase A results in juvenile and adult-onset gangliosidoses (Navon, 1991). It has been shown that the fibroblasts of the adult patients synthesize the alpha-subunit precursor but not the mature enzyme. The late-onset forms are due to point mutations within the protein coding region, which generate stable mRNA. (For further information on GM2 gangliosidosis, see Chapter 6.)

CHROMOSOME 16

Tuberous Sclerosis

There are believed to be at least two genes responsible for tuberous sclerosis. The TSC 2 gene has been isolated on chromsome 16. It is a large gene and currently work is focused on finding the mutations that may occur on TSC2. The TSC 1 gene is located on the long arm of chromsome 9 but has not yet been fully characterized. Both TSC genes are deletions.

The classic clinical triad of tuberous sclerosis is epilepsy, adenoma sebecum, and mental deficiency. According to a study at the Mayo Clinic, however, up to one-third of the patients may have normal intelligence (Gomez, 1979) and, when this group of intellectually normal patients develop psychiatric symptoms, occasionally they receive the diagnosis of chronic schizophrenia. Zlotlow and Kleiner (1965) described a 34-year-old regarded as a chronic schizophrenic, often incontinent, speaking incoherently, and with long episodes of mutism. In this individual, periods of irritable excitement alternated with catatonic stupor. Lishman (1987) reviewed the medical literature pointing out that psychotic features were common in individuals with tuberous sclerosis. He noted that some institutionalized patients with tuberous sclerosis received a diagnosis of a "primitive form of catatonic schizophrenia" (Lishman, 1987, p. 601). (For more detailed discussion of tuberous sclerosis, see Chapter 11.)

CHROMOSOME 18

A balanced translocation of chromosomes 2;18 (q21;q23) has been reported in two generations of a family with schizophrenia (Genes, Dumas, & Genest, 1976). In an individual with catatonic schizophrenia, deafness, and multiple physical abnormalities, a deleted segment of the short arm of the 18th chromosome (18p-) has been found (Ayraud et al., 1969). The long arm of the 18th chromosome (18q) has also been implicated in a patient with a schizophreniclike episode (Lejeune, 1977) as has a ring chromosome r(18) (Krag-Olsen, Hoeg Brask, Jacobsen, & Nielsen, 1981).

In a review of the literature, 18q was identified as a "possibly relevant" chromosomal region for further investigation in schizophrenia (Bassett, 1992) although a recent search was negative (Fang et al., 1995).

CHROMOSOME 19

When schizophrenics are studied as a single large group, genetic linkage analysis raised the question of whether the genes on chromosome 19 might be involved (Byerley et al., 1989). In a review of the literature, 19p was identified as a "possibly relevant" chromosomal region for further investigation in schizophrenia (Bassett, 1992).

CHROMOSOME 21

Pyridoxine Responsive and Nonresponsive Homocystinuria

One of the enzymes, cystathionine beta synthase, whose deficiency can cause homocystinuria has been located on chromosome 21. In a molecular biological study of 26 families with both pyridoxine-responsive and pyridoxine-nonresponsive members, specific mutations were observed (Hu et al., 1993). It is not considered likely today, however, in spite of the older literature, that deficiency of cystathione beta-synthase itself is directly associated with the symptoms of schizophrenia (see Chapter 6).

Other Studies Related to Chromosome 21

Jones and colleagues (1992) reported an alanine to valine substitution in codon 713 of the amyloid precursor protein gene (APP), which is on chromosome 21, in a single case of chronic schizophrenia. They were unable to detect this mutation in a further 100 unrelated patients with schizophrenia, however, 105 individuals with presenile dementia and 100 nondemented individuals. A further study of 191 individuals from 24 families containing multiple cases of schizophrenia and 58 unrelated individuals detected no abnormality (Mant, Asherson, Gill, McGuffin, & Owen, 1992). An additional 109 patients with schizophrenia were screened, including 24 patients from highly loaded pedigrees and again there were negative results (Nöthen et al., 1993). Mant and Nöthen and their colleagues concluded that if this mutation is indeed pathogenic, it must be an extremely rare cause of schizophrenia. Since then, additional studies summarized in Jonsson, Forsell, Lannfelt, and Sedval (1995) found negative results in more than 1000 individuals with schizophrenia.

CHROMOSOME 22

Metachromatic Leukodystrophy, Adult Type

Metachromatic leukodystrophy is a recessively inherited demyelinating disease caused by deficiency of arylsulfatase A, a lysosomal enzyme that hydrolyzes cerebroside sulfate (sulfatide). The demyelination is caused by lysosomal storage of sulfatide in Schwann cells and oligodendrocytes. The three clinical forms of the disease (late-infantile, juvenile, and adult) apparently are due to different levels of residual enzyme activity. The adult type of metachromatic leukodystrophy can present as schizophrenia (Betts, Smith, & Kelly, 1968; Kothbauer, Jellinger, Gross, Molzer, & Bernheimer, 1977; Manowitz, Kling, & Kohn, 1978). For example, even though it is a rare disease, determination of aryl-sulfatase A in a study of 18 chronic schizophrenics led to the detection of three cases of metachromatic leukodystrophy in that one study (Manowitz, Goldstein, & Nora, 1981).

The arylsulfatase A gene is located in the region of 22q13.31-qter. Alleles associated with some residual activity apparently delay the storage process considerably and are associated with a clinical presentation at a later age (Polten et al., 1991; Kappler, von Figura, & Gieselmann, 1992). (For a more-detailed discussion of metachromatic leukodystrophy, see Chapter 6.)

The Velo-Cardio-Facial Syndrome

The velo-cardio-facial syndrome (VCF) is an autosomal dominant multiple anomaly sydrome; the syndrome has been causally linked to a microdeletion at 22q11. It is not yet known if the deletion at 22q11 consists of a single gene or multiple contingous genes.

The current prevalence of schizophrenia or psychosis has been reported to occur in at least 20% of this patient group (Shprintzen, Goldberg, & Golding-Kushner, 1992; Motzkin et al., 1993; Mitnick, Bello, & Shprintzen, 1994). Chow, Bassett, and Weksberg (1994) have described in detail patients with VCF exhibiting either psychosis or schizophrenia and suggested chromosome 22q11 as a possible candidate region for other genetic studies of schizophrenia.

Dunham, Collins, Wadey, and Scambler (1992) found that Catechol-O-methyl transferase (COMT) gene was within the 450 kb YAC of the HP500 probe deleted in VCF patients. They hypothesized that hemizygosity for COMT, as might occur in individuals with VCF, might decrease metabolism of catecholamines including dopamine and norepinephrine, which could be a factor in the psychotic illnesses reported.

Because brain anomalies are now being reported in individuals with schizophrenia (see Chapter 12), patients with VCF and schizophrenia seemed to be a particularly useful group to evaluate by MRI. Although many patients with the VCF syndrome have brain anomalies visible on MRI, however, at least some of these patients with schizophrenia did not have detectable brain anomalies (Mitnick et al., 1994).

Other Studies Related to Chromosome 22

A genome-wide survey for schizophrenia susceptibility genes in nine multiplex families indicated a possible region of linkage on chromosome 22 but linkage testing using ten highly polymorphic chromosome 22 DNA markers was negative (Coon et al., 1994). Early linkage analysis suggested that chromsome 22q11 might be a suitable candidate region to search for genes reponsible for schizophrenia (Bassett, 1992). A suggestive linkage result has been reported for schizophrenia and markers from chromosome 22q12-q13 (Pulver et al., 1993). To date 105 families with schizophrenic members have been studied with genetic linkage analysis to examine whether a gene locus predisposing to schizophrenia can be located on chromosome 22—in those families results to date have been negative or inconclusive (Polymeropoulos et al., 1994).

SEX CHROMOSOMES (X, Y)

Changes in an Entire Chromosome: The X Chromosome

Klinefelter's syndrome

Klinefelter's syndrome is the result of the presence of at least one additional X chromosome in the nucleus of the male. The usual karyotype is 47 XXY although both mosaicism and variants, such as 47 XXXY and XXXXY are known. Klinefelter's syndrome is one of the relatively more frequent chromosomal anomalies. From a review of the literature, Crow (1988) has calculated an incidence of 0.55% of Klinefelter's syndrome with schizophrenia (5–6 cases per 1000) compared to an incidence of 0.13% of Klinefelter's syndrome in the general population (1 case per 1000).

The medical literature has many cases of patients with Klinefelter's syndrome who became schizophrenic (Tedeschi & Freeman, 1962; Raphel & Shaw, 1963; Judd & Brandkamp, 1967; MacLean, Court Brown, Jacobs, Mantle, & Strong, 1968; Anders et al., 1968; Forssman, 1970; Sperber, Salomon, Collins, & Stambler, 1972; Dasgupta, Dasgupta, & Balasubrahmanyan, 1973; Sorensen & Nielsen, 1977; Pomeroy, 1980; Roy, 1981). Nielsen (1969) found that 6% of the patients recorded in the psychiatric literature with Klinefelter's syndrome had been given the diagnosis of schizophrenia and another 7% had psychoses of an uncertain type but almost all with paranoid delusions. Mental hospital surveys, reviewed by Forssman in 1970, showed a 3-fold increase in patients with Klinefelter's syndrome compared with the general population. This increase was mainly caused by psychotic illnesses of a schizophrenic nature.

Patients with Klinefelter's syndrome are males with small testes and azoospermia or oligospermia. They may have a eunuchoid body shape and other signs of androgen deficiency, such as scanty beard growth or gynecomastia. Diagnosis is relatively easy to make by buccal smear.

THE XXX SYNDROME
(THE SUPER FEMALE SYNDROME)

A sex-chromosomal complement with three X chromosomes was first reported by Jacobs et al. (1959) in a normal woman studied because of secondary amenorrhea. Epidemiological studies have shown that there are no clinical features that can be considered typical for the XXX syndrome. Women with XXXX and XXXXX have also been reported.

Propping (1983) writes that the rate of schizophrenialike psychoses is probably increased by a factor of 3 in this population. Crow (1988) surveyed the medical literature and determined that there was an incidence of 0.37% (4 cases in 1000) of XXX women, including mosaics, who had schizophrenia compared to 0.10% (1 case in 1000) of XXX women in the general population. A number of patients with schizophrenialike psychosis have been reported in the medical literature (Raphel & Shaw, 1963; Asaka et al., 1967; Anders et al., 1968; Olanders, 1968; MacLean, Court-Brown, Jacobs, Mantle, & Strong, 1968; Forssman, 1970; Kaplan, 1970, 1972; Vartanian & Gendelis, 1972; Tsuang, 1974).

TURNER (XO) AND NOONAN SYNDROME

Case reports of both individuals with Turner syndrome (Slater & Zilkha, 1961; Mileu et al., 1964; Melbin, 1966; Kaplan & Cotton, 1968; Beaumont & Mayon, 1971; Propping, 1983) and Noonan syndrome (Krishna et al., 1977) with schizophrenia are reported in the literature. These are somewhat rare syndromes so the presence of this literature on schizophrenia is thought-provoking. In the case of Turner syndrome, diagnostic methods include buccal smear, standard chromosomal analysis and Y-chromosome specific DNA (SRY) probe.

Changes in an Entire Chromosome: The Y Chromosome

The XYY syndrome

Because of the ease of detection of an extra X chromosome by the simple procedure of a buccal smear for extra sex chromatin, the information on patients with an extra Y chromosome is more limited than on those with extra X chromosomes. Nevertheless, there are a number of patients with schizophrenia and the XYY karyotype in the medical literature (Abdullah, Jaruik, Kato, Johnston, & Lanzkron, 1969; Baker et al., 1970; Clark, Telfer, Baker, & Rosen, 1970; Forssman, Wahlström, Wallin, & Akesson, 1975; Faber & Abrams, 1975; Trixler, Kosztolanyi, & Mehes, 1976; Dorus, Dorus, & Telfer, 1977).

The question to consider is whether these patients have schizophrenia for some other reason or whether it is related to their chromosomal anomaly. XYY is one of the most frequent chromosomal anomalies in the general population, making its relevance to any individual case questionable. On the one hand, an extensive investigation of psychiatric patients left Nanko (1985) with the opinion that an association between schizophrenia and the XYY karyotype has not been established. On the other hand, Crowe (1988) writes that there is some evidence that individuals with additional Y-chromosomal material are over-represented in populations with psychosis.

A patient with schizophrenia, chronic-disorganized type, and a dicentric Y chromosome has been reported (Nanko, Konishi, Satoh, & Ikeda, 1993). Dicentric Y chromosomes are the most frequently encountered example of structural rearrangements of the Y chromosome. In this case, the break point was probably qll leaving two copies of the short arm and proximal long arm, which is genetically similar to XYY males.

Changes in Small Parts of Chromosomes

The fragile X syndrome

The clinical significance of fragile sites in chromosomes has been very difficult to interpret because of their frequency in normal populations. However, it is known that a fragile site on the X chromosome (Xq27.3) is found in approximately 8% of males with the autistic syndrome—data summarized in (Table 16.1, p. 190, Gillberg & Coleman, 1992). The genetic defect in autistic males appears to be an expansion of trinucleotide sequences (CGG) up to 600–1300 repeats, labeled a full mutation (Yu et al., 1991).

Much less is known about the behavioral phenotype in females. It has been found that some females, often obligate carriers, show alleles with about 33–600 trinucleotide repeats, labeled premutations (Yu et al., 1991). At this time, it is not clear whether these premutations are a factor in the question of a greater-than-chance occurrence of the fragile X syndrome and the schizophrenia spectrum disorders in female obligate carriers of the fragile X syndrome observed by some clinicians (Reiss, Hagerman, Vinogradov, Abrams, & King, 1988; Reiss & Freund, 1990; Steffenburg, 1991; Gillberg et al., 1992).

Adrenoleukodystrophy-X-linked and adrenomyeloneuropathy

Adrenoleukodystrophy (ALD) is a storage disorder that presents with intellectual, memory, and behavioral deterioration usually seen in children. A clinical subgroup of ALD is adrenomyeloneuropathy (AMN), which is seen in adults; the mean age of onset is 27.6 years and it is slowly progressive over the decades. In most instances these men present in their twenties or thirties with symptoms that may resemble schizophrenia, sometimes with dementia or a specific cerebral defect (Moser & Moser, 1989). When a peripheral neuropathy becomes apparent, the underlying diagnosis is more likely to be made.

These disease entities are known to be X-linked disorders and the primary gene defect for them has been mapped to chromosome X q28. A candidate gene has been isolated. For a clinical discussion of ALD and AMN, see Chapter 6.

Fabry disease

Fabry disease is an X-linked hereditary disease caused by a defect of a lysomal hydrolase alpha-galactosidase A. Because of the molecular heterogeneity of the alpha-glactosidase A gene, it is necessary to identify the site of mutation in the gene for each family with Fabry disease (Ishii et al., 1991). The majority of gene rearrangements were caused by small deletion/insertions or a single base substitution. For more clinical details on an interesting case of schizophrenia with Fabry disease, see Chapter 6.

Other studies related to X and Y chromosomes

Linkage studies were performed on 126 small families (with at least two schizophrenic members in one sibship). These studies were based on the hypothesis that a gene for schizophrenia exists with a homologous loci on both X and Y (X-Y linked) and the studies were consistent with the possible presence of a gene in this area; further studies were warranted (DeLisi et al., 1994).

Within what is called the psuedoautosomal region of the X chromosome (Xp22.3), a linkage study of three loci was performed on 85 families containing two or more siblings with schizophrenia or schizoaffective disorder. The data obtained did not support (but did not definitely exclude) a locus within the psuedoautosomal region (Crowe et al., 1994). Additional studies also failed to find linkage (Maier et al., 1995; Kolsi et al., 1995).

REFERENCES

Abdullah, S., Jarvik, L. F., Kato, T., Johnston, W. C., & Lanzkron, J. (1969). Extra Y chromosome and its psychiatric implications. *Archives of General Psychiatry, 21*, 497–501.

Alexsson, R., & Wahlström, J. (1984). Chromosomal aberrations in patients with paranoid psychosis. *Hereditas, 100*, 29–31.

American Psychiatric Association. (1987). *Diagnostic and statistical manual of mental disorders*, 3rd ed., rev. Washington, DC: American Psychiatric Press.

Anders, J. M., Jagiello, G., Polani, P. E., Gianelli, F., Hamerton, J. L., & Leiberman, D. M. (1968). Chromosome findings in chronic psychotic patients. *British Journal of Psychiatry, 114*, 1167–1174.

Andrew, S. E., Goldberg, Y. P., Kremer, B. et al. (1993). The relationship between trinucleotide (CAG) repeat length and clinical features of Huntington's disease. *Nature Genetics, 4*, 398–403.

Antonarakis, S. E., Blouin, J. C., Pulver, A. E., Wolyniec, P., Lasseter, V. K., Nestadt, G., Kasch, L., Babb, R., Kazaziou, H. H., Dombroski,

B. (1995). Schizophrenia susceptibility and chromosome 6p24–22 [letter]. *Nature Genetics, 11*, 235–236.

Arinami, T., Itokawa, M., Enguchi, H., Tagaya, H., Yano, S., Shimizu, H., Hamaguchi, H., & Toru, M. (1994). Association of dopamine D2 receptor molecular variant with schizophrenia. *Lancet, 343*, 703–704.

Asaka, A., Tsuboi, T., Inouye, E., Nagumo, Y., Hamada, S., & Okada, K. (1967). Schizophrenic psychosis in triple-X females. *Folia Psychiatric et Neurologica Japanica, 21*, 271–281.

Aschauer, H. N., Aschauer-Treiber, G., Isenberg, K. E., Todd, R. D., Knesevich, M. A., Garver, D. L., Reich, T., & Cloniger, C. R. (1990). No evidence for linkage between chromosome 5 markers and schizophrenia. *Human Heredity, 40*, 109–115.

Asherson, P., Walsh, C., Williams, J., Sargeant, M., Taylor, C., Clements, A., Gill, M., Owen, M., & McGuffin, P. (1994). Imprinting and anticipation: Are they relevant to genetic studies of schizophrenia? *British Journal of Psychiatry, 164*, 619–624.

Ayraud, N., Darcourt, G., Celsnitz, M. D. et al. (1969). Syndrome 18p-. Une novelle observation. *Annales de Génétique, 12*, 122–125.

Baker, D., Telfer, M. A., Inouye, E., Nagumo, Y., Hamada, S., & Okada, K. (1967). Chromosome errors in men with antisocial behavior. *Journal of the American Medical Association, 5*, 869–878.

Baron, M. (1976). Albinism and schizophreniform psychosis: A pedigree study. *American Journal of Psychiatry, 133*, 1273–1280.

Barr, C. L., Kennedy, J. L., Pakstis, A., Wetterberg, L., Sjogren, B., Bierut, L., Wadelius, C., Wahlstrom, J., Martinsson, T., Guiffra, L., et al. (1994). Progress in a genome scan for linkage studies of schizophrenia in a large Swedish kindred. *American Journal of Medical Genetics, 54*, 51–58.

Bassett, A. S. (1991). Linkage analysis of schizophrenia: Challenges and promises. *Social Biology, 38*, 186–2106.

Bassett, A. S. (1992). Chromosomal aberrations and schizophrenia autosomes. *British Journal of Psychiatry, 161*, 323–334.

Bassett, A. S., & Honer, W. G. (1994). Evidence for anticipation in schizophrenia. *American Journal of Human Genetics, 54*, 864–870.

Basset, A. S., McGillivray, B. C., Jones, B. D. et al. (1988). Partial trisomy chromosome 5 co-segregating with schizophrenia. *Lancet, 1*, 799–801.

Beaumont, P. J. V., & Mayon, R. (1971). Schizophrenia and XO/XX/XXX mosaicism. *British Journal of Psychiatry, 118*, 349–350.

Benzer, S. (1971). From gene to behavior. *Journal of the American Medical Association, 18*, 1015–1022.

Betts, T. A., Smith, T., & Kelly, R. E. (1968). Adult metachromatic leucod-ystrophy (sulphatide lipidosis) simulating acute schizophrenia. *Neurology*, *18*, 1140–1142.

Bolt, J. M. W. (1970). Huntington's chorea in the west of Scotland. *British Journal of Psychiatry*, *116*, 259–270.

Bowcock, A. M., Farrer, L. A., Hebert, J. M. et al. (1988). Eight closely linked loci place the Wilson disease locus within 13q14-q21. *American Journal of Human Genetics*, *43*, 664–674.

Brenner, S. (1973). The genetics of behaviour. *British Medical Bulletin*, *29*, 269–271.

Brewis, M., Poskanzer, D. C., Rolland, C., & Miller, H. (1966). Neurological disease in an English city. *Acta Neurologica Scandinavica (Suppl.)*, *24*, 42.

Burke, J. R., Enghild, J. J., Martin, M. E., Lou, Y-S., Myers, R. M., Roses, A. D., Vance, J. M., & Strictmatter, W. J. (1996). Huntington and DRPLA proteins selectively interact with the enzyme GAPDH. *Nature Medicine*, *2*, 347–350.

Byerley, W., Mellon, C., O'Connell, P., Lalouel, J-M., Nakumura, Y., Leppert, M., & White, R. (1989). Mapping genes for manic-depression and schizophrenia with DNA markers. *Trends in Neurosciences*, *12*, 46–48.

Cannon, T. D., Zorrilla, L. E., Shtasel, D. et al. (1994). Neuropsychological functioning in siblings discordant for schizophrenia and healthy volunteers. *Archives of General Psychiatry*, *51*, 651–661.

Chow, E. W. C., Bassett, A. S., & Weksberg, R. (1994). Velo-cardio-facial syndrome and psychotic disorders: Implications for psychiatric genetics. *American Journal of Medical Genetics, (Neuropsychiatric Genetics)*, *54*, 107–112.

Clark, G. R., Telfer, M. A., Baker, D., & Rosen, M. (1970). Sex chromosomes, crime and psychosis. *American Journal of Psychiatry*, *126*, 1659–1663.

Clarke, D. J., & Buckley, M. E. (1989). Familial association of albinism and schhizophrenia. *British Journal of Psychiatry*, *155*, 551–553.

Cloninger, C. R. (1994). Turning point in the design of linkage studies of schizophrenia. *American Journal of Medical Genetics (Neuropsychiatric Genetics)*, *54*, 83–92.

Conneally, P. M., Haimes, J., Tanzi, R. et al. (1989). No evidence of linkage heterogeneity between Huntington disease and G8. *Genomics*, *5*, 304–308.

Coon, H., Jensen, S., Holik, J., Hoff, M., Myles-Worsley, M., Reimherr, F., Wender, P., Waldo, M., Freedman, R., Leppert, M., & Byerley, W. (1994). Genomic scan for genes predisposing to schizophrenia. *American Journal of Medical Genetics*, *54*, 59–71.

Cossu, P., Pirastu, M., Nugaro, A., Figus, A., Balestriere, A., Borrone, C., Giacchino, R., Devoto, M., Monni, G., & Cao, A. (1992). Prenatal diagnosis of Wilson's disease by analysis of DNA polymorphism. *New England Journal of Medicine, 327,* 57.

Crow, T. J. (1988). Sex chromosomes and psychosis; the case for a pseudoautosomal locus. *British Journal of Psychiatry, 153,* 675–683.

Crow, T. J., Delisi, L. E., Lofthouse, R., Poulter, M., Lehner, T., Bass, N., Shah, T., Walsh, C., Boccio-Smith, A., Shields, G., & Ott, J. (1994). An examination of linkage of schizophrenia and schizoaffective disorder to the psuedoautosomal region (Xp22.3). *British Journal of Psychiatry, 164,* 159–164.

Dasgupta, J., Dasgupta, G., & Balasubrahmanyan, M. (1973). XXY, XY/XO mosaicism and acentric chromosomal fragments in male schizophrenics. *Indian Journal of Medical Research, 61,* 62–70.

Davis, M. B., Bateman, D., Quinn, N. P., Marsden, C. D., & Harding, A. E. (1994). Mutation analysis in patients with possible but apparently sporadic Huntington's disease. *Lancet, 344,* 714–717.

DeLisi, L. E., Devoto, M., Lofthouse, R., Poulter, M., Smith, A., Shields, G., Bass, N., Chen, G., Vita, A., Marganti, C., Ott, J., & Crow, T. J. (1994). Search for linkage to schizophrenia on the X and Y chromosomes. *American Journal of Medical Genetics (Neuropsychiatric Genetics), 54,* 113–121.

Detera-Wadleigh, S., Goldin, L. R., Sherrington, R. et al. (1989). Exclusion of linkage to 5q11-13 in families with schizophrenia and other psychiatric disorders. *Nature, 340,* 391–393.

Dorus, E., Dorus, W., & Telfer, M. A. (1977). Paranoid schizophrenia in a 47,XYY male. *American Journal of Psychiatry, 134,* 687.

Dunham, I., Collins, J., Wadey, R., & Scambler, P. (1992). Possible role for COMT in psychosis associated with velo-cardio-facial syndrome. *Lancet, 340,* 1361–1362.

Duyao, M., Ambrose, C., Meyers, R. et al. (1993). Trinucleotide repeat instability and age of onset in Huntington's disease. *Nature Genetics, 4,* 387–392.

Escobar, J. I. (1976). A cytogenetic study of children with psychiatric disorders. *Comprehensive Psychiatry, 17,* 309–313.

Faber, R., & Abrams, R. (1975). Schizophrenia in a 47,XYY male. *British Journal of Psychiatry, 127,* 401–403.

Fang, N., Coon, H., Hoff, M., Holik, J., Hadley, D., Reimherr, F., Wender, P., Myles-Worsley, M., Waldo, M., & Freedman, R. (1995). Search for a schizophrenia susceptibility gene on chromosome 18. *Psychiatric Genetics, 5,* 31–35.

Fletcher, J. M., Evans, K., Baillie, D., Byrd, P., Hanratty, D., Leach, S., Julier, C., Gosden, J. R., Muir, W., Porteous, St. Clair, D., & van

Heyningen, V. (1993). Schizophrenia-associated chromosome 11q21 translocation: Identification of flanking markers and development of chromosome 11q fragment hybrids as cloning and mapping resources. *American Journal of Human Genetics, 52,* 478–490.

Forssman, H. (1970). The mental implications of sex chromosome aberrations. The Blake March Lecture for 1970. *British Journal of Psychiatry, 117,* 353–363.

Forssman, H., Wahlström, J., Wallin, L., & Akesson, H. O. (1975). *Males with double Y-chromosmoes.* Göteborg, Sweden: Akademiförlaget.

Frosst, P., Blom, H. J., Milos, R., Goyette, P., Sheppard, C. A., Mathews, R. G., Boers, G. J., den Heijer, M., Kluijtmans, L. A. J., van den Heuvel, L. P., & Rozen, R. (1995). A candidate genetic risk factor for vascular disease: A common mutation in methylenetetrahydrofolate reductase. *Nature Genetics, 10,* 111.

Genest, P., Dumas, L., & Genest, F. B. (1976). Translocation chromosomique t(2;18) (q21; q23) chez un individu schizophrene et sa fille. *Union Medicale du Canada (Montreal), 105,* 1676–1681.

Gill, M., McGuffin, P., Parfitt, E., Mant, R., Asherson, P., Collier, D., Vallada, H., Powell, J., Shaikh, S., Taylor, C., Sargeant, M., Clements, A., Nanko, S., Takazawa, N., Llewellyn, D., Williams, J., Whatley, S., Murray, R., & Owen, M. (1993). A linkage study of schizophrenia with DNA markers from the long arm of chromosome 11. *Psychological Medicine, 23,* 27–44.

Gillberg, C., & Coleman, M. (1992). *The biology of the autistic syndromes,* second edition (p. 190). London: Mac Keith Press.

Goldfarb, L. G., Vasconcelos, O., Platonov, F. A., Lunkes, A., Kipnis, V., Kononova, S., Chabrashvili, T., Vladimintsev, V. A., Alexeev, V. P., & Gajdusek, D. C. (1996). Unstable triplet repeat and phenotypic variability of spinocerebellar ataxia type 1. *Annals of Neurology, 39,* 500–506.

Gomez, M. R. (1979). Neurologic and psychiatric symptoms. In M. R. Gomez (Ed)., *Tuberous sclerosis.* New York: Raven Press.

Gordon, C. T., Krasnewich, D., White, B., Lenane, M., & Rapoport, J. L. (1994). Brief report: Translocation involving chromosomes 1 and 7 in a boy with childhood-onset schizophrenia. *Journal of Autism and Developmental Disorders, 24,* 537–545.

Gottesman, I. I. (1991). *Schizophrenia genesis. Origin of madness.* San Francisco: Freeman.

Goyette, P., Sumner, J. S., Milos, R., Duncan, A. M. V., Rosenblatt, D. S., Mathews, R. G., & Rozen, R. (1994). Human methylenetetrahydrofolate reductase: Isolation of cDNA, mapping and mutation identification. *Nature Genetics, 7,* 19.

Goyette, P., Frosst, P., Rosenblatt, D. S., & Rozen, R. (1995). Seven novel mutations in the methylenetetrahydrate reductase folate gene and genotype/phenotype correlations in severe MTHFR deficiency. *American Journal of Human Genetics, 56,* 1052–1059.

Greenspan, R. J. (1995). Understanding the genetic construction of behavior. *Scientific American, 272,* 72–78.

Hall, J. C. (1994). The mating of a fly. *Science, 264,* 1702–1714.

Heston, L. L. (1966). Psychiatric disorders in foster home reared children of schizophrenic mothers. *British Journal of Psychiatry, 112,* 819–825.

Holland, T., & Gosen, C. (1990). A balanced chromosomal translocation partially cosegregating with pscyhotic illness in a family. *Psychiatry Research, 32,* 1–8.

Hu, F. L., Gu, Z., Kozich, V., Kraus, J. P., Ramesh, V., & Shih, V. E. (1993). Molecular basis of cystathionine beta synthase deficiency in pyridoxine responsive and nonresponsive homocystinura. *Human Molecular Genetics, 11,* 1857–1860.

Huntington's Disease Collaborative Research Group. (1993). A novel gene containing a trinucleotide repeat that is expanded and unstable on Huntington's disease chromosomes. *Cell, 72,* 971–983.

Ishii, S., Sakuraba, H., Shimmoto, M., Minamikawa-Tachino, R., Suzuki, T., & Suzuki, Y. (1991). Fabry disease: Detection of 13-bp deletion in alpha-galactoside A gene and its application to gene diagnosis in heterozygotes. *Annals of Neurology, 29,* 560–564.

Jacobs, P. A., Bailie, A. G., Court-Brown, W. M., McGregor, T. N., McLean, N., & Harden, D. C. (1959). Evidence for the existence of the human "superfemale." *Lancet, 2,* 423–425.

Jones, C. T., Morris, S., Yates, C., Moffoot, A., Sharpe, C., Brock, D. J. H., & St. Clair, D. (1992). Mutation in codon 713 of the β amyloid precursor protein gene presenting with schizophrenia. *Nature Genetics, 1,* 306–309.

Jonsson, E., Forsell, C., Lannfelt, L., & Sedval, G. (1995). Schizophrenia and APP gene. *Biological Psychiatry, 37,* 135–136.

Judd, L. L., & Brandkamp, W. W. (1967). Chromosome analyses of adult schizophrenics. *Archives of General Psychiatry, 16,* 316–324.

Kalsi, G., Curtis, D., Brynjolfsson, J., Butler, R., Sharma, T., Murphy, P., Read, T., Petursson, H., & Gurling, H. M. (1995). Investigation of linkage analysis of the XY pseudoautosomal region in the genetic susceptibility to schizophrenia. *British Journal of Psychiatry, 167,* 390–393.

Kalsi, G., Mankoo, B. S., Curtis, D., Brynjolfsson, J., Read, T., Sharma, T., Murphy, P., Petursson, H., & Gurling, H. M. (1995). Exclusion of linkage of schizophrenia to the gene for the dopamine D_2 receptor

(DRD2) and chromosome 11q translocation sites. *Psychological Medicine, 25*, 531–537.

Kaplan, A. R. (1970). Chromosomal mosaicisms and occasional acentric chromosomal fragments in schizophrenic patients. *Biological Psychiatry, 2*, 89–94.

Kaplan, A. R. (1972). Chromosomal aneuploidy, genetic mosaicism, occasional acentric fragments and schizophrenia: association of schizophrenia with rare cytogenetic anomalies. In A. R. Kaplan (Ed.), *Genetic factors in "schizophrenia."* Springfield, IL: Charles C. Thomas.

Kaplan, A. R., & Cotton, J. E. (1968). Chromosomal abnormalities in female schizophrenics. *Journal of Nervous and Mental Diseases, 147*, 402.

Kappler, J., von Figura, K., & Gieselmann, V. (1992). Late-onset metachromatic leukodystrophy: Molecular pathology in two siblings. *Annals of Neurology, 31*, 256–261.

Karlsson, J. L. (1970). The rate of schizophrenia in foster- reared children of schizophrenic index cases. *Biological Psychiatry, 2*, 285–290.

Kendler, K. S., Gruenberg, A. M. N., & Kinney, D. K. (1994). Independent diagnoses of adoptees and relatives as defined by DSM-III in the provincial and national samples of the Danish Adoption Study of Schizophrenia. *Archives of General Psychiatry, 51*, 456–468.

Kennedy, J. L., Guifra, L. A., Moises, H. W. et al. (1988). Evidence against linkage of schizophrenia to markers on chromosome 5 in a Northern Swedish pedigree. *Nature, 336*, 167–170.

Kety, S. S., Rosenthal, D., Wender, P. H., Schulsinger, F., & Jacobsen, B. (1975). Mental Illness in the biological and adoptive families of adopted individuals who have become schizophrenic: A preliminary report based on psychatric interviews. In R. Fieve, D. Rosenthal, & H. Brill (Eds.), *Genetic research in psychiatry* (pp. 147–165). Baltimore, MD: Johns Hopkins University Press.

Kety, S. S., Wender, P. H., Jacobsen, B., Ingraham, L. J., Jansson, L., Faber, B., & Kinney, D. K. (1994). Mental illness in the biological and adoptive relatives of schizophrenic adoptees. *Archives of General Psychiatry, 51*, 442–455.

Koide, R., Ikeuchi, T., Onodera, O., Tanaka, H., Igarashi, S., Endo, K., Takahashi, H., Kondo, R., Ishikawa, A., Hayashi, T., Saito, M., Tomoda, A., Miike, T., Naito, H., Ikuta, F., & Tsuji, S. (1994). Unstable expansion of CAG repeat in hereditary dentatorubal-pallidoluysin atrophy (DRPLA). *Nature Genetics, 6*, 9–13.

Korner, J., Schwanitz, G,. de Braganca, K., Roitzheim, B., Reitschel, M., Aschauer, H., Nothen, M. M., Propping, P., & Moller, H-J. (1993).

Screening for structural chromosomal abnormalities in psychotic and affectively ill patients. *Psychiatric Genetics, 3,* 167. (Abstract).

Kothbauer, P., Jellinger, K., Gross, H., Molzer, B., & Bernheimer, H. (1977). Adulte metachromatische leukodystrophie unter dem bild einer schizophrenen psychose. *Arch Psychiatr Nervenkr, 224,* 379–387.

Krag-Olsen, B., Hoeg Brask, B., Jacobsen, P., & Nielsen, J. (1981). Is there an increased risk of psychoses in patients with ring 18 and deletion long arm 18? In W. Schmid & J. Nielsen (Eds.), *Human behavior and genetics* (pp. 211–220). Amsterdam: Elsevier/North Holland.

Krishna, N. R., Abrams, R., Taylor, M. A., & Behar, D. (1977). Schizophrenia in a 46, XY male with Noonan syndrome. *British Journal of Psychiatry, 130,* 570–572.

La Spada, A. R., Paulson, H. L., & Fischbeck, K. H. (1994). Trinucleotide repeat expansion in neurological disease. *Annals of Neurology, 36,* 814–822.

Lee, J-S., Anvert, M., Floderus, Y., Gellerfors, P., Lannfelt, L., Linsten, J., Thunell, S., & Wetterberg, L. (1988). DNA polymorphism within the prophobilinogen deaminase gene in two Swedish families with acute intermittent porphyria. *Human Genetics, 79,* 379–381.

Lejeune, G. (1977). On the mechanism of mental deficiency in chromosomal deficiency. *Hereditas, 86,* 9–14.

Levy, D. L., Holzman, P. S., Matthysse, S., & Mendell, N. R. (1993). Eye tracking dysfunction and schizophrenia: A critical perspective. *Schizophrenia Bulletin, 19,* 461–536.

Lishman, W. A. (1987). *Organic psychiatry: The psychological consequences of cerebral disorder,* second edition. Oxford: Blackwell Scientific.

Llewellyn, D. H., Kalsheker, N. A., Elder, G. H., Goossens, M., Harrison, P. R., & Kalsheker, N. A. (1987). A Msp1 polymorphism for the human porphobilinogen deaminase gene. *Nucleic Acids Research, 15,* 1349.

MacLean, N., Court-Brown, W. M., Jacobs, P. A., Mantle, D. J., & Strong, J. A. (1968). A survey of sex chromatin abnormalities in an adult psychiatric population. *Journal of Medical Genetics, 5,* 165–172.

MacMillan, J. C., & Harper, P. S. (1991). Single-gene neurological disorders in south Wales: An epidemiological study. *Annals of Neurology, 30,* 411–414.

Maier, W., Schmidt, F., Schwab, S. G., Hallmayer, J., Minges, J., Ackenheil, M., Lichtermann, D., & Wildenauer, D. B. (1995). Lack of linkage between schizophrenia and markers at the telomeric end of the psuedoautosomal region of the sex chromosomes. *Biological Psychiatry, 37,* 344–347.

Manowitz, P., Kling, A., & Kohn, H. (1978). Clinical course of adult metachromatic leucodystroph presenting as schizophrenia. *Journal of
Nervous and Mental Diseases, 166,* 500–506.

Manowitz, P., Goldstein, I., & Nora, R. (1981). An arylsulfatase variant
in schizophrenic patients: preliminary report. *Biological Psychiatry,
16,* 1107–1114.

Mant, R., Asherson, P., Gill, M., McGuffin, P., & Owen, M. (1992). Schizophrenia scepticism. *Nature Genetics, 2,* 12.

McGuffin, P., & Sturt, E. (1986). Genetic markers in schizophrenia. *Human
Heredity, 36,* 65–88.

McGuffin, P., Asherson, P., Owen, M., & Farmer, A. (1994). The strength
of the genetic effect: Is there room for an environmental influence
in the aetiology of schizophrenia? *British Journal of Psychiatry,
164,* 593–599.

McHugh, P. R., & Folstein, M. F. (1975). Psychiatric syndromes of Huntington's chorea. In D. F. Benson & D. Blumer (Eds.), *Psychiatric
aspects of neurologic disease.* New York: Grune & Stratton.

McHugh, P. R., & Folstein, M. F. (1981). Psychiatric syndromes in Huntington's chorea. In D. F. Benson, & D. Blumer (Eds.), *Psychiatric
aspects of neurologic disease.* New York: Grune & Stratton.

Mellbin, G. (1986). Neuropsychiatric disorders in sex chromatin negative
women. *British Journal of Psychiatry, 112,* 145–148.

Mileu, S. M., Stancescu, V., Ionescu, V., Forea, I. Poenaru, S., & Maximilian
C. (1964). Turner-syndrome mit schizophrenia und XO-karyotypus.
Folia Psychiatrica et Neurologica Japonica (Tokyo), 34, 392–393.

Mitnick, R. J., Bello, J. A., & Shpritzen, R. J. (1994). Brain anomalies in the
velo-cardio-facial syndrome. *American Journal of Medical Genetics
(Neuropsychiatric Genetics), 54,* 100–106.

Moises, H. W., Yang, L., Kristbjarnarson, H., Wiese, C., Byerley, W.,
Macciardi, F., Arolt, V., Blackwood, D., Liu, X., & Sjogren, B. (1995).
An international two-stage genome-wide search for schizophrenia
suspectibility genes. *Nature Genetics, 11,* 321–324.

Moser, H., & Moser, A. (1989). Adrenoleukodystrophy—X-linked. In Stanbury et al. (Eds.), *The metabolic basis of inherited disease,* sixth
edition. New York: McGraw Hill.

Motzkin, B., Marion, R., Goldberg, R., Sprintzen, R., & Saenger, P. (1993).
Variable phenotypes in the velo-cardio-facial syndrome with chromosomal deletion. *Journal of Pediatrics, 123,* 406–410.

Murray, R. M., Lewis, S., & Reveley, A. M. (1985). Toward an aetiological
classification of schizophrenia. *Lancet, i,* 1023–1026.

Nagafuchi, S., Yanagisawa, H., Sato, K. et al. (1994). Dentatorubal and
pallidolusian atrophy expansion of an unstable CAG trinucleotide
on chromosome 12p. *Nature Genetics, 6,* 14–18.

Nanko, S. (1985). X and Y chromatin survey among 8000 inpatients in Japanese mental hospitals. In T. Sakai & T. Tsuboi (Eds.), *Genetic aspects of human behavior* (pp. 209–214). Tokyo: Igaku-Shoin.

Nanko, S. (1993). Schizophrenia with pericentric inversion of chromosome 9: A case report. *The Japanese Journal of Psychiatry and Neurology, 47,* 47–49.

Nanko, S., Hattori, M., Kuwata, S., Sasaki, T., Fukuda, R., Dai, X. Y., Yamaguchi, K., Shibata, Y., & Kazamatsuri, H. (1994). Neurotrophin-3 gene polymorphism associated with schizophrenia. *Acta Psychiatrica Scandinavica, 89,* 390–392.

Nanko, S., Konishi, T., Satoh, S., & Ikeda, H. (1993). A case of schizophrenia with dicentric Y chromosome. *Japanese Journal of Human Genetics, 38,* 229–232.

Navon, R. (1991). Molecular and clinical heterogeneity of adult GM2 gangliosidosis. *Developments in Neuroscience, 13,* 295–298.

Nielsen, J. (1969). Klinefelter's syndrome and the XXY syndrome. *Acta Psychiatrica Scandinavica (Suppl.), 209,* 1–353.

Nöthen, M. M., Erdmann, J., Propping, P., Lanczik, M., Rietschel, M., Körner, J., Maier, W., Albus, M., Ertl, M. A., & Wildenauer, D. B. (1993). Mutation in the β amyloid precursor protein gene and schizophrenia. (Correspondence) *Biological Psychiatry, 34,* 502.

Novelletto, A., Persichetti, F., Sabbadini, G. et al. (1994). Analysis of the trinucleotide repeat in Italian families affected with Huntington disease. *Human and Molelcular Genetics, 3,* 93–98.

Olanders, S. (1968). Excess of Barr bodies in patients in mental hospitals. *Lancet, ii,* 1244.

Ozcelik, T., Rosenthal, A., & Francke, U. (1991). Chromosomal mapping of brain-derived neurotrophic factor and neurotrophin-3 genes in man and mouse. *Genomics, 10,* 569–575.

Peltonen, L. (1995). All out for chromosome six. *Nature, 378,* 665–666.

Petrukin, K., Fischer, S. C., Pirastu, M., Tanzi, R. E., Chervov, I., Devoto, M., Brzustowski, L. M., Cayanis, E., Vitale, E., Russo, J. J., Matseoane, D., Boukhgalter, B., Wasco, W., Figus, A. L., Loudianos, J., Cao, A., Sternlieb, I., Evgrafov, O., Pavone, L., Warburtom, D., Ott, J., Penchaszadeh, G. K., Scheinberg, I. H., & Gilliam, T. C. (1993). Mapping, cloning and genetic characterization of the region containing the Wilson disease gene. *Nature Genetics, 5,* 338.

Polten, A., Fluharty, A. L., Fluharty, C. B., Kappler, J., von Figura, K., & Gieselmann, V. (1991). Molecular basis of different forms of metachromatic leukodystrophy. *New England Journal of Medicine, 324,* 18–22.

Polymeropoulos, M. H., Coon, H., Byerley, W., Gerson, E. S., Goldin, L., Crow, T. J., Rubenstein, J., Hoff, M., Holik, J., Smith, A. M., Shields,

G., Bass, N. J., Poulter, M., Lofthouse, R., Vita, A., Morganti, C., Merril, C. R., & DeLisi, L. E. (1994). Search for a schizophrenia susceptibility locus on human chromosome 22. *American Journal of Medical Genetics (Neuropsychiatric Genetics)*, *54*, 93–99.

Pomeroy, J. C. (1980). Klinefelter's syndrome and schizophrenia. *British Journal of Psychiatry*, *136*, 597–599.

Price, W. H., Burton, M., Buckton, K. et al. (1976). Chromosome survey of new patients admitted to the four maximum security hospitals in the United Kingdom. *Clinical Genetics*, *9*, 389–398.

Propping, P. (1983). Genetic disorders presenting as 'schizophrenia': Karl Bonhoeffer's early view of the pscyhoses in the light of medical genetics. *Human Genetics*, *65*, 1–10.

Pulver, A. E., Karayiorgou, M., Demarchi, N., Antonarakis, S., Housman, D., Kasch, L., Kazazian, H., Lamacz, M., Lasseter, V. K., McGrath, J., Meyers, D., Nestadt, G., Ott, J., Ramu, E., Wolyniec, P., & Childs, B. (1993). A potential linkage for schizophrenia on chromosome 22q12-q13. *Psychiatric Genetics*, *3*, 126.

Pulver, A. E., Lasseter, V. K., Lasch, L., Wolyniec, P., Nestadt, G., Blouin, J-L, Kimberland, M., Babb, R., Vourlis, S., Chen, H., Lalioti, M., Morris, M. A., Karayiorgo, M., Ott, J., Meyers, D., Antonarakis, S. E., Housman, D., & Karazian, H. H. (1995). Schizophrenia: A genome scan targets chromosomes 3p and 8p as potential sites of susceptibility genes. *American Journal of Medical Genetics* (Neuropsychiatric Genetics), *60*, 252–260.

Raphel, T., & Shaw, M. W. (1963). Chromosome studies in schizophrenia. *Journal of the American Medical Association*, *183*, 1022–1028.

Reiss, A. L., & Freund, L. (1990). Fragile X syndrome. *Biological Psychiatry*, *27*, 223–240.

Reiss, A. L., Hagerman, R. J., Vinogradov, S., Abrams, M., & King, R. J. (1988). Psychiatric disability in female carriers of the fragile X syndrome. *Biological Psychiatry*, *27*, 223–240.

Rosenberg, R. N. (1981). Biochemical genetics of neurologic disease. *New England Journal of Medicine*, *305*, 1181–1193.

Rosenberg, R. N. (1986). *Neurogenetics: Principles and practice* (p. 324). New York: Raven Press.

Ross, C. A., McInnis, M. G., Margolis, R. L. et al. (1993). Genes with triplet repeats: candidate mediators of neuropsychiatric disorders. *Trends in Neurosciences*, *16*, 254–260.

Rowland, L. P. (1992). The first decade of molecular genetics in neurology: Changing clinical thought and practice. *Annals of Neurology*, *32*, 207–214.

Roy, A. (1981). Schizophrenia and Klinefelter's syndrome. *Canadian Journal of Psychiatry*, *26*, 262–264.

Rubinsztein, D. C., Leggo, J., Goodburn, S., Barton, D. E., Ferguson-Smith, M. A., Ross, C. A., Li, S. H., Lofthouse, R., Crow, T. J., & DeLisi, L. E. (1994). B37 repeats are normal in most schizophrenic patients. *Lancet, ii*, 871–872.

Sanders, A. R., Hamilton, J. D., Fann, W. E., & Patel, P. (1991). Association of genetic variation at the porphobilinogen deaminase gene with schizophrenia. *American Journal of Human Genetics*, (Suppl.) *49*, 358. (abstract)

Saugstad, L., & Odegard, O. (1986). Huntington's chorea in Norway. *Psychological Medicine, 16*, 39–48.

Schwab, S. G., Albus, M., Hallmayer, J., Honig, S., Borrmann, M., Lichtermann, D., Ebstein, R. P., Achenheil, M., Lener, B., & Risch, N. (1995). Evaluation of a susceptibility gene for schizophrenia on chromosome 6p by multipoint affected sub-pair linkage analysis. *Nature Genetics, 11*, 325–327.

Seeman, P., Nizni,, H. B., Guan, H. C., Booth, G., & Ulpian, C. (1989). Link between D1 and D2 dopamine receptors is reduced in schizophrenia and Huntington diseased brain. *Proceedings of the National Academy of Science USA, 86*, 10156–10160.

Sherrington, R., Brynjolfsson, J., Petursson, H. et al. (1988). Locialzation of a suspectibility locus for schizophrenia on chromosome 5. *Nature, 336*, 164–167.

Shihabuddin, L., Silverman, J. M., Buchsbaum, M. S., Metzger, M., & Davis, K. L. (1995). Neuroimaging correlates of genetic marker for schizophrenia. *Biological Psychiatry, 37*, 662. (abstract)

Shpritzen, R. J., Goldberg, R. B., & Golding- Kushner, K. J. (1992). Letter to the editor: Late-onset psychosis in the velo-cardio-facial syndrome. *American Journal of Medical Genetics, 42*, 141–142.

Slater, E., & Zilkha, K. (1961). A case of Turner mosaic with myopathy and schizophrenia. *Proceedings of the Royal Society of Medicine, 54*, 674–675.

Smith, M., Wasmuth, J., McPherson, J. D., Wagner, C., Grandy, D., Civelli, O., Potkin, S. et al. (1989). Cosegregation of an 11q22.3-9p22 translocation with affective disorder: Proximity of the dopamine D2 receptor gene relative to the translocation breakpoint. *American Journal of Human Genetics, 45*, A220.

Snell, R. G., MacMillan, J. C., Cheadle, J. P. et al. (1993). Relationship between trinucleotide repeat expansion phenotypic variation in Huntington's disease. *Nature Genetics, 4*, 393–397.

Sorensen, K., & Nielsen, J. (1977). Twenty psychotic males with Klinefelter's syndrome. *Acta Psychiatrica Scandivica, 56*, 249–255.

Sperber, M. A. (1975). Schizophrenia and organic brain syndrome with trisomy 8 (group C trisomy 8[47,XX,8+]. *Biological Psychiatry, 10,* 27–43.

Sperber, M. A., Salomon, L., Collins, M. H., & Stambler, M. (1972). Childhood schizophrenia and 47,XXY Klinefelter's syndrome. *American Journal of Psychiatry, 128,* 1400–1408.

St. Clair, D., Blackwood, D., Muir, W., Carothers, A., Walker, M., Spowart, G., Gosden, C., & Evans, J. H. (1990). Association within a family of a balanced autosomal translocation with major mental illness. *Lancet, 336,* 13–16.

St. Clair, D., Blackwood, D., Muir, W. et al. (1989). No linkage of chromosome 5q11-5q13 markers to schizophrenia in Scottish families. *Nature, 339,* 305–309.

Steffenburg, S. (1991). Neuropsychiatric assessment of children with autism: A population-based study. *Developmental Medicine and Child Neurology, 33,* 495–511.

Straub, R. E., MacLean, C. J., O'Neill, F. A., Burke, J., Murphy, B., Duke, F., Shinkevin, R., Webb, B. T., Zhang, J., & Walsh, D. (1995). A potential vulnerability locus for schizophrenia on chromosome 6p24-22: Evidence for genetic heterogeneity. *Nature Genetics, 11,* 287–293.

Streletski, F. (1961). Psychosen im verlauf der Huntingtonschen Chorea inter besonderer berucksichtigung der wahnbilddungen. *Arch Psychiatr Nervenke, 202,* 202–214.

Tedeschi, L. G., & Freeman, H. (1962). Sex chromosomes in male schizophrenics. *Archives of General Psychiatry, 6,* 109–111.

Tienari, P. (1991). Interaction between genetic vulnerability and family environment: The Finnish adoptive family study of schizophrenia. *Acta Psychiatrica Scandinavica, 84,* 460–465.

Torry, E. F., Bowler, A. E., Taylor, E. H., & Gottresman, I. I. (1994). *Schizophrenia and Manic-Depressive Disorder: The biological roots of mental illness as revealed by the landmark study of identical twins.* New York: Basic Books.

Trixler, M., Kosztolanyi, G., & Mehes, K. (1976). Sex chromosome aberration screening among male psychiatric patients. *Archiv fur Psychiatrie und Nervenkrankheiten, 221,* 273–282.

Trottier, Y., Devys, D., Imbert, G., Saudou, F., An, I., Lutz, Y., Weber, C., Agid, Y., Hirsch, E. C., & Mandel, J-L. (1995). Cellular localization of the Huntington's disease protein and discrimination of the normal and mutated form. *Nature Genetics, 10,* 104–110.

Tsuang, M. T. (1974). Sex chromatin anomaly in Chinese females: Psychiatric characteristics of XXX. *British Journal of Psychiatry, 124,* 299–305.

Vartanian, M. E., & Gendelis, V. M. (1972). The role of chromosomal polymorphism of schizophrenia. *Indian Journal of Mental Health*, *1*, 93–106.

Wang, Z. W., Black, D., Andreasen, N. C., & Crowe, R. R. (1993). A linkage study of chromosome 11q in schizophrenia. *Archives of General Psychiatry*, *50*, 212–216.

Wang, Z. W., Black, D. W., Andreasen, N. C., & Crowe, R. R. (1994). No evidence of schizophrenia locus in a second pseudoautosomal region. (Letters to the editor) *Archives of General Psychiatry*, *51*, 427.

Wang, S., Sun, C., Walczak, C. A., Ziegle, J. S., Kipps, B. R., Goldin, L. R., & Diehl, S. R. (1995). Evidence for a susceptibility locus for schizophrenia on chromosome 6pter-p22. *Nature Genetics*, *10*, 41.

Warner, T. T., Williams, L. D., Walker, R. W. H., Flinter, F., Robb, S. A., Bundey, S. E., Honava, M., & Harding, A. E. (1995). A clinical and molecular genetic study of dentatorubropallidoluysian atrophy in four European families. *Annals of Neurology*, *37*, 452–459.

Yu, S., Kremer, E., Pritchard, M. et al. (1991). The fragile X genotype is characterised by an unstable region of DNA. *Science*, *252*, 1179–1181.

Zlotlow, M., & Kleiner, S. (1965). Catatonic schizophrenia associated with tuberose sclerosis. *Psychiatric Quarterly*, *39*, 466–475.

CHAPTER 11

Other Inherited Diseases

It has long been recognized that there are a number of families in which schizophrenia occurs more frequently than is seen in the general population; and this frequency appears to have a familial component (Figure 11.1). Hypotheses attempting to explain this phenomenon have ranged from environmental influences, the "schizophrenogenic mother" theory (Fromm-Reichmann, 1943) to genetic factors (see Chapter 10).

Such families are especially useful for studies by researchers attempting to find underlying etiologies of the schizophrenia syndrome. For example, recently a large Italian kindred segregating for schizophrenia was studied (unfortunately unsuccessfully) for the D_4 dopamine receptor gene (Macciardi et al., 1994). Family studies have given clear evidence of particular patterns of genetic transmission in some selected families (Guze et al., 1983). Adoption studies also have added credence to the evidence that, in some cases, schizophrenia is likely to be an inherited disorder (Kety, 1983) and that such families often also contain individuals with "latent," nonpsychotic forms of the illness (Tienari & Wynne, 1994).

The concordance of schizophrenia is high in monozygotic twins (40%—probandwise method; 28%—pairwise method). [There is a lower concordance (28%—probandwise method; 6%—pairwise method) in dizygotic twins (Torrey, Bowler, Taylor, & Gottesman, 1994; Kendler, 1983).] That the concordance rate is three to five times higher in identical twins appears to confirm that genetics must play a role in the causation of some cases of schizophrenia. Of course this is nowhere close to 100% concordance in the monozygotic twins and that would not be expected

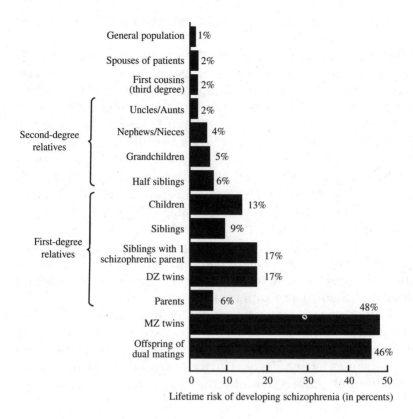

Figure 11.1 Grand average risks for developing schizophrenia compiled from the family and twin studies conducted in European populations between 1920 and 1987; the degree of risk correlates highly with the degree of genetic relatedness.
From *Schizophrenia genesis* by Gottesman. Copyright © 1991 by Irving I. Gottesman. Used with permission of W. H. Freeman and Company.

in a syndrome of so many different etiologies, including quite a few that are not genetic.

A study that investigated discordant identical twins found anatomical abnormalities in the brains of monozygotic twins discordant for schizophrenia (Suddath, Christison, Torrey, Casanova, & Weinberger, 1990). In Torrey Bowler, Taylor, and Gottesman's (1994) summary of the medical literature, the concordance rate of congenital anomalies of the brain in monozygotic twins was 17% compared to a concordance rate of 2% in dizy-gotic twins.

Genetic diseases can interfere with brain development even before birth. In the case of the reeler mouse, an autosomal reces-sive gene affects neuronal migration in many parts of the central nervous system (CNS); the abnormality can be detected by motor deficits in the mouse (Caviness, 1986). It is harder to be sure of behavioral abnormalities in mice. By inbreeding mice, however, researchers have been able to produce mice with eight mutants (actually seven mutations and one genetic variant) that disrupt neuronal migration and cause the presence of ectopic neurons in the developing hippocampal formation (Nowakowski, 1991). Each mutation causes a particular effect—they may effect either cell proliferation and/or migration of granule cells or pyramidal cells. The hippocampal formation and sometimes the cerebellum is effected. There is a fuller discussion of neurodevelopmental problems related to schizophrenia in Chapter 12.

Genetic diseases may present clinically at different develop-mental stages. In the case of metabolic diseases that present as schizophrenia (see Chapter 6), the age of onset may be as young as 10 years or as late as 50 years. In this chapter, inherited disease entities not fully covered in other chapters will be discussed.

DENTATORUBAL–PALLIDOLUYSIAN ATROPHY

Hereditary dentatorubal–pallidoluysian atrophy (DRPLA) is usu-ally a neurodegenerative disease characterized by a varying combination of epilepsy, progressive myoclonus, ataxia, choreo-athetosis, and dementia. A number of patients from families with DRPLA have been diagnosed by psychiatrists as schizophrenic or psychotic (Naito & Oyanagi, 1982; Koide et al., 1994; Warner et al., 1995). This is an example of how this disease entity is marked by clinical heterogeneity.

The genetic pattern of this disease is an autosomal dominant one and it appears to be a trinucleotide repeat disorder. The gene, found on chromosome 12p, has an unstable expansion of CAG repeats in the brain transcript CTG-B37. Normal chromo-somes have 7–34 repeats, whereas DRPLA is associated with

49–75 repeats. The Koide et al. patients who were schizophrenic had 57 repeats, near the lower end of the abnormal range (see Chapter 10). The DRPLA gene product, a ≈ 190 kD protein, is observed mainly in neuronal cytoplasm (Yazawa et al., 1955).

FAMILIAL BASAL GANGLIA CALCIFICATION

Cerebral calcification occurs in a wide variety of disorders and the basal ganglia are a common focus of calcification. Infections, hereditary folate malabsorption, toxins, trauma, and endocrine disorders all are associated with basal ganglia calcification. For bilateral forms, idiopathic hypoparathyroidism and psuedohypoparathyroidism I, II with resulting imbalances in calcium and phosphorus metabolism are common pathogenic factors. In the familial form of basal ganglia calcification not related to parathyroid disease, however, the pathogenesis of the calcification process is unknown. There is evidence to suggest that the basal ganglia play a role in motivational behavior through the striato–limbic system.

Konig (1989) studied the psychopathology of 70 patients with computed tomography (CT)-ascertained bilateral hyperdensities in basal ganglia structures. He found various psychiatric symptoms but only one case would have simulated the criteria of schizophrenia. The largest group (65%) had an affective syndrome. He noted that paranoid hallucinatory features are clinically more noticeable than depression and more likely to be recorded in the literature. In a study of 143 patients who underwent CT scanning at the Central Institute of Mental Health in Germany during a 10-year period, only 1% had bilateral basal ganglia mineralization and there was no evidence of an increased proportion of schizophrenia (Forstl, Krumm, Eden, & Kohlmeyer, 1991).

These studies are at variance with the report of Davison (1987) that schizophreniclike psychoses occur in up to 50% of patients with idiopathic calcification of the basal ganglia. Fernandez-Bouzas et al. (1990) reviewed CT scans of 45 DMS-III (APA, 1980) schizophrenic patients and found 3 bilateral and 1 unilateral calcification of the basal ganglia. They point out this is far in excess of the rate of basal ganglia calcification in large unselected series.

These contradictory studies make it difficult to know how to interpret the many cases of schizophrenia reported in the medical literature (Hall, 1972; Cummings, Gosenfeld, Houlihan, & McCaffrey, 1983). A family in which five of the eight members had basal ganglia calcification without any neurological findings also had a schizophrenialike psychosis (Francis, 1979; Francis & Freeman, 1984). A monozygotic twin pair who developed schizophrenia within 48 hours of each other had basal ganglia degeneration (West, 1973). A man with a XO/XY mosaic chromosomal pattern had symmetrical sclerosis of frontal white matter and the nucleus lentiformis with schizophrenia; he also had multiple urogenital malformations (Deckert, Strik, & Frtize, 1992). A patient with basal ganglia calcification who had a brother in a state mental hospital is described; this patient had a chronic depressive condition that included paranoia and auditory hallucinations (Lauterbach et al., 1994). Basal ganglia calcification also has been found at autopsy in individuals with schizophrenia (Davison, 1983).

FRIEDREICH'S ATAXIA

Friedreich's ataxia is one of the commonest hereditary diseases of the nervous system. A small subgroup of these patients develop a schizophrenialike illness characterized by paranoid delusions and outbursts of excitement although their specific relationship to the disease itself is unclear (Davies, 1949; Lishman, 1987). The term—Friedreich's psychosis—is used for outbreaks of paranoid beliefs, nocturnal hallucinations, aggressive impulsive behavior, and episodes of clouding of consciousness. This has not been conclusively shown to be related to the neurological disorder (Davison & Bagley, 1969).

Friedreich's ataxia starts with an unsteadiness of gait typically in the first or second decade of life. As nystagmus begins and speech becomes dysarthric, the characteristic deformities of kyphoscoliosis and pes cavus develop. The myocardium may become involved and the disease is often fatal in the third decade of life. Friedreich's ataxia is an autosomal recessive disease with a carrier frequency of about 1 in 110. Deoxyribose nucleic acid (DNA) testing in families is available by linkage analysis of a confirmed patient and the obligate carrier parents of this patient.

HUNTINGTON'S DISEASE

Huntington's disease, which is also known as Huntingdon's chorea, is an autosomal dominant disorder that begins in midlife and pursues an inexorable progression leading to complete disability and death, usually 15–20 years after the initial onset of symptoms. Choreiform movements combined with dementia are the hallmark of Huntington's chorea. Psychotic features can appear early in the course of the disease in some patients, however, and may even precede the onset of the chorea or dementia.

Some of the patients have been described as having a schizophrenic picture such as delusions of persecution with religiosity and sometimes grandiosity, sometimes very early in the course of the disease process (Streletzki, 1961). For such patients, McHugh and Folstein (1975, 1981) prefer the term "delusional-hallucinatory states" noting the emergence of psychotic symptoms from a pervasive delusional mood. They describe a typical progression as follows: the patient is overwhelmed by a vague impression of an uncanny change in reality that becomes laden with meaning of an uncertain nature. Delusions and hallucinations distil from this, often welling up suddenly and usually lasting for several months. Treatment with neuroleptics can lead to considerable improvement. McHugh and Folstein (1975) summarized Huntington's chorea as follows:

> The terms given to these disorders and issues of what they resemble are of less practical importance than the fact that they can be hard to distinguish from the standard "functional psychosis" and can appear before any choreic movements signal the diagnosis.

More recently, Folstein and Hedreen wrote "Schizophrenia is occasionally seen in adolescents or late in the course of the illness" (Folstein & Hedreen, 1995).

Huntington's disease may be confused with many other illnesses; psychiatric diagnoses are the most common, especially the label of schizophrenia or paranoid psychosis (Dewhurst, Oliver, & McKnight, 1970; Lishman, 1987). Bolt (1970) found that sometimes a diagnosis of schizophrenia or paranoid psychosis remained throughout the patient's life and was never revised prior to the patient's death; the diagnosis of Huntington's chorea was made on autopsy.

Onset of Huntington's disease is usually between the ages of 25 and 50 years; an average age of onset is in the mid-forties but the disease varies widely in age of onset sometimes even within members of the same family. There is evidence that the disease follows a more severe course when the onset is early; psychiatric disturbances in particular become more prominent as a premonitory feature (Lishman, 1987). These disturbances often are present for some considerable time before the chorea or intellectual impairment is apparent. Paranoid developments may be the earliest stage accompanied by depression and anxiety; in other cases a florid schizophrenic illness may be the presenting symptom. In some families, there is the phenomenon of anticipation, that is, the worsening of the disease phenotype over successive generations.

In 1983, Folstein, Abbott, Chase, Jensen, and Folstein surveyed the incidence of affective disorder among 88 patients of 63 kindreds from a defined geographical area in the state of Maryland. Fourty-one percent showed a major affective disorder, 32% depressive and 9% bipolar. These psychiatric symptoms had antedated the chorea by 2 to 20 years in almost two-thirds of the cases, apparently being confined to certain families. This 1983 study suggested a genetic heterogeneity within Huntington's disease.

Due to work in molecular biology, we now have a better understanding of these genetic patterns (see Chapter 10). Huntington's disease does not have genetic hetererogeneity in the sense that there is more than one gene involved. All the families so far studied worldwide have been mapped to the same location on chromosome 4p16.3 (Conneally et al., 1989). The gene has trinucleotide repeats. One molecular analysis of this repeat sequence revealed a range of 37–86 repeats in affected individuals and 11–34 repeats in normal controls (Duyau et al., 1993). The number of repeats correlates negatively with the age of onset, regardless of sex of the transmitting parent. In addition, in patients with maternally inherited Huntington disease, the length of the paternally inherited normal allele was also found to negatively correlate with the age of onset, raising the question whether in this situation the variation in repeat size within the normal ranges also might influence the function of the gene (Snell et al., 1993). The gene appears to have an expanded nucleotide repeat sequence, however, which is unstable. For example, in one Huntington's disease family, an affected male with a CAG repeat of 46 copies transmitted six different expanded alleles to each of his affected offspring, ranging from 48 to 120 repeats (Huntington's Disease Collaborative Research Group, 1993). The length of the trinucleotide repeat correlates positively with both age of onset and rapidity of clinical progression as well as neuropathological severity (Furtado et al., 1996).

Diagnosis of Huntington's chorea may be made during life by several techniques. One of these is through imaging techniques that show a marked dilation of the ventricular system, specially the frontal horns combined with a striking atrophy of the caudate nuclei, which may be represented only by a rim of tissue along the ventrolateral edge of the dilated anterior horns.

DNA testing also is available for the gene for Huntington's disease and the gene product called the huntingtin (Huntington's Disease Collaborative Group, 1993). The abnormal results are found in chromosome 4 in both familial and sporadic cases. There is a dynamic mutation in which trinucleotide repeats of CAG are expanded excessively; the run of CAGs in the gene encodes a polyglutamine tract. The length of the polyglutamine tract in normal individuals is 11 to 34; in individuals at risk for or with developed Huntington disease, the length is 37 to 121 (Novelletto et al., 1994). In families with the phenomenon of anticipation, there is evidence that the worsening of the disease in successive generations may be correlated with an increasing expansion of CAGs (Duyao et al., 1993; Snell et al., 1993; Andrew et al., 1993). Even in nonfamilial cases, it is worthwhile to search for the gene as some clinically doubtful sporadic cases were found to have the trinucleotide repeat (Davis et al., 1994).

KARTAGENER SYNDROME

Kartagener syndrome (immotile cilia syndrome) is an autosomal recessive disease with an incidence of about 1:4000 persons. The patients have situs inversus, chronic sinusitis, and chronic bronchitis with bronchiectasis due to a generalized disorder of ciliary motility. Male sterility can result from inadequate spermatozoal movement.

A number of patients have been described in the literature who have both Kartagener syndrome and schizophrenia (Kartagener & Horlacher, 1935; Kartagener & Stucki, 1962; Finkelstein, 1962; Glick & Graubert, 1964). It might just be coincidence that the two diseases coincide in some individuals, but because of the rarity of Kartagener syndrome, this remains an open question. How immotile cilia would relate to a disease of the central nervous system is far from clear; the failed ciliary activity of embryonal tissues are thought to be responsible for the situs inversus.

OCULOCUTANEOUS ALBINISM

Schizophrenia has been reported in patients with familial albinism (Baron, 1976; Clarke & Buckley, 1989). In the pedigree reported by Baron, five of the six albino individuals suffered from schizophrenia. Although these families may well represent two separate diseases (schizophrenia and albinism), which just happened to strike these unlucky families, the gene for tyrosinase, the enzyme responsible for albinism, is on the long arm of the eleventh chromosome, an area of intense investigation in schizophrenia research (see Chapter 10).

SCHILDER'S CEREBRAL SCHLEROSIS

Schilder's disease is a degenerative disease that usually presents with neurological signs; however, sometimes it can present as hebephrenic or catatonic schizophrenia with minimal or no neurological signs. In a number of these patients classified as schizophrenia prior to modern imaging techniques, the diagnosis of

Schilder's disease was not made until autopsy (Ferraro, 1934; Holt & Tedeschi, 1943; Roizin, Moriarty, & Weil, 1945; Peters, 1956; Jankowski, 1963); all these cases showed a hebephreno-catatonic picture. Schilder's disease mainly attacks the occipital lobes; however, in the schizophrenic cases, the predominant pathology often was in the frontal lobes, which may have been a factor in the clinical presentation of psychiatric rather than neurological symptoms.

Today imaging techniques such as CT or magnetic resonançe imaging (MRI) followed by a brain biopsy can lead to the correct diagnosis during life. Ramani (1981) reported on such a patient with a diagnosis of chronic schizophrenia who had disorganization of thinking, bizarre posturing, paranoid delusions, hallucinations and was refractory to treatment for 5 years. Finally a CT was performed that showed large symmetrically situated low-density areas in the frontal regions. Brain biopsy confirmed the diagnosis of Schilder's cerebral sclerosis (Ramani, 1981).

TOURETTE'S SYNDROME

There is evidence that a wide array of neuropsychiatric disturbances can result in individuals who carry the gene for Tourette's syndrome. The syndrome is a hereditary tic disorder whose manifestations often include hallucinations, paranoid ideation, schizotypical thinking, and schizophrenialike psychosis (Kerbeshian & Burd, 1985; Takeuchi et al., 1986; Comings & Comings, 1987; Kerbeshian & Burd, 1988; Comings, 1990).

Tourette's syndrome is also found in a small number of children with autism or fragments of the autistic syndrome (Gillberg & Coleman, 1992). One of the most interesting cases described a boy who was a savant calendrical calculator; he had learning difficulties but definitely was not an "idiot" (Moriarty, Ring, & Robertson, 1993). (The authors of this book deplore the use of the term "idiot savant" preferring the term "autistic savant" or just "savant.")

Sverd, Montero, and Gurevich (1993) have made an important contribution by documenting that the occasional patient with autism who, past adolescence, develops a schizophreniclike psychosis may carry the gene for Tourette syndrome. This will help put into perspective the debate about whether autism turns into schizophrenia. It is rare but when it does so, there may be an identifiable reason in some cases.

TUBEROUS SCLEROSIS

The classical triad of tuberous sclerosis is epilepsy, adenoma sebecum, and mental deficiency. According to a study at the Mayo Clinic, however, up to one-third of the patients may have normal intelligence (Gomez, 1979) and, when this group of intellectually normal patients develop psychiatric symptoms, occasionally they may receive the diagnosis of chronic schizophrenia.

Lishman (1987) reviewed the medical literature pointing out that psychotic features were common in individuals with tuberous sclerosis and that some institutionalized patients received a diagnosis of a "primitive form of catatonic schizophrenia" (Lishman, 1987, p. 601). Zlotlow and Kleiner (1965) have described a 34 year old regarded as a chronic schizophrenic, often incontinent, speaking incoherently and with long episodes of mutism; periods of irritable excitement alternated with catatonic stupor in this patient. Tuberous sclerosis has a heterogeneous genetic origin—the genes causing this symptom complex are located on chromosomes 16, 9, and possibly other chromosomes (see Chapter 10).

REFERENCES

Andrew, S. E., Goldberg, Y. P., Kremer, B. et al. (1993). The relationship between trinucleotide (CAG) repeat length and clinical features of Huntington's disease. *Nature Genet, 4*, 398–403.

Baron, M. (1976). Albinism and schizophreniform psychosis: A pedigree study. *American Journal of Psychiatry, 133*: 1273–1280.

Bolt, J. M. W. (1970). Huntington's chorea in the west of Scotland. *British Journal of Psychiatry, 116*, 259–270.

Caviness, V. S. (1986). Genetic abnormalities of the developing nervous system. In A. K. Asbury, G. M. McKann, & W. I. McDonald (Eds.), *Diseases of the nervous system* (pp. 22–35). Philadelphia: Saunders.

Clarke, D. J., & Buckley, M. E. (1989). Familial association of albinism and schizophrenia. *British Journal of Psychiatry, 155,*551–553.

Comings, D. E. (1990). *Tourette syndrome and human behavior.* Duarte, CA: Hope Publishing Co.

Comings, D. E., & Comings, B. G. (1987). A controlled study of Tourette syndrome, IV Obessions, compulsions and schizoid behaviors. *American Journal of Human Genetics, 41,* 782–803.

Conneally, P. M., Haimes, J., Tanzi, R. et al. (1989). No evidence of linkage heterogeneity between Huntington disease and G8. *Genomics, 5,* 304–308.

Cummings, J. L., Gosenfeld, L. F., Houlihan, J. P., & McCaffrey, T. (1983). Neuropsychiatric disturbances associated with idiopathic calcification of the basal ganglia. *Biological Psychiatry, 18,* 591–601.

Davies, D. L. (1949). Psychiatric changes associated with Freidreich's ataxia. *Journal of Neurology, Neurosurgery and Psychiatry, 12,* 246–250.

Davis, D. L., Bateman, D., Quinn, N. P., Marsden, C. D., & Harding, A. E. (1994). Mutation analysis in patients with possible but apparently sporadic Huntington's disease. *Lancet, 344,* 714–717.

Davison, K. (1983). Schizophrenia-like psychoses associated with organic cerebral disorders: A Review. *Psychiatric Developments, 1,* 1–34.

Davison, K. (1987). Organic and toxic concomitants of schizophrenia: Association or chance. In H. Helmchen, & F. Henn (Eds.), *Biological perspectives on schizophrenia.* Chichester: Wiley.

Davison, K., & Bagley, C. R. (1969). Schizophrenia-like psychoses associated with organic disorders of the central nervous system: A review of the literature. In R. N. Herrington (Ed.), *British Journal of Psychiatry,* Special Publication No. 4.

Deckert, J., Strik, W. K., & Fritze, J. (1992). Organic schizophrenic syndrome associated with symmetrical basal ganglia sclerosis and XO/XY mosaic. *Biological Psychiatry, 31,* 401–403.

Dewhurst, K., Oliver, J. E., & McKnight, A. L. (1970). Sociopsychiatric consequences of Huntington's disease. *British Journal of Psychiatry, 116,* 255–258.

Duyao, M., Ambrose, C., Myers, R. et al. (1993). Trinucleotide repeat length instability and age of onset in Huntington's disease. *Nature Genetics, 4,* 387–392.

Fernandez-Bouzas, A., Angrist, B., Hemdal, P., Adler, L. A., & Rotrosen, J. (1990). Basal ganglia calcification in schizophrenia. *Biological Psychiatry, 27,* 671–685.

Ferraro, A. (1934). Histopathological findings in two cases clinically diagnosed as dementia praecox. *American Journal of Psychiatry, 90* (part 2) 883–903.

Ferraro, A. (1943). Pathological changes in the brain of a case of clinically diagnosed dementia praecox. *Journal of Neuropathology and Experimental Neurology, 2,* 84–94.

Finkelstein, B. (1962). Mental symptoms occuring in Kartagener's syndrome. *American Journal of Psychiatry, 118,* 745.

Folstein, S., & Hedreen, J. (1995). The psychopathology of Huntington's disease. *Biological Psychiatry, 37,* 593–683.

Folstein, S. E., Abbott, M. H., Chase, G. A., Jensen, B. A., & Folstein, M. F. (1983). The association of affective disorder with Huntington's disease in a case series and in families. *Psychological Medicine, 13,* 537–542.

Forstl, H., Krumm, B., Eden, S., & Kohlmeyer, K. (1991). What is the psychiatric significance of bilateral basal ganglia mineralization? *Biological Psychiatry, 29,* 827–833.

Francis, A. F. (1979). Familial basal ganglia calcification and schizophreniform psychosis. *British Journal of Psychiatry, 135,* 360–362.

Francis, A., & Freeman, H. (1984). Psychiatric abnormality and brain calcification over four generations. *Journal of Nervous and Mental Diseases, 172,* 166.

Fromm-Reichmann, F. (1943). Psychoanalytic psychiatry with psychotics. *Psychiatry, 6,* 277–279.

Furtado, S., Suchnowersky, O., Rewcastle, B., Graham, L., Klimek, M. L., & Garber, A. (1996). Relationship between trinucleotide repeats and neuropathological changes in Huntington's disease. *Annals of Neurology, 39,* 132–136.

Gillberg, C., & Coleman, M. (1992). *The biology of the autistic syndromes.* London: Mac Keith Press.

Glick, I. D., & Graubert, D. N. (1964). Kartagener's syndrome and schizophrenia: a report of a case with chromosomal studies. *American Journal of Psychiatry, 121,* 603–605.

Gomez, M. R. (1979). Neurologic and psychiatric symptoms. In M. R. Gomez (Ed.), *Tuberous sclerosis.* New York: Raven Press.

Gottesman, I. I. (1991). *Schizophrenia genesis.* New York: W. H. Freeman & Co.

Guze, S. B., Cloninger, C. R., Martin, R. L. et al. (1983). A follow-up and family study of schizophrenia *Archives of General Psychiatry, 40,* 148–152.

Hall, P. (1972). Calcification of the basal ganglia apparently presenting as a schizophreniform psychosis. *Postgraduate Medical Journal, 48,* 636–639.

Holt, E. K., & Tedeschi, C. (1943). Cerebral patchy demyelination. *Journal of Neuropathology and Experimental Neurology, 2*, 306–314.

Huntington's Disease Collaborative Research Group. (1993). A novel gene containing a trinucleotide repeat that is expanded and unstable on Huntington's disease chromosomes. *Cell, 72*, 971–983.

Janowski, K. (1963). A case of Schilder's diffuse sclerosis diagnosed clinically schizophrenia. *Acta Neuropathologica, 2*, 302–305.

Kartagener, M., & Horlacher, A. (1935). Bronchiektasien bel Situs viscerum inversus. *Schweizerische Medizinische Wochenschrift, 65*, 782–784.

Kartagener, M., & Stucki, P. (1962). Brochiectasis with situs inversus. *Archives of Pediatrics, 79*, 193–207.

Kendler, K. S. (1983). Twin studies in schizophrenia, a current perspective. *American Journal of Psychiatry, 140*, 1413–1419.

Kerbeshian, J., & Burd, L. (1985). Auditory hallucinations and atypical tic disorder: Case reports. *Journal of Clinical Psychiatry, 46*, 398–399.

Kerbeshian, J., & Burd, L. (1988). Tourette disorder and schizophrenia in children. *Neuroscience and Behavioral Reviews, 12*, 267–270.

Kety, S. S. (1983). Observations on genetic and enviornmental influences in the etiology of mental disorders from studies on adoptees and their families. In S. S. Kety, L. P. Rowland, R. L. Sedman, & S. W. Matthyesse (Eds.), *Genetics of neurological and psychiatric disorders* (pp. 105–114). New York: Raven Press.

Koide, R., Ikeuchi, T., Onodera, O., Tanaka, H., Igarashi, S., Endo, K., Takahashi, H., Kondo, R., Ishikawa, A., Hayashi, T., Saito, M., Tomoda, A., Miike, T., Naito, H., Ikuta, F., & Tsuji, S. (1994). Unstable expansion of CAG repeat in hereditary dentatorubal-pallidoluysin atrophy (DRPLA) *Nature Genetics, 6*, 9–13.

Konig, P. (1989). Psychopathological alterations in cases of symmetrical basal ganglia sclerosis. *Biological Psychiatry, 25*, 459–468.

Lauterbach, E. C., Spears, T. E., Prewett, M. J., Price, S. T., Jackson, J. G., & Kirsh, A. D. (1994). Neuropsychiatric disorders, myoclonus and dystonia in calcification of basal ganglia pathways. *Biological Psychiatry, 35*, 345–351.

Lishman, W. A. (1987). *Organic psychiatry; The psychological consequences of cerebral disorder*, second edition. Oxford: Blackwell Scientific Publications.

Macciardi, F., Petronis, A., Van Tol, H. H. M., Marimo, C., Cavallini, C., Smeraldi, E., & Kennedy, J. L. (1994). Analysis of the D_4 dopamine receptor gene variant in an Italian schizophrenia kindred. *Archives of General Psychiatry, 51*, 288–293.

McHugh, P. R., & Folstein, M. F. (1975). Psychiatric syndromes of Huntington's chorea. In D. F. Benson & D. Blumer (Eds.), *Psychiatric aspects of neurologic disease*. New York: Grune & Stratton.

McHugh, P. R., & Folstein, M. F. (1981). Psychiatric syndromes in Huntington's chorea. In D. F. Benson & D. Blumer (Eds.), *Psychiatric aspects of neurologic disease*. New York: Grune & Stratton.

Moriarty, J., Ring, H. A., & Robertson, M. M. (1993). An idiot savant calendrical calculator with Gilles de la Tourette syndrome: Implications for an understanding of the savant syndrome. *Psychological Medicine, 23*, 1019–1021.

Naito, H., & Oyanagi, S. (1982). Familial myoclonus epilepsy and choreoathetosis: Hereditary dentatorubral-pallidoluysian atrophy. *Neurology, 32*, 798–807.

Novelletto, A., Persichetti, F., Sabbadini, G. et al. (1994). Analysis of the trinucleotide repeat expansion in Italian families affected with Huntington disease. *Human Molecular Genetics, 3*, 93–98.

Nowakowski, R. S. (1991). Genetic disturbances of neuronal migration: Some examples from the limbic system of mutant mice. In S. A. Mednick, T. D. Cannon, C. E. Barr, & M. Lyon (Eds.), *Fetal neural development and adult schizophrenia* (pp. 69–96). Cambridge: Cambridge University Press.

Peters, G. (1956). Dementia praecox. In Luborsch, Henke (Eds.), *Erkrankungen des ZNS IV. Handbuch der Speziellen Pathologogischen Anatomie und Histologie, Bd XIII*. Berlin: Springer.

Ramani, S. V. (1981). Psychosis associated with frontal lobe lesions in Schilder's cerebral sclerosis. *Journal of Clinical Psychiatry, 42*, 250–252.

Roizin, L., Moriarty, J. D., & Weil, A. A. (1945). Schizophrenic reaction syndrome in the course of acute demylination of central nervous system: Clinicopathological report of a case, with brief review of the literature. *Archives of Neurology and Psychiatry, 54*, 202–211.

Snell, R. G., MacMillan, J. C., Cheadle, J. P. et al. (1993). Relationship between trinucleotide repeat expansion phenotypic variation in Huntington's disease. *Nature Genetics, 4*, 393–397.

Streletzki, F. (1961). Psychosen im verlauf der Huningtonschen Chorea inter besonderer berücksichtigung der wahnbilddungen. *Archives für Psychiatrie und Nervenkrankheiten, 202*, 202–214.

Suddath, R. L., Christison, G. W., Torrey, E. F., Casanova, M. F., & Weinberger, D. R. (1990). Anatomical abnormalities in the brains of monozygotic twins discordant for schizophrenia. *New England Journal of Medicine, 322*, 791–794.

Sverd, J., Montero, G., & Gurevich, N. (1993). Brief Report: Cases for an association between Tourette syndrome, autistic disorder and schizophrenic-like disorder. *Journal of Autism and Developmental Disorders*, *23*, 407–413.

Takeuchi, K., Yamashita, M., Morikyo, M., Takeda, N., Morita, K., Tamura, T., & Karya, H. (1986). Giles de la Tourette's syndrome and schizophrenia. *Journal of Nervous and Mental Diseases*, *174*, 247–248.

Tienari, P. J., & Wynne, L. C. (1994). Adoption studies of schizophrenia. *Annals of Medicine, 26*, 233–237.

Torrey, E. F., Bowler, A. E., Taylor, E. H., & Gottesman, I. I. (1994). *Schizophrenia and manic-depressive disorder.* New York: Basic Books.

Warner, T. T., Williams, L. D., Walker, R. W. H., Flinter, F., Robb, S. A., Bundey, S. E., Honava, M., & Harding, A. E. (1995). A clinical and molecular genetic study of dentatorubropallidoluysian atrophy in four European families. *Annals of Neurology, 37*, 452–459.

West, A. (1973). Concurrent schizophrenia-like psychosis in monozygotic twins suffering from CNS disorder. *British Journal of Psychiatry*, *122*, 675–677.

Yazawa, I., Nukina, N., Hashida, H., Goto, J., Yamada, M., Kanazawa, I. (1995). Abnormal gene product identified in hereditary dentatorubral-pallidoluysian atrophy (DRPLA) brain. *Nature Genetics, 10*, 99.

Zlotlow, M., & Kleiner, S. (1965). Catatonic schizophrenia associated with tuberose sclerosis. *Psychiatric Quarterly, 39*, 466–475.

CHAPTER 12

Structural, Static, and Malignant Entities

Structural lesions of the central nervous system can be associated with schizophrenic symptoms. These changes in brain structure can be initiated at any time in life from abnormalities in utero to the senile degenerations at the end of life. In general, males who develop schizophrenia show more premorbid deficits, earlier onset, and poorer outcome than females (Szymanski et al., 1995). One explanation suggested for this difference between the sexes is that males with schizophrenia are more likely to have structural brain abnormalities (Castle & Murray, 1991) or delays in myelination (Benes, Turtle, Khan, & Farol, 1994).

GESTATIONAL LESIONS

There is an increasing amount of evidence building to suggest that one subgroup of patients who present with schizophrenia—primarily during late adolescence and early adulthood—may have an apparently static encephalopathy that was already present at the time of birth and may be due to an insult to the central nervous system as early as the second trimester of gestation. It is known that brain growth increases dramatically at the end of the second trimester.

It is difficult for many physicians to imagine that an insult 15 to 20 years or more earlier and even prior to birth could cause the onset of such a major chronic illness, such as schizophrenia in adult life. However, the early clinicians may have had an inkling about this as described in the paper "Neurodevelopmental Schizophrenia: Rediscovery of Dementia Praecox" (Murray, 1994). A recent clue was that a study of schizophreniclike psychoses in patients with chronic temporal lobe epilepsy showed they did not occur at random; they were significantly associated with lesions that originated in the fetus or perinatally (Roberts, Done, Bruton, & Crow, 1990). Another piece of evidence was a study of monozygotic twin pairs discordant for schizophrenia in which 30% of the twins who later developed schizophrenia had permanent changes in motor skills and showed unusual behavior by 5 years of age (Torrey et al., 1994). Then another surprise from childhood home movies not only revealed a higher rate of neuromotor abnormalities in preschizophrenic children compared to their healthy siblings but that the group differences were significant only in the first 2 years of life (Walker, Savole, & Davis, 1994).

One way of coming to terms with this concept of such an early lesion is thinking about the brain in anatomical developmental terms as an always changing organ. For example, in the neuropathological study of myelination, a progressive increase has been reported in the myelination of the superior medullary lamina of the parahippocampal gyrus during childhood, adolescence, and even adulthood (Benes et al., 1994). The superior medullary lamina showing the late postnatal myelination is involved in the relay of information among several brain regions thought to be implicated in the pathophysiology of schizophrenia (the hippocampal formation, the parahippocampal gyrus and the anterior cingulate region). In some of these systems, for example, cortical hippocampal relays, abnormal patterns of myelination have been reported in patients with schizophrenia (Benes, 1989). These relay areas, also known as the heteromodal association cortex system, are the areas of the greatest grey matter reduction in schizophrenics according to a recent paper (Schlaepher et al., 1994). The control group, bipolar disorder patients, did not exhibit heteromodal gray matter reduction. This paper adds additional evidence, already reported that the brains of schizophrenic individuals taken as a group, are smaller than those of controls (Bruton et al., 1990) and have a 20–30% decrease in the volume of the medial temporal lobe structures.

Benes and associates in their 1994 paper speculate that myelination in this region may be a protective, rather than a potentiating framework for the appearance of the symptoms of schizophrenia, a result they call paradoxical. In other words, any delay in the myelination could lead to failure in adequately developing the inhibitory systems needed to suppress the pathology already present in the brain.

Other reports consistent with a disorder of brain development describe reduced tempolimbic and thalamic structure volumes and nerve cell numbers without accompanying gliosis, cytoarchitectural anomalies in the hippocampal formation, frontal cortex, entorhinal cortex, and left lateralized temporal horn enlargement. These findings are well described and discussed in Bogerts and Falkai (1991). In 1993, Bogerts reviewed 50 neuroanatomical postmortem studies and came to the conclusion that a number of factors, including lack of gliosis in limbic strucutres, probably reflects a disorder of prenatal brain development in schizophrenia (Bogerts, 1993).

Other disciplines have reported abnormal findings in adolescents with schizophrenia. In neurophysiology, there have been reports that during the late adolescence of individuals developing schizophrenia, both position emission tomography (PET) and [51]P MRS (magnetic resonance spectroscopy) high-energy phosphate findings indicate frontal hypometabolism, which could suggest either an exaggeration or loss of control of the synaptic pruning that is normally occurring at this time (Pettegrew et al., 1991; Keshaven et al., 1994). As early as 1982/1983, Feinberg raised the question of whether schizophrenia could be due to a fault in programmed synaptic elimination during adolescense (Feinberg, 1982/1983). An abnormally high neuronal density in prefrontal area 9 and occipital area 17 has been reported in the cortex of some individuals with schizophrenia (Selemon et al., 1995).

To move from the adolescent or adult brain all the way back to before birth certainly seems like a very major leap. However, focused evidence of a midtrimester gestational insult in some patients with schizophrenia can be seen in several different disciplines—neuropathology (neuronal migration defects without gliosis, static ventriculomegaly), clinically (in the presence of second trimester physical anomalies), and in epidemiological studies (viral infections).

Neuronal Migration Defects

As the central nervous system develops in a fetus, brain cells undergo proliferation, migration, and differentiation in order to become functional neurons. It is likely that the overwhelming majority of the cells of the brains of humans are present and in place by 6 months of gestational age. However, this statement is made with caution as there are reports of production of neurons in the adult rat (Bayer, Yackel, & Puri, 1982).

In the first trimester, proliferation of new brain cells occurs in specialized zones that line the ventricular system. In the case of the temporal cortex, all of the neurons of the major subdivisions (areas CA1, CA2, and CA3) of the hippocampus are derived from the ventricular zone (Nowakowski & Rakic, 1981).

Primarily during the second trimester, after proliferation from neuroblasts to young neurons, cells need to migrate to their final location, a process accomplished by either passive *cell displacement* or active *neuronal migration* (Sidman & Rakic, 1973). In active neuronal migration, neurons may be guided to their final position by radial glial fibers, the scaffolds of the cerebral cortex. When the neurons reach the vicinity of their final position, the complex job of differentiation begins. Neurons must grow an axon—often over a long distance—and produce dendritic processes in a characteristic arborization pattern. As one example, the cells in the striatal–thalamic–cortical dopamine system proliferate and migrate to their target structures in the second trimester. It should be noted that the afferent connections of the dopamine system to the prefrontal cortex are not established until after birth, however.

Sometimes during fetal life the process of neuronal migration is disrupted before some neurons have reached their final position; the neurons are disoriented. A major disruption results in lissencephaly (smooth brain), often a form of profound retardation, in which there is serious disruption of neuronal migration of cortical layers combined with normal myelination and, consequently, adequate glial migration (Barkovich, Koch, & Carrol, 1991). Less major disruptions may cause missing neuronal sections, such as porencephalic cysts or heterotopic (or ectopic) clumps of cells.

In some patients with severe schizophrenia, cytoarchitectural anomalies have been described (Falkai, Bogerts, Roberts, & Crow, 1988). In a computed tomography (CT) scan project of chronic schizophrenics, a 3/5cm right parieto-temporal porencephalic cyst and mild right cerebral atrophy was found in a patient with a mild left hemiparesis from birth (Cunningham Owens, Johnstone, Bydder, & Kreel, 1980). Anomalies have been found in a the hippocampal formation (McLardy, 1974; Altshuler, Conrad, Kovelman, & Scheibel, 1987) and heterotopic neurons specifically have been described bilaterally in area CA1 of the hippocampus (Kovelman & Scheibel, 1984, 1986; Conrad, Abebe, Austin, Forsythe, & Scheibel, 1991; Conrad & Scheibel, 1987). Missing or abnormally sized neurons also have been described (Benes, Majocha, Bird, & Marotta, 1987; Benes, Sorensen, & Bird, 1991; Benes, McSparren, Bird, San Giovanni, & Vincent, 1991b). In clinical–anatomical correlations in postmortem studies, cytoarchitectural changes in the limbic allocortex have been reported to occur more frequently in hebephrenic than in paranoid patients (Jakob & Beckmann, 1986).

A recent sophisticated study using immunocytochemistry [neurons that contain nictotinamide-adenine dinucleotide phosphate-diaphorase (NADPH-d)] have shown cellular displacement of neurons in the frontal lobe, temporal lobe, and hippocampal formation in four out of five brains of individuals with schizophrenia (Akbarian et al., 1993a, 1993b). Based on the timing for the migration of these neurons containing NADPH-d in the developing brain of the rhesus monkey, it is expected that the perturbation occurred at some point in the middle to later part of the second trimester of gestation (Bloom, 1993).

Recently there is a report that at least one of the neurotrophins, the growth factors that play important developmental roles for the central nervous system, may be different in individuals with schizophrenia compared to controls (Nanko et al., 1994). For full details, see Chromosome 12 in Chapter 10. Individuals with schizophrenia have been found to have increases in a serum fragment of the neural cell adhesion molecule floating around in their serum in one study (Lyons et al., 1988), whereas another study reports decreased expression of the embryonic form of the neural cell adhesion molecule in schizophrenic brains (Barbeau, Liang, Robitalille, Quirion, & Srivastava, 1995).

An increased incidence of psychosis has been demonstrated in Japanese individuals who were exposed during the second trimester of gestation to the radiation from the atomic explosions in Nagasaki and Hiroshima (Otake & Schull, 1984). Studies of these patients have noted disturbed patterns of cell migration in their brains (Radic, 1991).

Abnormalities of the corpus callosum and septum pellucidum are manifestations of defective neuronal migration and are usually accompanied by pervasive neuronal abnormalities. The septum pellucidum serves as a relay structure between the limbic system and diencephalon. Such abnormalities can be seen with many clinical presentations not limited to but including schizophrenia—abnormalities of the septum pellucidum (Mathews et al., 1985; Lewis & Mezey, 1985; George et al., 1989; Luaute et al., 1992; Degreef et al., 1992; Scott, Price, George, Brillman, & Rothfus, 1993) and agenesis of the corpus callosum (Mathews et al., 1985; Andreasen, 1988; Lewis, Reveley, David, & Ron, 1989; Scott et al., 1993). It is relevant to keep in mind that these midline cerebral malformations can also be seen in normal controls; however, in the two series in which patients with schizophrenia were compared to controls (Degreef et al., 1992; Scott et al., 1993), there was an increased incidence in patients with schizophrenia. In a study of patients with epilepsy, however, the morphology of the corpus callosum was not related to the presence of psychosis (Conlon & Trimble, 1988). Reversal of the usual asymmetry of the planum temporale is under investigation (Falkai et al., 1995; Petty et al., 1995). Porencephalic and arachnoid cysts have been reported in a patient with an atypical psychosis (Blackshaw & Bowen, 1987).

In addition to classical neuronal migration defects, other gestational lesions have been documented in individuals with schizophrenic symptoms (Owens, Johnstone, Bydder, & Kreel, 1980). One girl, who, at the age of 14 years had both intractable seizures and schizophrenia, was found to have a cavernous angioma after a left anterior temporal lobectomy. Her seizures were markedly improved and she was no longer classified as schizophrenic after the surgical procedure (Bruton, 1988). There are cases in the medical literature in which an arteriovenous malformation (Vallant, 1965) and a cerebral arterial malformation (Reimer & Nagaswami, 1974) appeared as possible causes of an individual's diagnosis of schizophrenia.

One surprise in all these developmental reports was the measurement of lobules of the cerebellum in patients with schizophrenia. Because of reports of cerebellar vermal atrophy in autism (Courchesne, Young-Courchesne, Press, Hesselink, & Jernigan, 1988), Nasrallah, Schwarzkopf, Olson, and Coffman (1991) measured the lobules in 30 men with schizophrenia and found the patients had consistently larger cerebellar structures than controls.

Minor Physical Anomalies

Minor physical anomalies are slight deviations in external physical characteristics that are noted frequently in developmental disorders. Because the brain and the skin develop embryologically from the same germinal layer—the ectoderm—visable anomalies in individuals have been postulated possibly to serve as evidence for nonvisible brain anomalies in the same individual. Organogenesis is mostly complete in the first trimester, before the massive neural migration begins. One of the few organs whose prenatal development is simultaneous with the neuronal migration to the cortex is the distal upper limb. The ectodermal cells of the fetal upper limb migrate to form the skin of the hand between 14 and 22 weeks of gestation. Scalp hair patterning is determined slightly earlier during weeks 10–16 of fetal development.

There has been a consistent finding of more minor physical anomalies in patients with schizophrenia compared to controls (Gualtieri, Adams, Shen, & Louiselle, 1982; Guy, Majorski, Wallace, & Guy, 1983; Green, Satz, & Soper, 1987; Lohr & Flynn, 1993; Cannon et al., 1994; Green et al., 1994). The neurodevelopmental timing of the insults causing these minor physical anomalies is suggested by the case of monozygotic twins discordant for schizophrenia; higher scores of second trimester dysmorphological hand anomalies have been found in the psychotic twin (Bracha,

Torrey, Bigelow, Lohr, & Linington, 1991). A counterclockwise scalp hair whorl also has been reported in individuals with schizophrenia (Alexander, Breslin, Molnar, Richter, & Mukherjee, 1992).

The presence of these minor physical anomalies may have a practical implication in that there is some evidence that patients with high scores for physical anomalies are more likely to develop tardive dyskinesia; that is, preexisting central nervous system damage may place patients with schizophrenia at increased risk for side effects of drugs attempting to control their symptoms (Barnes, 1988).

Ventriculomegaly and Occult Hydrocephalus

Many, many studies have reported enlarged ventricles and reduction of cortical volume in many schizophrenic patients using a variety of methodologies—pneumoencephaly (PEG), computerized tomography, and magnetic resonance imaging (Harvey et al., 1993; Nopoulos et al., 1995). Neither the meaning or the timing of the enlarged ventricles are yet understood but it is quite possible that they were part of the neurodevelopmental pattern of the brain of the individuals who later became schizophrenic and are therefore included under the "gestational lesions" section. Ventriculography has been found in the youngest patients; for example, a 10 year-old with a recent onset of the DSM-III (APA, 1980) criteria for schizophrenia was found to have lateral, third, and fourth ventricular enlargement (Woody, Bolyard, Eisenhauer, & Altschuler, 1987). That these lesions may be static is suggested by the case of a boy who had a CT scan because of a possible sports injury 15 months prior to his development of schizophrenia. There was no change at all in the size of the ventriculomegaly when he later had a repeat CT because of the development of symptoms of schizophrenia. A multipatient 7-year follow-up study clearly states "Cerebral ventricular enlargement in schizophreniform disorder does not progress" (Jaskiw et al., 1994, p. 23).

Pneumoencephaly was first used in 1927 to study schizophrenic patients (Haug, 1962). Because the technique involves the injection of air, the dilated ventricles seen in many early PEG studies were considered controversial, but later techniques have confirmed the ventriculomegaly often demonstrated in these early studies is a consistent finding in many schizophrenic patients.

Computerized tomography was first used in a study of schizophrenic patients in 1976 (Johnstone, Crow, Frith, Husband, & Kreel, 1976). A review performed a decade later on 80 studies noted that 75% of the studies that measured the lateral ventricles and 80% of those that measured the the third ventricle reported enlargement in schizophrenia (Shelton & Weinberger, 1986).

After magnetic resonance imaging was introduced, the presence of ventriculomegaly in many patients with schizophrenia was confirmed by this imaging technique (Andresasen et al., 1990). For example, a recent study of 81 individuals with schizophrenia again demonstrated that they had higher ventricle-brain ratios (i.e., larger ventricular volumes) than controls (Gur et al., 1994). The relevance of the increased ventricular size was emphasized by a study of monozygotic twins discordant for schizophrenia—in nearly all the cases, the schizophrenic twin was found to evidence larger third and lateral ventricles on MRI (Suddath, Christison, Torrey, Casanova, & Weinberger, 1990). Several investigators have recorded that increased ventricle-brain ratios and third ventricle widths in adulthood are significantly related to evidence of perinatal complications recorded by midwives on an average of 33 years prior to the actual measurement (Silverton, Finello, Mednick, & Schulsinger, 1985; Cannon, Mednick, & Parnas, 1989). As magnetic resonance imaging methods have been refined, very thin slices of brain can be visualized and there have been reports of finding small reductions in volume in particular brain areas, areas that might even correlate with detailed, specific symptoms of schizophrenia (Shenton, Kikinis, McCarley, & Jolesz, 1992) although this report has been challenged (Sullivan et al., 1996).

According to one study, the enlargement of the third ventricle may be more relevant than the enlargement of the lateral ventricles. Bornstein et al (1992) found highly significant associations between cognitive deficits and third-ventricular volume while neuropsychological performance was not highly associated with lateral ventricular size (Bornstein, Schwartzkopf, Olson, & Nasrallah, 1992).

Ventriculomegaly has been called the most consistently replicated neuropathological finding in schizophrenia. A majority of studies agree with the finding that schizophrenic patients as a whole have signficantly larger ventricles and smaller limbic brain structures; however, there is overlap with a normal population so that about 50% of the patients fall within normal ranges. A review of the literature shows that if you compare patients with schizophrenia with their unaffected first-degree relatives there is a higher percentage of ventricular enlargement in the persons with schizophrenia, from 70% to 100% (Cannon & Marco, 1994).

Daniel, Goldberg, Gibbons, and Weinberger (1991) decided to see if the large ventricles were a marker that characterizes a subgroup of patients with schizophrenia. Using a Gaussian mixture analysis of 1,056 cases, they found no evidence of bimodality in venticular size. The classic more-or-less bell-shaped curve was present; it has just moved as a whole to a higher plane compared to medical controls and normal controls. Their conclusion was that "distinct subpopulations of schizophrenia based on ventricular size do not exist" (p. 887). Of course the authors did not mean to imply that schizophrenia did not have subpopulations because that would be based on the ridiculous assumption that all the medical controls with their beautiful bell-shaped curve in their same study also all had only one disease. One interpretation of this data for both the medical controls and the persons with schizophrenia as well as the normal controls is that when many, many subpopulations exist within a large group of human brains, ventricular size tends to create a bell-shaped curve. From the ventricular data on schizophrenia, one also could speculate that the disease entities that result in expression of this particular final common pathway called schizophrenia have a tendency to atrophy the neuronal pathways lining the ventricles.

It is known that enlarged ventricles and reduction of brain volume can be a sign of a variety of different disease processes. In sorting out what causes the ventriculography, the specific location of the abnormalities (cortical sulci, lateral ventricles, third ventricle, sylvian fissures, interhemispheric fissures, etc.) needs to be defined.

Hydrocephalus [in which the outflow of cerebral spinal (CSF) fluid is blocked] is the best known etiology of enlarged ventricles, but failure of adequate development or later atrophy secondary to hemorrhage, infections, or other insults are also possibilities in any particular case. For each individual with schizophrenia who also has ventriculomegaly and reduction of brain volume, a serious attempt should be made to determine the etiology of the abnormality. It is important because, for example, the use of electroconvulsive therapy (ECT) as therapy for the symptoms of schizophrenia may raise the CSF pressure and cause further deterioration of a patient with increased CSF pressure (O'Flaithbheartaigh, Williams, & Jones, 1994).

Classical hydrocephalus has been reported in the brains of patients with schizophrenia. Aqeductal stenosis, in particular, may fail to declare itself until adolescence or adulthood; asymptomatic cases have even been found on autopsy. The stenosis is usually the result of a congenital defect although some may be traced to episodes of meningitis in childhood. Intraventicular pressure may be elevated or normal.

Schizophrenic symptoms have been reported in the adult presentation of aqueductal stenosis (Roberts, Trimble, & Robertson, 1983; Smith, 1990; O'Flaithbheartaigh et al., 1994). In one study, CT scans of patients with schizophrenia found three with aqueductal stenosis (Reveley & Reveley, 1983). Two were known to be hydrocephalic from birth but in the third patient, the condition was entirely unsuspected. A male with schizophrenia and cystic enlargement of the pineal body, a condition that can be associated with blockage of the aqeduct, presented at the early age of 11 years (Cunningham Owens et al., 1980). In both of the cases reported by O'Flaithbheartaigh et al. (1994), episodes of raised intracranial pressure were relieved neurosurgically, but there is no evidence from their paper that these procedures were effective in preventing reoccuring psychiatric deterioration.

Schizophrenia is also reported in normal-pressure hydrocephalus (Lying-Tunell, 1979). The classic triad used to identify normal pressure hydrocephalus is (1) urinary incontinence, (2) gait disturbance, and (3) dementia—not schizophrenia. There is a question of whether to treat occult hydrocephalus; a literature search by Dewan and Bick (1985, p. 1130) came to the conclusion that "normal pressure hydrocephalus can sometimes undoubtedly cause, or contribute to, 'schizophrenia.' The literature indicates that when the complete triad is present, surgical intervention may be remarkably rewarding."

Lishman (1987) also pointed out that in spite of a considerable failure rate, shunt operations can occcasionally be dramatically successful in relieving symptoms whether or not the intraventricular pressure has been raised.

A STATIC ENCEPHALOPATHY

First-episode neuroimaging studies in young people with schizophrenia suggest that there are abnormalities that predate the onset of the illness and are fixed in some cases (Keshaven et al., 1994). A review by Bogerts (1991) has revealed a lack of gliosis in the limbic structures of the temporal lobe in the brains of many schizophrenics, which could be interepreted as compatible with a gestational lesion rather than a degenerative disorder or a viral infection after birth. This information combined with evidence of neuronal migration defects and static ventriculomegaly suggests the possibility that many individuals with schizophrenia may have a static disease process that began before they were born, perhaps in the second trimester of gestation. If so, the first question to ask is *what kind of disease processes* would be likely to cause such injuries?

Based on information about gestational insults that specifically effect the brain from the field of neurology, there are a number of possibilities. Maternal viral infections are one distinct possibility for any given patient. The influenza virus and pestiviruses are currently under investigation as culprits (see Chapter 5). Another major possibility is genetic misprogramming, particularly in patients with positive family histories (see Chapter 10).

Dietary deficiency is also a possibility (Butler et al., 1994). Apparently, there is an increased risk of schizophrenia among female children exposed during gestation to the Dutch Hunger Winter of World War II when Dutch women were severely deprived of food during pregnancy (Susser & Lin, 1992). Reevaluation of the data raises the possibility that the same findings may hold true for male fetuses also (Jones, 1994; Susser, 1994).

Maternal exposure to toxins, intrauterine bleeding, and toxemia also might be considered in any individual patient. In the case of twins, the twin transfusion syndrome might be a factor. It is relevant to remember that once the fetus is injured in the second trimester, the chances of anoxia and perinatal difficulties at the end of third trimester subsequently increase.

A second, important question to ask is *when did the injury occur* to the fetal brain? The data from the neuronal migration defects and the minor physical anomalies point to the later months of the second trimester of pregnancy. It is interesting to note that the major psychiatric illness of childhood—autism— also has a significant subgroup of patients with evidence of second-trimester injury to the fetal brain; however, there is preliminary evidence that the timing of the injury in autism possibly may be nearer the beginning than the end of the second trimester (Gillberg & Coleman, 1992). A summary of some of the innovative thinking currently underway regarding neurodevelopmental lesions and schizophrenia is seen in Table 12.1.

CHILDHOOD LESIONS

Childhood Cranial Trauma

Wilcox and Nasrallah (1987) have presented evidence that childhood head trauma may, in some cases, be associated with the later development of schizophrenia. They compared the prevalence of head injury in 200 schizophrenics, 325 manic-depressives, and 134 normal subjects. They found head injury to be most common in the schizophrenic group, whereas almost all injuries were received before 10 years of age; in fact, two-thirds occurred before the age of 3 years. Earlier studies had suggested that head injury may be an age-dependent risk factor in psychosis (Achte, Hillbom, & Aalberg, 1969). A study from Nigeria that compared individuals with mania to those with schizophrenia found a history of early brain trauma was associated with an adult diagnosis of schizophrenia (Gurejeo, Bamidele, & Raji, 1994). Injury to the

TABLE 12.1 Neurodevelopmental Paths to Schizophrenia and Their Correlates

	Medial fronto–limbic defect	Periventricular damage	Cerebral specialization failure
Hypothetical Mechanism	Faulty migration of elements in the dorsal cytoarchitectonic trend	Delivery complications periventricular anoxia or hemorrhage	Failure of hemisphere specific or tertiary cortical growth and cellular "pruning"
Gross Morphologic Indices	Sulcal enlargement, volume reductions in anterior hippocampal formation	Ventricular enlargement	Absence or reversal of normal asymmetry, "thick" corpus callosum, small brain size?
Histopathologic Indices	Cytoarchitectonic variations in hippocampus, cingulate, and dorsomedial frontal cortex	Periventricular thinning	Altered asymmetry of planum temporale, frontal operculum, decreased relative volume of isocortical fields
Early Developmental "Markers"	If severe, attentional and motor disturbance	If severe, social withdrawal	Poor acquisition of language competence, early academic deficits
Pattern of psychotic decompensation	Florid, active, "paranoid"	Blunted, withdrawn, "flat"	Regressive, simple, "hebephrenic"
Response to Neuroleptics	Good	Fair/poor	Fair/poor
Deterioration?	Most likely	Possible	Least likely
Risk for TD	Highest	High?	Least likely
Neuropsychological profile after compensation	Executive and motor deficits; defects in response preparation and organization	Learning and memory deficits	Language deficits, "primitive" cognitive style; anomalous dominance

Table 12.1 *(cont.)*

	Medial fronto–limbic defect	Periventricular damage	Cerebral specialization failure
Psychophysiologic abnormalities	Reduced CNV; alteration of "processing negativity"	Orienting response dysfunction; alteration of mismatch negativity?	???

From R. M. Bilder & G. Degreef. (1991). Morphologic markers of neurodevelopmental paths to schizophrenia. In S. A. Mednick, T. D. Cannon, C. E. Barr, & J. M. LaFosse (Eds.), *Developmental neuropathology in schizophrenia*. New York: Plenum Press. Reproduced with permission.

immature brain appears to be more likely to be associated with schizophrenia than injury closer to the age of presentation.

ADULT LESIONS

Tumors of the Central Nervous System

Any form of psychotic illness may accompany a cerebral tumor and this includes tumors that may present as schizophrenia (Lishman, 1987). Those patients with predominately psychiatric features are usually those with tumors involving the limbic portions of the temporal and frontal lobes; some observers believe that those with the schizophreniform presentation are more likely to have a temporal than a frontal loci (Strub & Black, 1981).

Factors such as increased intracranial pressure, the rate of growth of the tumor, and the location of the tumor (Malamud, 1967) may influence the clinical presentation. Regarding intracranial pressure, there is a distinction between tumors arising above and below the tentorium—those above the tentorium are more likely to have mental symptoms even without increased intracranial pressure, whereas those below the tentorium may have relatively few mental symptoms in the presence of high levels of increased intracranial pressure (Hecaen & Ajuriaguerra, 1956).

The nature of a tumor and the rapidity of its growth is a factor in relation to the incidence and severity of mental symptoms. Tumors that produce no mental symptoms are mainly of the slow-growing type (Keschner, Bender, & Strauss, 1938). However, it is important to keep in mind that *very slow growing tumors can be more liable to present with mental symptoms but without neurological signs so that they may more easily be missed*. There is a greater incidence of mental disturbances among malignant as compared to benign cerebral tumors; malignant tumors invade the brain more widely. Gliomas have been found to produce a higher incidence of mental disturbance than meningiomas (Hecaen & Ajuriaguerra, 1956).

Regarding cancers originating outside the central nervous system, metastatic tumors with several deposits scattered throughout the brain have proved to be associated with a higher incidence of mental disturbance than any variety of primary intercerebral tumor (Keschner et al., 1938). There also are nonmetastatic CNS complications of malignant tumors; carcinoma of the lung is said to have a particularly high incidence of CNS nonmetastatic presentations (Croft & Wilkinson, 1965). A paranoid, delusional patient with auditory hallucinations and squamous carcinoma of the lung was reported by Johnstone, Mac Millan, and Crow, 1987) in their series of first-episode schizophrenias; however, the patient also had two cerebral infarctions.

Regarding the location of tumors, hallucinations seen in association with tumors of the brain often occur as part of an epileptic disturbance caused by the tumor. Sometimes they are seen without any evidence of paroxysmal activity, however. The type of hallucination can be suggestive of the location of the tumor, particularly if it is a circumscribed, focal lesion. Visual hallucinations are suggestive of tumors of the occipital lobe or of subtenorial tumors, presumably by pressure effects on the adjacent occipital lobe. Auditory hallucinations, accompanied sometimes by visual and/or gustatory and/or olfactory hallucinations, usually originate in the temporal lobe or in the adjacent frontal lobe. Medial–frontal lobe lesions also can discharge directly to the temporal lobe, mimicking its symptoms. Parietal lobe tumors have been associated with tactile and kinesthetic hallucinations.

Attempts at precise anatomical location can be misleading or even damaging, however. The approach to treatment of space-occupying lesions in the brain of patients is an area that needs a most sophisticated clinical judgment. For example, removing some types of structural masses—such as ganglioglial lesions in the temporal lobe in patients with intractable epilepsy who were treated by anterior temporal lobectomy—resulted in the development of de novo schizophrenia in some individuals (Bruton, 1988). (See discussion of Bruton cases in Chapter 13.)

Temporal Lobe Tumors

Patients with temporal lobe tumors may present with schizophrenia as the initial manifestation of the tumor. A review of the literature was performed by Davison and Bagley (1969) regarding the location of the tumor in 77 cases originally diagnosed as schizophrenia. They found a significantly higher proportion of temporal lobe and pituitary tumors compared to control groups of tumor patients without psychiatric symptoms. (In the case of pituitary tumors, the psychiatric picture may be attributable, least in part, to the endocrine disturbances secondary by the tumor, see Chapter 8.)

Epilepsy is more common in patients with temporal lobe tumors than tumors in other locations. In a review of 249 temporal lobectomies performed because of epilepsy, gangliogliomas—developmental lesions of the medial temporal lobe containing aberrant neurons—were disproportionately ($p < 0.001$) associated with the risk of psychosis (Roberts, Done, Bruton, & Crow, 1990). Hallucinatory auras in temporal lobe tumors are thought by the patient to be real at the time of their occurrence thus often resulting in a psychiatric diagnosis. Any type of malignant or benign tumor can be found in the temporal lobe.

In the Bruton study (1988), three of the 16 patients who had both intractable epilepsy and schizophrenia prior to neurosurgery had good relief from both clinical problems following treatment by temporal lobectomies. Case examples follow for two of these patients, who were adults at the time of the neurosurgery.

Bruton patient 42

Seizures began at age 15 years in this boy and a diagnosis of schizophrenia was made. After left anterior temporal lobectomy at age 45 years, seizures were "improved" and his personality and social adjustment was "improved" and he was no longer classified as schizophrenic. Neuropathology of the resected material disclosed a white-matter cyst anterior to the inferior horn of the ventricle. The cyst wall of neuroglial tissue was lined by ependyma.

Bruton patient 67

Seizures began at age 40 years in this woman and a diagnosis of schizophrenia was made. Three years later, a left anterior temporal lobectomy resulted in her permanent return to a normal life, free of both seizures and schizophrenia. Neuropathology disclosed a lesion whose predominant cell type was protoplasmic astrocytic; it was located in the parahippocampal and fusiform gyri.

Before ending the subject of the temporal lobe and schizophrenia, however, a note of caution is in order. A sophisticated neuropsychological analysis comparing patients with schizophrenia to those with medically intractiable focal temporal lobe epilepsy suggested that lateralized temporal lobe dysfunction does not provide an adequate model of the cognitive impariments seen in schizophrenia (Gold et al., 1994).

Tumors in Other Locations

Besides the temporal lobe, the schizophrenic pattern of symptoms is more likely to occur in certain other locations in the brain. Tumors of the frontal lobe, particularly menigiomas, can present as chronic schizophrenia. Because meningiomas arise from the coverings of the central nervous system rather than the brain itself, they are among the most accessible tumors for treatment. Thus it is a tragedy when meningiomas are missed; there is a case in the literature in which a very slow-growing meningioma took 43 years to diagnose (Hunter, Blackwood, & Bull, 1968) (see Appendix A). Individuals with corpus callosum tumors may appear to have catatonic schizophrenia (Alpers, 1936; Elliot, 1969).

In parietal lobe tumors, hallucinatory disturbances consist of tactile or kinesthetic hallucinations usually confined to the opposite side of the body (Lishman, 1987). The epileptic manifestations of parietal lobe tumors may be quite bizarre and may antedate the appearance of neurological signs. Examples of such hallucinatory auras include transformation of a limb into a mechanical object or the phantom appearance of a third limb (Hecaen & Ajuriaguerra, 1956).

Treatment of brain tumors has been primarily surgical in the past. Brain tumors have been missed in psychiatric patients on a number of occasions; this is particularly unfortunate when the tumor is a benign meningioma, which often is the easiest type of brain tumor to remove. In the historical era before CT and MRI scans were readily available, it appears that the majority of CNS neoplasms causing schizophrenic symptoms often were not diagnosed during life. A review of several mental hospital autopsy studies in the first half of the century revealed that up to 72% of the tumors were not recognized before autopsy (Waggoner & Bagchi, 1954).

In an autopsy study from the State Mental Hospitals of Denmark, two-thirds of the brain tumors found on autopsy had been missed during life; moreover the great majority of these patients had been hospitalized for less than 6 months prior to death so presumably the tumor had been present at the time of admission. The tumor frequency on autopsy for the whole series was 3% (Andersson, 1970). This finding replicated an earlier study in America, which suggested that the chance of finding a cerebral tumor was significantly greater among patients dying in State Mental Hospitals in North America than in nonmental hospitals (3.7% vs. 2.4%). This difference was particularly great for benign meningiomas, which constituted 33% of the tumors in mental hospitals but only 14% in nonmental hospitals (Patton & Sheppard, 1956). Although the percentages of this study were challenged by Klotz (1957), he did agree that meningiomas were about twice as frequent in comparison to other forms of tumor as seen in neurological practice and that approximately half the tumors had been unsuspected during life in the mental patients. Other studies have confirmed that meningiomas appear to be overrepresented among autopsies of psychiatric patients (Raskin, 1956; Hunter et al., 1968). The frontal lobe is an area to check for meningiomas in patients with schizophrenia (Hunter et al., 1968). Malamud (1967, 1975) in his series of individuals with functional diagnoses who were found to have autopsy-proven tumors after death emphasized that a seizure disorder often accompanied the diagnosis of schizophrenia.

This history reflects the importance of a complete neurological work-up including an imaging study for a first-time psychotic episode in a previously healthy person (Nasrallah, 1986).

Adult Cranial Trauma

All forms of schizophrenia have been reported after head injury: hebephrenic, paranoid, and catatonic. Cases indistinguishable from the naturally occurring disorder may be seen (Lishman, 1987). In other cases the sequelae of the head injury, such as a hemiparesis, accompany the psychiatric symptoms (Johnstone et al., 1987). Paranoid forms are reported to be especially frequent. Another frequent pattern is a schizophrenialike hallucinosis in which affect is preserved and thought disorder is not intrusive. Sometimes the psychiatric symptoms occur only during a time-limited phase of the recovery (Silverman, 1949). Thompson (1970) has suggested, in his three cases reports, that traumatic lesions sometimes can be the specific triggering or precipitating factor for the development of overt schizophrenia in individuals who were at risk for schizophrenia because of latent schizophrenic factors present.

A number of surveys have addressed the question of the relationship between head trama and schizophrenia; the most extensive was a Finnish study that followed 3,552 soldiers with brain injuries from the war over a 22–26-year period (Achté et al., 1967, 1969). Their conclusion was that 2.6% of the patients developed psychoses resembling schizophrenia, which is well above the incidence to be expected in the general population. The authors reported that only 0.84% developed what they called primary or malignant schizophrenia (not dissimilar to the population as a whole), however, the remainder being what they called schizophreniform or borderline cases. The possibility of a special association with temporal lobe damage in some of these injured veterans has been reviewed by a number of investigators (Hilbom,

1951; Davison & Bagley, 1969). An early study had suggested that the rates of psychosis are similar in head-injured and non-head-injuried adults (Feuchtwanger & Maver-Gross, 1938).

With the development of recent imaging techniques, subdural hematomas are being reported in patients with some of the symptoms of schizophrenia (i.e., Woods, 1980). Their relevance, if any, remains to be determined.

REFERENCES

Achté, K. A., Hillbom, E., & Aalberg, V. (1969). *Posttraumatic psychoses following war brain injuries.* Helsinki: Reports from the Rehabilitation Institute for Brain-injured Veterans in Finland, vol. 1.

Achté, K. A., Hillbrom, E., & Aalberg, V. (1969). Psychosis following war brain injuries. *Acta Psychaitrica Scandinavica, 45,* 1–18.

Achté, K. A., Hillbom, E., & Aalberg, V. (1969). Psychoses following war brain injuries. *Acta Psychiatiatrica Scandinavica, 45,* 1–18.

Akbarian, S., Vinuela, A., Kim, J. J., Potkin, S. G., Bunney, W. E., Jr., & Jones, E. G. (1993a). Distorted distribution of nicotinamide-adenine dinucleotide phosphate-diaphorase neurons in temporal lobe of schizophrenics implies anomalous cortical development. *Archives of General Psychiatry, 50,* 178–187.

Akbarian, S., Bunney, W. E., Jr., Potkin, S. G., Wigal, S. B., Hagman, J. O., Sandman, C. A., & Jones, E. G. (1993b). Altered distribution of nicotinamide-adenine dinucleo phosphate-diaphorase cells in frontal lobe of schizophrenics implies anomalous cortical development. *Archives of General Psychiatry, 50,* 169–177.

Alexander, R. C., Breslin, N., Molnar, C., Richter, J., & Mukherjee, S. (1992). Counter clockwise scalp hair whorl in schizophrenia. *Biological Psychiatry, 32,* 842–845.

Alpers, B. J. (1936). A note on the mental syndrome of corpus callosum tumours. *Journal of Nervous and Mental Disorders, 84,* 621–627.

Altshuler, L., Conrad, A., Kovelman, J. A., & Scheibel, A. (1987). Hippocampal pyramidal cell orientation in schizophrenia. *Archives of General Psychiatry, 44,* 1094–1098.

American Psychiatric Association (1980). *Diagnostic and statistical manual of mental disorders, 3rd ed.* Washington, DC: American Psychiatric Press.

Andersson, P. G. (1970). Intracranial tumors in a psychiatric autopsy material. *Acta Psychiatrica Scandinavica, 46,* 213–224.

Andreasen, N. (1988). Paper Presented at the 4th Biennial Winter Workshop on Schizophrenia, Badgastein.

Andreasen, N. C., Ehrhardt, J. C., Swayze, V. W., II, Alliger, R. J., Yuh, W. T., Cohen, G., & Ziebell, S. (1990). Magnetic resonance imaging of the brain in schizophrenia: The pathophysiolologic significance of structural abnormalities. *Archives of General Psychiatry, 47*, 35–44.

Barbeau, D., Liang, J. J., Robitalille, Y., Quirion, R., & Srivastava, L. K. (1995). Decreased expression of the embronic form of the neural cell adhession molecule in schizophrenic brains. *Proceddings of the National Academy of Sciences of the United States of America, 92*, 2785–2789.

Barkovich, A. J., Koch, T. K., & Carrol, C. L. (1991). The spectrum of lissencephaly: Report of ten patients analyzed by magnetic reosnance imaging. *Annals of Neurology, 30*, 139–146.

Barnes, T. R. E. (1988). Tardive dyskinesia: Risk factors, pathophysiology and treatment. *Recent Advances in Clinical Psychiatry, 6*, 185–207.

Bayer, S. A., Yackel, J. W., & Puri, P. S. (1982). Neurons in the rat dentate gyrus granular layer substantially increase during juvenile and adult life. *Science, 216*, 890–892.

Benes, F. M. (1989). Myelination of cortical hippocampal relays during late adolescence. *Schizophrenia Bulletin, 15*, 585–593.

Benes, F. M., McSparren, J., Bird, E. D., SanGiovanni, J. P., & Vincent, S. (1991). Deficits in small interneurons in prefrontal and cingulate cortices of schizophrenic and schizoaffective patients. *Archives of General Psychiatry, 48*, 996–1001.

Benes, F. M., Majocha, R., Bird, E. D., & Marotta, C. A. (1987). Increased vertical axon numbers in the cingulate cortex of schizophrenics. *Archives of General Psychiatry, 44*, 1017–1021.

Benes, F. M., Sorensen, I., & Bird, E. D. (1991). Reduced neuronal size in posterior hippocampus of schizophrenic patients. *Schizophrenia Bulletin, 17*, 597–608.

Benes, F. M., Turtle, M., Khan, Y., & Farol, P. (1994). Myelination of a key relay zone in the hippocampal formation occurs in the human brain during childhood, adolescence and adulthood. *Archives of General Psychiatry, 51*, 477–484.

Bilder, R. M., & Degreef, G. (1991). Morphologic markers of neurodevelopmental paths to schizophrenia. In S. A. Mednick, T. D. Cannon, C. E. Barr, & J. M. LaFosse (Eds.), *Developmental neuropathology of schizophrenia*. New York: Plenum Press.

Blackshaw, S., & Bowen, R. C. (1987). A case of atypical psychosis associated with alexithymia and a left fronto-parietal lesion. *Canadian Journal of Psychiatry, 32*, 688–692.

Bloom, F. E. (1993). Advancing a neurodevelopmental origin for schizophrenia. *Archives of General Psychiatry, 50,* 224–227.

Bogerts, B., & Falkai, P. (1991). Clinical and neurodevelopmental aspects of brain pathology in schizophrenia. In S. Mednick, T. Cannon, C. Barr, & M. Lyon (Eds.), *Fetal neural development and adult schizophrenia.* Cambridge, UK: Cambridge University Press.

Bogerts, B. (1991). The neuropathology of schizophrenia: Pathophysiological and neurodevelopmental implications. In S. A. Mednick, T. Cannon, C. Barr, & M. Lyon (Eds.), *Fetal neural development and adult schizophrenia.* Cambridge, UK: Cambridge University Press.

Bogerts, B. (1993). Recent advances in the neuropathology of schizophrenia. *Schizophrenia Bulletin, 19,* 431–445.

Bornstein, R. A., Schwarzkopf, S. B., Olson, S. C., & Nasrallah, H. A. (1992). Third-ventricle enlargement and neuropsychological deficit in schizophrenia. *Biological Psychiatry, 31,* 954–961.

Bracha, S. H., Torrey, E. F., Bigelow, L. B., Lohr, J. B., & Linington, B. B. (1991). Subtle signs of prenatal maldevelopment of the hand ectoderm in schizophrenia: A preliminary monozygotic twin study. *Biological Psychiatry, 30,* 719–725.

Bruton, C. J. (1988). *The neuropathology of temporal lobe in epilepsy.* Oxford: Oxford University Press.

Bruton, C. J., Crow, T. J., Frith, C. D. et al. (1990). Schizophrenia and the brain. *Psychological Medicine, 20,* 285–304.

Butler, P. D., Susser, E. S., Brown, A. S., Kaufmann, C. A., & Gorman, J. M. (1994). Prenatal nutritional deprivation as a risk factor in schizophrenia: Preclinical evidence. *Neuropsychopharmacology, 11,* 227–235.

Cannon, M., Byrne, M., Cotter, D., Sharm, P., Larkin, C., & O'Callaghan, E. (1994). Further evidence for anomalies in the hard-prints of patients with schizophrenia: A study of secondary creases. *Schizophrenia Research, 13,* 179–184.

Cannon, T. D., & Marco, E. (1994). Structural brain abnormalities as indicators of vulnerability to schizophrenia. *Schizophrenia Bulletin, 20,* 89–102.

Cannon, T. D., Mednick, S., & Parnas, J. (1989). Genetic and prenatal determinants of structural brain deficits in schizophrenia. *Archives of General Psychiatry, 46,* 883–889.

Castle, D. J., & Murray, R. M. (1991). The neurodevelopmental basis of sex differences in schizophrenia. *Psychological Medicine, 21,* 565–575.

Conlon, P., & Trimble, M. R. (1988). A study of the corpus callosum in epileptic psychosis using magnetic resonance imaging. *Biological Psychiatry, 24,* 852–857.

Conrad, A. J., & Scheibel, A. S. (1987). Schizophrenia and the hippocampus: The embryological hypothesis extended. *Schizophrenia Bulletin, 17*, 597–608.

Conrad, A. J., Abebe, T., Austin, R., Forsythe, S., & Scheibel, A. B. (1991). Hippocampal pyramidal cell disarray in schizophrenia as a bilateral phenomenon. *Archives of General Psychiatry, 40*, 413–417.

Courchesne, E., Yeung-Courchesne, R., Press, G. A., Hesselink, J. R., & Jernigan, T. L. (1988). Hypoplasia of cerebellar vermal lobules VI and VII in autism. *New England Journal of Medicine, 318*, 1349–1354.

Croft, P. B., & Wilkinson, M. (1965). The incidence of carcinomatous neuromyopathy with special reference to carcinoma of the lung and breast. In W. R. Brain & F. H. Norris (Eds.), *The remote effects of cancer on the nervous system. Contemporary neurology symposia*, Volume 1, pp. 44–54. New York: Grune and Stratton.

Cunningham Owens, D. G., Johnstone, E. C., Bydder, G. M., & Kreel, L. (1980). Unsuspected organic disease in chronic schizophrenia demonstrated by computed tomography. *Journal of Neurology, Neurosurgery and Psychiatry, 43*, 1065–1969.

Daniel, D. G., Goldberg, T. E., Gibbons, R. D., & Weinberger, D. R. (1991). Lack of bimodal distribution of ventricular size in schizophrenia. *Biological Psychiatry, 30*, 887–903.

Davison, K., & Bagley, C. R. (1969). Schizophrenia-like psychoses associated with organic disorders of the central nervous system: a review of the literature. In R. N. Herrington (Ed.), *Current problems in neuropsychiatry. British Journal of Psychiatry* Special Publication, no. 4. Ashford, Kent: Headley Brothers.

Degreef, G., Lantos, G., Bogerts, B. et al. (1992). Abnormalities of the septum pellucidum on MR scans in first-episode schizophrenic patients. *American Journal of Neuroradiology, 13*, 835–840.

Dewan, M. J., & Bick, P. A. (1985). Normal pressure hydrocephalus and psychiatric patients. *Biological Psychiatry, 20*, 1127–1131.

Elliot, F. A. (1969). The corpus callosum, cingulate gyrus, septum pellcidum, septal area and fornix. In P. J. Vinken, & G. W. Bruyn (Eds.), *Handbook of clinical neurology*, vol 2. Amsterdam: North-Holland.

Falkai, P., Bogerts, B., Roberts, G. W., & Crow, T. J. (1988). Measurement of the alpha-cell-migration in the entorhinal region: A marker for developmental disturbances in schizophrenia? *Schizophrenia Research, 1*, 157–158.

Falkai, P., Bogerts, B., Schneider, T., Greve, B., Pfeiffer, U., Pilz, K., Gonsiorzcyk, C., Majtenyi, C., & Ovary, I. (1995). Disturbed planum temporale asymmetry in schizophrenia. A quantative post-mortem study. *Schizophrenia Research, 14*, 161–176.

Feinberg, I. (1982/1983). Schizophrenia: Due to a fault in programmed synaptic elimination during adolescence? *Journal of Psychiatry Research, 17,* 319–334.

Feuchtwanger, E., & Maver-Gross, W. (1938). Hirnverletzung und schizophrenie. *Schweizer Archiv fur Neurologie und Psychiatrie, 41,* 17–99.

George, M. S., Scott, T. F., Kellner, C. H. et al. (1989). Abnormalities of the septum pellucidum in schizophrenia. *Journal of Neuropsychiatry and Clinical Neuroscience, 1,* 385–390.

Gillberg, C., & Coleman, M. (1992). *The biology of the autistic syndromes,* second edition. London: Mac Keith Press.

Gold, J. M., Hermann, B. P., Randolph, C., Wyler, A. R., Goldberg, T. E., & Weinberger, D. R. (1994). Schizophrenia and temporal lobe epilepsy; a neuropsychological analysis. *Archives of General Psychiatry, 51,* 265–272.

Green, M. F., Satz, P., & Christenson, C. (1994). Minor physical anomalies in schizophrenia patients, bipolar patients and their siblings. *Schizophrenia Bulletin, 20,* 433–440.

Green, M. F., Satz, P., Soper, H. V., & Kharabi, F. (1987). Relationship between physical anomalies and age of onset in schizophrenia. *American Journal of Psychiatry, 144,* 666–667.

Gualtieri, C. T., Adams, A., Shen, C. D., & Louiselle, D. (1982). Minor physical anomalies in alcoholic and schizophrenic adults and hyperactive and autistic children. *American Journal of Psychiatry, 139,* 640–643.

Gur, R. E., Mozley, D., Shtasel, D. L., Cannon, T. D., Gallacher, F., Turetsky, B., Grossman, R., & Gur, R. C. (1994). Clinical subtypes of schizophrenia: Differences in brain and CSF volume. *American Journal of Psychiatry, 151,* 343–350.

Gureje, O., Bamidele, R., & Raji, O. (1994). Early brain trauma and schizophrenia in Nigerian patients. *American Journal of Psychiatry, 151,* 386–371.

Guy, J. D., Majorski, L. V., Wallace, C. J., & Guy, M. P. (1983). The incidence of minor physical anomalies in adult male schizophrenics. *Schizophrenia Bulletin, 9,* 571–582.

Harvey, I., Ron, M. A., Du Boulay, G., Wicks, D., Lewis, S. W., & Murray, R. M. (1993). Reduction of cortical volume in schizophrenia on magnetic resonance imaging. *Psychological Medicine, 23,* 591–604.

Haug, J. O. (1962). Pneumoencephalographic studies in mental disease. *Acta Psychiatrica Scandinavica, 38* (Suppl.), 11–104.

Hecaen, H., & Ajuriaguerra, J. (1956). *Troubles mentaux au cours des tumeurs intracraniennes.* Paris: Masson.

Hilbom, E. (1951). Schizophrenia-like psychosis after brain trauma. *Acta Psychiatrica et Neurologica Scandinavica, (Suppl.), 60,* 36–47.

Hunter, R., Blackwood, W., & Bull, J. (1968). Three cases of frontal lobe meningiomas preesented psychiatrically. *British Medical Journal, 3*, 9–16.

Jakob, J., & Beckmann, H. (1986). Prenatal developmental disturbances in the limbic allocortex in schizophrenics. *Journal of Neural Transmission, 65*, 303–326.

Jaskiw, G. E., Juliano, D. M., Goldberg, T. E., Hertzman, M., Urow-Hamell, E., & Weinberger, D. R. (1994). Cerebral ventricular enlargement in schizophreniform disorder does not progress. A seven year follow-up study. *Schizophrenia Research, 14*, 23–28.

Johnstone, E. C., Crow, T. J., Frith, C. D., Husband, J., & Kreel, L. (1976). Cerebral ventricular size and cognitive impairment in chronic schizophrenia. *Lancet, ii*, 924–927.

Johnstone, E. C., Mac Millan, J. F., & Crow, T. J. (1987). The occurrence of organic disease of possible or probable etiological significance in a population of 268 cases of first episode schizophrenia. *Psychological Medicine, 17*, 371–379.

Jones, P. (1994). Schizophrenia after prenatal exposure to the Dutch Hunger Winter of 1994–1945. (Letter). *Archives of General Psychiatry, 51*, 333.

Keschner, M., Bender, M. B., & Strauss, I. (1938). Mental symptoms associated with brain tumour: A study of 530 verified cases. *Journal of the American Medical Association, 110*, 714–718.

Keshaven, M. S., Anderson, S., & Pettegrew, J. W. (1994). Is schizophrenia due to excessive synaptic pruning in the prefrontal cortex? The Feinberg hypothesis revisited. *Journal of Psychiatric Research, 28*, 239–265.

Keshavan, M. S., Pettegrew, J. W., Beckwith, K. et al. (1994). Grey matter abnormalities in first-epidosde schizophrenia. *Schizophrenia Research, 11*, 136.

Klotz, M. (1957). Incidence of brain tumors in patients hospitalized for chronic mental disorders. *Psychiatric Quarterly, 31*, 669–680.

Kovelman, J. A., & Scheibel, A. B. (1984). A neurohistological correlate of schizophrenia. *Biological Psychiatry, 19*, 1601–1621.

Kovelman, J. A., & Scheibel, A. B. (1986). Biological substrates of schizophrenia. *Acta Neurologica Scandinavica, 73*, 1–32.

Lewis, S. W., & Mezey, G. C. (1985). Clinical correlates of septum pellucidum cavities. *Psychological medicine, 15*, 45.

Lewis, S. W., Reveley, M. A., David, A. S., & Ron, M. A. (1989). Agenesis of the corpus callosum and schizophrenia: A case report. *Psychological Medicine, 18*, 341–347.

Lishman, W. A. (1987). *Organic psychiatry.* Oxford: Blackwell Scientific.

Lohr, J. B., & Flynn, K. (1993). Minor physical anomalies in schizophrenia and mood disorders. *Schizophrenia Bulletin, 19,* 551–556.

Luaute, J. P., Sanabria, E., Bauge, J. P. et al. (1990). Abnormalities of the septum pellucidum in schizophrenia (letter). *Journal of Neuropsychiatry and Clinical Neuroscience, 2,* 461–462.

Lying- Tunell, U. (1979). Psychotic symptoms in normal-pressure hydrocephalus. *Acta Psychiatrica Scandinavica, 59,* 415.

Lyons, F., Martin, M. L., Maguire, C., Jackson, A., Regan, C. M., & Shelley, R. K. (1988). The expression of an N-CAM serum fragment is positively correlated with the severity of negative features in Type II schizophrenia. *Biological Psychiatry, 23,* 769–775.

Malamud, M. (1967). Psychiatric disorder with intracranial tumors of the limbic system. *Archives of Neurology, 17,* 113–123.

Malamud, N. (1975). Organic brain disease mistaken for psychiatric disorder: A clinicopathologic study In D. F. Benson & D. Blumer (Eds.), *Psychiatric aspects of neuorologic disease.* New York: Grune & Stratton.

Mathews, R. J., Partain, C. L., Penwash, R. et al. (1985). A study of the septum pellucidum and corpus callosum in schizophrenia with MR imaging. *Acta Psychiatrica Scandinavica, 72,* 414–421.

McLardy, T. (1974). Hippocampal zinc and structural deficits in brains from chronic alcoholics and some schizophrenics. *Journal of Orthomolecular Psychiatry, 4,* 32–36.

Murray, R. M. (1994). Neurodevelopmental schizophrenia: The rediscovery of dementia praecox. *British Journal of Pdsychiatry (Suppl), (25),* 6–12.

Nanko, S., Hattori, M., Kuwata, S., Sasaki, T., Fukuda, R., Dai, X. Y., Yamaguchi, K., Shibata, Y., & Kazamatsuri, H. (1994). Neurotrophin-3 gene polymorphism associated with schizophrenia. *Acta Psychiatrica Scandinavica, 89,* 390–392.

Nasrallah, H. A. (1986). The differential diagnosis of schizophrenia: Genetic, perinatal, neurological, pharmacological and psychiatric factors. In H. A. Nasrallah & D. R. Weinberger (Eds.), *The neurology of schizophrenia.* Amsterdam: Elsevier.

Nasrallah, H. A., Schwarzkopf, S. B., Olson, S. C., & Coffman, J. A. (1991). Perinatal brain injury and cerebellar vermal lobules I-X in schizophrenia. *Biological Psychiatry, 29,* 567–574.

Nopoulos, P., Torres, I., Flaum, M., Andreasen, N. C., Ehrhardt, J. C., & Yuh, W. T. (1995). Brain morphology in first-episode schizophrenia. *American Journal of Psychiatry, 152,* 1721–1723.

Nowakowski, R. S., & Rakic, M. (1981). The site of origin and route and rate of migration of neurons to the hippocampal region of the rhesus monkey. *Journal of Comparative Neurology, 196,* 129–154.

O'Flaithbheartaigh, S., Williams, P. A., & Jones, G. H. (1994). Schizophrenic psychosis and associated aqueduct stenosis *British Journal of of Psychiatry, 164*, 684–686.

Otake, M., & Schull, W. I. (1984). In utero exposure to A-Bomb radiation and mental retardation: A reassessment. *British Journal of Radiology, 57*, 409–414.

Owens, D. G. C., Johnstone, E. C., Bydder, G. M., & Kreel, L. (1980). Unsuspected organic disease in chronic schizophrenia demonstrated by computed tomography. *Journal of Neurology, Neurosurgery and Psychiatry, 43*, 1065–1069.

Patton, R. B., & Sheppard, J. A. (1956). Intracranial tumors found at autospy in mental patients. *American Journal of Psychiatry, 113*, 39–324.

Pettegrew, J. W., Keshavan, M. S., Panchalingam, K., Strychor, S., Kaplan, D. B., Tretta, M. G., & Allen, M. (1991). Alterations in brain high-energy phosphate and membrane phospholipid metabolism in first-episode, drug-naive schiophrenics. *Archives of General Psychiatry, 48*, 563–568.

Petty, R. G., Barta, P. E., Pearlson, G. D., McGilchrist, I. K., Lewis, R. W., Tien, A. Y., Pulver, A., Vaughn, D. D., Casanova, M. F., & Powers, R. E. (1995). Reversal of asymmetry of the planum temporale in schizophrenia. *American Journal of Psychiatry, 152*, 715–721.

Radic, P. (1991). Quoted as a "personal communication." In S. A. Mednick, T. D. Cannon, C. E. Barr, & J. M. LaFosse (Eds.), *Developmental neuropathology of schizophrenia* (p. 139). New York: Plenum Press.

Raskin, N. (1956). Intracranial neoplasms in psychotic patients. *American Journal of Psychiatry, 112*, 481–484.

Reimer, D. R., & Nagaswami, S. (1974). Catatonic schizophrenia associated with cerebral arterial malformations and with membranous glomerulonephritis. *Psychosomatics, 15*, 39–40.

Reveley, A. M., & Reveley, M. A. (1983). Aqeduct stenosis and schizophrenia. *Journal of Neurology, Neursurgery and Psychiatry, 46*, 18–22.

Roberts, J. K. A., Trimble, M. R., & Robertson, M. (1983). Schizophrenic psychosis associated with aqueduct stenosis in adults. *Journal of Neurology, Neurosurgery and Psychiatry, 46*, 892.

Roberts, G. W., Done, D. J., Bruton, C., & Crow, T. J. (1990). A "mock up" of schizophrenia: Temporal lobe epilepsy and schizophrenic-like psychosis. *Biological Psychiatry, 28*, 127–143.

Schlaepfer, T. E., Harris, G. J., Tien, A. Y., Peng, L. W., Lee, S., Federman, E. B., Chase, G. A., Barta, P. E., & Pearlson, G. D. (1994). Decreased regional cortical gray matter volume in schizophrenia. *American Journal of Psychiatry, 151*, 842–848.

Scott, T. F., Price, T. R. P., George, M. S., Brillman, J., & Rothfus, W. (1993). Midline cerebral malformations and schizophrenia. *Journal of Neuropsychiatry and Clinical Neurosciences, 5,* 287–293.

Selemon, L. O., Rajkowska, G., & Goldman-Rakic, P. S. (1995). Abnormally high neuronal density in the schizophrenic cortex. A morphometric analysis of prefrontal area 9 and occipital area 17. *Archives of General Psychiatry, 52,* 805–818.

Shelton, R. C., & Weinberger, D. R. (1986). X-ray computerized tomography studies in schizophrenia: A review and synthesis. In H. A. Nasrallah & D. R. Weinberger (Eds.), *Handbook of schizophrenia, Vol. 1: The neurology of schiziophrenia* (pp. 207–250). Amsterdam: Elsevier.

Shenton, M. E., Kikinis, R., McCarley, R. W., & Jolesz, F. A. (1992). Abnormalities of the left temporal lobe and thought disorder in schizophrenia. *New England Journal of Medicine, 327,* 604–612.

Sidman, R. L., & Rakic, P. (1973). Neuronal migration with special reference to developing human brain: A review. *Brain Research, 62,* 1–35.

Silverman, M. (1949). Paranoid reaction during the phase of recovery from subarachnoid haemorrhage. *Journal of Mental Science, 95,* 706.

Silverton, L., Finello, K. M., Mednick, S. A., & Schulsinger, F. (1985). Low birth weight and ventricular enlargement in a high-risk sample. *Journal of Abnormal Psychology, 94,* 405–409.

Smith, K. H. (1990). Aqueduct stenosis and schizophrenia (letter). *Australian and New Zealand Journal of Psychiatry, 24,* 163–164.

Strub, R. L., & Black, F. W. (1981). *Organic brain syndromes: An introduction to neurobehavioral disorders* (p. 384). Philadelphia: F. A. Davis.

Suddath, R. L., Christison, D. A., Torrey, E. F., Casanova, M. F., & Weinberger, D. R. (1990). Anatomical abnormalities in the brains of monozygotic twins discordant for schizophrenia. *New England Journal of Medicine, 322,* 791–794.

Sullivan, E. V., Shear, P. K., Luw, K. O., Zipursky, R. B., & Pfefferman, A. (1996). Cognitive and motor impairments are related to gray matter volume deficits in schizophrenia. *Biological Psychiatry, 39,* 234–240.

Susser, E. (1994). Letters to the editor—in reply. *Archives of General Psychiatry, 51,* 1994.

Susser, E. S., & Lin, S. P. (1992). Schizophrenia after prenatal exposure to the Dutch winter of 1944–1945. *Archives of General Psychiatry, 49,* 983–988.

Szymanski, S., Lieberman, J. A., Alvir, J. M., Mayerhoff, D., Loebel, A., Geisler, S., Chakos, M., Koreen, A., Jody, D., & Kane, J. (1995). Gender differences in onset of illness, treatment response, course, and biological indices in first episode schizophrenic patients. *American Journal of Psychiatry, 152,* 698–703.

Thompson, G. N. (1970). Cerebral lesions simulating schizophrenia: Three case reports. *Biological Psychiatry, 2*, 59–64.

Torrey, E. F., Taylor, E. H., Bracha, H. S., Bowler, A. E., McNeil, T. F., Rawlings, R. R., Quinn, P. O., Bigelow, L. B., Rickler, K., Sjostrom, K., Higgins, E. S., & Gottesman, I. I. (1994). Prenatal origin of schizophrenia in a subgroup of discordant monozygotic twins. *Schizophrenia Bulletin, 20*, 423–432.

Vallant, G. (1965). Schizophrenia in a woman with temporal lobe artiovenous malformation. *British Journal of Psychiatry, 111*, 307.

Waggoner, R. W., & Bagchi, B. K. (1954). Initial masking of organic brain changes by psychic symptoms. *American Journal of Psychiatry, 110*, 904.

Walker, E. F., Savole, T., & Davis, D. (1994). Neuromotor precursors of schizophrenia. *Schizophrenia Bulletin, 20*, 441–451.

Wilcox, J. A., & Nasrallah, H. A. (1987). Childhood head trauma and schizophrenia. *Psychiatry Research, 10*, 303–306.

Woods, S. W. (1980). Catatonia is a patient with subdural hematomas. *American Journal of Psychiatry, 137*, 983–984.

Woody, R. C., Bolyard, K., Eisenhauer, G., & Altschuler, L. (1987). CT scan and MRI findings in a child with schizophrenia. *Journal of Child Neurology, 22*, 105–110.

CHAPTER 13

The Schizophreniclike Psychoses
of Epilepsy

There is a well-documented pattern in the medical literature of psychoses occurring in relationship to epilepsy. A number of studies have emphasized the schizophreniclike nature of many of the chronic psychoses seen in patients with epilepsy (Hoch, 1943; Mulder & Daly, 1952; Ervin, Epstein, & King, 1955; Pond, 1957; Rodin, Dejong, Waggoner, & Bagchi, 1957; Slater & Beard, 1963; Bruens, 1971, 1980; Taylor, 1975; Shukla, Srivastava, & Katiyar, 1979; Dorr-Zegers & Rauh, 1980; Logsdail & Toone, 1988).

Most puzzling has been the fact that in some patients there appears to be an opposite relationship between abnormal mental states versus seizures and that, in some, there is documented electroencephalographic (EEG) evidence of what is called "forced normalization" (Landolt, 1958). In the subgroup of patients who show the phenomenon of forced normalization, seizure therapy suppresses seizures with EEG normalization during the clinical presentation of psychiatric symptoms. [This phenomenon may underlie the attempt to treat schizophrenia by inducing seizures or seizurelike phenomenon that began in 1937 and continues to the modern era (Potter & Rudorfer, 1993).]

The psychotic states can occur both after seizure[s]— postictally—and between seizures—interictally. The postictal states and the interictal psychoses share several characteristics in common—overrepresentation of complex partial seizures, lack of family history for psychoses, and a roughly similar interval between the age of onset of epilepsy followed by the age of onset of psychosis (Logsdail & Toone, 1988).

Stevens and Lonsbury-Martin (1985) have suggested that subclinical limbic seizures could mediate apparent interictal psychopathology. There also is some very preliminary evidence related to kindling and dopamine-hyperfunction that might help us understand how seizures can induce psychosis but interfere with psychotic symptoms (Adamec, 1990); however, this work is based on hypotheses not yet proven.

POSTICTAL PSYCHOSES

In the clinical practice of epilepsy, postictal psychoses are the most commonly observed psychotic events. Patients sometimes can emerge from the ictas with confusion, automatisms, wandering, and inappropriate behavior. The change of affect, especially associated with hypomanic presentation, in association with right-sided epileptic activity, can be striking (Trimble, 1991).

One set of criteria for postictal psychoses:

1. An episode of confusion or psychosis manifested immediately upon a seizure or has emerged within a week of the return of apparently normal mental function.
2. Length of duration of psychosis—minimum of 24 hours and maximum of 3 months.
3. Mental state characterized by one or more criteria: clouding of consciousness, disorientation, delirium, delusions, and/or hallucinations in clear consciousness.
4. No evidence of extraneous factors that might have contributed to the abnormal mental state (anticonvulsant, alcohol, or other drug toxicity, EEG evidence of minor status, recent history of head injury, or a previous history of an interictal psychosis) (Logsdail & Toone, 1988).

In one early study of patients who suffered from postictal psychoses, the peak age of onset was between 30–40 years. In the majority of cases the psychoses developed within 24 hours of the seizure(s) although it could occur as much as 7 days later.

Hallucinations (mainly auditory) were reported in 36% of the patients and delusions (mainly persecutory) in 24% of patients (Levin, 1952). In a more recent study of postictal psychoses, up to half the patients had paranoid delusions (Logsdail & Toone, 1988). In this study the mean age of onset of epilepsy was 16.7 years and onset of psychosis was 32.2 years. Logsdail and Toone (1988) write that "mental state phenomena occur that are identical to those which are found in, and are diagnostic of, the functional psychoses, and they occur frequently in clear consciousness" (p. 246).

Are these postictal psychoses a psychiatric variant of Todd's phenomenon (motor, sensory, and memory abnormalities that occur following seizures in some patients)? Savard, Andermann, Remillard, and Oliver (1987) reported nine cases of postictal psychosis after complex partial seizures raised this interesting question.

INTERICTAL PSYCHOSES

Regarding interictal psychoses, one definition of this phenomenon is a psychosis lasting longer than a month in a setting of clear consciousness in a patient with a seizure disorder. The syndrome profile of the patients with schizophrenia and epilepsy compared to those with schizophrenia alone show few significant differences, emphasizing the similarities of the clinical presentation of these two disorders (Trimble, 1991). Perez and Trimble (1980) have described the mental state of 24 interictal patients, using the PSE evaluation (Wing, Cooper, & Sartorius, 1974). They found that 50% of these patients with epilepsy and psychosis were categorized as having schizophrenic psychosis with 92% of those having a profile of nuclear schizophrenia based on the first rank symptoms of Schneider (Perez & Trimble, 1980). Other diagnoses in this study included residual schizophrenia/mania, manic psychosis, psychotic depression, and psychotic psychosis.

TEMPORAL LOBE EPILEPSY

There are many studies that attempt to delineate a specific EEG focus, which increases the likelihood of later development of a psychiatric syndrome. The majority of studies show a much greater incidence in temporal lobe epilepsy compared to other focal disorders. The literature on this topic and controversies surrounding it are well reviewed in Trimble (1991).

It is interesting to note that pathological studies of the brain in temporal lobe epilepsy have reported abnormalities in the same small section of the brain—the hippocampus—that is also described as abnormal in patients with schizophrenia (see Chapter 12). However, in schizophrenia, while the hippocampal neuronal somata appears to be in disarray with haphazard placements (Conrad, Trufat, Austin, Forsythe, & Scheibel, 1991), in temporal lobe epilepsy, there may be a different look—long stretches of hippocampal dendrites all leaning in one direction, a "wind-blown look" (Scheibel et al., 1974). When unilateral temporal lobe epilepsy is studied, glucose hypometabolism can be demonstrated by imaging studies ([18F]fluorodeozyglucose positron emission tomography [PET]) and is useful in presurgical epilepsy evaluations (Theodore et al., 1992). However, postsurgical neuroanatomical studies show that this hypometabolism apparently is not based on neuronal loss per se in the hippocampal or accompanying diaschisis (distant effects of regional insult) (Henry et al., 1994).

The absence of family history in the majority of the studies of patients with psychoses related to epilepsy might be considered a somewhat unexpected finding (Slater & Glithero, 1963; Flor-Henry, 1969; Perez, Trimble, Murray, & Reider, 1985). The only exception so far is a study of patients with epilepsy so severe they were being evaluated for temporal lobectomy (Jensen & Larsen, 1979).

When one combines (1) the absence of family history and (2) the long interval between the onset of epilepsy and the psychotic episodes, the possibility comes to mind of gradually developing metabolic failure in the central nervous system—possibly due to seizures themselves or to the chronic use of anticonvulsant medication. In considering this problem, it is important to note that the organic psychosyndrome produced by toxic levels of anticonvulsants is quite different from the kind of psychoses being discussed here. The schizophrenialike illnesses usually occur after many years of long-term but therapeutic, presumably nontoxic, levels of anticonvulsants. They also do not resolve by lowering the dose of the anticonvulsant as can be seen in the organic psychosyndromes that occur secondarily to clearly toxic levels of a drug.

Psychoses have been reported in association with most anticonvulsant drugs; these are mostly individual cases reported anecdotally (Trimble, 1991). In these cases, the drugs include phenytoin, primidone, carbamazepine, vigabatrin, sodium valproate, and ethosuximide. Sander, Hart, Trimble, and Shorvon (1991) note that the psychoses associated with ethosuximide and vigabatrin are often directly seizure-related, occurring as a consequence of forced normalization or as postictal psychoses associated with clustering.

Metabolites, known to be related to psychoses and sometimes to be adversely affected by long-term use of anticonvulsant drugs, are folic acid (see Chapters 6 and 7) and calcium (Richens & Rowe, 1970; Coleman & Brown, 1976). Reynolds (1967) first postulated that a deficiency of folate, brought about by anticonvulsant treatment, might be one factor leading to the the schizophrenialike illnesses in epilepsy. He described a series of cases involving schizophrenialike psychoses with anticonvulsant-drug-induced megaloblastic anemia or nonanemic folate deficiency (Reynolds, 1967). Since then, this question has been looked at by a number of investigators who came to the conclusion that there was no association between the prescribed drugs and interictal psychoses, even if the patients were found to have lowered folate levels (Flor-Henry, 1969; Bruens, 1971; Ramani & Gumnit, 1982; Perez et al., 1985).

Regarding calcium, a number of studies long ago established the effect of anticonvulsants on calcium metabolism. Low serum levels of calcium (Richens & Rowe, 1970) and 25-hydroxycholecaliciferol (Hahn, Hendin, Scharp, & Haddad, 1972); elevation of bone isoenzyme fractions of alkaline phosphatase levels (Hunter, Maxwell, Stewart, Parsons, & Williams, 1971); gross radiological evidence of rickets or osteomalacia (Marsden, Reynolds, Parson, Harris, & Duchen, 1973); and reduced mineral content as measured by photon absorptiometry (Christianson, Kristensen, & Rodbro, 1972) have all been recorded on long-term anticonvulsant therapy. The symptoms of disorientation, confusion, and active visual and auditory hallucinations have been described in cases in which calcium metabolism is altered by hypoparathyroidism (Bartter, 1953; Aurbach, 1973).

In the Coleman and Brown (1976) case, a girl developed a seizure disorder at the age of 4, which was followed by bizarre behavior, loss of previously acquired academic skills, and visual and auditory hallucinations 7 years later, at the beginning of adolescence. The family history was positive only for seizures, not for psychosis—the two brothers of the patient both had mild seizure disorders without progression to any form of mental dysfunction. After hypocalcinuria was documented in the patient at 21 years of age, the initiation of 1200 units of vitamin D orally led to successful seizure control and a reversal of the psychiatric disorder.

TEMPORAL LOBE EPILEPSY SO SEVERE IT REQUIRED TEMPORAL LOBECTOMY

Pathological or imaging studies of this patient group often does not reveal a specific underlying etiology. Some of the best neuropathological information comes from a small subgroup of epileptic patients diagnosed both as having schizophrenia and a type of epilepsy so severe that it could not be controlled with drugs. A neuropathologist, C. J. Bruton (1988), has recently reported on such a series of patients with intractable temporal lobe epilepsy who were referred as candidates for anterior temporal lobectomy. Before lobectomy, 16 of these patients were considered to be suffering from a schizophrenic illness and another three had an unspecified psychosis.

This neurosurgical procedure results in tissue taken from the temporal lobe of a living patient and provided a valuable opportunity to study the view that a focal temporal lobe abnormality specially predisposes to the developmental of an epileptic psychiatric syndrome. In the Bruton series, on neuropathological examination of the sections of the temporal lobe removed at operation of the 16 schizophrenic epileptics, one-half (8) were found to have Ammon's horn sclerosis (also known as mesial temporal sclerosis, pararhinal sclerosis, or incisural sclerosis).

This is a patterned loss of nerve cells in the hippocampus accompanied by fibrous gliosis, usually most severe in the Sommer sector and the end folium although some cases show an almost "global" destruction of hippocampal neurons. Four of the schizophrenic patients, however, had an indefinite neuropathological result or no apparent abnormality at all. The remainder of the patients had (one each) an astrocytic lesion, a mixed glial lesion, a vascular lesion, and a developmental lesion (Bruton, 1988).

After the operations, the schizophrenic symptoms disappeared in 3 patients—the ones with the developmental lesion (a white matter cyst separate from the ventricle), the vascular lesion (a cavernous angioma in the parahippocampal gyrus), and the astrocytic lesion. The other patients were not helped psychiatrically and in fact, additional patients developed schizophrenia postoperatively including ones who had a ganglioglial lesion in their resected temporal lobes. A review of Bruton's book points out that some of the patients who developed schizophrenia *after* the operation were operated on before the usual age of onset of schizophrenia, suggesting that the operation may not have been relevant in these particular patients (Taylor, 1989). The removal of a hamartoma by temporal lobectomy has been reported to induce psychosis (Stevens, 1988). Regarding seizures in the Bruton series, the majority, but not all, of patients with preoperative schizophrenia were improved, including many who became seizure-free.

ARE THESE PSYCHOTIC EPISODES SEEN IN EPILEPTIC PATIENTS A TYPE OF SCHIZOPHRENIA?

In both the postictal (Logsdail & Toone, 1988) and the interictal (Perez et al., 1985) psychoses, authors have noted that, in many patients, the mental phenomena seen are identical with, and diagnostic of, the so-called functional psychoses. The many authors reviewed here often note the schizophreniclike phenomena they are dealing with in some of the patients. As noted above, not all patients with epilepsy and a psychiatric disorder have schizophrenic symptoms, but there appears to be a large subgroup who do. From a phenomenological viewpoint, Pond (1957) has noted a tendency for the patients with schizophrenic symptoms to differ from process schizophrenia by two characteristics—they may maintain some affective warmth and usually have a lack of hebephrenic deterioration with personality dilapidation.

DISEASE ENTITIES THAT CAN PRESENT WITH BOTH SCHIZOPHRENIC SYMPTOMS AND A SEIZURE DISORDER

Finally, it is relevant to keep in mind that there are some established disease entities that present both with schizophrenia and seizures. Sprinkled throughout the other chapters of this book are a number of diseases that can present with a combination of the symptoms of schizophrenia and a seizure disorder. A list of these diseases follows.

- acute encephalitis (Chapter 5)
- acute intermittent porphyria (Chapter 6)
- Addison's disease (Chapter 8)
- dentatorubal-pallidoluysian atrophy (DRPLA) (Chapter 11)
- systemic lupus erythematosus (Chapter 9)
- tuberous sclerosis (Chapter 11)
- tumors of the central nervous system (Chapter 12)
- vitamin D deficiency (Chapter 7)
- Wilson's disease (Jacksonian type) (Chapter 6)

REFERENCES

Adamec, R. E. (1990). Does kindling model anything clinically relevant? *Biological Psychiatry, 27,* 249–279.

Aurbach, G. D. (1973). Clinical conference: Hyperparathyroidism: Recent studies. *Annals of Internal Medicine, 79,* 566–581.

Bartter, F. C. (1953). *Proceedings of the Association for Research in Nervous and Mental Disorders, 32,* 1.

Bruens, J. H. (1971). Psychosis in epilepsy. *Psychiatrica, Neurologica, Neurochirurgica, 74,* 174–192.

Bruens, J. H. (1980). Different kinds of psychosis as related to different kinds of epilepsy. *12th International Epilepsy Congress,* Copenhagen.

Bruton, C. J. (1988). The neuropathology of temporal lobe epilepsy. In *Maudsley monograph no. 31.* Oxford: Oxford University Press.

Christianson, C., Kristensen, M., & Rodbro, P. (1972). Latent osteomalacia in epileptic patients on anti-convulsants. *British Medical Journal, 3,* 738–739.

Coleman, M., & Brown, W. M. (1976). Apparent reversal of a familial syndrome of seizures and later dementia by administration of Vitamin D. In D. V. Siva Sankar (Ed.), *Psychopharmacology of childhood* (pp. 59–67). Westbury, NY: PJD Publications.

Conrad, A. J., Trufat, A., Austin, R., Forsythe, S., & Scheibel, A. B. (1991). Hippocampal pyramidal cell disarray in schizophrenia as a bilateral phenomenon. *Archives of General Psychiatry, 48,* 413–417.

Dorr-Zegers, O., & Rauh, J. (1980). Different kinds of psychoses as related to different kinds of epilepsy. Presented at the study group of psychosis in epilepsy. *12th International Epilepsy Congress,* Copenhagen.

Ervin, F., Epstein, A. W., & King, H. E. (1955). Behaviour of epileptic and non-epileptic with temporal spikes. *Archives of Neurology and Psychiatry, 74,* 488–497.

Flor- Henry, P. (1969). Psychosis and temporal lobe epilepsy. *Epilepsia, 10,* 363–395.

Hahn, T. J., Hendin, B. A., Scharp, C. R., & Haddad, J. G. (1972). Effect of chronic anticonvulsant therapy on serum 25 hydroxy calciferol levels in adults. *New England Journal of Medicine, 287,* 900.

Henry, T. R., Babb, T. L., Engel, J., Jr., Mazziotta, J. C., Phelps, M. E., & Crandall, P. H. (1994). Hippocampal neuronal loss and regional hypometabolism in temporal lobe epilepsy. *Annals of Neurology, 36,* 925–927.

Hoch, P. J. (1943). Clinical and biological interrelations between schizophrenia and epilepsy. *American Journal of Psychiatry, 100,* 507–512.

Hunter, J., Maxwell, J. D., Stewart, D. A., Parsons, V., & Williams, R. (1971). Altered calcium metabolism in epileptic children on anticonvulsants. *British Medical Journal, 4,* 202.

Jensen, I., & Larsen, J. K. (1979). Psychoses in drug reistant temporal lobe epilepsy. *Journal of Neurology, Neurosurgery and Psychiatry, 42,* 948–954.

Landolt, H. (1958). Serial EEG investigations during psychotic episodes in epileptic patients and during schizophrenic attacks. In A. M. Lorentz De Haas (Ed.), *Lectures on epilepsy* (pp. 91–133). Amsterdam: Elsevier.

Levin, S. (1952). Epileptic clouded states. *Journal of Nervous and Mental Disease, 116,* 215–225.

Logsdail, S. J., & Toone, B. K. (1988). Post-ictal psychoses. *British Journal of Psychiatry, 152,* 246–252.

Marsden, C. D., Reynolds, E. H., Parson, V., Harris, R., & Duchen, L. (1973). Myopathy associated with anti-convulsant osteomalacia. *British Medical Journal, 4,* 526.

Mulder, D. W., & Daly, D. (1952). Psychiatric symptoms associated with lesions of the temporal lobes. *Journal of the American Medical Association, 150,* 173–176.

Perez, M. M., & Trimble, M. R. (1980). Epileptic psychoses—diagnostic comparison with process schizophrenia. *British Journal of Psychiatry, 137,* 245–249.

Perez, M. M., Trimble, M. R., Murray, N. M. F., & Reider, I. (1985). Epileptic psychosis: An evaluation of PSE profiles. *British Journal of Psychiatry, 146,* 155–163.

Pond, D. A. (1957). Psychiatric aspects of epilepsy. *Journal of the Indian Medical Profession, 3,* 1441–1451.

Potter, W. Z., & Rudorfer, M. V. (1993). Electroconvulsive therapy—a modern medical procedure (editorial). *New England Journal of Medicine, 328,* 882–883.

Ramani, V., & Gumnit, R. J. (1982). Intensive monitoring of interictal psychosis in epilepsy. *Annals of Neurology, 11,* 613–622.

Reynolds, E. H. (1967). Schizophrenia-like psychoses of epilepsy and disturbances of folate and vitamin B12 metabolism induced by by anticonvulsant drugs. *British Journal of Psychiatry, 113,* 911–919.

Richens, A., & Rowe, D. J. F. (1970). Disturbance of calcium metabolism with anti- convulsant drugs. *British Medical Journal, 4,* 73.

Rodin, E. A., Dejong, R. N., Waggoner, R. W., & Bagchi, B. K. (1957). Relationship between certain forms of pscyhomotor epilepsy and schizophrenia. *Archives of Neurology and Psychiatry, 77,* 449–463.

Sander, J. W., Hart, Y. M., Trimble, M. R., & Shorvon, S.D. (1991). Vigabatrin and psychosis. *Journal of Neurology, Neurosurgery and Psychiatry, 541,* 435–439.

Savard, G., Andermann, F., Remillard, G. M., & Oliver, A. (1987). Postictal psychosis following partial complex seizures is analgous to Todd's paralyses. In P. Wolf, D. Dam, D. Janz, & F. E. Dreifuss (Eds.), *Advances in epileptology,* vol. 16 (pp. 603–660). New York: Raven Press.

Scheibel, M., Crandall, P., & Scheibel, A. B. (1974). The hippocampal-dendate complex in temporal lobe epilepsy. *Epilepsia, 15,* 55–80.

Shukla, G. D., Srivastava, O. N., Katiyar, B. C., Joshi, V., & Mohan, P. K. (1979). Psychiatric manisfestations in TLE: A controlled study. *British Journal of Psychiatry, 135,* 411–417.

Slater, E., & Beard, A. W. (1963). The schizophrenia-like psychoses of epilepsy. *British Journal of Psychiatry, 109,* 95–150.

Slater, E., & Glitheroe, E. (1963). The schizophrenia-like psychoses of epilepsy. iii. Genetical aspects. *British Journal of Psychiatry, 109*, 143–133.

Stevens, J. (1988). Paper presented at the 4th Biennial Winter Workshop on Schizophrenia, Badgastein.

Stevens, J. R., & Lonsbury-Martin, B. (1985). Limbic system, epilepsy and psychosis: Experimental studies and clinical correlations. *Psychiatry J Univ Ottawa, 10*, 193–203.

Taylor, D. C. (1975). Factors influencing the occurrence of schizophrenic-like psychosis in patients with temporal lobe epilepsy. *Psychological Medicine, 5*, 249–254.

Taylor, D. C. (1989). Book review: The neuropathology of temporal lobe epilepsy by C. J. Bruton. *Psychological Medicine, 19*, 525–527.

Theodore, W. H., Sato, S., Kufta, C. et al. (1992). Temporal lobectomy for uncontrolled seizures: The role of positron emission tomography. *Annals of Neurology, 32*, 789–794.

Trimble, M. R. (1991). *The psychoses of epilepsy.* New York: Raven Press.

Wing, J. K., Cooper, J. E., & Sartorius, N. (1974). *The measurement and classification of psychiatric symptoms.* Cambridge, London: University Press.

CHAPTER 14

Toxic Factors in Schizophrenia

The induction of schizophrenic symptoms by drugs and other toxins is a subject fraught with difficulty. The problem is that an individual with schizophrenia is ten times as likely to have an alcohol problem and seven times as likely to have a current problem with another drug compared to someone who does not have schizophrenia (Drake, 1994). The explanation of why this happens is not fully understood.

Some researchers believe that substance abuse may precipitate mental illness in vulnerable individuals. Some of these patients appear to be extremely sensitive to the effects of cocaine, alcohol, or even nicotine and caffeine (Lake, 1991). Others investigators think that many apparent drug-induced cases of schizophrenia may be misguided attempts by patients already psychiatrically ill to self-medicate their symptoms away. Another possible precipitating factor may be temporary withdrawal symptoms when addicted patients try to break their habit.

Tsuang et al. (1982) studied the question of how to determine if a drug abuser had a preexisting psychiatric illness. They found that the risk for schizophrenia in the families of 45 drug abusers with prolonged psychosis was 6.5%. This was similar to the risk for families of 46 schizophrenics (6.8%). They and others have pointed out that the drug abuse may precipitate the illness in the genetically predisposed. The summary of their position is that "a psychosis in a drug abuser that does not remit after prolonged cessation of drug abuse and that otherwise meets criteria for schizophrenia probably is schizophrenia" (Tsuang & Faraone, 1994).

ALCOHOL

In their paper discussing individuals with first episodes of schizophrenia, Johnstone, MacMillan, and Crow, 1987 report three cases of alcohol abuse. In two of the cases, the symptoms of schizophrenia developed following prolonged heavy intake of alcohol and, in the third case, began 48 hours after a sudden termination of alcohol intake. In all three cases the psychotic symptoms were resolved during a short period of time while the patient remained alcohol-free in the hospital.

The incidence of schizophrenic symptoms in alcoholics has been investigated. In one study a subgroup of alcoholics with Irish backgrounds were found to have a higher incidence than those with British backgrounds (Lipsedge & Littlewood, 1979). Other papers investigating the psychiatric consequences of excessive alcohol intake include Nagao (1964), Cook and Winokur (1985), and Cohen (1995). In evaluating psychiatric symptoms in alcoholics, the possibility of Wernicke-Korsakoff psychosis and thiamine deficiency must be kept in mind.

PRESCRIPTION DRUGS

The catecholaminergic drugs, used for therapy in a variety of illnesses, can occasionally cause a psychosis similar to schizophrenia. These drugs include amantadine (Borison, 1979), L-DOPA (Klawans, 1978), dopamine by catheter into the ventricle (Kulkarni, Horne, Butler, Keks, & Copolov, 1992), and ephedrine.

Anticholingeric drugs can produce a toxic psychosis resembling schizophrenia (Dysken, Merry, & Davis, 1978). These drugs include atropine, tricyclic antidepressants, some neuroleptics, and also drugs used to combat neuroleptic-induced extrapyramidal side effects, such as benzatropine and trihexyphenidyl. It is no surprise (see Chapter 8) that glucocorticosteroids can produce psychotic symptoms (Ling, Perry, & Tsuang, 1981).

Other drugs associated with psychosis in the medical literature—often when they are given in overdosage—are cimetidine (Adler, Sadja, & Wilets, 1980), clonazepam (Browne, 1978), digitalis (Gorelick, Kussin, & Kahn, 1978), disulfiram (Nasrallah, 1979), isoniazid, phenylpropanolamine (Lake, 1991), procaine, and sal-butamol. A series of new drugs created to block N-methyl-D,L-aspartic acid (NMDA) receptors also are under investigation because of the possibility that they may induce a schizophrenialike psychosis in adults (Olney & Farber, 1995).

Withdrawal of prescription drugs has also been associated with psychoses. Three patients have been reported (Patterson, 1985; Golden, Hoffman, Falk, Provenzale, & Curtis, 1989) with a florid psychotic syndrome secondary to the withdrawal of propranolol, a beta-adrenergic receptor blocking agent, widely used in the treatment of hypertension and ischemic heart disease.

ABUSE OF ILLEGAL DRUGS

Analysis of the 1982 National Survey data indicate that approximately one-third of the household population, or about 60 million Americans aged 12 or older, have at least tried illicit drugs, or used drugs nonmedically (Blanken, Adams, & Durell, 1987).

Sometimes schizophrenia appears to be precipitated by illicit drug use. In many cases of drug abuse, the patient has taken an array of illegal drugs over time, making it most difficult to determine which drug or which combination of drugs may have touched off the schizophrenic episode. It is also possible that such patients with schizophrenic symptoms who use so many drugs may be self-medicating an already present illness that it disturbing them. Often it is a challenge to decide if the psychosis is autonomous or not (Bowers, Imirowicz, Druss, & Mazure, 1995).

Amphetamines and Methamphetamine

The amphetamines are some of the most potent psychostimulants. Small or moderate doses given orally to normal subjects commonly produces wakefulness, alertness, decreased sense of fatigue, and elevation of mood. Prolonged use or large doses can cause symptoms considered to be a model of schizophrenia, however (Snyder, 1973). A recent epidemic of methamphetamine abuse in Japan resulted in a dramatic increase of admissions to a psychiatric hospital for a methamphetamine psychosis said to be similar to schizophrenia (Iwanami et al., 1994). In 6.5% of the patients, the symptoms persisted despite the individuals' abstinence from methamphetamine.

Cocaine

Inca legends state that Manco Capac, the Divine Child of the Sun, gave the Incas the coca leaf as a gift. The coca leaf was to give new strength to the weary, satisfy the hungry, and succor the unhappy (Blanken et al., 1987). Alas, cocaine can do other things—it can act as a psychotogen, inducing an acute behavioral disorder characterized by agitation, paranoia, and hallucinations with serious consequences (Siegel, 1978; Bron, 1982; Cohen, 1984; Sherer, 1988). The DSM-III-R (APA, 1987) drew a distinction between cocaine delirium and cocaine delusional disorder. Cocaine can also precipitate seizure disorders. There is a case in the literature in which chronic cocaine abuse precipitated an episode of prolonged partial complex status epilepticus, which was initially misdiagnosed as a psychotic or schizophrenic disorder due to cocaine (Merriam, Medalia, & Levine, 1988). Treatment programs for cocaine addicts have been developed (Angres & Benson, 1987). Buprenorphine may be more successful than methadone in these therapy programs (Kosten et al., 1989).

Lysergic Acid Diethylamide

Lysergic acid diethylamide (LSD) has been reported to precipitate the symptoms of schizophrenia in susceptible individuals (Anastasopoulos & Photiades, 1962; Hatrick & Dewhurst, 1970; Bron, 1982). According to Goldstein (1973), nicotinic acid or niacin can be used as an antidote to the acute psychedelic psychosis of LSD.

Phencyclidine

Drugs such as phencyclidine (PCP) that interact with PCP binding sites and sigma binding sites in the brain can produce psychomimetic effects that resemble symptoms of schizophrenia (Javitt, 1987). It is an antagonist of glutamate at the NMDA receptor (Anis et al., 1983). This drug also exacerbates symptoms in schizo-phrenic patients (Luby, Cohen, Rosenbaum, Gottlieb, & Kelley, 1959).

Multiple Drug Use

In the Johnstone, MacMillan, and Crow (1987) series of first-epi-sode schizophrenics, two patients with multiple drug use were included. In a 17-year-old man, who had taken heroin, amphet-amine, cocaine, barbiturates, cannabis, LSD, and psilocybin for some years, the schizophrenic symptoms completely resolved over a drug-free period of 2 months while in the hospital. In a 33-year-old homeless man, who had taken heroin, LSD, morphine, physeptone, amphetamines, barbiturates, and benzodiazepines, there were intermittent drug-free admissions over many months without good result; the patient did not respond to neuroleptics.

HEAVY METALS AND TOXINS

Heavy metals and toxins can cause symptoms that mimic schizo-phrenia, such as mania and hallucinations (see Table 14.1).

Bismuth

Bismuth is used by colostomy patients who occasionally become deranged from it.

Carbon Monoxide

Carbon monoxide is a colorless, odorless gas with 200 times more affinity for the oxygen-carrying hemoglobin site than oxygen itself. Carbon monoxide poisoning thus produces hypoxia throughout the body, which selectively affects the central nervous system. An example of carbon monoxide's effects follows.

An officer who was intoxicated by carbon monoxide during World War I went into a deep coma. Shortly afterward, a psychosis developed that was diagnosed as schizophrenia even by Kurt

TABLE 14.1 Heavy Metals and Toxins

Substance	Psychosis	Mania	Depression	Organic	Hallucinations	Other
Lead			xx	xx		Lower IQ and hyperactivity in children
Mercury	xx		xx	xx		Extreme anxiety, strange form of xenophobia
Arsenic	xx	xx	xx	xx	Visual	
Manganese	xx	xx	xx			Destruction of nigro striatum
Bismuth	xx		xx	xx	Visual	Anxiety
Thallium	xx		xx	xx		
Aluminum			xx	xx	xx	
Tin (Organo)			xx			Unprovoked rage attacks
Magnesium	xx		xx	xx		
Copper	xx	xx	xx	xx	xx	
Vanadium	??		xx			
Cadmium						Associated with learning disabilities in children
Bromine	xx	xx	xx	xx	Auditory and Visual	
Anticholinergics	xx		xx	xx		Prominent anxiety
Carbon monoxide	xx		xx	xx		Catatonia, borderline personality, panic attack
Carbon dioxide						Precipitate panic attack
Volatile hydrocarbons	xx	xx		xx	Auditory and Visual	Conduct disorder, panic anxiety, personality change

From I. Extein & M. S. Gold (1988). *Medical Mimics of Psychiatric Disorders*. Washington, DC: American Psychiatric Press, p. 180. Reproduced with permission from American Psychiatric Press.

Schneider (Propping, 1983). After 22 years of continuous psychiatric illness, the patient died from pulmonary tuberculosis and was found to have a wide-spread necrosis in the central nervous system (Roeder-Kutsch & Scholz-Wolfing, 1941).

Manganese

Psychiatric symptoms, often of a dramatic nature, have been recorded in victims, such as manganese miners, who experience excessive exposure to this toxin. The earliest signs of manganese poisoning are usually a generalized severe malaise and psychiatric signs (Estroff & Gold, 1986). Manganese-poisoned patients often are diagnosed as schizophrenic (Chandra, 1983). Various terms have been applied to the psychiatric symptoms they exibit, which tend to be hypomanic in nature with mental excitement, aggressive behavior, and incoherent speech as prominent features. These terms are manganese mania (Rodier, 1955), manganic madness (Edwards, 1980), and locura manganica (Mena et al., 1967). All of this information may have led to the manganese hypothesis of schizophrenia and neurodegenerative disorders suggested by Donaldson (1987). Diagnosis of manganese poisoning is established by quantitative serum levels greater than 0.05 ppm.

Mercury

The saying, "mad as a hatter," refers to felt-hat makers of the ninetieth century who had a heavy exposure to mercury vapor (Freeman, 1860). The psychiatric symptoms of mercury poisoning are many, including irritability and and a unique form of xenophobia in which patients avoid contact with strangers (Estroff & Gold, 1986).

Thallium

Thallium poisoning was much more common in the past when thallium was used as a treatment for ringworm, syphilis, and as a depilatory agent. It continued to be used in rat and insect poisons in the United States until the 1970s when it was banned (Estroff & Gold, 1986). Psychiatric symptoms include hallucinations and other symptoms that may be diagnosed as schizophrenia (Munch, 1984). Other symptoms commonly seen are alopecia and gastrointestinal distress (Edwards, 1980).

REFERENCES

Adler, L. E., Sadja, L., & Wilets, G. (1980). Cimetidine toxicity manifested as paranoia and hallucinations. *American Journal of Psychiatry,* *137,* 1112.

American Psychiatric Association (1987). *Diagnostic and statistical manual of mental disorders,* third ed., revised. Washington, DC: American Psychiatric Press.

Anastasopoulos, G., & Photiades, H. (1962). Effects of LSD-25 on relatives of schizophrenic patients. *Journal of Mental Science, 108,* 95–98.

Angres, D. H., & Benson, W. H. (1987). Cocainism—a workable model for recovery. *Psychiatric Medicine,* vol 3. Longwood, FL: Ryandic Publishing Co.

Anis, N. A., Berry, S. C., & Barton, N. R. (1983). The dissociation anesthetics, ketamine and phencyclidine, selectively reduce excitation of central mammalian neurons by N-methyl-aspartate. *British Journal of Pharmacology, 79,* 565–575.

Blanken, A. J., Adams, E. H., & Durell, J. (1987). Drug abuse: Implications and trends. *Psychiatric medicine,* vol 3. Longwood, FL: Ryandic Publishing Co.

Borison, R. L. (1979). Amantadine-induced psychosis in a geriatric patient with renal disease. *American Journal of Psychiatry, 136,* 111.

Bowers, M. B. Jr., Imirowicz, R., Druss, B., & Mazure, C. M. (1995). Autonomous psychosis following psychotogenic substance abuse [letter]. *Biological Psychiatry, 37,* 136–137.

Bron, B. (1982). *Drogenabhängigkeit un Psychoses.* Berlin: Springer Verlag.

Browne, T. R. (1978). Clonazepam. *New England Journal of Medicine, 299,* 812.

Chandra, S. V. (1983). Psychiatric illness due to manganese poisoning. *Acta Psychiatrica Scandinavica, 67,* 49–54.

Cohen, S. (1984). Cocaine: Acute medical and psychiatric complications. *Psychiatric Annals, 14,* 747.

Cohen, S. (1995). Overdiagnosis of schizophrenia: Role of alcohol and drug misuse. *Lancet, 346,* 1541–1542.

Cook, B. L., & Winokur, G. (1985). Separate heritability of alcoholism and psychotic symptoms. *American Journal of Psychiatry, 142,* 360.

Donaldson, J. (1987). The physiopathologic significance of manganese in the brain: Its relation to schizophrenia and neurodegenerative disorders. *Neurotoxicology, 8,* 451–462.

Drake, R. E. (1994). Substance abuse and mental illness: Recent research. *Decade of the Brain, 5,* 4–6.

Dysken, M. W., Merry, W., & Davis, J. M. (1978). Anticholinergic psychosis. *Psychiatric Annals, 8,* 30.

Edwards, N. (1980). Mental disturbances related to metals. In R. C. W. Hall (Ed.), *Psychiatric presentations of medical illness.* New York: Spectrum.

Estroff, T. W., & Gold, M. S. (1986). Medication-induced and toxin-induced psychiatric disorders. In I. Extein, & M. S. Gold (Eds.), *Medical mimics of psychiatric disorders,* Washington, DC: American Psychiatric Press.

Freeman, J. A. (1860). Mercurial disease among hatters. *Transactions of the New Jersey State Medical Society, 61,* 61–64.

Golden, R. N., Hoffman, J., Falk, D., Provenzale, D., & Curtis, T. E. (1989). Psychoses associated with propranolol withdrawal. *Biological Psychiatry, 25,* 351–354.

Goldstein, J. A. (1973). Treatment of a trip. *Emergency Medicine, 5,* 13.

Gorelick, D. A., Kussin, S. Z., & Kahn, I. (1978). Paranoid delusions and auditory hallucinations associated with digoxin intoxication. *Journal of Nervous Mental Disorder, 166,* 817.

Hatrick, J. A., & Dewhurst, K. (1970). Delayed psychosis due to LSD. *Lancet, ii,* 742–744.

Iwanami, A., Sugiyama, A., Kuroki, N., Toda, S., Kato, N., Nakatani, Y., Horita, N., & Kaneko, T. (1994). Patients with methamphetamine psychosis admitted to a psychiatric hospital in Japan. *Acta Psychiatrica Scandinavica, 89,* 428–432.

Javitt, D. C. (1987). Negative schizophrenic symptomology and the PCP (phencyclidine) model of schizophrenia. *Hillside Journal of Clinical Psychiatry, 9,* 12–35.

Johnstone, E. C., MacMillan, J. F., & Crow, T. J. (1987). The occurrence of organic disease of possible or probable etiological significance in a population of 268 cases of first episode schizophrenia. *Psychological Medicine, 17,* 371–379.

Klawans, H. L. (1978). Levodopa-induced psychosis. *Psychiatric Annals, 8,* 19.

Kosten, T. R., Kleber, H. D., & Morgan, C. (1989). Treatment of cocaine abuse with buprenorphine. *Biological Psychiatry, 26,* 637–639.

Kulkarni, J., Horne, M., Butler, E., Keks, N., & Copolov, D. (1992). Psychotic symptoms resulting from intraventricular infusion of dopamine in Parkinson's disease. *Biological Psychiatry, 31,* 1225–1227.

Lake, C. R. (1991). Manic psychosis after coffee and phenylpropanolamine. *Biological Psychiatry, 30,* 401–404.

Ling, M. H., Perry, P. J., & Tsuang, M. T. (1981). Side effects of corticosteroid therapy: Psychiatric aspects. *Archives of General Psychiatry, 38,* 471.

Lipsedge, M., & Littlewood, R. (1979). Transcultural psychiatry. *Recent Advances in Clinical Psychiatry, 3,* 91–134.

Luby, E. D., Cohen, B. D., Rosenbaum, G., Gottlieb, J. S., & Kelley, R. (1959). Study of a new schizophrenomimetic drug—Sernyl. *Archives of Neurology Psychiatry, 81,* 363–366.

Mena, I., Marin, O., Fuenzalida, S. et al. (1967). Chronic manganese poisoning—clincial picture and manganese turnover. *Neurology, 17,* 128–136.

Merriam, A. E., Medalia, A., & Levine, B. (1988). Partial complex status epilepticus associated with cocaine abuse. *Biological Psychiatry, 23,* 515–518.

Munch, J. C. (1984). Human thallotoxicosis. *Journal of the American Medical Association, 102,* 1929–1934.

Nagao, S. (1964). Clinico-genetic study of chronic alcoholism. *Japanese Journal of Human Genetics, 9,* 111–135.

Nasrallah, H. A. (1979). Vulnerability to disulfiram psychosis. *Western Juornal of Medicine, 130,* 575.

Olney, J. W., & Farber, N. B. (1995). NMDA receptor hypofunction and schizophrenia. *Biological Psychiatry, 37,* 667. (abstract)

Patterson, J. R. (1985). Psychosis following discontinuation of a long-acting propranolol preparation. *Journal of Clinical Psychopharmacology, 5,* 125–126.

Propping, P. (1983). Genetic disorders presenting as "schizophrenia." Karl Bonhoeffer's early view of the psychoses in the light of medical genetics. *Human Genetics, 65,* 1–10.

Rodier, J. (1955). Manganese poisoning in Moroccan miners. *British Journal of Indian Medicine, 12,* 21–35.

Roeder-Kutsch, T., & Scholz-Wolfing, J. (1941). Schizophrenes siechtum auf der grundlage ausgedehnter hirnveranderungen nach kohlen-oxydvergiftung. *Zhurnal Neuropatalogii Psikiatrii, 173,* 702–730.

Sherer, M. A. (1988). Intravenous cocaine: psychiatric effects, biological mechanisms. *Biological Psychiatry, 24,* 865–885.

Siegel, R. K. (1978). Cocaine hallucinations. *American Journal of Psychiatry, 132,* 225–231.

Snyder, S. H. (1973). Amphetamine psychosis: a 'model' schizophrenia mediated by catecholamines. *American Journal of Psychiatry, 130,* 61.

Tsuang, M. T., & Faraone, S. V. (1994). Schizophrenia. In G. Winokur, & P. J. Clayton (Eds.), *The medical basis of psychiatry.* Philadelphia: Saunders.

Tsuang, M. T., Simpson, J. C., et al. (1982). Subtypes of drug abuse with psychosis: Demographic characteristics, clinical features, and family history. *Archives of General Psychiatry, 39,* 141–147.

CHAPTER 15

Miscellaneous Topics

THE DEMENTIAS

The dementias generally are not misdiagnosed as a form of schizophrenia. In many cases the clinical distinction between schizophrenia and dementia can be based on the difference between the thought disorders of the two entities. Schizophrenic thinking, although grossly distorted, usually is adequate for the day-to-day tasks of living and retains those basic cognitive functions that deteriorate early in dementias. From another point of view the presence of the first rank symptoms of schizophrenia are usually missing in the dementias.

However, the two syndromes occassionally are confused particularly in cases presenting before 60 years of age. The early impairment of memory in Alzheimer disease and the conspicuous neurological signs of Creutzfeldt-Jakob disease usually preclude such misdiagnoses. Nevertheless, in the case of Pick's disease, memory is preserved for a long time and sensorimotor neurological signs often are absent. In a series published by Malamud (1975), a functional disorder was diagnosed 9% of the time in Alzhemier's disease, 10% of the time in Creutzfeldt-Jakob disease, but 23% of the time with Pick's disease. In the occasional relatively young adult who develops Pick's disease—at 29 years of age (Winkelman & Book, 1949) or at the age of 34 years (Malamud, 1975)—schizophrenia can be the clinical diagnosis during life and Pick's disease is found only at autopsy, much to the surprise of the neuropathologists. Pick's disease is characterized by atrophy of the frontal and temporal lobes.

There has been a controversy about whether there is a dementia of schizophrenia itself because of the cognitive impairment now demonstrated on neuropsychological tests (Kirkpatrick, Golden, & Fletcher, 1987). This is likely to be a discussion that does little to illuminate the underlying disease entities in either group, however.

Eventually, the new molecular biological studies being developed may help sort out the dementias. Creutzfeldt-Jakob has turned out to be a prion disease (Hsiao & Prusiner, 1990). In one case of chronic schizophrenia with cognitive impairment, a missense mutation at codon 713 of the beta amyloid precursor protein gene has been found (Lawrie, 1993), but is unlikely to be etiological to the schizophrenia as a silent nonpathogenic variant has been found at codon 705 (Forsell & Lannfelt, 1995). (For further discussion of this case, see page 181.) This is just the beginning of understanding the dementias.

NARCOLEPSY

Narcolepsy is a strange disorder that consists of attacks of daytime somnolence that are irresistible in intensity, causing the individual to suddenly fall asleep during the day, sometimes even while standing up. The syndrome may also include hypnagogic hallucinations and episodes of sleep paralysis as well as attacks of cataplexy, in which the patient abruptly loses muscle tone and may fall briefly to the ground. Narcolepsy can be idiopathic or secondary to other brain disorders such as encephalitis, hypothalamic tumor or the Kleine-Levin syndrome.

Schizophrenia appears to develop in patients with narcolepsy frequently enough to indicate it may be more than chance expectation; there can be a clinical problem deciding if a patient has narcolepsy or schizophrenia (Shapiro & Spitz, 1976). The association of a schizophrenialike psychosis with narcolepsy was first recognized as early as 1884 and cases were reported in the older medical literature before the introduction of amphetamine therapy in 1930 began to obscure the picture (Davison, 1983).

In one review of the literature, which identified 18 patients with schizophrenia, only one had a family history of schizophrenia (Davison & Bagley, 1969). The question arose whether the psychiatric symptoms had been touched off by the ingestion of amphetamines but only 5 of the 18 patients were taking such medication. In some patients, the persistent delusions and hallucinations appear to be direct extensions of the vivid dreams or hypnagogic experiences; however, a study exploring this question found no greater degree of sleep hallucinosis in the patients who developed schizophrenic reactions than in those who did not (Sours, 1963). The evidence in the literature suggests that some of the patients met classical DSM-III (APA, 1980) criteria of schizophrenia, whereas others have a deteriorating paranoid-hallucinatory state in which hypnagogic experiences become interwoven into the content of the psychosis (Coren & Strain, 1965).

THE PIP SYNDROME

It has been reported that 25% of institutionalized patients with schizophrenic symptoms can be observed to consume greater than average amounts of water (deLeon, Verghese, Tracy, Josiassen, & Simpson, 1994). These patients fall into three categories:

1. Primary polydipsia—patients who consume and excrete large quantities of water but maintain normal serum sodium levels (Vieweg, David, Rowe, Yank, & Spradlin, 1986).
2. The PIP syndrome—patients with polydipsia and intermittent hyponatremia (Vieweg, Rowe, David, Sutker, & Spradlin, 1984).
3. Reset osmostat syndrome—patients with polydipsia who consistently maintain abnormally low serum sodium levels (Robertson, 1985).

The syndrome of psychosis, intermittent hyponatremia, and polydipsia (PIP syndrome) is found in seriously mentally ill persons but is not limited to schizophrenia; the syndrome also has been seen in neurosis, depression, hysteria, delusional hypochondriasis, and bulimia (Zubenko, 1987). It is estimated that approximately 7% of psychotic patients suffer from episodes of intermittent hyponatremia (PIP syndrome) (Leadbetter, Shutty, Higgins, & Pavalonis, 1994). Characteristically PIP patients reside in state mental hospitals and are readily identified by the staff as consuming fluids almost constantly throughout the day and they frequently arise at night to urinate and consume additional fluids (Vieweg et al., 1986).

Chronic medical sequelae include bowel and bladder distention, hypotonic bladder, urinary incontinence, urinary tract infections, hydronephrosis, vomiting, malnutrition, hypocalcemia, osteopenia, fractures, edema, and congestive cardiac failure. Acute signs of hyponatremia include impaired cognition, seizures, delirium, coma, and death.

Diagnosis of the PIP syndrome is made by observing the polydipsia and recording the subsequent intermittent hyponatremia. It appears that 6:00-P.M. urine specimens are most predictive of 24-hour urine volumes in this population, despite the fact that there appears to be some variability in their daily drinking patterns (Vieweg et al., 1986).

Polydipsia has been observed for 60 years but is far from being fully understood. It has been known since 1933 that patients with schizophrenic disorders excrete almost twice the daily urine volume of normal subjects (Hoskins & Sleeper, 1933). Studies of the pathophysiology of the PIP syndrome have found defects involving abnormal thirst regulation, inappropriate arginine vasopressin (AVP) secretion, and excessive response to AVP by the renal tubules (Goldman, Luchins, & Robertson, 1988; Riggs, Dysken, Kin, & Opsahl, 1991). It also may be associated with inappropriate secretion of antidiuretic hormone (Suzuki, Takeuchi, Mori, Takegoshi, & Kurachi, 1992) or hippocampal pathology (Umbricht, 1994). One of the most hopeful aspects of the PIP syndrome is that it can sometimes disappear if the patient responds to treatment for the underlying mental illness.

SARCOIDOSIS

Sarcoidosis ended up in the Miscellaneous Topics chapter because of the disagreement in the literature about the cause of this syndrome, which mimics tuberculosis in some regards. Neurological involvement in sarcoidosis is around 5% (Delaney, 1977; Stern et al., 1985), but the clinical picture of sarcoidosis is known to be quite variable; sometimes it occurs in a relapsing–remitting pattern similar to multiple sclerosis (Scott, Seay, & Goust, 1989).

In the medical literature, patients are reported who have both sarcoidosis and schizophrenia (Delaney, 1977; Stoudemire, Linfors, & Houpt, 1983; Johnstone, MacMillan, & Crow, 1987). Whether the sarcoidosis is responsible for the symptoms of schizophrenia in these patients is far from clear. There is a report in the medical literature of paranoid psychosis and auditory hallucinations, labeled schizophreniclike, in patients with central nervous system (CNS) sarcoidosis remitting with steroid treatment (Suchenwirth & Dold, 1969). (CNS involvement in sarcoidosis may be underreported.) Because of the relapsing–remitting pattern in this disease entity, the interpretation of these cases raises, but does not settle, the question of treatment of psychiatric symptoms in sarcoidosis.

UREMIA

Uremia is caused by anything that causes a prolonged and severe reduction of blood flow through the kidneys, either of renal or extrarenal origin, and usually is associated with disordered mental functioning. If the uremia develops quickly, there rarely is any diagnostic difficulty identifying the kidney dysfunction because the patient is clearly unwell. If the uremia develops slowly, however, occasionally the picture may present as a uremic encephalopathy, which can appear as a primary mental illness. Uremic encephalopathies frequently have features that suggest a functional psychiatric illness (Fraser, 1992). Mental state abnormalities have been noted as an early and sensitive index of upcoming neurological abnormalities (Locke, Merrill, & Tyler, 1961).

In the medical literature, a patient with uremia is described with a mental state fluctuating between psychotic and normal periods who was diagnosed as suffering from catatonic schizophrenia (Baker & Knutson, 1946). Uremia may also present as a mounting paranoia over many months (Menninger, 1924).

A major treatment for uremia—kidney dialysis—can itself sometimes be accompanied by short-lived psychotic episodes usually in clear consciousness, but often marked by features such as loosely held delusions or visual hallucinations (Lishman, 1987; Fraser & Arieff, 1988). Patients sometimes develop full-blown dialysis dementia, a progressive and often fatal encephalopathy. These patients sometimes have symptoms of paranoia, hostility, and other psychotic symptoms. The etiology of these psychiatric symptoms is apparent, however.

VASCULAR LESIONS

Older individuals with schizophrenia sometimes are found to have vascular lesions in the brain and this inevitably raises the question of whether the infarct is related to the schizophrenia (von Janzarik, 1957; Tippin & Dunner, 1981; Levine & Finklestein, 1982; Peroutka, Sohmer, Kumer, Folstein, & Robinson, 1982; Minabe, Kadonor, & Kurachi, 1990). There have been reports of paranoid–hallucinatory psychoses developing soon after subarachnoid hemorrhage (Silverman, 1949) and bilateral carotid artery occlusion (Shapiro, 1959). The timing of cerebrovascular accidents sometimes makes the consequent psychiatric symptoms seem related in that particular case.

One computed tomography (CT) survey of 136 chronic schizophrenics found seven cases with unsuspected cerebral infarction, some with evidence of multiple infarcts (Cunningham Owens, Johnstone, Bydder, & Kreel, 1980). Because these patients were all under 40 years of age when admitted to the psychiatric hospital and had been living there for up to 47 years, it is far from clear when these previously undetected infarctions had occurred or if they were relevant to the individuals' psychiatric symptoms. In fact, autopsy studies of chronic schizophrenics have found no excess of cerebrovascular disease (Corsellis, 1962; Hussar, 1966). Because the frequency of cerebrovascular disease is so high in first world countries, one tends to discount reports of cerebrovascular disease in a patient with schizophrenia unless there is a direct time sequence or other unequivocable data.

There is a very rare syndrome classified as peduncular hallucinosis, involving vascular lesions in the cerebral peduncles or adjacent midbrain structures (Lhermitte, Levy, & Trelles, 1932;

Nakajima, 1983; Geller & Bellur, 1987). This is unlikely to be confused with schizophrenia because the cranial nerves are involved, hallucinations are always visual, and there are associated disturbances of consciousness.

REFERENCES

American Psychiatric Association (1980). *Diagnostic and statistical manual of mental disorders, 3rd ed.* Washington, DC: American Psychiatric Press.

Baker, A. B., & Knutson, J. (1946). Psychatric aspects of uremia. *American Journal of Psychiatry, 102,* 683–687.

Coren, H. Z., & Strain, J. J. (1965). A case of narcolepsy with psychosis (paranoid state of narcolepsy). *Comprehensive Psychiatry, 6,* 191–199.

Corsellis, J. A. N. (1962). *Mental illness and the aging brain.* London: Oxford University Press.

Cunningham Owens, D. G., Johnstone, E. C., Bydder, G. M., & Kreel, L. (1980). Unsuspected organic disease in chronic schizophrenia demonstrated by computed tomography. *Journal of Neurology, Neurosurgery and Psychiatry, 43,* 1065–1969.

Davison, K., & Badley, C. R. (1969). Schizophrenia-like psychoses associated with organic disorders of the central nervous system: A review of the literature. In R. N. Herrington (Ed.), *British Journal of Psychiatry special publication no. 4.* Ashford, Kent: Headley Brothers.

Davison, K. (1983). Schizophrenia-like psychosis associated with organic cerebral disorders: A review. *Psychiatric Developments, 1,* 1–34.

Delaney, P. (1977). Neurological manifestations in sarcoidosis. *Annals of Internal Medicine, 87,* 336–345.

deLeon, J., Verghese, C., Tracy, J., Josiassen, R., & Simpson, G. M. (1994). Polydipsia and water intoxication in psychiatric patients: A review of the epidemiological literature. *Biological Psychiatry, 35,* 408–419.

Forsell, C., & Lannfelt, L. (1995). Amyloid precursor protein mutation at codon 713 (Ala—>Val) does not cause schizophrenia: Non-pathogenic variant found at codon 705 (silent). *Neuroscience Letters, 184,* 90–93.

Fraser, C. L. (1992). Neurologic manifestations of the uremic state. In A. I. Arieff & R. C. Griggs (Eds.), *Metabolic brain dysfunction in systemic disorders.* New York: Little, Brown & Co.

Fraser, C. L., & Arieff, A. I. (1988). Nervous system complications in uremia. *Annals of Internal Medicine, 109,* 143.

Geller, T. J., & Bellur, S. N. (1987). Pedunclar hallucinosis: Magnetic resonance imaging confirmation of mesencepahlic infarction during life. *Annals of Neurology, 21*, 602–604.

Goldman, M. B., Luchins, D. J., & Robertson, G. L. (1988). Mechanisms of altered water metabolism in psychotic patients with polydipsia and hyponatremia. *New England Journal of Medicine, 318*, 397–403.

Hoskins, R. G., & Sleepr, F. H. (1933). Organic functions in schizophrenia. *Archives of Neurology and Psychiatry, 30*, 123–140.

Hsiao, K., & Prusiner, S. B. (1990). The inherited prion diseases. *Neurology, 40*, 1820–1827.

Hussar, A.E. (1966). Gross anatomic lesions of the brain in 1275 autopsies of long-term hospitalized schizophrenic patients. *Diseases of the Nervous System, 27*, 743–747.

Johnstone, E. C., MacMillan, J. F., & Crow, T. J. (1987). The occurrence of organic disease of possible or probable etiological significance in a population of 268 cases of first episode schizophrenia. *Psychological Medicine, 17*, 371–379.

Kirkpatrick, B., Golden, R. N., & Fletcher, R. H. (1987). Is there a dementia of schizophrenia? *Psychiatric medicine*, vol. 4. Longwood, FL: Ryandic Publishing Co.

Lawrie, S. M. (1993). Clinical, psychological and neuroradiological findings in a case of schizophrenia with cognitive impairment: Missense nutation at codon 713 of the beta amyloid precursor protein gene. (letter) *Schizophrenia Research, 10*, 273–275.

Leadbetter, R. A., Shutty, M. S., Higgins, P. B., & Pavalonis, D. (1994). Multidisciplinary approach to psychosis, intermittent hyponateremia and polydipsia. *Schizophrenia Bulletin, 20*, 375–385.

Levine, D. N., & Finklestein, S. (1982). Delayed psychosis after right temporoparietal stroke or trauma: Relation to epilepsy. *Neurology, 32*, 267.

Lhermitte, J., Levy, G., & Trelles, J. (1932). L'hallucinose pedonculaire (etude anatomique d'un cas). *Revue Neurologique, (Paris)* 1, 382.

Lishman, W. A. (1987). *Organic psychiatry: The psychological consequences of cerebral disorder.* second edition. Oxford: Blackwell Scientific.

Locke, S. J., Merrill, J. P., & Tyler, H. R. (1961). Neurological complications of acute uremia. *Archives of Internal Medicine, 108*, 75.

Malamud, N. (1975). Organic brain disease mistaken for psychiatric disease; A clinicopathologic study. In D. F. Benson & D. Blumer (Eds.), *Psychiatric aspects of neurologic disease* (pp. 287–307). New York: Grune & Stratton.

Menninger, K. A. (1924). Paranoid psychosis with uremia. *Journal of Nervous and Mental Disease, 60*, 26–34.

Minabe, Y., Kadono, Y., & Kurachi, M. (1990). A schizophrenic syndrome associated with a midbrain tegmental lesion. *Biological Psychiatry*, *27*, 661–663.

Nakajima, K. (1983). Clinicopathological study of pontine hemorrhage. *Stroke*, *14*, 485–493.

Peroutka, S. J., Sohmer, B. H., Kumer, A. J., Folstein, M., & Robinson, R. G. (1982). Hallucinations and delusions following a right temporoparieto-occipital infarction. *Johns Hopkins Medical Journal*, *151*, 181.

Riggs, A. T., Dysken, M. W., Kin, S. W., & Opsahl, J. A. (1991). A review of disorders of water homeostasis in psychiatric patients. *Psychosomatics*, *32*, 133–148.

Robertson, G. L. (1985). Osmoregulation of thirst and vasopressin secretion: Functional properties and their relationship to water balance. In R. W. Schrier (Ed.), *Vasopressin*. New York: Raven Press.

Scott, T. F., Seay, A. R., & Goust, J. M. (1989). Pattern and concentration of IgG in cerebrospinal fluid in neurosarcoidosis. *Neurology*, *39*, 1637–1639.

Shapiro, B., & Spitz, H. (1976). Problems in the differential diagnosis of narcolepsy versus schizophrenia. *American Journal of Psychiatry*, *133*, 1321.

Shapiro, S. K. (1959). Psychosis due to bilateral carotid artery occlusion. *Minnesota Medicine*, *42*, 25–27.

Silverman, M. (1949). Paranoid reaction during the phase of recovery from subarachnoid hemorrhage. *J Ment Sci*, *95*, 706–708.

Sours, J. A. (1963). Narcolepsy and other disturbances in the sleep-waking rhyrhm: A study of 115 cases with review of the literature. *Journal of Nervous and Mental Disease*, *137*, 525–542.

Stern, B. J., Krumholz, A., Johns, C. et al. (1985). Sarcoidosis and its neurological manifestations. *Archives of Neurology*, *42*, 909.

Stoudemire, A., Linfors, E., & Houpt, J. L. (1983). Central nervous system sarcoidosis. *General Hospital Psychiatry*, *5*, 129–132.

Suchenwirth, R., & Dold, V. (1969). Functional psychoses in sarcoidosis (Funktionspsychosen bei der Sarkoidose). *Verhandlungen Deutschen Gesellschaft für Innere Medizin*, *75*, 757–759.

Suzuki, M., Takeuchi, O., Mori, I., Takegoshi, K., & Kurachi, M. (1992). Syndrome of inappropriate secretion of antidiuretic hormone associated with schizophrenia. *Biological Psychiatry*, *31*, 1057–1061.

Tippin, J., & Dunner, F. (1981). Biparietal infarctions in a patient with catatonia. *American Journal of Psychiatry*, *138*, 10.

Umbricht, D. (1994). Polydipsia and hippocampal pathology [letter]. *Biological Psychiatry*, *36*, 709–710.

Vieweg, W. V. R., Rowe, W. T., David, J. J., Sutker, L. H., & Spradlin, W. W. (1984). Evaluation of patients with self-induced water intoxication and schizophrenic disorders (SIWIS). *Journal of Nervous Mental Disease, 172,* 552–555.

Vieweg, W. V. R., David, J. J., Rowe, W. T., Yank, G. R., & Spradlin, W. W. (1986). Diurnal variation of urinary excretion for patients with psychosis, intermittent hyponatremia and polydipsia (PIP syndrome). *Biological Psychiatry, 21,* 1031–1042.

von Janzarik, W. (1957). Zur problematik schizophrener psychosen im loheren lebensalter. *Nervenarzt, 28,* 535–542.

Winkelman, N. W., & Book, M. H. (1949). Asympyomatic extra-pyramidal involvement in Pick's disease. *Journal of Neuropathology and Experimental Neurology, 8,* 30–42.

Zubenko, G. S. (1987). Water homeostasis in psychiatric patients (Editorial). *Biological Psychiatry, 22,* 121–125.

CHAPTER 16

The Medical Work-Up of Patients with Schizophrenia

At the present time it is standard practice for a patient who presents with the possible diagnosis of schizophrenia to receive a complete psychiatric and neurological examination (Rubin et al., 1994) supplemented with thorough neuropsychological testing. These examinations follow standard examination forms. For example, the neurological examination includes an emphasis on frontal lobe signs and so-called soft signs, such as mirror movements, graphesthesia, and palmomental reflex (Bartko, Zador, Horvath, & Herczeg, 1988). Table 16.1 shows a well known differential diagnosis of hallucinations (Cadet, Rickler, & Weinberger, 1986). There are entire books on these subjects that do not need recounting here. At the risk of being repetitious, however, this work-up reemphasizes the signs and symptoms (Lieberman, 1995) of some of the underlying disease entities that can present with the symptoms of schizophrenia.

Interpretation of neurological signs focused on diagnosable forms of schizophrenia is listed here:

NEUROLOGICAL SIGNS

Adventitious movements
- chorea—Huntington disease, DRPLA (dentatorubalpallidoluysian atrophy)
- tics—Tourette syndrome
- wing flapping—Wilson's disease

TABLE 16.1 Perceptual Disturbances

Hallucinations

Auditory	(temporal lobe, schizophrenia)
Gustatory	(complex partial seizures, Briquet's syndrome, schizophrenia)
Heautoscopic	(parieto-occipital)
Lilliputian	(temporal lobe, toxic states, hypnogogic, schizophrenia)
Peduncular	(intoxication, encephalitis upper brainstem, pulvinar)
Olfactory	(epilepsy, migraine, Alzheimer's disease, alcoholic psychoses, manicdepressive illness, schizophrenia)
Somatic	(phantom limb, phantom breasts, toxic encephalopathies, schizophrenia)
Visual	(retinal diseases, optic nerve lesion, epilepsy, migraine, toxic-metabolic, Briquet's syndrome, sensory and sleep deprivation, schizophrenia)

From Jean Lud Cadet et al. (1986). The clinical neurologic examination in schizophrenia. In Vol. 1, H. A. Nasrallah & D. Weinberger (Eds.), *Handbook of schizophrenia* (p. 11). Amsterdam: Elsevier. Reprinted with permission.

Dysarthria—Wilson's disease, DRPLA
Dystonia—Wilson's disease
Myoclonus—DRPLA
Opsoclonus—DRPLA
Peripheral neuropathy
  • acute intermittent porphyria
  • adrenomyeloneuropathy
  • Fabry disease
  • GM_2 gangliosidosis
  • homocystinuria—methylenetetrahydrofolate   reductase deficiency type
  • systemic lupus erythematosus
Reflexes
  • depressed ankle jerk—hypothyroidism
  • pathological reflexes—encephalitis, tumor
Seizures
  • acute encephalitis
  • acute intermittent porphyria
  • Addison's disease
  • DRPLA

- systemic lupus erythematosus
- tuberous sclerosis
- tumor of the central nervous system
- vitamin D deficiency
- Wilson's disease (Jacksonian type)

Stroke—Fabry's disease
Tremor (finger)—DRPLA
Unusual gait
    ataxia
- argininosuccinic aciduria
- DRPLA
- Friedreich's ataxia
- GM2 gangliosidosis
- Hartnup disease
- Wilson's disease

Supplementary general examination recommendations focus on a specific search for treatable etiologies of schizophrenia .

GENERAL EXAMINATION: SIGNS AND SYMPTOMS

Symptoms

Acute epigastric/abdominal pain
- acute intermittent porphyria
- Addison's crisis
- Fabry disease
- systemic lupus erythematosus
Chronic bronchitis, sinusitis, and bronchiectasis
- Kartagener's syndrome
Cold intolerance
- Addison disease
- hypothyroidism
Constipation (severe)
- acute intermittent porphyria
- hypothyroidism
Headache
- acute encephalitis
- acute intermittent porphyria

- tumor of the central nervous system

Loss of appetite/anorexia/weight loss
  - Addison's disease
  - hyperthyroidism
  - systemic lupus erythematosus

Vomiting
  - acute intermittent porphyria
  - Addison's crisis
  - systemic lupus erythematosus

Sexual dysfunction
  amenorrhea
    - Cushing's syndrome
    - Addison's disease
  menorrhagia
    - hypothyroidism

Signs

Anemia
  - systemic lupus erythematosus
  - uremia

Arthritis
  - systemic lupus erythematosus

Cardiac symptoms
  - cardiac dysrhythmias, tachycardia exceeding 90 beats per
    minute, palpitations
      hyperthyroidism
      systemic lupus erythematosus

Evidence of dehydration
  - Addison's crisis

Glossitis
  - pellegra

Goiter
  - hyperthyroidism, hypothyroidism

Hair
  - unusual tufting and friability—argininosuccinic aciduria
  - hirsute—Cushing's syndrome
  - axillary & pubic hair absent—hypopituitarism

Hypertension
- Cushing's syndrome
- systemic lupus erythematosus

Hypotension
- Addison's disease

Immune system depressed
- Cushing's syndrome
- Addison's disease

Liver involvement
- jaundice/hepatosplenomegaly—Wilson's disease

Lymphadenopathy
- systemic lupus erythematosus

Mutism
- Wilson's disease

Moon face
- Cushing's syndrome

Obesity
- of recent onset—Cushing's syndrome, hypothyroidism

Ophthalmological signs
- exophthalmos, lid retraction, lid-lag—hyperthyroidism
- Kayser-Fleischer ring—Wilson's disease

Pyrexia
- Addison's crisis
- acute encephalitis
- (low grade)—systemic lupus erythematosus

Retinopathy
- systemic lupus erythematosus

Skin
- alopecia—systemic lupus erythematosus
- angiectasia—Fabry's disease
- butterfly eruption on the face—systemic lupus erythematosus
- dry, rough—hypothyroidism, hypopituitarism
- purple striae on the abdomen and thighs—Cushing's syndrome
- edematous—hypothyroidism, Fabry's disease, Wilson's disease
- excessive bruising—Cushing's syndrome, systemic lupus erythematosis

- pigmentation on exposed surfaces—Addison's disease, pellagra
- reddening of the dorsum of the hands—pellegra, Hartnup disease
- sebaceous adenoma on the face—tuberous sclerosis
- sweating—hyperthyroidism

Spinal column
- kyphotic "buffalo hump"—Cushing's syndrome
- stiff neck—acute encephalitis

Stomatitis—pellegra

Testicular atrophy/impotence
- Cushing's syndrome, Addison's disease, hypothyroidism

LABORATORY TESTING

The laboratory testing is presented in two sections. Work-up A is a laboratory evaluation of diseases that have known treatments. Work-up B completes the work-up for illnesses without known present therapies. A full work-up is recommended as genetic counseling and the possibility of future therapies in any disease makes it worthwhile to diagnose every patient as accurately as possible.

Work-Up A: Laboratory Evaluation of Treatable Diseases

Blood tests:

All Patients

1. CBC
2. Tests of immune function
3. Electrolytes
4. Blood urea nitorgen (BUN)
5. Glucose
6. Calcium, phosphorus
7. Thyroid-stimulating hormone (TSH)—if abnormal, T3, T4, thyroid-reducing hormone (TRH) stimulation test

8. Liver-function tests
9. A test for neurosyphilis (TPI, TPHA, or FTA-ABS)
10. Erythrocyte sedimentation rate
11. LE cells
12. Serum vitamin A
13. Serum vitamin B_{12}
14. Serum 1, 25 dihydroxy vitamin D_3
15. Serum copper, ceruloplasmin
16. Serum methionine and phenylalanine
17. Serum zinc
18. Porphobilinogen deaminase measured in erthyrocytes

Male Patients Only

19. Level of saturated very long chain fatty acids (VLCFA) in plasma (Moser et al., 1981; Alberghina, Fiumara, Pavone, & Giuffrida, 1984), red cells (Antoku, Sakai, Goto, Iwashita, & Kuroiwa, 1984), or white cells (Molzer, Bernheimer, Heller, Toifi, & Vetterlein, 1982).
20. Test of alpha-galactosidase A level in lymphoblasts for Fabry disease

Urine tests

1. Screening for drugs
2. Twenty-four hour urinary level of copper, quantitative amino acids including homocystine, end-products of vitamin B_3, adrenal steroids
3. Test for levels of urinary porphyrins (porphobilinogen, delta-aminolevulinic acid) once psychiatric symptoms turn on

Chest X-ray

Electrophysiological testing
- Electroencephalogram

Ophthalmological testing
- slit lamp testing—Wilson, Fabry

Lumbar Puncture (when indicated)
- (acute case)—test for encephalitis, PCR for herpes simplex

- (chronic case)—test for neurosyphilis if blood tests ambiguous; protein level elevated may indicate chronic encepalopathy

Imaging tests
- Magnetic resonance imaging or computed tomography

Skin biopsy
- if skin lesions of Fabry disease are present

Future tests
- analysis of deoxyribose nucleic acid (DNA) extracted from hair roots for diagnosis of the porphyrias (Schreiber, Fong, & Jamani, 1994)

Work-Up B: Additional Laboratory Evaluation for Diseases Without Established Treatments at this Time

Blood tests

1. chromosomal karyotype
2. molecular biological testing if indicated DNA testing (looking for trinucleotide repeats) for Huntington's Disease (Huntington's Disease Collaborative Research Group, 1993) and, in females, for fragile X. Allele testing for GM2 gangliosidosis and metachromatic leukodystrophy.

Urine tests
1. aryl-sulfatase A levels

REFERENCES (Includes References for Laboratory Procedures not Available in Standard Laboratories)

Alberghina, M., Fiumara, A., Pavone, I., & Giuffrida, A. M. (1984). Determination of C20-C30 fatty acids by reversed-phase chromatographic techniques: An efficient method to quantitate minor fatty acids in the serum of patients with adrenoleukodystrophy. *Neurochemical Research, 9,* 1719.

Antoku, Y., Sakai, T., Goto, I., Iwashita, H., & Kuroiwa, Y. (1984). Adreno-leukodystrophy: Abnormality of very long chain fatty acids in erythrocyte membrane phospholipids. *Neurology, 34,* 1499.

Bartko, G., Zador, G., Horvath, S., & Herczeg, I. (1988). Neurological soft signs in chronic schizophrenic patients: Clincial correlates. *Biological Psychiatry, 24,* 458–460.

Cadet, J. L., Rickler, K. C., & Weinberger, D. R. (1986). The clinical neurological examination in schizophrenia. In H. A. Nasrallah & D. R. Weinberger (Eds.), *The neurology of schizophrenia.* Amsterdam: Elsevier.

Huntington's Disease Collaborative Research Group (1993). A novel gene containing a trinucleotide repeat that is expanded and unstable on Huntington's disease chromosomes. *Cell, 72,* 971–983.

Lieberman, J. (1995). Signs and symptoms. What can they tell us about the clinical course and pathophysiologic processes of schizophrenia. *Archives of General Psychiatry, 52,* 361–363.

Molzer, B., Bernheimer, H., Heller, R., Toifi, K., & Vetterlein, M. (1982). Detection of adrenoleukodystrophy by increased C26:0 fatty acid levels in leukocytes. *Clinica Chimica Acta, 125,* 299.

Moser, H. W., Moser, A. B., Frayer, K. K., Chen, W., Schulman, J. D., O'Neill, B. P., & Kishimoto, Y. (1981). Adrenoleukodystrophy: Increased plasma content of saturated very long chain fatty acids. *Neurology, 31,* 1241.

Rubin, P., Vorstrup, S., Hemmingsen, R., Andersen, H. S., Bendsen, B. B., Stromso, N., Larsen, J. K., & Bolwig, T. G. (1994). Neurological abnormalities in patients with schizophrenia or schizophreniform disorder at first admission to hospital: Correlations with computerized tomography and regional cerebral blood flow findings. *Acta Psychiatrica Scandinavica, 90,* 385–390.

Schreiber, W. E., Fong, F., & Jamani, A. (1994). Molecular diagnosis of acute intermittent porphyria by analysis of DNA extracted from hair roots. *Clinical Chemistry, 40,* 1744–1748.

CHAPTER 17

Conclusions

Schizophrenia has the same root as *schism*, referring to an intrapsychic split. Yet an additional split with regard to schizophrenia also has existed between neurology and psychiatry for too long a time. Schizophrenia is, after all, a legitimate concern of neuroscientists, whatever their professional orientation (Hackinski, 1993). It now appears that schizophrenia forms a behavioral syndrome that represents the final common pathway of a number of different developmental, physical, enzymatic, infectious, and other injuries. It is relevant to note that these various injuries are expressed clinically primarily in the adolescent and adult age groups.

There is evidence suggesting that many patients have a structural static encephalopathy of lifelong duration. Others have clearly reversible etiologies of their psychiatric symptoms. Reversibility is most clearly seen in the metabolic and endocrine subgroups of schizophrenia. Therapies are also possible in some of the infectious and autoimmune subgroups. Tumors and abscesses presenting as schizophrenia have been successfully treated.

The search for the genetic basis in families with two or more members with schizophrenia is now underway, but progress is slow as the huge human genome is painstakingly investigated. In medicine, the new tools of molecular biology have already begun to allow the arguments between lumpers and splitters to be eroded. Take, for example, tuberous sclerosis and Huntington's disease. It is now known that although tuberous sclerosis has genetic heterogeneity with genes on different chromosomes, all families with Huntington's disease worldwide so far have been mapped to the same location on only one chromosome—number 4.

It appears at this time in medical history that there may be two distinctly different molecular biological mechanisms for families with several members with schizophrenia. In those families where the genetic pattern most closely fits a recessive model, a tiny genetic mutation between alleles may account for the onset of schizophrenia in adults. Molecular biology has revealed that the adult onset of metabolic diseases, such as metachromatic leukodystrophy, have an increasing chance to present with symptoms suggestive of schizophrenia if one particular allele is present; whereas the more common neurological childhood presentation of this disease entity is usually linked to other, slightly different alleles. A similar pattern is seen in GM2 gangliosidosis.

A second genetic pattern is seen in other families with a number of adult members, who are located somewhere on the schizophrenia spectrum. In these families, the exact genetic pattern in the family doesn't fit previously established models or, at best in some families, appears to be a variant of a dominant model. It is theoretically possible that some of the families have trinucleotide-repeat disorders. Ten out of the 11 inherited diseases (identified at the time of publication of this book) associated with expansion of trinucleotide repeats affect the central nervous system (La Spada, Paulson, & Fischbeck, 1994; Willems, 1994). In two of the diseases associated with trinucleotide expansions—Huntington's disease and dentatorubal–pallidoluysin atrophy—subgroups of individuals diagnosed as schizophrenic have been found. A third trinucleotide repeat expansion disease—the fragile X syndrome (FRAXA)—has been identified in 8% of the children with the psychiatric diagnosis of autism. These children with autism carry a full mutation; a few of their mothers with premutations have been found to have a schizophrenia spectrum disorder.

In these trinucleotide-repeat expansion diseases, a numerical explanation (the actual number of repeats of the trinucleotide) exists that sometimes directly relates to the clinical presentation of disease symptoms from mild to severe manifestations. New intriguing possibilities now present themselves regarding the schizophrenia spectrum. For instance, will the different clinical manifestations of two adult individuals in the same family—one with chronic schizophrenia and one with schizotypal personality disorder—someday be understood by this new genetics? Is it even possible that the trinucleotide group of diseases might be helpful in deciphering apparently nonhereditary cases of schizophrenia since premutations of asymptomatic parents already have been identified in sporadic cases of Huntington's disease?

There is no substitute for the hard work of a specific identification of the primary, underlying etiology or etiologies of the disease process affecting the brain of each individual with one of the schizophrenias. This is the future.

REFERENCES

Hachinski, V. (1993). Schizophrenia as a brain disease. *Archives of Neurology*, *50*, 1097.

La Spada, A. R., Paulson, H. L., & Fischbeck, K. H. (1994). Trinucleotide repeat expansion in neurological disease. *Annals of Neurology*, *36*, 814–822.

Willems, P. J. (1994). Dynamic mutations hit double numbers. *Nature Genetics*, *8*, 213–215.

Glossary of Terms

Although the terms used in this book will be obvious to most professional readers, for the student and educated lay reader we have tried to define the meaning of a number of terms. This glossary particularly emphasizes the terms used in genetics.

Acrocentric chromosome: Refers to a chromosome with the centromere near the end of the chromosome. Acrocentric autosomal chromosomes are satellited.

Anticipation: (in a family history) This is the phenomenon of worsening of the disease phenotype over successive generations. The trinucleotide-repeat disorders show instability in transmission of the expanded repeat from parents to children (see *Trinucleotide-Repeat Expansion*). Further expansion of the repeat is typical, with larger repeats associated with more severe disease. Increasing repeat length in successive generations explains the phenomenon of anticipation.

Alleles: (allelomorphic gene) Alleles are genes that are located at the same locus of the same chromosome and that are concerned with the same category of information by a very slight variation from each other. For example, the genes of blood groups A, B, and O are alleles.

Autosomes: Chromosome pair numbers 1 to 22, in contrast to the gonosomes.

Centromere: Constricted portion of the chromosome that divides it into a long and short arm.

Chromosomes: Microscopic threadlike concentrations of nuclear chromatin visible during meiosis and mitosis. Chromosomes are the structures bearing the genes.

Codon: A triplet of bases in a DNA or RNA molecule that codes for one amino acid.

Deletion: Part of a chromosome arm broken off and usually lost. The symbol for a deletion from the short arm of the chromosome is p- (from the French "petit," meaning small) and for a deletion from the long arm is q-.

Diploid: Two haploid sets of 23 chromsomes each = 46 chromsomes.

DNA: Deoxyribonucleic acid: a sequence of nucleotides, usually double-stranded. Each DNA molecule is a long chain made up of four basic chemical building blocks called nucleotides. The base of each nucleotide can be any of the four different bases: adenine (A), thymine (T), guanine (G), or cytosine (C). These nucleotides, in sets of three called trinucleotides or DNA triplets, are the alphabet of inheritance.

Dominant trait: One expressed in the phenotype in the heterozygous condition.

G proteins: G proteins are so named because of their ability to bind the guanine nucleotides guanosine triphosphate (GTP) and guanosine diphosphate (GDP). The family of proteins known as G proteins may be involved in all the transmembrane signaling in the nervous system with the exception of synaptic transmission via receptors that contain intrinsic ion channels. G proteins serve to couple receptors to specific intracellular effector systems.

Gamete: Mature germ cell of either sex—ovum or sperm—with a haploid set of 23 chromsomes (in normal circumstances).

Genes: Units of genetic information consisting of DNA.

Genetic mutation: Error in the exact sequence of the DNA. (It is like a misspelling of the DNA sequence.)

Genome: All the chromsomal DNA (in humans, about 3×10^9 base pairs of DNA).

Genotype: The genome (exact pattern of genes) of an individual.

Gonosomes: The sex chromosomes X and Y, also called the 23rd pair of chromosomes.

Haploid: One set of 23 chromsomes.

Haplotype: A set of linked alleles inherited together from one parent.

Heterozygote: An individual with different alleles at a specific locus.

Homozygote: An individual with identical alleles at a specific locus.

Idiopathic schizophrenia: Patients with the clinical symptoms of schizophrenia who do not have an exact diagnosis.

Karyotype: Chromosomal complement of an individual usually arranged and analyzed according to size and banding patterns.

Linkage: Association on the same chromosome of two alleles (e.g., a marker allele and a disease-susceptiblility allele), such that they are inherited together.

Meiosis: This is a process of two cell divisions as a haploid gamete originates from a diploid gametic stem cell. Meiosis I—reduction division; Meiosis II—equational division.

Mitosis: Division of a cell resulting in two daughter cells with the same chromosomal complement as the mother cell.

Monosomy: When one chromsome is missing; a complement of only 45 chromosomes.

Monozygotic (identical) twins: Monozygotic twins orginate from a single zygote and are the only individuals with identical genotypes.

Mutation: Permanent heritable change in the amino acid sequence of DNA.

Phenotype: The observed (physical) expression of the genotype in the individual.

Recessive trait: A trait expressed in the phenotype in the homozygous condition.

Satellite: A small mass of chromatin separated from the short arm of the acrocentric autosomes by a small stalk (secondary constriction).

Translocation: Transfer of a piece of one chromosome to another nonhomologous chromosome. If two nonhomologous chromosomes exchange pieces, the translocation is said to balanced. (Robertsonian translocation—fusion of two autosomal acrocentric chromosomes. The fusion occurs between two fragments, one with a centromere and one without a centromere.)

Trinucleotide-Repeat Expansion: The trinucelotides that make up DNA often repeat within a gene. The number of repeats can increase (expand) beyond the usual number of repeats. Such expansions (and rarely contractions) are associated with malfunction of the gene and a subsequent genetic disease. Examples are the repeats of the C (cytosine) A (adenine)

G (guanine) sequence in Huntington disease and the repeats of the C (cytosine) G (guanine) G (guanine) sequence in the fragile X syndrome.

Trisomy: Two haploid sets of 23 chromosomes plus one extra chromosome. For a patient with a trisomy syndrome, the total number of chromsomes is 47—instead of the usual 46.

Zygote: The product of fusion of sperm and egg.

APPENDIX A

Case Histories of
Patients with the Symptoms
of Schizophrenia and
an Underlying Disease Entity

ADDISON'S DISEASE/PERNICOUS ANEMIA
[TYPE II AUTOIMMUNE POLYGLANDULAR
SYNDROME (APS)]

(McFarland, 1963) A young man in his early 20's was diagnosed and treated for pernicous anemia successfully for 20 years until the age of 44 years when a diagnosis of schizophrenic reaction, acute undifferentiated type, was made. He received chlorpromazine and electroshock treatments intermittently until he lapsed into coma. Found to have a severe hyponatremia and infections, he remained hypotensive in spite of corticosteroid treatments and developed a seizure disorder a month later. A transfer to a University hospital resulted in a work-up revealing the diagnoses of adrenocortical insufficiency (Addison's disease), pernicous anemia, and subacute combined system disease as well as malnutrition. Treatments of dexamethasone, 9-alpha-fluorodrocortisone, sodium chloride, and vitamin supplements, including vitamin B_{12} resulted in a gradual improvement until the patient became completely asymptomatic. He was maintained successfully on the vitamin B_{12}, hydrocortisone, and 9-alpha-fluorohydrocortisone.

AQUEDUCTAL STENOSIS

(O'Flaithbheartaigh, Williams, & Jones, 1994) A 51-year-old woman, who had a brother in a mental hospital and a mother with multiple sclerosis, experienced second- and third-person auditory hallucinations and paranoid delusions leading to hospitalization. She recoverd on neuroleptic medication but was readmitted 2 years later and received electroconvulsive therapy (ECT). She appeared more withdrawn and weaker after her second set of ECT treatments, however. At this point, a computed tomography (CT) scan was performed revealing hydrocephalus secondary to aqueductal stenosis. A ventriculoparietal shunt was inserted revealing cerebrospinal fluid (CSF) under raised pressure. The authors note that deterioration after each ECT administered was probably caused by the convulsions further raising the CSF pressure.

SPACE-OCCUPYING LESIONS (BRAIN TUMORS)

Astrocytic Tumor

(Bruton, 1988) A woman who was epileptic was diagnosed as having schizophrenia at 40 years of age; electroencephalogram (EEG) showed a temporal-lobe EEG focus. Three years later, a surgical procedure of anterior temporal lobectomy was performed and an astrocytic lesion was found. This patient is part of the Bruton series (she is #76) and she is the only one who fully recovered following anterior temporal lobectomy out of 16 epileptic/schizophrenic patients with temporal lobe EEG foci in the series, although two others were said to have lost their schizophrenic traits.

Meningioma

(Hunter, Blackwood, & Bull, 1968) This patient had a brain tumor of the type that is usually most easily removed because it arises from the covering (meninges) of the brain rather than being inside the cerebrum itself, as is true of the other tumors discussed here. The patient was not accurately diagnosed for 43 years, however, surviving a very slow-growing tumor. She lived through eras of changes of terminology in psychiatry—her symptoms started at age 32 years—her diagnoses through the years were successively dementia praecox, dementia paranoides, delusional insanity, and finally schizophrenia. Nineteen years after admission to a mental hospital she began developing optic atrophy, 26 years after admission she began grand mal seizures, and 43 years after admission, a right carotid arteriogram and gamma scan disclosed a subfrontal mass. At the age of 75 years, neurosurgery disclosed a large meningioma on the floor of the anterior fossa and entering the middle fossa posteriorly. After this surgery, she failed to recover consciousness and died 2 days later. This same paper by Hunter et al. presents two other cases of frontal meningiomas that presented psychiatrically—their course was 3 and 25 years until accurate diagnosis. Another more-recent example of a frontal lobe meningioma presenting as schizophrenia is reported by (Andy, Webster, & Carranza, 1981).

Cerebral Cyst

(Johnstone, Macmillan, & Crow, 1987) An 18-year-old girl had a nocturnal convulsion, auditory hallucinations, and depressed thoughts. Fifteen years later, she admitted to the hospital with a diagnosis of schizophrenia. A diagnosis of cerebral cysticercosis was established by CT scan in this patient who had been brought up in India. She responded to phenobarbtone and benzodiazepine therapy.

CUSHING'S DISEASE

(Johnson, 1975) A 25-year-old woman was diagnosed with schizophrenia and was confined in a mental hospital for 25 years. When she was 50 years old, a physician made the diagnosis of Cushing's disease and she underwent the treatment for Cushing's disease—a bilateral adrenalectomy. This resulted in full recovery of her symptoms of schizophrenia and she was released from the hospital. A very similar case in a man who was hospitalized with schizophrenia at 23 years of age is described by Hertz, Nadas, and Wojtkowski (1955).

FABRY DISEASE

(Liston, Levine, & Philippart, 1973) A 26-year-old man was hospitalized with severe paranoid schizophrenia; a diagnosis of Fabry disease was made and his mental status improved dramatically when placed on phenoxybenazime. He was discharged on the medication. He did well for 6 months until he discontinued the phenoxybenazime; 2 weeks after the discontinuation, he was readmitted with a severe paranoid schizophrenia. After 3 weeks of hospitalization during which he remained psychotic, phenoxybenzamine was again started and coincident with this regimen, his psychosis began to remit. Five weeks later he was discharged without evidence of psychosis. The authors state "If it were not for the known existence of Fabry disease in this patient, the diagnosis of paranoid schizophrenia would have been made without equivocation" (p. 403).

HARTNUP DISEASE

(Navab & Asatoor, 1970) A 25-year-old woman (who had a cousin with with a diagnosis of chronic schizophrenia) became withdrawn, lost contact with reality, was hypomanic, and made strange meaningless utterances in a loud and high-pitched voice; she also had a red, scaly rash typical of pellegra in all areas of skin exposed to direct sunlight. Urinary amino acid testing led to the diagnosis of Hartnup disease. Treatment with nicotinamide improved her abnormal mental state dramatically within 24 hours and she is now described as clinically normal and is an intelligent, happy, and well-adjusted young lady. A similar case (with hallucination, delusion, and incomprehensible words followed by an excellent response to nicotinamide) is described by Oyanagi et al. (1967).

HOMOCYSTINURIA—^{5,10}N-METHYLENE-TETRAHYDROFOLATE REDUCTASE DEFICIENCY (MTHFR DEFICIENCY)

(Pasquier, Lebert, Petit, Zittoun, & Marquet, 1994) A Chinese woman developed a schizophrenic disorder that occurred intermittently starting at age 19. At age 30 years, she moved to France. At age 45 years, she developed a severe neuropathy as well as a reoccurrence of her psychiatric symptoms, which were then treated with chlorpromazine. A medical work-up was initiated only because of the neuropathy. The work-up revealed homocystinuria, however, an abnormally low level of serum and red cell folate and a decrease of MTHFR activity to 25% of the mean control value. She received a vitamin cocktail including folic acid; neuroleptic drugs were stopped. The homocystinuria, neuropathy, behavior problems, and delusions remitted. There was one more paranoid episode 6 weeks later successfully treated with loxapine and folic acid and then she refused further examinations, although the authors remark that 1 year later her state was unchanged (Freeman, Finkelstein, & Mudd, 1975). This is another case with a decrease of MTHFR activity to 18% where the schizophrenic symptoms responded to the folic acid (alone or in combination with pyridoxine) on different four occasions.

HYDROCEPHALUS, NORMAL PRESSURE

(Lying-Tunell, 1979) Starting at 49 years of age, a woman developed an intermittent pattern of hallucinations, anxiety, depression, and a paranoid psychosis. At 52 years of age, she was hospitalized and the pneumoencephalogram (PEG) was reported as "normal." At 65 years of age, a disorder of memory and gait was noted; at 66 years of age, she became incontinent of urine. She required admission to a mental hospital one or more times every year until the age of 69 years, when a PEG and isotope cisternography showed pictures typical of normal-pressure hydrocephalus. At the age of 71 years, a ventriculo-atrial shunt *ad modum* Pudenz with a low-pressure value was inserted. A month later, her gait was improved "she got around surprisingly fast by herself" (p. 416), she became continent, her memory improved and "her earlier recognized long-standing psychiatric symptoms disappeared" (p. 416). At the age of 73 years, she died in sespis, probably from an infected shunt. This patient had the classic triad for normal-pressure hydrocephalus of gait disturbance, urinary incontinence, and dementia.

HYPERPARTHYROIDISM

(Alarcon & Franceschini, 1984) A 53-year-old woman reported that her neighbors were plotting to kill her and her employer was planning to poisen her; she also heard imaginary phone calls. Haloperidol (4 mg a day) showed only negligible improvement; after beginning trifluoperazine (2 mg in the morning and 5 mg at bedtime), her delusions worsened and she announced that her father was Jesus Christ. Parathyroidectomy with excision of a left inferior parathyroid adenoma resulted in the complete disappearance of her delusions after 3 days, however, and auditory hallucinations after less than 2 months. She returned to normal life.

HYPERTHYROIDISM

(Greer & Parsons, 1968) A 28-year-old man lost weight and was admitted to the hospital with sinus tachycardia, bilateral exopthalmos, and a goiter over which a bruit could be heard. He was correctly oriented for time and place and his memory for recent and remote events was unimpaired. He had a paranoid delusional state, however, was hearing accusatory and warning voices in his head, and had loosening of the association of ideas, derealization, and déjà vu. Treated initially by 400 mg of chlorpromazine, his mental state remained normal for 2 years of follow-up only on the therapy for his thyroid disease (methylthiouracel and thyroxine).

HYPOPITUITARISM

(Hanna, 1970) At 53 years of age, a woman began delusions and auditory hallucinations. She would not go out of the house because she thought she was followed by a car and she heard voices from airplanes and meeting halls. After 2 years, she was admitted to a psychiatric hospital, placed on thioridazine, developed a grand mal seizure a week later, and became semi-comatose. Her absence of axillary and public hair led to the diagnosis of hypopituitarism and she had a dramatic recovery when placed on cortisone and thyroxine. In this case, when she was admitted to the hospital, her age combined with her muddled and inaccurate account of recent events led the doctors to diagnose her as paranoid state with organic dementia, not schizophrenia.

NEUROSYPHILIS

(Johnstone et al., 1987) Three cases of neurosyphilis were discovered in the Johnstone et al. (1987) study of 268 cases of first-episode schizophrenia. All three were women in their fifties. Case 1 sought hospital admission because of unpleasant smells in her house, vibration of the walls of her house, and electrical sensations in her own body. Case 2, a married housewife, attributed her hallucinations to a conspiracy of traffic wardens, police, space agents, soldiers, and doctors all organized by witchcraft. Case 3 was kept awake at night by voices talking about her and described herself as a subject of persecution by the Children of Christ, organized by her sister-in-law and estranged spouse.

SYSTEMIC LUPUS ERYTHEMATOSUS

(Lief, 1960) A 25-year-old woman was diagnosed as having lupus erythematosus (LE) disseminatus with the presenting symptoms of joint pain and epitaxis. LE smears and latex fixation were both positive. She was prescribed steriod therapy but did not take it. Three months later she presented with acute renal failure, cardiac enlargement, and visual and auditory hallucinations. Her psychiatric symptoms cleared in 4 days when she was placed on 40 mg of prednisone. A year later, in association with a colpotomy for pelvic abscess, she deteriorated psychiatrically and became unmanageable requiring transfer to the Psychiatric Service. A week later prednisone was increased to 100 mg daily with prompt clearing of her psychiatric symptoms. She was successfully discharged on a daily dose of 40 mg of prednisone and did well. Lief also describes two other more chronic cases in psychiatric wards; one of them had the classic butterfly rash on her face.

RHEUMATIC FEVER/CHOREA/DISEASE

(Breutsch, 1940) A 25-year-old lawyer was thought to have developed his psychiatric symptoms because of overstudy in college. He became seclusive, restless, and unmanageable. He had periods during which he tore up clothing and bedding, went into other patients' rooms and carried off objects that he would hide or throw out the window. Institutionalized for 29 years, he gradually had a marked intellectual deterioration. He died from myocardial infarction due to chronic rheumatic heart disease (confirmed on autopsy) although he had no history of rheumatic fever or an audible heart murmer. Diffuse degeneration of ganglion cells, intimal proliferation of some small cortical vessels, and occasional endarteritic meningeal arties were found in the brain. This is one of four cases in this paper. [Fessel and Solomon (1960) have raised the question whether some of these cases might have been systemic lupus erthematosus rather than rheumatic fever.]

VITAMIN A DEFICIENCY

(Coleman, unpublished manuscript) A young man developed the symptoms of schizophrenia at the age of 18 years. He did not respond to phenothiazines or haloperidol and remained in a chronic psychiatric hospital for 10 years. At the age of 28 years, he received a full medical evaluation, which disclosed a total absence of vitamin A in his serum. He was prescribed 10,000 units of vitamin A daily; possibly coincidentally his hallucinations and delusions disappeared within 6 weeks. Discharged from the hospital, he lives independently but remains an odd person. The family did not allow a crossover; he is maintained on 10,000 units of vitamin A daily with monitoring of his serum level.

WILSON'S DISEASE

(Modal, Karp, Liberman, & Munitz, 1985) A hospitalized 22-year-old woman had a schizophreniform psychosis as the main manifestation of Wilson's disease. A controlled trial with penicillamine (the specific treatment for Wilson's disease) revealed a clear priority of this drug over phenothiazines in abolishing the psychotic features of the disease. The effective dose of penicillamine in this case was found to be over 1650 mg/day.

ZINC DEFICIENCY?

(Staton, Donald, & Green, 1976) This 26-year-old patient had a diagnosis of catatonic schizophrenia, which failed to respond to phenothiazines (and he also developed severe extrapyramidal side effects) and had only transient improvement with electroconvulsive therapy. The discovery of a low serum zinc level and treatment with oral zinc sulfate and pyridoxine led to a satisfactory reversal of his symptoms of schizophrenia.

REFERENCES

Alarcon, R. D., & Francheschini, J. A. (1984). Hyperparathryoidism and paranoid psychosis: Case report and review fo the literature. *British Journal of Psychiatry, 145,* 477–486.

Andy, O. J., Webster, J. S., & Carranza, J. (1981). Frontal lobe lesions and behavior. *Southern Medical Journal, 74,* 968–972.

Breutsch, W. L. (1940). Chronic rheumatic brain disease as a possible factor in the causation in some cases of dementia praecox. *American Journal of Psychiatry, 97,* 276–296.

Bruton, C. J. (1988). The neuropathology of temporal lobe epilepsy. *Maudsley monograph no. 31.* Oxford: Oxford University Press.

Coleman, M. *Case history: Total absence of vitamin A in the serum of an individual with schiziophrenia.* Unpublished manuscript.

Fessel, W. J., & Solomon, G. F. (1960). Psychosis and systemic lupus erythematosus: A review of the literature and case reports. *California Medicine, 92,* 266–270.

Freeman, J. M., Finkelstein, J. D., & Mudd, S. H. (1975). Folate-responsive homocystinuria and "schizophrenia." *New England Journal of Medicine, 292,* 491–496.

Greer, S., & Parsons, V. (1968). Schizophrenia-like psychosis in thyroid crisis. *British Journal of Psychiatry, 114*, 1357–1362.

Hanna, S. M. (1970). Hypopituitarism (Sheehan's syndrome) presenting with organic psychosis. *Journal of Neurology, Neurosurgery, Psychiatry, 33*, 192–193.

Hertz, P. E., Nadas, E., & Wojtkowski, H. (1955). Cushing's syndrome and its management. *American Journal of Psychiatry, 112*, 144–239.

Hunter, R., Blackwood, W., & Bull, J. (1968). Three cases of frontal meningiomas presenting psychiatrically. *British Medical Journal, 3*, 9–16.

Johnson, J. (1975). Schizophrenia and Cushing's syndrome cured by adrenalectomy. *Psychological Medicine, 5*, 165–168.

Johnstone, E. C., Macmillan, F., & Crow, T. J. (1987). The occurrence of organic disease of possible or probable aetiological significance in a population of 268 cases of first episode schizophrenia. *Psychological Medicine, 17*, 371–379.

Lief, V. F. (1960). Psychosis associated with lupus erythematosus disseminatus. *Archives of General Psychiatry, 3*, 608–611.

Liston, E. H., Levine, M. D., & Philippart, M. (1973). Psychosis in Fabry disease and treatment with phenoxybenzamine. *Archives of General Psychiatry, 29*, 402–403.

Lying-Tunell, U. (1979). Psychotic symptoms in normal-pressure hydrocephlus. *Acta Psychiatrica Scandinavica, 59*, 415–419. McFarland, H. R. (1963). Addison's disease and related psychoses. *Comprehensive Psychiatry, 4*, 90–95.

Modal, I., Karp, L., Liberman, U. A., & Munitz, H. (1985). Penicillamine therapy for a schizophreniform psychosis in Wilson's disease. *Journal of Nervous and Mental Disease, 173*, 698–701.

Navab, A., & Asatoor, A. M. (1970). Studies on intestinal absorption of amino acids and a dipeptide in a case of Hartnup disease. *Gut, 11*, 373–379.

O'Flaithbheartiagh, S., Williams, P. A., & Jones, G. H. (1994). Schizophrenic psychosis and associated aqueduct stenosis. *British Journal of Psychiatry, 164*, 684–686.

Oyanagi, K., Takagi, M., Kitabatake, M., & Nakao, T. (1967). Hartnup disease. *Tohoku Journal of Experimental Medicine, 91*, 383–395.

Pasquier, F., Lebert, F., Petit, H., Zittoun, J., & Marquet, J. (1994). Methylenetetrahydrofolate reductase deficiency revealed by a neuropathy in a psychotic adult. *Journal of Neurology, Neurosurgery and Psychiatry, 57*, 765–766.

Staton, M. A., Donald, A. G., & Green, G. B. (1976). Zinc deficiency presenting as schizophrenia. *Current Concepts in Psychiatry, 2*, 11–14.

Index

abscesses, cerebral, 74, 288
accidents, 43
Addison's disease, 54, 134–136, 148,
  255, 280, 281, 282, 283, 284,
  autoimmune form, 135, 148, 295
  replacement therapy, 136
adoption studies, 166–167
adrenocorticotrophic hormone
  (ACTH), 136
adrenoleukodystrophy-X-linked(ALD),
  85–86, 93, 168, 187, 285
adrenomyeloneuropathy(AMN), 56,
  85–86, 135, 168, 187, 285
affect — blunted, flat, inappropriate,
  12, 13, 20, 23, 24, 25, 26, 44,
  128,
affective symptoms/disorders in general, 10, 28, 29, 43, 44, 89, 134,
  137, 139, 205, 208
  unimodal, 29
  bimodal, 29, 219
amyloid disease, 135
anterior cingulate region, 219
anticipation (genetically), 165, 170,
  171, 208, 209
anosmia, 73
arachnoid cyst, 74, 223
argininosuccinic aciduria, 87, 281,
  282
Asperger syndrome, 17, 25, 26, 30,
  40
Ataxia, dominant type, 57

attention deficit hyperactivity disorder (ADHD), 30, 44, 47
attention deficits in schizophrenia,
  20, 30, 47
autism — infantile autism/autistic dis-
  order/autistic syndromes/autism
  spectrum disorders/autisticlike
  conditions, 11, 13, 17, 25, 30–31,
  40, 44, 90, 122, 211
autism as a symptom of schizophrenia, 11, 43
autoimmune disorders, 146–163, 288
autoimmune polyglandular syndrome
  (APS), 135, 295
automatisms, 21

bipolar affective disorder/manic-de-
  pressive disease, 44, 152, 170
bone marrow transplants, 86, 96
borderline personality disorder, 45,
Borrelia burgdorferi, spirochete, 72
brain, structural abnormalities, 29,
  32, 67, 203–204, 218–238

calcium, 125–126, 138, 140, 205, 252
catalepsy, 21
catatonia, see schizophrenia
catechol-O-methyl transferase
  (COMT), 183
celiac disease, 122
cerebellar cortex of the brain, 67, 89,
  90, 204, 224

⑤ *Springer Publishing Company*

SCREENING FOR BRAIN IMPAIRMENT, 2nd Edition
A Manual for Mental Health Practice

Richard A. Berg, PhD, **Michael Franzen**, PhD, and **Danny Wedding**, PhD

Written for the general clinician, this fully revised volume provides a concise and useful outline for the evaluation of patients with suspected central nervous system dysfunction. The second edition has been updated to reflect the recent proliferation of neuropsychological assessment devices as well as to include discussion of AIDS-related cognitive disorders. The non-specialist practitioner will find helpful explanations of terms and a useful glossary.

Screening for
Brain Impairment
Second Edition

A Manual for Mental Health Practice

Richard A. Berg
Michael Franzen
Danny Wedding

⑤
Springer Publishing Company

Contents:

Neurological Disorders • Psychiatric Disorders with Neurological Implications • Approaches to Neurological Assessment • The Neuropsychological History • The Mental Status Examinations • Screening Tests of Perceptual and Motor Functions • Screening Tests for Verbal Functions • Screening for Memory Functions • Screening Tests for Higher Cognitive Functions • Neuropsychological Screening

1994   264pp   0-8261-5741-6   hard

536 Broadway, New York, NY 10012-3955 • (212) 431-4370 • Fax (212) 941-7842

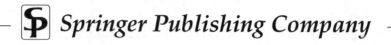 **Springer Publishing Company**

STRESS IN PSYCHIATRIC DISORDERS
Robert Paul Liberman, MD,
and **Joel Yager**, MD, Editors

This unique and expertly written volume describes how specific factors increase vulnerability or protect against the impact of stressors in a variety of clinical and social settings, such as depression, schizophrenia, Post Traumatic Stress Disorder, political torture, natural disasters, and the rapidly changing medical profession.

Contents:

1994   208pp   0-8261-8310-7   hardcover

536 Broadway, New York, NY 10012-3955 • (212) 431-4370 • Fax (212) 941-7842